Stefan Kratzsch

Forms and Performance of Foreign Direct Investments in Sub-Saharan Africa

Nomos

The Deutsche Nationalbibliothek lists this publication in the Deutsche Nationalbibliografie; detailed bibliographic data are available on the Internet at http://dnb.d-nb.de

a.t.: Leipzig, Univ., Diss., 2017

ISBN 978-3-8487-4948-5 (Print)
978-3-8452-9160-4 (ePDF)

British Library Cataloguing-in-Publication Data
A catalogue record for this book is available from the British Library.

ISBN 978-3-8487-4948-5 (Print)
978-3-8452-9160-4 (ePDF)

Library of Congress Cataloging-in-Publication Data
Kratzsch, Stefan
Forms and Performance of Foreign Direct Investments in Sub-Saharan Africa
Stefan Kratzsch
347 p.
Includes bibliographic references.

ISBN 978-3-8487-4948-5 (Print)
978-3-8452-9160-4 (ePDF)

1st Edition 2018

Annotation

This Book represents a Doctoral Thesis submitted to and accepted by the Leipzig University, Faculty of History, Arts and Oriental Studies – Institute of African Studies (Universität Leipzig, Fakultät für Geschichte, Kunst- und Orientwissenschaften – Institut für Afrikastudien) for granting the degree of PhD (Dr. phil.). The Thesis was successfully defended on 3 November 2017 in Leipzig, Germany and received a degree of "magna cum laude".

The two reviewers were Prof. Dr. Helmut Asche (first reviewer) and Prof. Dr. Katja Werthmann (second reviewer).

Acknowledgements

I take this opportunity to express my gratitude to the many individuals whose support has been essential for the completion of the PhD Thesis which forms the basis of this Book. My deep appreciation goes to my supervisor, Professor Helmut Asche who has relentlessly supported me with his wisdom and insights and who has provided the necessary reassurance and guidance to bring this academic journey of mine to a successful termination.

I also wish to thank Leipzig University, particularly the Institute of African Studies at the Faculty of History, Arts and Oriental Studies, for accepting me as an external doctorate student and for providing me with the means to undertake the research for my PhD Thesis. I owe gratitude to my employer, the United Nations Industrial Development Organisation (UNIDO), including former and current colleagues at UNIDO, for creating a professional framework that enabled me to learn and eventually apply my acquired knowledge in the thematic area of my PhD Thesis.

Most of all, however, I am indebted to all members of my family without whom I would never have reached this point in my life. All of them contributed in their own individual way and pushed me to go beyond what I thought would be possible. I am conscious of all the sacrifices they had to make in encouraging and supporting me over such a long period of time while selflessly subordinating their own expectations and needs – in me as husband, father, son and son-in-law. Especially my wife Šárka has never ceased to believe in my ability to finish what I started and she has provided continued moral encouragement and generous understanding during the most difficult periods of writing this Thesis. I will forever be grateful for that. Needless to say, I am also thankful to many others who in one way or another have contributed in no small measure to the successful completion of this Thesis.

I dedicate this Book to my family.

Abstract

This Book sheds light on different forms of foreign direct investment (FDI) in Sub-Saharan Africa (SSA) at the macro-level as well as the micro-level. The understanding of these different FDI forms provides the foundation for a detailed analysis of the multifaceted dimensions of FDI performance through an OLS regression model. The Book posits that the understanding of FDI performance determinants is indispensable in the debate about the contribution of FDI to SSA's economic development and its technological transformation. It claims that the formulation of ambitious FDI impact targets would be futile unless the foreign investor experiences subjectively acceptable growth and profit levels and sees a business rationale in maintaining the longevity and stability of its operations in SSA.

An extensive literature review provides the basis for the formulation of eleven hypotheses drawing primarily from resource-based, institutional and transaction cost theories. The sample is derived from the UNIDO 2010/11 Africa Investor Survey database and comprises 2,692 foreign subsidiaries. The results are at odds with the majority of the macro-level literature on FDI inflow determinants to SSA in that they bring into question the exclusive focus on institutional and business climate determinants. Instead, firm-level results point to the relevance of R&D intensity, brands, prior or parallel experience in SSA, cultural proximity and product diversification in explaining FDI performance. Being an older and larger foreign subsidiary also has a positive impact on FDI performance as well as local market orientation. JVs perform better than greenfield foreign investors.

Another contribution is made in the detailed analysis of macro-level FDI flow and stock statistics from the four main sources IMF, UNCTAD, the World Bank and OECD. The Book divulges deviations between different data sources and provides an account of the main reasons for the under- and overestimation in FDI statistics. It concludes that SSA's national statistics offices and central banks require further capacity building. In this context, FDI surveys in SSA should be continued in order to build up a firm-level panel database to advance research on FDI typology, FDI performance and other related topics.

Keywords: Sub-Saharan Africa, foreign direct investment, determinants, performance, entry mode

JEL Classifications: F21, F23, L22, L25.

Table of Contents

List of Figures

List of Tables

List of Boxes

Abbreviations

AGOA	African Growth and Opportunity Act
ANOVA	Analysis of Variance
BIT	Bilateral Investment Treaty
BPM	Balance of Payments and International Investment Position Manual
BOP	Balance of Payments
CDIS	Coordinated Direct Investment Survey
CEO	Chief Executive Officer
DAC	Development Assistance Committee (of the OECD)
DRC	Democratic Republic of the Congo
DSBB	Dissemination Standards Bulletin Board
EAC	East African Community
EBA	Everything But Arms
ECOWAS	Economic Community of West African States
EDDI	Enhanced Data Dissemination Initiative
EPZ	Export Processing Zone
EU	European Union
FDI	Foreign Direct Investment
FE	Foreign Entrepreneur
FIFA	Fédération Internationale de Football Association
GDDS	General Data Dissemination System
GDP	Gross Domestic Product
GSP	Generalized System of Preferences
GTZ	Gesellschaft für Technische Zusammenarbeit (now GIZ)
GVC	Global Value Chain
ICT	Information and Communications Technology
IIA	International Investment Agreement
IIP	International Investment Position

IMF	International Monetary Fund
INV	International New Venture
IO	International Organization
IPA	Investment Promotion Agency
ISIC	International Standard Industrial Classification
IT	Information Technology
ITRS	International Transaction Reporting System
IZ	Industrial Zone
JV	Joint Venture
KMO	Kaiser–Meyer–Olkin Measure
LDC	Least Developed Country
M&A	Merger & Acquisition
MDGs	Millennium Development Goals
MF	Manufacturing
MNC	Multinational Corporation
MNE	Multinational Enterprise
NIP	New Industrial Policy
NSO	National Statistics Office
OECD	Organisation for Economic Cooperation and Development
OLI	Ownership–Location–Internalization (Paradigm)
OLS	Ordinary Least Squares
PCA	Principals Component Analysis
R&D	Research & Development
REC	Regional Economic Community
ROA	Return On Assets
ROI	Return On Investments
ROS	Return On Sales
SA	South Africa
SADC	Southern African Development Community
SDDS	Special Data Dissemination Standard
SDGs	Sustainable Development Goals
SEZ	Special Economic Zone

SIMSDI	Survey of Implementation of Methodological Standards for Direct Investment
SME	Small and Medium-sized Enterprises
SPE	Special Purpose Entity
SSA	Sub-Saharan Africa
TNC	Transnational Corporation
UBO	Ultimate Beneficial Ownership
UK	United Kingdom
UNCTAD	United Nations Conference on Trade and Development
UNECA	United Nations Economic Commission for Africa
UNIDO	United Nations Industrial Development Organization
US	United States
USD	United States Dollar
VIF	Variance Inflation Factor
WDI	World Development Indicators (of the World Bank)
WIR	World Investment Report (of UNCTAD)
WOS	Wholly-Owned (Foreign) Subsidiary

1. Introduction

1.1 The foreign direct investment (FDI) scenario in Sub-Saharan Africa

Classical development theories consider the scarcity of capital and resulting low levels of investments into productivity-enhancing technological progress as a fundamental impediment to economic development. From a developing country perspective, the process of catching up with the developed part of the world requires continued expenditures on knowledge accumulation, product and process innovation and human capital formation (UNCTAD 1999b, UNIDO 2005). Since the conversion of domestic savings into domestic investments alone is insufficient to accomplish ambitious economic development goals, developing countries have put additional emphasis on the attraction of various types of foreign direct investments (FDI) (Wells and Wint 2000, Harding and Javorcik 2007, Harding and Javorcik 2011). Compared to cross-border bank lending or portfolio investments, FDI constitutes a lasting investment interest and is, under normal circumstances, the least volatile form of transferring foreign savings from one country to another (Lipsey 1999, Morrissey and Osei 2004, IMF 2009). This characteristic makes FDI in principle an ideal conduit for bridging technological and know-how gaps between developed and developing countries thus contributing to the achievement of developing countries' social and economic development objectives.

Sub-Saharan Africa (SSA), the region with the world-wide largest number of least developed countries (LDCs) and the focus of this Book, is perhaps in the direst need of attracting "quality" FDI. SSA is not alone in this endeavour. The purported positive impact of FDI on economic development has paved the way for the emergence of different actors and stakeholders whose principal mandate is FDI attraction and promotion. Investment promotion has become a tough and competitive business in which developed and developing countries, spearheaded by specialized investment promotion agencies (IPAs), are vying for the attention of a growing but nonetheless finite number of multinational enterprises (MNE) in order to persuade them to invest in their own country and not in another. SSA is now an active player in the investment promotion arena as indicated by a remarkable increase of ratified bilateral investment treaties (BITs) as well as the proliferation of IPAs and special economic zones (SEZs) across the continent (UNCTAD 2008b, Farole 2011, UNIDO 2012a).

The extent to which a developing country is able to attract or retain more of "quality" FDI as opposed to another will ultimately determine the aggregated impact that the group of foreign-owned companies has on the local economy. A frequent policy recommendation for developing countries has been to improve the conditions for attracting the "right" mix of FDI along different desirable dimensions of economic impact in terms of capital formation, employment creation, skills enhancements, global value chain integration, infrastructural or ICT development, linkages, local content development and others. In this environment of stiff competition, there is a strong temptation for SSA countries to adopt an almost cynical stance over such selective investor targeting following the adage of *"Beggars can't be choosers"*. Within this reasoning, the neoliberal investment policy paradigms of the 1990's fell on fertile grounds and have prompted SSA countries to deregulate their local markets and actively tout the most visible national business reforms in accordance with the World Bank's "Doing Business" logic, thereby often masking the lack of a genuine policy resolve to address the underlying structural and intertwined challenges of the African continent. While most SSA countries have most likely surpassed the peak of neoliberal investment policy-making, the continent continues to have one of the world's most relaxed FDI entry or local content regulations (OECD 2005b, UNCTAD 2006a, World Bank et al. 2010, De la Medina Soto and Ghossein 2013). Very rarely will investment laws force foreign investors to choose a suboptimal mode of entry or to utilize a certain proportion of input factors such as locally available human resources or local supply chains.

The global financial crisis of 2008/2009 evidently led to a global contraction of FDI volumes during the following few years (UNCTAD 2009f, UNCTAD 2009e). Developing countries were relatively less affected by the global financial crisis and recorded a decline of FDI inflows of 24 per cent in 2009 as opposed to a 44 per cent drop in FDI inflows to developed countries (UNCTAD 2010b). FDI inflows to Africa decreased by even less, namely 19 per cent in 2009. This nurtured optimism that the crisis could mark the beginning of a sustained catching-up process and turn the essence of the Official 2010 FIFA World Cup Song "*Waka Waka (This Time for Africa)*" into concrete action once and for all. According to this thinking, multinational enterprises would undertake a global business risk re-assessment resulting in closing the perceived risk gap between SSA and hitherto misleadingly perceived "low"-risk locations in developed countries. At the same time, the emergence of MNEs from developing countries resulted in a higher proportion of South-South FDI flows (Akyut and Ratha 2003, Aykut and Goldstein 2006, UNCTAD 2006b, UNCTAD and UNDP 2007, Henley et al. 2008, Saunders 2008, Draper et al. 2010, Gómez-Mera et al. 2015). This nurtured further optimism that investors from developing countries would be more tolerant with regard to imperfections in the host country's investment climate as they would be used to operating in such conditions in their own country of origin (UNIDO 2007, Cuervo-Cazurra and Genc 2008, Desbordes et al. 2011).

For the period 2014 to 2016, 15.9 per cent of international investors consider SSA as a "very important" or "extremely important" investment destination compared to 14.1 per cent of international investors during the period from 2012 to 2014 (UNCTAD 2012a, UNCTAD 2014c). Moreover, relaxed FDI entry regulations promise minimal interference by government authorities hence making it easier for MNEs to choose from a list of potential investment locations in SSA. At the same time, most countries in SSA were able to show robust improvements of the set of macro-economic fundamentals (AFDB 2014). Since the beginning of the millennium, real annual GDP has grown at an average of 5 per cent and real income per capita has increased by 2.1 per cent. An African middle class, estimated at 34 per cent of Africa's population (AFDB 2011b) has presumably emerged as an engine of transformation of the urban parts of Africa into attractive consumer markets. The proportion of people living below the poverty line has fallen from over 50 per cent to less than 45 per cent. Of the 20 economies narrowing the gap with the Doing Business regulatory frontier the most since 2009, nine are in SSA (World Bank 2013).

SSA's economic performance and its robustness even during the global financial crisis, its relative improvements in the Doing Business rankings and the continent's liberal FDI regulations were sufficient ingredients for papers and press to pitch a chorus of praise on Africa's staggering transformation from "The Hopeless Continent" (The Economist 2000) to "The Hopeful Continent" (The Economist 2013a). By the same token, the continent's future investment potential was compared to "Lions on the move" (McKinsey Global Institute 2010), "A Sea of Opportunities" (UNECA 2014) or the "African growth miracle" (McMillan and Harttgen 2014). As a matter of fact, soaring nominal FDI inflows to SSA seem to somehow confirm the euphoria. In 2013 and according to the database of the United Nations Conference on Trade and Development (UNCTAD), FDI inflows amounted to 44.8 billion USD in nominal levels rising from 41 billion USD in 2012 and 42.2 billion USD in 2011. SSA's total FDI inward stock has never been higher and accounted for 474.3 billion USD in 2013. The proportion of developing country investments in SSA is rapidly increasing (UNCTAD 2010a, UNOSAA 2010). This creates a situation whereby African host country governments or Investment Promotion Agencies (IPAs) proudly present year-by-year FDI inflow statistics as a purported indicator of successful business climate reforms without however providing further evidence of concrete FDI performance and impact.

While SSA's nominal FDI growth trajectory appears impressive at first sight, it masks the fact that, in 2013, SSA's, including South Africa's (SA), FDI inward stock reached a minuscule 1.9 per cent of the world's FDI inward stocks and 1.3 per cent if SA is excluded from the group of SSA countries. Compared to 20 years ago, the relative importance of SSA has virtually stagnated. In 1992, the share of SSA's FDI inward stocks in world FDI inward stocks was 1.8 per cent, including SA and 1.3 per cent, excluding SA. Besides, the majority of FDI inward stocks remain primarily concentrated in the natural resource extraction sectors regardless of whether the foreign investment has entered as an M&A or as a greenfield investment (UNCTAD 2004b, UNCTAD 2008b, UNCTAD 2011a). As a consequence, countries in SSA without considerable deposits of natural resources as well as other sectors within resource-rich SSA countries play considerably less of a role in the FDI location decision of MNEs. In its 1999 World Investment Report (WIR), UNCTAD has been asking the question "There are about 60,000 TNCs [transnational corporations]: where does one start?" (UNCTAD 1999b, p. 183), which has been a timely question prior to the launch of the 2000–2015 Millennium Development Goals (MDGs). In this context, the 2012 WIR called for the need to have "A New Generation of Investment Policies" which puts *specific* and *targeted* FDI promotion at the heart of the development policy agendas of developing countries (UNCTAD 2012b). In view of the next generation of 2015–2030 Sustainable Development Goals (SDGs) that succeeded the MDGs, policy makers and investment promotion stakeholders in developing countries have been reminded once again that pursuing the SDGs implies "targeting investors in sectors or activities that are particularly conducive to SDGs" (UNCTAD 2014d, p.170).

As plausible as these different sets of policy recommendations may appear, its actual implementation is a tall order. FDI can affect and permeate all levels of the SSA host economy at the macro-economic level, the meso-level as well as the micro- or firm-level. Macro-level economic factors as well as geographic factors determine the relative success of a country in attracting FDI and keeping such factors right can prevent foreign investors from divesting (Dunning 1993, UNCTAD 1998, Dunning 2000). At the meso-level, the quality and transparency of the interaction between a specific group of already established foreign investors and the host country's regulatory and supporting institutions determines long-term foreign subsidiary success or failure (Kostova 1999, Meyer and Nguyen 2005, Bénassy-Quéré et al. 2007, Chan et al. 2008, Dunning and Lundan 2008a). At the micro-level, the foreign investor governs the extent to which its subsidiary is interwoven into the host country's domestic fabric of other private and public enterprises. In this connection, FDI spill-over effects are often measured in terms of backward or forward linkages or the foreign investor's propensity to engage in equity partnerships with indigenous partners (Makino and Delios 1996, Javorcik 2004, Blalock and Simon 2009, Meyer and Sinani 2009).

Issues related to firm-level performance of FDI and its ensuing impact on host country growth and spill-overs need to be analysed not only against a well-defined classification of different forms of FDI but also from a macro-, meso- and firm-level perspective. While this is well recognized at global level, international business researchers with a focus on Africa have kept an astonishingly narrow research focus on the classical macro-level FDI determinants analyses revolving mainly around answers to the question of "*what location factors attract (or do not attract) FDI flows to SSA?*" (Pigato 2000, Cotton and Ramachandran 2001, Pigato 2001, Asiedu 2002, Bende-Nabende 2002, Naudé and Krugell 2003, Asiedu 2004b, Onyeiwu and Shrestha 2004, Akinkugbe 2005, Mlambo 2005, Anyanwu 2006, Asiedu 2006, Dupasquier and Osakwe 2006, Naudé and Krugell 2007, Suliman and Mollick 2009, Kolstad and Wiig 2011, Sichei and Kinyondo 2012) or "*to what extent does FDI contribute to macroeconomic growth in SSA?*" (Lumbila 2005, UNECA 2006, Adams 2009, Gohou and Soumaré 2009). All studies have in common that they use either SSA's FDI inflows or FDI inward stocks as the dependent variable. There are some variations in that sometimes FDI inflows/inward stocks as a percentage of world FDI inflows/inward stocks, FDI inflows/GDP, FDI inflows as a percentage of gross fixed capital formation or FDI inflows per capita are deployed as dependent variable. The most frequently reported results are that political determinants and the general institutional business climate (Agodo 1978, Morisset 2000, Cotton and Ramachandran 2001, Pigato 2001, Bende-Nabende 2002, Asiedu 2004b, Mlambo 2005, Asiedu 2006, Naudé and Krugell 2007), the educational level of SSA's population (Naudé and Krugell 2003, Asiedu 2006, Naudé and Krugell 2007, Suliman and Mollick 2009) as well as market size and growth (Cotton and Ramachandran 2001, Onyeiwu and Shrestha 2004, Akinkugbe 2005, Mlambo 2005, Asiedu 2006, Sichei and Kinyondo 2012) matter most in attracting higher volumes of FDI inflows. However, even in instances of tangible business climate improvements, resulting FDI inflows are far from guaranteed especially in SSA countries with low natural resource endowments (Asiedu 2002). The review of the FDI literature on SSA thus confirms a strong skew towards macro-economic determinants.

Against this scenario, the well-meant advice of international organizations (IOs) and non-governmental organizations (NGOs) towards more selectivity in SSA's FDI promotion and attraction process is in stark contrast to the large body of FDI determinants studies that, in failing to distinguish between different types of FDI, continue to provide rather general and unspecific policy recommendations to promote literally *all types* of FDI and *at the same time*. An exception is the study of Samuel Adams who comes to the conclusion that FDI, unlike domestic investment, does not have a positive impact on economic growth in SSA and thus notes that "FDI is not inherently virtuous – its impact depends on the overall incentive and capability structure of the host country. Thus, attracting FDI is only one part of the story. The other is how FDI impacts on the wider local economy. In this respect, we have argued that SSA countries need to be cautious and critical in the kind of FDI they attract; that the open door policy to attract all kinds of FDI will not yield the desired benefits" (Adams 2009, p. 947).

Generally speaking, the results of inferential data analysis are as good as the data that is being entered into econometric models. One preoccupation of researchers is therefore to mitigate the risk of a "garbage in, garbage out" scenario. In his acclaimed book "Poor Numbers" Morten Jerven summarizes the problem in African development statistics, although without being specific about FDI statistics: "The state of the scholarly literature today, particularly in African studies and International development but also more generally in the social sciences, is deeply and doubly unsatisfactory. To date it has either neglected the issue of data quality and therefore accepted data at face value or dismissed the data as unreliable and therefore irrelevant. Numbers are too important to be ignored, and the problems surrounding the production and dissemination of numbers are too serious to be dismissed" (Jerven 2013, p. 110). Turning towards the quality of FDI statistics based on SSA's Balance of Payments (BOP), UNCTAD states that "the muddle is even greater with FDI, where methodological snags are compounded by serious data gaps arising from the loose definition of what is being measured, as well as collection and coverage problems. [...] Such fundamental definitional problems are aggravated by the fact that aggregate FDI flows are a composite of different sources including equity flows from abroad, undistributed profits and inter-company loans" (UNCTAD 2005c, p. 17-19).

Against this background, the large and growing body of the macro-economic FDI determinants literature in SSA deserves to be given more critical scrutiny. Some scepticism is in order to take a closer look at the policy relevance of macro-economic FDI studies in Africa. The problems in terms of FDI data collection and availability in SSA appear to be too fundamental for researchers to simply persist in briefly addressing them in the obligatory section on statistical constraints and limitations. In line with Jerven's reasoning, researchers should not be criticized for analysing available data as long as a vigilant approach is maintained and findings are not exaggerated to the point of dogma (Jerven 2013). Seeing FDI solely through macro-economic lenses will certainly not do justice to its complex and intertwined nature and its respective contribution to the host country's social and economic development through its various meso- and firm-level impact channels. Even in the context of fast-growing FDI inflows and inward stocks (the macro-channel), the economic and social benefits resulting from certain MNE activities with a potentially positive impact on the host country may not materialize at the meso- or micro-level.

1.2 Research objective

The majority of serious FDI scholars would certainly agree that it is not ideal to analyse FDI in SSA from a solely macro-economic perspective but that it is necessary to put much more emphasis on the firm-level analysis of FDI in SSA. As concerns official FDI statistics, there is wide consensus that firm-level enterprise surveys are needed to complement or improve BOP statistics (Bellak 1998, Stephan and Pfaffmann 2001, UNCTAD 2005d, Zhan 2006, Fujita 2008, UNCTAD 2009b). Until recently however, firm-level FDI research was based on relatively small sample sizes of FDI subsidiaries based in individual African countries

(Boateng and Glaister 2002, Bhaumik and Gelb 2005, Aryeetey et al. 2008, World Bank 2012), of foreign investor subsidiaries from a specific home country in a single or a group of SSA countries (Gilroy et al. 2001, Grobbelaar 2004, Kabelwa 2004, Prabhakar 2008, Saunders 2008, Schroeder 2008, Dobler 2009) or at the level of multinational headquarters with a focus on SSA (Bartels et al. 2002, Naidu and Lutchman 2004, MIGA 2014, Gómez-Mera et al. 2015).

UNIDO was the first IO that undertook specialized multi-country surveys of foreign subsidiaries in SSA aiming to generate a hitherto unavailable firm-level data set for studying different foreign investor types. Four rounds of foreign subsidiary surveys have been conducted and an Investor Survey Report was launched after each survey round (UNIDO 2002a, UNIDO 2003, UNIDO 2007, UNIDO 2012a). The sample allows for the classification of foreign investors by their entry modes, their home countries, their sizes, their organizational structures and investment motives. For instance, concerning FDI motives, a distinction is made between whether the foreign investor is primarily attracted by raw materials and the natural resource endowment of the host country (natural-resource-seeking FDI), the size and growth potential of the market (market-seeking FDI), the availability of low-cost work force and favourable infrastructure conditions for exports (efficiency- or export-seeking FDI) or assets that strengthen the firm's market position and augment knowledge (strategic asset-seeking FDI) (Dunning 1993). Unsurprisingly, the availability of such an unprecedented dataset of FDI subsidiaries in SSA has sparked the publication of numerous other articles e.g. with regard to South-South FDI (Henley et al. 2008), firm-level FDI determinants (Bartels et al. 2008, Bartels et al. 2009) and supply chain linkages (Amendolagine et al. 2013, Görg and Seric 2013).

The classification of different types of FDI is a prerequisite for the laudable but ambitious concept of foreign investment targeting. For SSA countries to take a pro-active rather than a reactive approach to investment promotion, they first need to understand *who* is to be targeted (UNIDO 2012a). An improved predictive capacity as to the likely economic contribution of specific MNE segments would be of great support in crafting successful FDI-host country combinations. This framework explains the focus of this Book on FDI performance of different FDI types. MNEs are rational in entering a particular foreign market if the return of investment is anticipated to be higher than in other competing FDI locations (Dunning 1993, Dunning 1998, Brouthers et al. 1999). At the same time, MNEs self-select the entry mode that they consider superior for future profit maximization (Shaver 1998, Brouthers 2002, Brouthers et al. 2003, Brouthers and Nakos 2004, Slangen and Hennart 2008). After successfully concluding the preparatory stage (i.e. the stage during which the foreseen FDI project is registered and approved, construction work is undertaken, recruitments are made, etc.), the parent company expects its subsidiary to meet or exceed predetermined performance targets within the shortest possible time. On the one hand, an enduring period of high performance of the subsidiary might be rewarded through sequential FDI which is often financed from reinvested earnings (Lundan 2006, UNCTAD 2007a). On the other hand, a long period of underperformance will eventually lead to a partial or full divestment (Boddewyn 1983).

Subsidiary-level FDI performance determines the growth and longevity of the foreign investment and is therefore of paramount importance in the debate on FDI impact and the attraction of "quality" FDI. The formulation of ambitious FDI impact targets will be futile unless the foreign investor meets a subjectively acceptable performance target. UNIDO formulates: "improved productivity [of foreign investment], at all levels of aggregation, is a necessary – even if not sufficient – condition of economic development and plays a significant role in improving social welfare" (UNIDO 2012a, p.33). Despite the strikingly simple causality between FDI performance and ensuing FDI impact in all its variations, the attempts to approach the topic of FDI performance in SSA has, until now, again solely been undertaken from a macro-level perspective. Studies with focus on the topic of "FDI performance" allude to an analysis at the firm-level but what is measured is the extent of diversion of FDI from other parts of the world into Africa i.e. once again a macro-economic construct (UNCTAD 1999a, Dupasquier and Osakwe 2006, UNCTAD and UNDP 2007). Likewise, studies with a focus on the contribution of FDI inflows on GDP growth in SSA overlook the endogenous character of foreign firm-level performance and its wider cumulative outcomes, for instance, in terms of domestic and export sales growth or the increase of employment and wages (Lumbila 2005, UNECA 2006, Gohou and Soumaré 2009).

In recognition of the tenable role that FDI performance plays for the attainment of SSA's higher-ranking social and economic development objectives, the empirical analysis in the second part of this Book focuses on factors that are affecting such performance. The methodological design overcomes the almost exclusive focus in the macro-economic FDI determinants literature on institutional and host country determinants of FDI inflows. Dunning's eclectic or ownership (O), location (L) and internalization (I) paradigm posits that location factors are only *one* of at least three dimensions that determine whether an FDI project is implemented and remains successful over time (Dunning 1993, Dunning 1998, UNCTAD 1998). The literature review is expected to prepare the ground for the formulation of hypotheses with attribution to different theoretical domains forming the building blocks of the OLI paradigm:

- *Resource-based theories (the "O"-dimension):* These theories describe the foreign enterprise as an efficient bundle of assets including technologies, codified and non-codified process and product knowledge, financial capital and organizational networks (Penrose 1959, Caves 1971, Hymer 1976, Barney 1991). The theory follows the notion that the foreign investor (i.e. its management, its core strategies, its attitude towards learning and innovation, its entrepreneurial culture, etc.) is to a large extent responsible for its own success. In this context, it will be hypothesized that foreign subsidiaries will perform better if:
  a. they have access to inimitable resources such as patents and trademarks (Combs and Ketchen 1999, De Carolis 2003, Newbert 2007);
  b. they undertake R&D activities (Lu and Beamish 2001, Andras and Srinivasan 2003, UNCTAD 2005e);
  c. they employ a greater share of high-skilled workers (UNIDO 2007);
  d. they have subsidiary experience in other SSA countries (Delios and Beamish 1999a, Luo and Peng 1999, Ogasavara and Hoshino 2009).

  The effective deployment of internal firm resources combined with R&D activities support the foreign firm's objective of product diversification (Hitt et al. 1997). It will therefore be hypothesized that:
  e. diversification leads to an increase in aggregate local demand for the range of available foreign products which, in turn, impacts positively on FDI subsidiary performance (Khanna and Palepu 1997, Chakrabarti et al. 2007).
- *Institution-based theories (the "L"-dimension):* The list of SSA host country-level determinants (business climate indicators, human capital, market size, market growth, etc.) is well known from the macro-economic FDI literature. A prudent methodological design requires the inclusion of at least some of them in the FDI firm-level analysis. Two hypotheses are attributable to *institution-based theories*, namely that:

a. the stability of the political, economic and legal business climate has a positive effect on firm-level FDI performance;
b. the existence of a BIT between the foreign investor home country and the SSA host country should be irrelevant for FDI performance (Hallward-Driemeyer 2003, Gallagher and Birch 2006, Yackee 2007).

– *Transaction cost-based theories (the "I"-dimension):* Transaction cost theory analyses the choice of MNEs to carry out business transactions through external markets (e.g. international trade) as opposed to the internalization of international market transactions to overcome costs related to market failures and information asymmetry (Williamson 1975, Buckley and Casson 1976, Buckley and Casson 1985). The foreign firm's asset specificity in terms of its product or technological complexity plays a crucial role in transaction-based theories. In this context, contract enforcement costs and the costs of accessing local input factors of production, in particular raw materials, are also important. It will be hypothesized, that:
  a. FDI performs better in environments where transaction costs of contract enforcement are lower (Brouthers 2002, Brouthers and Nakos 2004);
  b. FDI performs better in environments where factor input costs are lower (Heide and Stump 1995, UNCTAD 2009f).

The majority of FDI performance determinants are indeed attributable to the three components of the eclectic paradigm and, unsurprisingly, the majority of hypotheses of this Book are subsumed under it. Despite various later extensions of the eclectic paradigm (e.g. Dunning and Lundan 2008b, Dunning and Lundan 2008a), other theories deserve closer scrutiny as they may also play a role in explaining a sizable portion of FDI performance. For example, there is an understanding that FDI performance will also depend on the industry and its prevalent entry barriers as well as its concentration and degree of competition amongst firms (Porter 1985, Rumelt 1991, McGahan and Porter 1997). In some instances, the extent of cultural distance between the foreign investor's home country and the FDI host country (Hofstede 1980, Li and Guisinger 1991, Tihanyi et al. 2005, Wang and Schaan 2008) or the degree of subsidiary autonomy (Birkinshaw 1998, Birkinshaw 2000, Gammelgaard et al. 2012) can also have an impact on FDI performance. Moreover, a very large body of literature has analysed the nexus between the FDI entry mode and subsequent FDI performance (Chowdhury 1992, Woodcock et al. 1994, Li 1995, Pan et al.

1999, Brouthers 2002, Delios and Beamish 2004, Chung and Beamish 2005a, Brouthers et al. 2008a, Slangen and Hennart 2008, Tan 2009, Chang et al. 2013, Brouthers et al. 2015). In the case of joint ventures (JVs), real options theory asserts that one or more changes in the ownership structure in the post-entry stage occur out of an expectation of higher performance and are hence quite common (Kogut 1991, Arino and de la Torre 1998, Chi 2000, Kumar 2005, Brouthers et al. 2008a). The literature review leads to the formulation of two more hypotheses:

a. An increase in foreign equity share in a JV will entail higher FDI performance;
b. A lower cultural distance between the home country and the SSA host country of the foreign investor will entail higher FDI performance.

The majority of variables will be constructed from the UNIDO 2010/11 Investor Survey questionnaire that formed the basis of UNIDO's "Africa Investor Report 2011: Towards Evidence-Based Investment Promotion Strategies" (UNIDO 2012a). Descriptive statistics, particularly frequency statistics and cross-tabulation, are used to arrive at an accurate classification of the most important types of FDI in SSA. This classification is necessary for the design of a robust ordinary least squares (OLS) regression model in the final part of this Book.

The chosen empirical approach is expected to provide an answer to the main research question, which is the following:

"To what extent and in what direction do resource-based, institution-based, transaction cost-based and other determinants affect the performance of different types of FDI in SSA?"

1.3 Structure of the Book

This Book is structured into six main chapters.

Following this introduction, Chapter 2 provides an extensive update on the status of macro-economic FDI statistics with regard to the four recognized sources, the IMF, the World Bank, UNCTAD, and in the case of SSA's outflow or outwards FDI statistics, the OECD. The macro-economic review of available FDI statistics serves two purposes: First, to assess the reliability of *existing* FDI data in SSA based on available BOP statistics and, second, to assess whether other and hitherto unnoticed types of FDI with a potential relevance for SSA's economic development might be at play and whether they can or should be measured through macro-economic lenses. The purpose of this part of the Book is not to refute or even discredit the contributions of SSA's FDI determinants literature but to raise critical issues.

Chapter 3 shifts the focus away from the macro-economic towards a firm-level dimension of FDI measurement. It is expected that this firm-level dataset helps to overcome the challenges that are likely to be encountered during the first part of this Book in developing a reliable typology of FDI flows and stocks based on patchy macro-economic BOP FDI statistics. The UNIDO 2010/11 Investor Survey sample is analysed to provide cross-combinations of FDI characteristics in SSA. This includes a closer look at the industrial subsector composition as well as the most important countries of FDI origin. Frequency tables and cross-tabulations are presented with regard to the most preferred entry modes, the MNEs' organizational structures, the market orientations as well as the ages and sizes of foreign subsidiaries in SSA.

Chapter 4 presents and discusses the extant literature in the area of firm-level performance. It starts by reviewing the intricate relationship between the MNE's strategic decision of entry mode and resulting FDI performance. The heterogeneous facets of FDI performance are discussed in Chapter 4.2. Six further sub-chapters follow to present the main spheres of literature which form the basis for the development of the hypotheses.

Chapter 5 presents the empirical analysis which is centred on an OLS hierarchical regression model. On the basis of the UNIDO 2010/11 Investor Survey data and in line with the proposed classification of Hult et al. (Hult et al. 2008), three dependent variables of FDI performance are constructed, namely the profit margin of the FDI subsidiary, its capacity utilization as well as an indicator of a subjective performance assessment. Independent variables are defined and sometimes transformed in order to produce robust proxies for the testing of hypotheses. In addition, a Principal Components Analysis (PCA) is carried out to deliver a missing set of independent variables and with the aim of increasing the explanatory value of the regression model. Several control variables with varying combinations are included and lead to four different model specifications. The final part makes the connection between regression results and the list of proposed hypotheses while recalling the most salient findings of other research fellows in the given research areas.

The final Chapter 6 summarises the main findings and outlines limitations. It concludes to suggest extensions for future research.

2. A macro-economic perspective of FDI in SSA

2.1 Definitions

The underlying concepts and definitions of FDI are provided in the "4th Edition of the OECD Benchmark Definition of Foreign Direct Investment", which is compatible with the International Monetary Fund's (IMF) Balance of Payments and International Investment Position Manual (BPM), whose 6th revision was released in 2009 (OECD 2008, IMF 2009). IMF defines FDI as a "category of cross-border investment associated with a resident in one economy having control or a significant degree of influence on the management of an enterprise that is resident in another economy" (IMF 2009, p. 100). The term "control or a significant degree of influence on the management" underscores the investor's lasting interest in the enterprise and it is assumed to be achieved "when a direct investor directly owns equity that entitles it to 10 per cent or more of the voting power in the direct investment enterprise" (IMF 2009, p. 101). In the case of less than 10 per cent equity ownership, the foreign investment is no longer a *direct* investment but should under normal circumstances be classified as *portfolio* investment. The foreign portfolio investor holds a share certificate which could be sold in the stock market at any time and hence does not fulfil the criteria of a lasting interest of a foreign direct investor in a particular enterprise.

BPM-6 states that "direct investment covers most financial transactions and positions between affiliates resident in different economies. Investment income associated with direct investment positions is also included in direct investment" (IMF 2009, p. 104). The main statistics for recording FDI comprise FDI *flows* i.e. FDI transactions that are carried out within an accounting period, usually the calendar year, as well as FDI *stocks* that are recorded as positions referring to the level of assets or liabilities at a given point in time (IMF 2009). As a result, macro-economic statistics of FDI flows are reported from the BOP whereas FDI stocks can be found in the International Investment Position (IIP) (IMF 2011a). Ideally, both should be integrated in a manner "so that all changes in positions between two points in time are fully explained by the recorded flows" (IMF 2009, p. 29), captured as transactions in the financial account and adjusted to consider changes in volume, exchange rate and price. In such a scenario, the difference of FDI stock data under the IIP between two consecutive years should exactly match the FDI transaction data captured by the BOP during that particular year. Or, more specifically and following IIP logic, the country's direct investment *liabilities* towards foreign parents' equity investments in affiliates resident in the reporting country (i.e. claims that foreigners have on their assets in the reporting country) between two consecutive years should reflect net FDI *inflows* for the reporting country. The direct investment liability position of the IIP corresponds to FDI inward stocks. In contrast, a country's direct investment *assets* include equity investments by parent companies resident in that country in its affiliates abroad and they reflect FDI *outward* stocks whereas the difference of the direct investment asset positions during two consecutive years describe the country's outward FDI flow during that year.

According to BPM-5, direct investment can be sub-classified into equity capital, reinvested earnings and other capital (intercompany transactions). Equity capital comprises equity that the foreign parent invests in its branches as well as all shares it owns in its subsidiaries and associates. Reinvested earnings "consist of the direct investor's share (in proportion to direct equity participation) of earnings not distributed as dividends by subsidiaries or associates and earnings of branches not remitted to the direct investor" (IMF 1993, p. 87–88). A foreign investor who decides to reinvest all or parts of its earnings in the FDI project makes a deliberate decision against repatriating these profits back to its source (Lundan 2006). As such, reinvested earnings originate in the host country of FDI and do not entail a cross-border financial transfer which poses challenges for its recording, as will be discussed in detail in Chapter 2.3.6. The third category of FDI comprises "other capital" and pertains to intercompany transactions that represent a permanent borrowing and lending of funds in the sense of loans granted from direct investors to its subsidiaries and, vice versa, loans from subsidiaries to direct investors.[1] The BPM-6 expands the concept of direct investment in the form of equity shares in that it specifically includes the case of international investment funds which are normally not engaged in any or little production and which hold assets and liabilities on behalf of groups of owners. Moreover, BPM-6 goes into

1 Other capital as the third form of FDI is particularly prevalent for so-called Special Purpose Entities (SPEs) whose main purpose is to serve as financial intermediary for spreading risks, reissuing loans, etc.

more detail by specifying equity capital investment which may in some cases take the form of reverse investment i.e. in cases when the "direct enterprise may acquire an equity or other claim on its own immediate or indirect investor" (IMF 2009, p. 107), and also direct equity investment between fellow enterprises. Fellow enterprises are enterprises "that are under the control or influence of the same immediate or indirect investor, but neither fellow enterprise controls or influences the other fellow enterprise" (IMF 2009, p.103). IMF claims that both data on reverse investment and investment between fellow enterprises should be separately published under BPM-6 and be presented as two additional sub-categories under "equity and investment fund shares" of the financial account. The category of reinvested earnings has been maintained between BPM-5 and BPM-6. The BPM-5 category of "other capital" is now labelled as "debt instruments" in the BPM-6 and is sub-divided into debt instruments from the direct investor into the direct investment enterprise, reverse investment and debt instruments between fellow enterprises. Figure 2.1 below provides the recommended breakdown of the main categories of FDI in the financial account of the BOP which is recorded on a directional basis as an asset for the economy of the direct investor and a liability for the economy of the direct investment enterprise.

Figure 2.1: Direct investment presentation in the financial account of the BOP following BPM-6

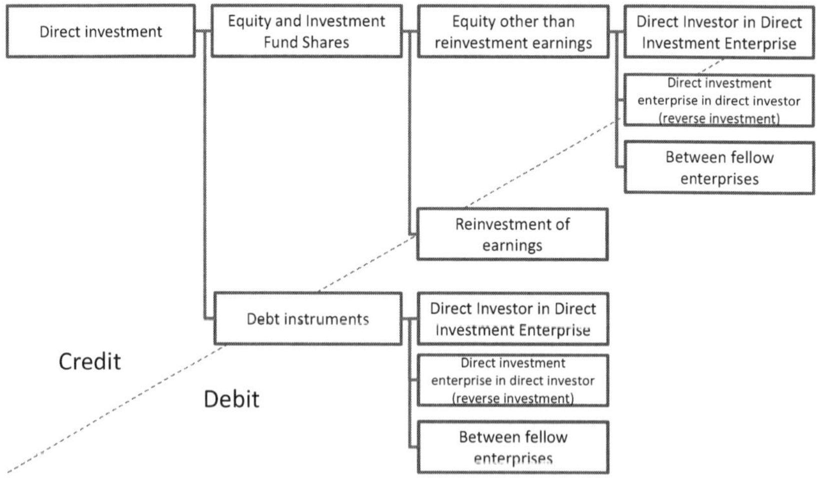

Source: IMF (2009), presentation simplified by author.

2.2 The state of FDI statistics in SSA

FDI statistics on SSA are collected and disseminated by different organizations, of which the IMF, the World Bank and UNCTAD are the most relevant in terms of coverage of countries and frequency of statistics updates. The OECD also plays an important role not because it would collect SSA's inward statistics at BOP level but because it provides an important source of approximation of FDI inflow statistics from FDI outflows of OECD member countries (OECD 2014b, OECD 2014a).

With a few recent exceptions to be addressed in Chapter 2.3.1, the IMF reports its FDI statistics in SSA based solely on data collected in the BOPs by the respective SSA central banks. More specifically, the IMF reported the "Standard Balance of Payments Components" on its web site according to BPM-5 format covering all statistics until end of 2008 and according to BPM-6 format from 2009 onwards.[2] It is worth mentioning that post 2009-data reported to the IMF on a BPM-5 basis is re-arranged to a BPM-6 presentational basis, solely for publication purposes and not necessarily because SSA countries would have already fully adopted the BPM-6 reporting standard. As a matter of fact, even the full adherence to the standards and provisions stipulated by BPM-5 and its ensuing International Transaction Reporting System (ITRS) is currently the exception in SSA. The most recently available study which gives country-level information about the status and quality of implementation of BPM-5 is contained in IMF's 2003 Report "How Countries Measure FDI". Two SSA countries, namely SA and Nigeria participated in the IMF Survey of Implementation of Methodological Standards for Direct Investment (SIMSDI). In the case of SA, the IMF attested overall good levels of improvement although reinvested earnings remains one critical aspect of direct investment income data that is supposedly collected but not officially reported. In the case of Nigeria, reinvested earnings are neither collected nor reported and the recognized 10 per cent FDI threshold is not applied (IMF 2003). As for the other countries, UNCTAD claims that only seven SSA economies (Lesotho, Mauritius, Namibia, SA, Seychelles, Sierra Leone and Togo) have adopted the IMF BOP definition (UNCTAD 2005c). The former does not, however, give evidence that the formal adoption has actually led to

2 Online at http://elibrary-data.imf.org/DataExplorer.aspx (accessed on 9 January 2015).

the implementation of a stringent set of measures for capturing or reporting FDI statistics following IMF's BPM-5 in a consistent and frequent manner, especially since the SIMSDI Survey Instrument has not been applied since 2003. As concerns the majority of the 48 SSA countries, some authors conjecture that approximately one half of African countries have no system in place for capturing FDI at the level of the BOP (Patterson et al. 2004). UNCTAD assumes that the proportion of African countries that work in non-conformity with the IMF-BOP manual is even higher and comprises 35 countries (UNCTAD 2005c).

A review of the direct investment component of financial account statements publicized on IMF's online database corroborates aforementioned findings and confirms blatant statistical gaps in recording direct investment according to BPM-5 or BPM-6. Table 2.1 on the following page highlights that there is currently no single SSA country that would capture FDI liability transactions (FDI "inflows") as per classification proposed by BPM-6 and following the breakdown presented before in Figure 2.1.

Fourteen SSA economies (Burkina Faso, Central African Republic, Chad, Comoros, Congo (Rep.), DRC, Equatorial Guinea, Eritrea, Gabon, Madagascar, Mauritania, Somalia, South Sudan and Zimbabwe) do not publicize a BOP. The reason for this lies in the absence of a viable institutional framework to systematically record and disseminate FDI macroeconomic statistics. In contrast, several SSA countries have in the recent past improved their methods of FDI statistics compilation and reporting. Nowadays, a fairly large number of SSA countries are *in principle* compliant with the direct investment breakdown stipulated by BPM-5 since they report on these three direct investment components, namely equity capital, reinvested earnings and other capital (intercompany transactions).[3] In total, 24 countries in SSA have in the past for at least one single year reported direct investment following BPM-5 but at changing frequency and with many omissions between consecutive years. For example, Côte d'Ivoire complied with BPM-5 until 2010 but stopped reporting any direct investment figures after that. Guinea and Liberia have never reported on all three components together during the same year but reported either on equity capital, reinvested earnings or direct investment debt during one particular year. Many economies, including large SSA economies such as

3 "Other capital" under BPM-5 is denoted "debt instruments" under BPM-6, which was the term used before in Figure 2.1.

Ethiopia, Kenya, Sudan, SA and Mauritius do not collect BOP information on reinvested earnings in spite of the significant cumulative monetary effects that can emanate from sequential investments from the pool of existing foreign investors (Lundan 2006, UNCTAD 2007a). Moreover, it is still the exception that SSA countries report on reverse investments both in terms of direct investment equity and debt. Only six countries (Benin, Botswana, Mali, Mozambique, Niger and Senegal) have at least for one past year reported on reverse equity investment and nine SSA countries on reverse investment via debt instruments.

Table 2.1: BOP reporting of SSA countries on the direct investment components of FDI liabilities (FDI inflows)

Country	Equity and Investment Fund Shares				Debt instruments		
	Equity other than reinvested earnings						
	DI in DIE	DIE in DI (reverse inv.)	Between fellow enterprises	Reinv. Earnings	DI in DIE	DIE in DI (reverse inv.)	Between fellow enterprises
Angola				X	X		
Benin	X	X		X	X	X	X
Botswana	X	X		X	X	X	
Burkina Faso							
Burundi	X						
Cameroon	X			X	X	X	
Cape Verde	X			X	X	X	
Central African Republic							
Chad							
Comoros							
Congo, Rep.							
Côte d'Ivoire	X			X	X	X	
Djibouti	X			X			
DRC							
Equatorial Guinea							
Eritrea							
Ethiopia					X		
Gabon							
Gambia, The	X			X			
Ghana	X			X	X		
Guinea	X			X	X		

Guinea-Bissau	X			X			
Kenya	X				X		
Lesotho	X			X	X		
Liberia	X			X	X		
Madagascar							
Malawi	X			X	X		
Mali	X	X		X	X	X	
Mauritania							
Mauritius	X				X		
Mozambique	X	X		X	X	X	
Namibia	X			X	X		
Niger	X	X		X	X	X	
Nigeria	X			X	X		
Rwanda	X						
São Tomé and Príncipe	X				X		
Senegal	X	X		X	X	X	X
Seychelles	X			X	X		
Sierra Leone	X			X	X		
Somalia							
South Africa	X				X		
South Sudan							
Sudan	X				X		
Swaziland	X			X	X		
Tanzania	X			X	X		
Togo	X			X	X	X	
Uganda	X			X	X		
Zambia	X			X	X		
Zimbabwe							

Source: Financial account breakdown for direct investment, presented on http://elibrary-data.imf.org (accessed on 9 January 2015). Reported if SSA country has collected the direct investment item at least once between 2009 and 2013; DI – Direct Investment; DIE – Direct Investment Enterprise.

With the exception of Senegal, which reported on direct investment debt instruments among fellow enterprises in 2011[4], no other SSA country seems to have adjusted its statistical FDI recording systems to capture the transaction volumes among fellow enterprises.

4 Senegal stopped reporting direct investment BOP figures after 2011.

The blatant absence of statistical figures related to the two additional dimensions of direct investment introduced by BPM-6, namely equity investment and debt instruments among fellow enterprises, shows that SSA countries still have a long way to go before becoming compliant to BPM-6. As yet it is unclear why IMF's World Economic Outlook 2014 gives the misleading impression that nine SSA countries (Burundi, Côte d'Ivoire, Djibouti, Guinea, Guinea-Bissau, Niger, Senegal, Uganda, Zambia) already use the new BPM-6 "at source" because the in-depth review of the direct investment components of these nine countries does not come to such a conclusion (IMF 2014d). Neither does IMF's 2014 classification of 37 SSA countries as being BPM-5 compliant (with the exception of Gambia and Zimbabwe as the only SSA countries compliant to BPM-4) match with the BOP analyses presented in Table 2.1 above.

Prospects for BPM-6 compliance within a reasonable timeframe do realistically exist for those countries that have already ushered in the first steps towards BPM-5 compliance, which is the case for 24 SSA countries. As concerns the other group of SSA countries, in particular those that have not at all reported on FDI figures, it is unlikely that they could leapfrog previous BOP guidelines and would have the capacities to immediately adopt the most complex methodology of the BPM-6. IOs such as the IMF or UNCTAD are making efforts to mitigate the capacity shortcomings in FDI statistics and have provided advice and training support for improving data collection according to the BOP Definition of the IMF (IMF 1993, Patterson et al. 2004, OECD 2008, IMF 2009, Morrison 2013, Quin et al. 2013).

The IMF frames its capacity building support and methodological guidance through its General Data Dissemination System (GDDS) which has the majority of SSA countries as members, with the exceptions of Equatorial Guinea, Eritrea and South Sudan.[5] In short, GDDS attempts to tackle another main challenge of statistical systems of developing countries, namely the *reliability* of data that appears in the financial account of the respective BOPs. To this end, GDDS member countries are urged to update and revise their metadata to describe the current practices of data compilation and dissemination techniques and allow external entities to track a country's convergence towards the best statistical practice, as

5 Membership of GDDS is taken from http://dsbb.imf.org/ (accessed on 18 January 2015).

demonstrated by the superior Special Data Dissemination Standard (SDDS) of the IMF (IMF 2013). SA and Mauritius are the only SSA countries that have managed to graduate from the GDDS to the SDDS and to join the same group as e.g. the OECD member countries. The SDDS with currently 71 member countries world-wide, puts forward the highest standard for the compilation and presentation of BOP statistics and the IIP according to BPM-6 and other related guidelines (IMF 2009, IMF 2011a, IMF 2014a). Against this background, the gestation period of SSA countries is likely to be very long when it comes to the methodologically accurate, however, more complex BPM-6 Guide and its practical companion document, the "Balance of Payments and International Investment Position Compilation Guide" launched in 2014 (IMF 2014a). As a result, the majority of SSA countries are currently members of the GDDS and not the SDDS.

IMF's assessment of the quality and hence reliability of statistical practices and, more particularly, the BOP, strongly depends on the metadata that GDDS member countries are willing to divulge via IMF's "Dissemination Standards Bulletin Board" (DSBB).[6] As Table 2.2 on the next page shows, many of SSA's central banks or NSOs have unfortunately not shared metadata information for a long time. 21 of 48 SSA countries have reported statistical metadata more than 10 years ago i.e. 2005 or before, 6 countries between 2006 and 2010 and 17 countries have reported metadata information after 2011.

A careful review of the DSBB further reveals that, in the majority of cases, the IMF seems to dispose of no means to validate the exact data collection methods and estimation and approximation methodologies because the respective Central Bank or National Statistics Office does not accurately and exhaustively reflect such methodologies as part of their metadata reporting practices. Half of all SSA countries do not disclose any methodological notes to the public. Conversely, about one third of SSA countries publish their statistical methodologies in national publications and/or the IMF BOP Statistics Yearbook thereby allowing statisticians and researchers to comprehend collection, estimation and compilation methods.

6 Online at http://dsbb.imf.org/ (accessed on 18 January 2015).

Table 2.2: Main facts on BOP statistics in SSA

Membership in IMF Dissemination Standard		Statistical Manual employed at source[1]	
Not a member	3	BPM-4	2
Member of GDDS	43	BPM-5	37
Member of SDDS	2	BPM-6	9
TOTAL	**48**	**TOTAL**	**48**
Most recent meta data reporting year		**Extent of BOP disclosure**	
2005 or before	21	Public	14
2006 to 2010	6	Not public	24
2011 to present	17	Shared upon request (but not public)	3
Unknown[2]	4	Unknown[2]	7
TOTAL	**48**	**TOTAL**	**48**

Main Source: IMF's "Dissemination Standards Bulletin Board" (DSBB), online at http://dsbb.imf.org/ (accessed on 18 January 2015).
[1] Based on Statistical Appendix (Table G) in IMF (2014d).
[2] Category "Unknown" covers cases of missing information; countries outside GDDS standard (Equatorial Guinea, Eritrea and South Sudan) were also classified as "Unknown".

The publicized DSBB information sheds further light on data collection and estimation practices particularly for the direct investment components of the BOP and the IIP. These practices differ amongst SSA countries. Certain SSA countries are more advanced in that they aim to adopt a regular and rather stringent approach to collect the required FDI data through FDI flow and stock surveys undertaken either jointly or individually by the Central Bank, the NSO and the IPA. Amongst the first countries that collected information on FDI stocks and flows through specific surveys were Cameroon, Ethiopia, Kenya, Madagascar, Malawi, Mauritius, Mozambique, Namibia, Nigeria, SA, Tanzania and Uganda. The latest reporting years covered the early 2000's (UNCTAD 2008b). A new impetus to FDI stock and flow data collection came in 2010, when the IMF "identified direct investment as an area of large and growing importance, as well as where data can and should be improved" (IMF 2010, p. 7) and launched its "Coordinated Direct Investment Survey (CDIS)" Programme aiming to provide comprehensive and harmonized data on FDI stocks and flows.[7] Until the end of 2013, the CDIS had coverage of 19 SSA countries.

7 Online at http://cdis.imf.org/ (accessed on 29 March 2015).

In contrast to the first group of countries, more than half of SSA countries are neither part of the CDIS nor do they have a regular data collection system in place to capture FDI transactions. The metadata review reveals different and highly fragmented methods of data estimation which poses a challenge in comparing FDI statistics amongst different SSA countries. In the absence of regular survey mechanisms, the most common method of estimating FDI inflows or outflows are through voluntary reports of purchases and sales of foreign exchange by commercial banks in the framework of national ITRSs. While it is acknowledged that ITRSs form a good basis for estimating FDI, their quality of reporting generally deteriorates when exchange control requirements are loosened resulting in a larger number of foreign exchange transactions outside the national banking systems (Quin et al. 2013). On the one hand, FDI can be underestimated because of a large number of small value and over-the-counter transactions not properly captured through the ITRS, complex and cascading transactions or transactions through foreign bank accounts. One the other hand, large domestic transactions in foreign currency can be wrongly interpreted as FDI under the ITRS and may result in an overestimation of FDI (Quin et al. 2013). SSA countries basing their BOP statements primarily on the ITRS include large economies like Côte d'Ivoire, Ethiopia, Madagascar, Sudan[8] and the majority of small SSA economies not covered by the CDIS initiative.[9] Beyond that, there are several other methods applied that follow neither a survey logic nor an ITRS logic. For example, the DRC estimates that 20 per cent of the income of oil-exporting companies is considered to be FDI inflow and 10 per cent of recorded investments by the Ministry of Planning are considered actual foreign investment. No survey instruments are in place to validate such information and to cover sectors outside the petroleum sector. Zimbabwe compiles FDI figures mainly from approval figures received from the Zimbabwe Investment Authority. Liberia calculates its FDI flow figures in a similar way, based on approvals from the Liberian National Investment Commission. In several cases, information reported in the financial press of the respective SSA country is screened on an ad hoc basis to capture high-value direct investments and make subsequent adjustments to available FDI data.

8 For example, Sudan estimates FDI inflow data in the form of cash collected from the commercial banks and the Bank of Sudan (BOS) as well as capital goods imported under the investment concession as recorded by Sudanese customs.

9 Source: http://dsbb.imf.org/ (accessed on 18 January 2015).

2.3 Aggregated FDI statistics in SSA from different sources

The most important sources of FDI statistics in SSA are the IMF, the World Bank, UNCTAD and the OECD. Although the four main FDI reporting organizations subscribe to the same FDI definition, there are nonetheless significant discrepancies which stem from the degree to which statistical adjustments and validation are made to FDI statistics derived from the BOP or IIP. In the following, statistics on SSA's FDI flows and stocks will be provided on the basis of these different available sources and with the aim of unearthing the extent of the discrepancies in the observed FDI statistics data. The previous sub-chapter pinpointed the different challenges that SSA's central banks or NSOs have yet to overcome in terms of data quality, development plans for statistical systems as well as data dissemination. SSA's FDI statistics as presented in the following chapters should thus be looked at in the light of the aforementioned statistical caveats.

2.3.1 SSA FDI statistics reported by the IMF

The IMF does not carry out any *ex post* adjustments to the FDI positions in the respective BOPs. FDI inflow statistics for a respective year can be extracted under "liabilities in reporting economy" (BOP denotation up to the year 2008) and "net incurrence of liabilities" (BOP denotation from 2009 onwards) from the direct investment position of the financial account. The unadjusted direct investment liability positions of the BOP are presented in Table 2.3 on the next page from 2006 to 2013 for those countries where such information was available from the IMF.

There has been considerable variation of FDI inflows year-by-year with the lowest FDI inflows of 15.84 billion USD recorded in 2006 and the largest FDI inflows of 92.12 billion USD recorded in 2011. The BOP liability position of Mauritius has been subject to major corrections of the country's ITRS in the light of deviating results from rounds of the foreign assets and liabilities surveys organized within IMF's CDIS Programme. These corrections have largely influenced the aggregated FDI inflows for SSA especially for the years 2010 until 2013 when Mauritius' direct investment liability position made up between 50 to 65 per cent of SSA's total. Interestingly, the outbreak of the global crisis in 2008/2009 coincided with a peak in FDI inflows in Angola (2.21 billion USD), Nigeria (8.55 billion USD) and SA (9.64 billion USD).

Table 2.3: Aggregated BOP direct investment liability positions (FDI inflows) for SSA, 2006–2013, in billions of USD

Country	2006	2007	2008	2009	2010	2011	2012	2013
SSA[1]	**15.84**	**26.15**	**34.38**	**31.27**	**56.40**	**92.12**	**53.75**	**48.34**
of which:								
Angola	-0.04	-0.89	1.68	2.21	-3.23	-3.02	-6.90	-7.12
Ghana	0.64	1.38	2.71	2.37	2.53	3.22	3.29	3.23
Mauritius	0.11	0.34	0.38	0.26	34.25	60.00	27.16	27.26
Mozambique	0.15	0.43	0.59	0.90	1.26	3.65	5.64	6.70
Nigeria	4.85	6.03	8.20	8.55	6.05	8.84	7.10	
South Africa	-0.18	5.74	9.64	7.62	3.69	4.14	4.63	8.12
Sudan	3.53	2.43	2.60	1.73	2.06	2.31	2.31	2.18
Zambia	0.62	1.32	0.94	0.69	1.73	1.11	1.73	1.81

Source: IMF, http://elibrary-data.imf.org (accessed on 9 January 2015); Own calculations.
[1]Following SSA countries and years were not available and are not included in the aggregated figures: Benin (2013), Burkina Faso (all years), Central African Republic (all years), Chad (all years), Comoros (all years), Congo, Rep.(2008–2013), Côte d'Ivoire (2011–2013), DRC (all years), Equatorial Guinea (all years), Eritrea (all years), Ethiopia (2013), Gabon (all years), Gambia (2013), Guinea-Bissau (2013), Kenya (2013), Madagascar (all years), Malawi (2013), Mali (2012–2013), Mauritania (all years), Niger (2013), Nigeria (2013), Senegal (2012–2013), Somalia (all years), South Sudan (all years), Togo (2011–2013), Zimbabwe (all years).

A dramatic increase of inflows is evident in the case of Mozambique from less than 1 billion USD per year before 2009 to 5.64 billion USD in 2012 and 6.7 billion USD in 2013. The bulk of recent FDI investments in Mozambique targeted coal mining as well as natural gas and oil extraction (IMF 2014b). Ghana had relatively constant FDI inflows of more than 2 billion USD over recent years with a further upward trend driven by Ghana's new role as a large producer of crude oil and natural gas starting in 2011.

FDI inward *stocks* can be derived from the direct investment liability position of the IIP whenever available in SSA economies.[10] The following Table 2.4 displays the results. Accordingly, SSA had an FDI inward stock of at least 527.05 billion USD in 2013, dropping from 696.83 billion USD in 2012. Many SSA countries, including large economies like Cameroon,

10 Source: http://elibrary-data.imf.org (accessed 30 January 2015).

DRC, Ethiopia and Kenya do not have an IIP and were excluded from the aggregation of FDI inward stocks at the continental-level resulting in a likely underestimation. Similar to the case of FDI flows, Mauritius stands out as having a proportionally very large share of SSA's inward stock, namely between 30 and 45 per cent depending on the year of observation. Mauritius adheres to IMF's SDDS and establishes its international direct investment liability position on the basis of foreign asset and liability surveys (Quin et al. 2013).

Table 2.4: Aggregated IIP direct investment liability positions (FDI inward stocks) for SSA, 2009–2013, in billions of USD

Country	2009	2010	2011	2012	2013
SSA[1]	**494.22**	**558.18**	**669.50**	**696.83**	**527.05**
of which:					
Angola	44.25	41.02	38.00	31.10	23.98
Ghana	8.52	11.48	13.17	13.26	
Mauritius	179.04	185.27	299.70	312.57	238.00
Mozambique	3.87	4.69	8.26	13.91	20.60
Nigeria	54.23	60.33	69.24	76.75	
South Africa	138.75	179.56	159.39	163.51	152.12
Sudan	20.45	22.90	32.05	36.85	42.12
Tanzania	8.07	8.76	9.39	10.84	11.29
Uganda	5.03	5.58	6.47	7.67	8.87
Zambia	8.88	9.96	10.92	12.45	14.26

Source: IMF, http://elibrary-data.imf.org (accessed on 9 January 2015); Own calculations.
[1]Following SSA countries and years were not available and are not included in the aggregated figures: Benin (2013), Burkina Faso (all years), Cameroon (all years), Central African Republic (all years), Chad (all years), Comoros (all years), Congo, Rep.(all years), Côte d'Ivoire (2011–2013), DRC (all years), Equatorial Guinea (all years), Eritrea (all years), Ethiopia (all years), Gabon (all years), Gambia (all years), Ghana (2013), Guinea-Bissau (2012–2013), Kenya (all years), Lesotho (all years), Liberia (all years), Madagascar (all years), Mali (2012–2013), Mauritania (all years), Niger (2013), Nigeria (2013), São Tomé and Príncipe (all years), Senegal (2012–2013), Seychelles (all years), Somalia (all years), South Sudan (all years), Togo (2011–2013), Zimbabwe (all years).

As an SDDS member, Mauritius valuates its FDI inward position according to market values[11] whereas most other SSA countries apply book values as a source for valuation of inward FDI stock, with the only exception of the SDDS member South Africa. FDI stocks at current market values

11 Source: http://dsbb.imf.org/Pages/SDDS/DQAFBase.aspx?ctycode=MUS&catcode=IIP00 (accessed on 18 January 2015).

often exceed book values (Zhan 2006, UNCTAD 2008b, UNCTAD 2009b). This may partially explain the large share of Mauritius in the aggregated IIP direct investment liability positions of SSA.

Several countries had a considerable growth in FDI inward stocks between 2009 and 2013. For example, FDI stocks grew by 432 per cent in Mozambique, by 106 per cent in Sudan, by 76 per cent in Uganda and by 61 per cent in Zambia. Angola has experienced several years of FDI divestments resulting in almost halving the FDI inward stock from 2009 to 2013.

In the aftermath of the release of BPM-6, the IMF gives SSA countries the freedom of choice to either continue to use the ITRS or to turn towards the consistent application of FDI surveys as a means to collect the required data for BOP statistics (IMF 2014a). The previous methodological approach of sole reliance on ITRSs has been brought into question by the IMF itself and prompted the launch of the CDIS Programme in order to collect information on inward direct investment positions in aggregated form or cross-classified by investment origin (see also Chapter 2.4.2).[12] 19 SSA countries (Benin, Botswana, Burkina Faso, Cape Verde, Ghana, Guinea-Bissau, Mali, Mauritius, Mozambique, Niger, Nigeria, Rwanda, SA, Senegal, Seychelles, Tanzania, Togo, Uganda and Zambia) have carried out at least one round of the yearly CDIS. Annex Table 1 gives an overview of the CDIS data coverage as of end of 2013. The majority of these 19 countries have repeated the Survey every consecutive year between 2009 and 2013, attempting to capture the inward direct investment positions in terms of equity and debt and, in some cases, also the outward investment positions (Benin, Burkina Faso, Mali, Mauritius, Mozambique, Senegal, South Africa and Togo).

The following Table 2.5 provides the results from the CDIS Survey undertaken in 2012 and 2013 in selected SSA countries. Accordingly, the total FDI inward stock of 19 SSA countries was 562.3 billion USD in 2012/2013 which is the highest figure amongst all IOs that report FDI stocks (see following sub-Chapter 2.3.5). Mauritius and SA host the largest inward FDI stock on the African continent. The effect of Mauritius' and SA's membership in IMF's SDDS shows itself because the IIP direct investment liability positions of both countries in Table 2.4 are per-

12 See: http://www.imf.org/external/np/sec/pr/2010/pr10510.htm (accessed 9 July 2016).

fectly congruent with the CDIS results. Regular inward stock surveys have thus superseded the less reliable ITRSs in both countries. Inconsistencies remain for other SSA countries in the sense that CDIS data does not fully match official IIP statistics in the same year.[13]

Table 2.5: Inward direct investment positions of SSA countries participating in CDIS

Country	Inward FDI stock (in USD million)	Per cent of inward FDI equity position in total FDI stock (1 minus FDI inward debt instruments position)	Latest Reporting year
Benin	977.2	80.8	2012
Botswana	4,921.1	65.7	2013
Burkina Faso	1,327.8	42.3	2013
Cape Verde	1,611.0	99.8	2013
Ghana	13,075.9	40.2	2012
Guinea-Bissau	150.4	100.0	2012
Mali	2,355.1	63.1	2013
Mauritius	238,002.1	62.3	2013
Mozambique	13,792.7	28.9	2012
Niger	1,551.9	72.2	2012
Nigeria	94,960.5	77.0	2013
Rwanda	715.5	48.9	2012
Senegal	1,158.1	88.2	2012
Seychelles	1,080.4	95.8	2013
South Africa	152,124.2	81.3	2013
Tanzania	12,741.3	Not available	2012
Togo	458.3	69.5	2013
Uganda	9,213.5	88.3	2013
Zambia	12,114.4	65.3	2013
TOTAL	**562,332.6** [1]	69.5	

Source: IMF Coordinated Direct Investment Survey (CDIS); http://cdis.imf.org (accessed on 29 March 2015).
[1] Total calculated based on latest reporting year

In 2012/2013, the percentage of the inward FDI equity position was on average 69.5 per cent. This statistic reveals interesting information about the degree of integration of direct investment enterprises in the MNE network.

13 For example, Zambia's FDI inward stock measured through CDIS was 12.11 billion USD in 2013 comparing to 14.26 billion USD in the country's IIP.

The inward FDI equity position behaves inversely to the FDI debt instrument position (intercompany loans). Related to intercompany loans, the IMF states in the BPM-6: "Although debt and other claims that do not involve voting power are not relevant to defining a direct investment relationship, they are included in direct investment transactions and positions if a direct investment relationship exists between the parties" (IMF 2009, p. 105). As a consequence, almost any type of intercompany loans issued by in-house banks, including short-term loans such as overnight deposits and supplier credits, are statistically treated as if they were FDI provided there exists an underlying investment relationship between the foreign parent and its affiliate subsidiary that fulfils the minimum criteria of a significant degree of influence and a minimum of 10 per cent equity ownership.[14] This statistical practice has not been free of criticism (De Nederlandsche Bank 2004, Patterson et al. 2004). A high proportion of FDI accumulation in the form of intercompany loans implies a loosened relationship between the affiliate and the parent company in comparison to a foreign investment that takes the form of foreign equity capital. Intercompany loans, especially if they involve short term loans, are subject to higher volatility than equity capital and can lead to pro-cyclical capital drains similar to cross-border portfolio investments in situations of a looming economic recession of the FDI host country (Ocampo et al. 2007). Against this background, SSA countries with a high proportion of inward FDI through intercompany loans (low proportion of equity related FDI) may be exposed to a larger risk of a sudden foreign capital drain. For example, only 28.9 per cent of Mozambique's FDI inward stock is related to foreign equity which makes the country vulnerable to a sudden foreign capital withdrawal, especially since the majority of the country's recent FDI inflows are concentrated in megaprojects in the natural resource sector, in particular oil, gas and coal mining and where prices are exogenously dictated by the world market (IMF 2014b). This exacerbates the risk of potential foreign divestments as a reaction to a drop in global market prices of the country's most prominent natural resources. Other SSA countries with a proportion of FDI equity inward stock of less than 50 per cent are Ghana (40.2 per cent), Burkina Faso (42.3 per cent) and Rwanda (48.9 per cent). The majority of FDI inward stocks of Guinea-Bissau, Cape Verde,

14 This includes a scenario in which the foreign investor owns only a minority equity share of 10 per cent but provides large-scale and short-term loans to the subsidiary which may even exceed its actual equity share – but would still be counted as FDI.

Seychelles, Uganda and Senegal have been a result of equity transactions and not intercompany loans.

2.3.2 SSA FDI statistics reported by the World Bank

Amongst its World Development Indicators (WDI), the World Bank reports "net FDI inflows"[15] and "net FDI"[16]. The FDI data is largely based on BOP data reported by the IMF but is also "supplemented by the World Bank staff estimates using data from the United Nations Conference on Trade and Development (UNCTAD) and official national sources".[17] There is a pattern in the sense that the World Bank tends to adopt the IMF BOP results for those countries where BOP statements exist and are at the disposal of the IMF. For example, this is the case for Cape Verde, Gambia, Liberia, Mozambique, Nigeria, SA, Seychelles and Sudan leading to a scenario of convergence between World Bank and IMF data and divergence in relation to available UNCTAD data. Alternatively, in cases where such BOP statements are not publicized or do not exist, the World Bank tends to utilize estimations from UNCTAD. This is the case for countries such as Central African Republic, Chad, Comoros, Equatorial Guinea, Eritrea, Gabon, Madagascar, Mauritania, Somalia and Zimbabwe. In the majority of cases, however, the World Bank reporting represents a mix of data collected by the IMF and UNCTAD as shown in Annex Table 2.[18] With the exceptions of South Sudan and Gambia (2000–2002), data is available for all years after 2000.

As the following Figure 2.2 illustrates, SSA has overall seen a rapid growth of yearly FDI inflows from 6.73 billion USD in 2000 to 44.73 billion USD in 2013. FDI inflows dipped in 2006 and in the aftermath of the financial crisis in 2009/10 but reached a new record of 42.95 billion USD in 2011 which was further exceeded in the consecutive years 2012 and

15 See: http://data.worldbank.org/indicator/BX.KLT.DINV.CD.WD (accessed on 24 January 2015).

16 See: http://data.worldbank.org/indicator/BN.KLT.DINV.CD_(accessed on 24 January 2015).

17 See metadata information taken from http://wdi.worldbank.org/table/6.9# (accessed on 24 January 2015).

18 There are some exceptions where World Bank data is different to both IMF and UNCTAD data, e.g. in Burkina Faso from 2006–2010, in DRC from 2006–2012, in Namibia from 2006–2011 or in Zambia from 2010–2011.

2013. Amongst the largest recipients of FDI inflow are Angola, Congo (Rep.), Ghana, Mozambique, Nigeria, SA and Sudan. These seven countries usually account for around 50 per cent of yearly FDI inflows into SSA. Within the last decade, Ghana and Mozambique have risen to join the group of African countries as prime destination for FDI inflows.

Figure 2.2: FDI inflows into SSA countries between 2000 and 2013

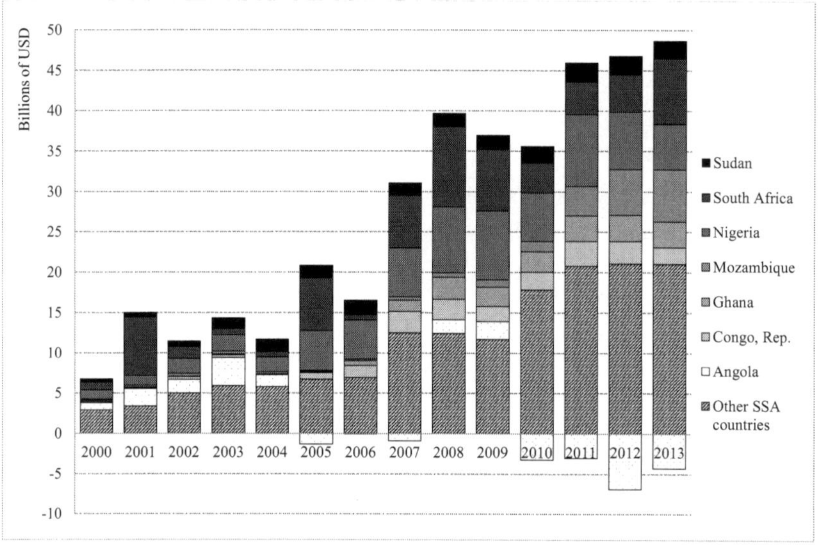

Source: WDI database (World Bank)

Still, until 2006, both countries would not exceed a share of 5 per cent in FDI inflows to SSA compared to 2012/13 when their share already accounted for 22 per cent of FDI inflows to SSA.

FDI inflow statistics of the World Bank exceed those of the aggregated BOP direct investment liability positions of the IMF by 659 million USD in 2006, 4.03 billion USD in 2007, 5.28 billion USD in 2008 and 5.68 billion USD in 2009.[19] This is to be expected because many SSA countries have not been covered by the IMF whereas the World Bank covered all of them with the exception of South Sudan. This is reversed for the years

19 World Bank classifies Djibouti under Middle East & North Africa and not SSA; Djibouti has been re-classified as SSA for comparative reasons.

2010 to 2013 when aggregated BOP direct investment liability positions of the IMF were considerably higher than FDI inflows of the World Bank. The major reason for this discrepancy is a massive downward adjustment that the World Bank has made to the BOP direct investment liability data of Mauritius. If Mauritius is removed, the difference between FDI inflow data of the World Bank and available aggregate BOP direct investment liability data of the IMF is widening year-by-year and reaches a positive difference of around 10 billion USD for the years 2010 and 2011, 12.73 billion USD in 2012 and 23.03 billion USD in 2013, again keeping in mind the important caveat that the World Bank covers all countries (with the exception of South Sudan) and IMF covers around 36 SSA countries depending on the year.

The World Bank also reports on net FDI i.e. FDI in SSA from foreign sources (FDI inflows) less FDI by SSA to the rest of the world (FDI outflows). In BOP terms, the net FDI from a particular SSA country would be positive if FDI outflows i.e. the acquisition of financial assets abroad from a particular SSA country would exceed its FDI inflows i.e. the incurrence of liabilities in the country for a specific year. No data on net FDI before 2005 is available. As Table 2.6 on the next page shows, net FDI has been negative every year since 2005, which supports the assumption that the few emerging SSA multinational companies investing outside the continent do not offset the assets held by non-SSA foreign investors in SSA, not accounting for the emergence of increasing levels of intra-SSA investments (UNIDO 2007, UNIDO 2012a, UNCTAD 2014d). In the case of Angola, the net FDI is positive which is a result of divestments between 2010 and 2013 (negative FDI inflows) and not due to a hike of outward FDI projects by Angolan-based multinationals. Otherwise, a positive net FDI for a particular year constitutes a rather rare scenario in SSA. Noteworthy are the relatively low FDI net figures for SA in 2012 and 2013 with minus 1.73 billion USD in 2012 and minus 2.58 billion USD in 2013 respectively. FDI inflows of the same years were 4.67 billion USD in 2012 and 8.12 billion USD in 2013 which implies that SA had quite large FDI outflows of 2.9 billion USD in 2012 and 5.54 billion USD in 2013, large proportions of which are likely to appear as FDI inward flows in Southern African economies in the geographic vicinity of SA.

Table 2.6: Net FDI in SSA, 2005–2013, in billions of USD

Country	2005	2006	2007	2008	2009	2010	2011	2012	2013
SSA[1]	**-16.15**	**-8.47**	**-23.13**	**-33.47**	**-28.03**	**-34.93**	**-29.67**	**-30.15**	**-14.05**
of which:									
Angola	1.52	0.23	1.81	0.89	-2.20	4.57	5.12	9.64	13.16
Ghana	-0.14	-0.64	-1.38	-2.71	-2.37	-2.53	-3.20	-3.29	-3.23
Mauritius	0.01	-0.10	-0.28	-0.33	-0.22	-13.84	0.99	-5.67	-2.19
Mozambique	-0.11	-0.15	-0.43	-0.59	-0.86	-1.02	-3.56	-5.63	-6.18
Nigeria	-4.97	-4.53	-5.17	-7.15	-7.03	-5.13	-8.03	-5.56	
South Africa	-5.61	5.31	-3.60	-12.00	-6.31	-3.85	-4.29	-1.73	-2.58
Sudan	-1.56	-1.84	-1.50	-1.65	-1.73	-2.06	-2.31	-2.31	-2.18
Tanzania	-0.94	-0.40	-0.58	-1.38	-0.95	-1.84	-1.23	-1.80	-1.87
Zambia	-0.36	-0.62	-1.32	-0.94	-0.43	-0.63	-1.11	-2.43	-1.63

Source: WDI database (World Bank), online at http://data.worldbank.org/indicator/BN.KLT.DINV.CD (accessed on 24 January 2015).
[1]Following SSA countries and years were not available and are not included in the aggregated figures: Benin (2013), Burkina Faso (2011–2013), Central African Republic (all years), Chad (all years), Congo Rep. (2008–2013), Côte d'Ivoire (2011–2013), Equatorial Guinea (all years), Eritrea (all years), Ethiopia (2013), Gabon (2006–2013), Gambia (2013), Guinea-Bissau (2013), Kenya (2013), Madagascar (2006–2013), Malawi (2013), Mali (2012–2013), Mauritania (2005–2011), Niger (2013), Nigeria (2013), Senegal (2012–2013), Somalia (all years), South Sudan (all years), Togo (2011–2013) and Zimbabwe (all years).

From a theoretical point of view, net FDI figures reported by the World Bank should correspond to the direct investment component of the BOP, as reported by the IMF under BPM-6 starting from 2009. For available BPM-5 data from 2006-2008 when the directional reporting system has still been maintained, net FDI can be calculated by subtracting "direct investment into reporting economy" from "direct investment abroad". A comparative analysis was undertaken on the basis of the same underlying data sets from both the World Bank and IMF.[20] The discrepancy between World Bank net FDI data and IMF data accounts for 1.14 billion USD in 2006, 152 million USD in 2007 and 864 million USD in 2008. Between

20 Excluding the following countries and years: Benin (2013), Burkina Faso (all years), Central African Republic (all years), Chad (all years), Comoros (all years), Congo Rep. (2008–2013), Côte d'Ivoire (2011–2013), DRC (all years), Equatorial Guinea (all years), Eritrea (all years), Ethiopia (2013), Gabon (all years), Gambia (2013), Guinea-Bissau (2013), Kenya (2013), Madagascar (2006–2013), Malawi (2013), Mali (2012–2013), Mauritania (all years), Niger (2013), Nigeria (2013), Senegal (2012–2013), Somalia (all years), South Sudan (all years), Togo (2011–2013) and Zimbabwe (all years).

2009 and 2013, there is perfect congruency between FDI net figures reported by the World Bank and the aggregated direct investment component of the BOP. In this context, it is worth mentioning that the breakdown of direct investment components for foreign investors' extra-territorial assets is even sketchier compared to the FDI liability components of the BOP, as reported in Annex Table 3. A total of 20 SSA countries have not compiled any information about direct investment abroad, including large countries such as DRC, Ethiopia, Sudan and Tanzania. In certain cases, the World Bank refrains from reporting net FDI for countries that are not regularly reporting BOPs to the IMF.[21] A detailed analysis unveils some statistical flaws related to the World Bank's computation of net FDI which conjectures that countries that do not display any data on outward direct investment assets do not possess any of such outward direct investment assets. This has been the case for countries like Djibouti, Ethiopia, Gambia, Rwanda, Sudan and Tanzania even though it is impossible that none of these countries, especially economies with active membership in a regional economic community (REC) such as the East African Community (EAC), did not have any outward direct investment flows as a result of fast-growing intra-regional trade relations (UNIDO 2007, AFDB 2010, UNIDO 2012b, EAC 2013). Consequently, the negative tendency of net FDI figures in SSA might be overestimated because it does often not account for outward direct investment or it captures only some dimensions of outward direct investment leaving out others such as outward investments into fellow enterprises.

2.3.3 SSA FDI statistics reported by UNCTAD

UNCTAD reports FDI data for inward and outward FDI flows and inward and outward FDI stocks through its "FDI-TNC-GVC Information System".[22] While IMF relies exclusively on FDI data as shown in the country's BOP, UNCTAD taps into numerous data sources making it globally the most authoritative and reliable provider of FDI statistics within an overall context of chronic paucity of FDI data in SSA. Published and un-

21 For example, in 2012, FDI Net data was not reported for Central African Republic, Chad, Côte d'Ivoire, Equatorial Guinea, Eritrea, Mali, Senegal, Somalia, South Sudan and Zimbabwe.

22 Available at: www.unctad.org/fdistatistics (accessed on 11 February 2015).

published national official FDI data directly from central banks, statistical offices or national authorities on an aggregated and disaggregated basis constitute the priority data source for the compilation of UNCTAD's FDI/TNC flow and stock database. The data is further complemented by data obtained from other IOs such the IMF, the World Bank, OECD as well as UNCTAD's own estimates. UNCTAD also uses OECD outflows statistics as proxies for its FDI inflow statistics. As a last resort and when all other data sources have been exhausted, UNCTAD may use "FDI data from large recipients and investors"[23] or the M&A database of the Thomson Reuters Corporation as proxies.[24] In reality, however, changes to the FDI greenfield database or the M&A database do not trigger significant corrections of UNCTAD's FDI inflow database and, as sub-Chapter 2.3.5 after next will show, do generally not result in drastic deviations from FDI inflow figures from the direct investment liability component of SSA's BOPs.

An analysis of UNCTAD's FDI inflow data shows similar trends to what had already emerged from the analysis of FDI inflows of the World Bank data (see Figure 2.3). The only exception is observable when UNCTAD reported an increase of 900 million USD from 38.7 billion USD to 39.6 billion USD between 2008 and 2009 whereas the World Bank saw a decline of 2.7 billion USD during the same period. An all-time record inflow of 44.8 billion USD (World Bank: 44.4 billion USD) was achieved in 2013 (UNCTAD 2014d).

---

23 Presumably referring to the "fDi Markets" greenfield projects database, see Chapter 2.4.3.

24 http://unctad.org/en/Pages/DIAE/Investment%20and%20Enterprise/FDI_Flows.aspx (accessed on 11 February 2015).

Figure 2.3: FDI inflows into SSA, comparing UNCTAD vs. World Bank data, 2000–2013

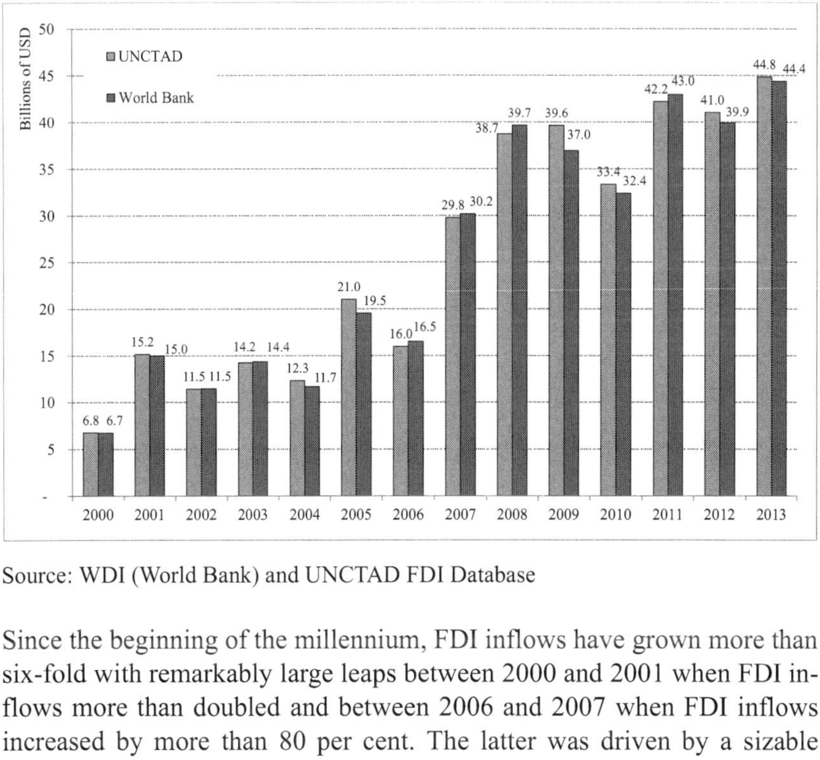

Source: WDI (World Bank) and UNCTAD FDI Database

Since the beginning of the millennium, FDI inflows have grown more than six-fold with remarkably large leaps between 2000 and 2001 when FDI inflows more than doubled and between 2006 and 2007 when FDI inflows increased by more than 80 per cent. The latter was driven by a sizable number of mega greenfield projects in the oil and gas sectors of Angola, Mozambique and Uganda as well as large M&As in Sudan's telecommunication sector (see Annex Table 4 and Table 2.18). In 2010, it was evident that the contraction in global demand and the resulting financial constraints of large multinationals had also negatively impacted the volume of FDI inflows into SSA, albeit to a much lesser extent than most other regions in the world. As a result, FDI inflows slumped from 39.6 billion USD in 2009 to 33.4 billion USD in 2010 (UNCTAD 2014d).

Figure 2.4: FDI inflows into SSA, disaggregated by regions, 2000–2013

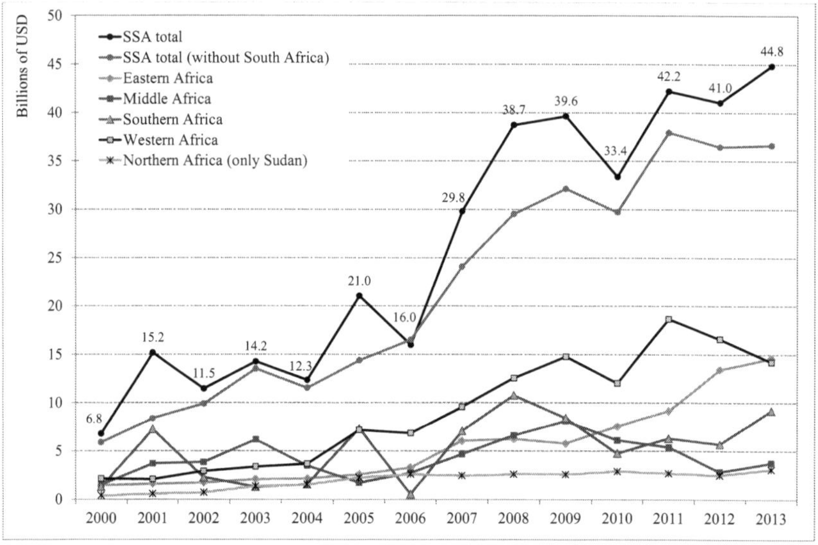

Source: UNCTAD FDI Database

Not all regions in SSA have experienced the same growth trajectory (see Figure 2.4 above). This is particularly blatant when comparing Eastern Africa[25] to Middle Africa[26]. While Eastern Africa experienced a nearly undisrupted year-by-year growth from 2000 to 2013, the contagious effect of the financial crisis seemed to be more structural and long-term in the case of Middle Africa which has seen declining new FDI inflows over the past years. Due to major FDI disinvestments in Angola, FDI inflows to Middle Africa have been highly volatile and dropped to 3.76 billion USD in 2013 shrinking the region's share to less than 10 per cent of total FDI inflows to SSA. In contrast, Eastern Africa has become the prime FDI destination attracting nearly one third of FDI inflows in 2013 and surpassing

25 UNCTAD's classification of "Eastern Africa" comprises the following economies: Burundi, Comoros, Djibouti, Eritrea, Ethiopia, Kenya, Madagascar, Malawi, Mauritius, Mozambique, Rwanda, Seychelles, Somalia, South Sudan (no data available), Tanzania, Uganda, Zambia and Zimbabwe.

26 UNCTAD's classification of "Middle Africa" comprises the following economies: Angola, Cameroon, Central African Republic, Chad, Congo, DRC, Equatorial Guinea, Gabon and São Tomé and Príncipe.

Western Africa[27] which had been in first position since 2006. In 2012 and 2013, the most attractive FDI destination in East Africa and second most attractive destination in SSA was Mozambique with FDI inflows of nearly 6 billion USD and 5.6 billion USD respectively. Other Eastern African FDI growth poles are Tanzania, Uganda and Zambia.

Over the ten year time span of 2004 to 2013, Nigeria absorbed on average an annual 6.3 billion USD of new FDI inflows, making it SSA's largest single country FDI destination before South Africa attracting an average annual volume of 5 billion USD. Until only a few years ago Nigeria had an overarching position in Western Africa, absorbing at least half of the region's FDI inflows. Following the discovery of oil and gas deposits in Ghana, FDI inflows of more than 3 billion USD between 2011 and 2013 boosted the country to become the second largest recipient of FDI inflows in Western Africa after Nigeria and the fourth largest in SSA.

FDI inflows to Southern Africa[28] correlate strongly with those of SA that in itself acts as an important outward investor in the region (Games 2004, Naidu and Lutchman 2004, UNCTAD 2005b, Saunders 2008, Draper et al. 2010). A particularly drastic decline in the immediate aftermath of the financial crisis was observable for SA where new FDI inflows dropped from 9.2 billion USD in 2008 to 7.5 billion USD in 2009 and further down to 3.6 billion USD in 2010. As a result, once SA is excluded from the SSA group, the dip in 2010 appears less dramatic although it still accounted for 8 per cent less than 2009 inflows. While other countries have been subject to highly volatile FDI inflows, year-by-year FDI inflows to Sudan have been constant even during the financial crisis and, since 2005, never dropped below an average annual 2 billion USD.[29]

Turning from FDI flows to stocks, UNCTAD reports FDI inward and outward stocks as book value or historical costs from the liability and asset positions in the IIPs whenever they are available and published by the IMF. To mitigate persistent problems related to incomplete or unavailable IIPs from SSA countries, UNCTAD also resorts back to cumulate FDI

27 UNCTAD's classification of "Western Africa" comprises Benin, Burkina Faso, Cape Verde, Côte d'Ivoire, Gambia, Ghana, Guinea, Guinea-Bissau, Liberia, Mali, Mauritania, Niger, Nigeria, Senegal, Sierra Leone and Togo.

28 UNCTAD's classification of "Southern Africa" comprises Botswana, Lesotho, Namibia, SA and Swaziland.

29 Some of these FDI inflows may however be attributable to South Sudan after the 2011 period for which data does still not exist.

flows and reports them as stocks.[30] This is a statistically problematic practice since cumulated FDI flows do not consider valuation changes or inflation rate adjustments and a priori exclude FDI not resulting in a BOP transaction such as reinvested earnings. As a result, FDI inward stocks calculated in this manner are most probably underestimated (Bellak 1998).

Table 2.7: FDI inward stocks (in billions of USD) and shares, 1992–2013

Region	1992	1995	1998	2001	2004	2007	2010	2013
	in billions of USD and per cent							
World	2,423.4	3,425.9	5,754.4	7,589.7	11,299.6	18,136.2	20,370.7	25,464.2
Developing countries	610.2	850.4	1,230.4	1,875.6	2,431.5	4,660.2	6,597.1	8,483.0
Africa	69.1	89.3	110.3	155.0	256.4	414.6	596.8	687.0
SSA	42.6	56.1	70.1	106.9	187.1	279.5	411.5	474.3
SSA (SA excl.)	31.9	41.1	54.4	72.2	106.9	147.6	232.0	334.3
SSA in World	1.8%	1.6%	1.2%	1.4%	1.7%	1.5%	2.0%	1.9%
SSA in dev. countries	7.0%	6.6%	5.7%	5.7%	7.7%	6.0%	6.2%	5.6%
SSA in Africa	61.6%	62.8%	63.6%	68.9%	73.0%	67.4%	69.0%	69.0%
SSA (SA excl.) in world	1.3%	1.2%	0.9%	1.0%	0.9%	0.8%	1.1%	1.3%
SSA (SA excl.) in dev. countries	5.2%	4.8%	4.4%	3.8%	4.4%	3.2%	3.5%	3.9%
SSA (SA excl.) in Africa	46.2%	46.0%	49.3%	46.6%	41.7%	35.6%	38.9%	48.7%
SSA (SA excl.) in SSA	75.0%	73.2%	77.6%	67.5%	57.1%	52.8%	56.4%	70.5%
Source: Own calculations based on UNCTAD 2014 FDI Database								

Accordingly, the total FDI inward stock for SSA was 474.3 billion USD in 2013 (UNCTAD 2014d). It has more than doubled compared to 2006, when FDI inward stock amounted to 229.3 billion USD. Due to relative insensitivity to year-by-year outliers, FDI inward stocks lend themselves to a fairly robust descriptive trend analysis both at regional as well as at

30 http://unctad.org/en/Pages/DIAE/Investment%20and%20Enterprise/FDI_Stocks.aspx (accessed 11 February 2015).

global level. As Table 2.7 on the previous page indicates, the share of SSA's FDI inward stocks in global FDI inward stocks has over the past 20 years vacillated between 1 and 2 per cent and stood at 1.9 per cent in 2013.

After the financial crisis in 2010, SSA's share in world FDI inward stocks jumped up rapidly from 1.5 to 2 per cent and has since then remained close to the 2 per cent mark. The same trend can be recognized if SA is excluded from SSA in which case the share of SSA increased from 0.8 per cent in 2007 to 1.1 per cent in 2010 and to 1.3 per cent in 2013 compared to world FDI inward stocks. Likewise, the share of SSA (excl. SA) FDI inward stock rose to nearly 50 per cent of Africa's inward stocks with a particularly drastic gain from 2010 to 2013, which was certainly influenced by the political turmoil associated with the 2011 "Arab spring" movements in several Northern African countries and ensuing foreign investors' reluctance for new FDI investments or reinvestments. SSA's (excluding SA) share in developing countries' inward stock has in recent years risen to 3.9 per cent thus slowly returning to the shares the region had in the 1990s. Figure 2.5 on the next page shows how the FDI inward stocks of the main subregions of SSA[31] have changed in relation to SSA's total FDI inward stock.

The largest FDI inward stock of SSA is concentrated in SA. It accounted for 140 billion USD in 2013 which translates into a share of 29.5 per cent of SSA's total FDI inward stock. SA's FDI inward stock accounts for the lion's share (93.5 per cent) in the FDI inward stock of Southern Africa. Southern Africa's share in SSA has been volatile, reaching 50 per cent in 1999 and 2005–2007 only to drop sharply in the years to follow. The most populous country in Africa, Nigeria, follows second after SA and hosted an FDI inward stock of close to 82 billion USD in 2013 which equates to a share of 17.3 per cent in total SSA FDI inward stocks. Nigeria is by far the most dominant FDI host in Western Africa, followed by Ghana (19.8 billion USD FDI inward stocks, 4.2 per cent share in SSA in 2013), Côte d'Ivoire and Liberia. The recent hike from a 23.4 per cent share of Western Africa to a 30.6 per cent share between 2010 and 2013 is especially attributable to a rapid FDI inward stock increase in Ghana's oil and gas sector and also the doubling of FDI inward stocks in Niger and Mauritania

31 Classification of subregions underlying FDI inward stock calculations is the same as for FDI inflows, see footnotes no. 25 to 28.

due to large investments into the mining, oil and natural gas extraction sectors.

Figure 2.5: FDI inward stocks of SSA subregions in relation to SSA's total FDI inward stocks, 1995–2013

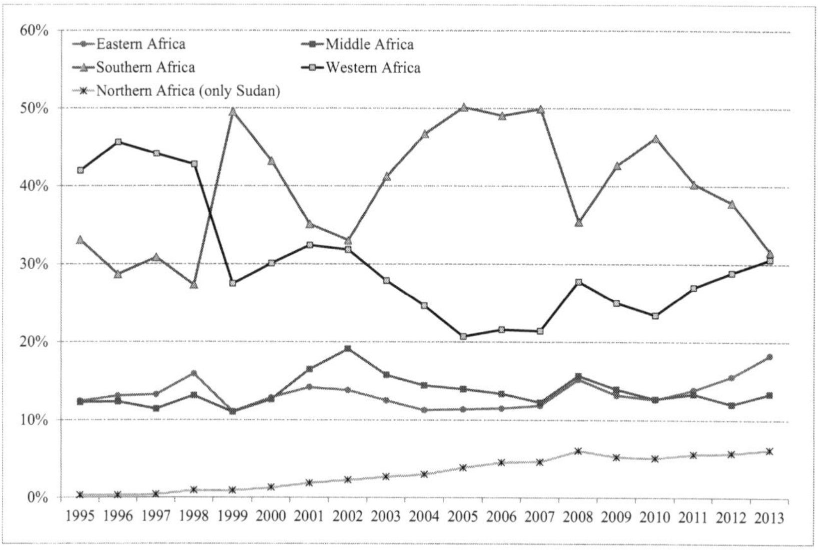

Source: UNCTAD 2014 FDI Database

The shares of both Eastern and Middle Africa have not considerably changed and have been at around 15 per cent on average. Middle Africa's share could have been considerably higher if Angola had not dropped from a summit FDI inward stock of 13.4 billion USD in 2004 to a meagre 2.3 billion USD in 2013. All other economies in Middle Africa increased their FDI inward stock. Noteworthy is the Republic of Congo which has grown its FDI stock from 2.9 billion USD in 2004 to 23 billion USD in 2013, making it the fourth largest FDI host economy in SSA. Eastern Africa's recent increase in SSA's FDI inward stock is primarily attributable to sizable FDI inflows in the mining and petroleum sector of Mozambique and to a lesser extent to Uganda, Tanzania and Zambia. With a share of 6.1 per cent, Sudan is SSA´s third largest host of FDI inward stocks and, in 2013, was host to an FDI inward stock of 29.1 billion USD.

2.3.4 SSA FDI statistics reported by OECD

FDI outflow and outward stock statistics can constitute a useful complement to FDI inflow and inward stock statistics especially in situations where the ITRSs at host county-level are non-existent or unreliable. The most comprehensive and harmonized statistics on FDI outflows are being compiled and reported by the OECD in its two yearly publications, the "Geographical Distribution of Financial Flows to Developing Countries 2013: Disbursements, Commitments, Country Indicators" and "International Direct Investment Statistics" (OECD 2014b, OECD 2014a). In these publications, OECD reports the aggregated OECD outflows of the current 29 members of the OECD Development Assistance Committee (DAC).[32]

These statistics are convenient although they mask the full extent of global FDI outflows into SSA because they are biased towards developed countries' outflows and omit the rapid soaring of FDI that has its origin in developing countries. According to UNCTAD, the latter accounted for an estimated 20.8 per cent of FDI flows into Africa over the 2000–2008 period and 7.4 per cent of 2008 FDI stocks (UNCTAD 2010a). A further caveat of OECD statistics is related to the statistical phenomenon of a widening global gap between total FDI inflows reported by recipient countries and total FDI outflows reported by source countries (UNCTAD 2005d, Zhan 2006). This phenomenon is vividly referred to as FDI "deficit to the moon" (Bellak 1998, p. 243) and stems from differing reporting practices at the outward and inward level in terms of distinguishing FDI from portfolio investments, treatment of unremitted subsidiary profits and other discrepancies between statistical recording practices. Over the past years, this gap has leaned towards global inward flows being remarkably higher than global FDI outflows for a given year (Fujita 2008).[33] Applied to OECD outward statistics directed to SSA, it would mean that OECD outflow statistics are likely to be lower than the real but unknown OECD

32 DAC members comprise: Australia, Austria, Belgium, Canada, Czech Republic, Denmark, European Union, Finland, France, Germany, Greece, Iceland, Ireland, Italy, Japan, Korea, Luxembourg, the Netherlands, New Zealand, Norway, Poland, Portugal, Slovak Republic, Slovenia, Spain Sweden, Switzerland, UK, and US. See http://www.oecd.org/dac/dacmembers.htm#members (accessed on 28 February 2015).

33 For example, in 2013, the reported global FDI outflows were 1,411 billion USD and the global FDI inward flows were 1,452 billion USD, see UNCTAD 2014d.

proportion in SSA's FDI inward flows. In practice, this hypothesis is not verifiable because only very few SSA countries provide breakdowns for countries of origin in their respective inflow statistics. In 2008, only 12 African countries had such a breakdown in their FDI inflow or inward stock statistics (Fujita 2008, UNCTAD 2008b). OECD explains these discrepancies quite cryptically to be "largely due to the timing of revisions" in the case of differences with IMF's BOP data and "due to adjustments" in comparison to UNCTAD.[34]

Table 2.8 below shows total OECD outflows to SSA and for selected main destination economies from 2006 to 2013. Unlike other FDI data sources such as IMF, the World Bank and UNCTAD, OECD statistics show a gradual decline of FDI outflows after two major peaks in 2007 and 2010.

Table 2.8: OECD outflows to SSA, 2006–2013, in billions of USD

Country	2006	2007	2008	2009	2010	2011	2012	2013
SSA, total[1]	4.45	19.51	4.94	10.32	9.07	7.65	2.00	3.26
of which:								
Angola	0.42	-0.63	0.39	2.85	2.02	1.96	-2.12	1.55
Congo (Rep.)	0.55	0.89	0.17	0.23	0.31	-1.12	0.50	0.56
Ghana	0.01	0.26	0.03	0.20	0.28	0.59	0.61	0.51
Mauritius	0.65	9.87	0.05	0.51	1.48	0.49	-0.98	0.06
Nigeria	-0.13	-0.02	0.89	2.53	-0.15	1.47	3.63	-0.34
South Africa	2.30	6.23	4.95	2.33	2.27	3.08	0.62	-0.28
Other SSA	0.65	2.91	-1.53	1.67	2.86	1.18	-0.26	1.21

[1]Excluding St. Helena, Mayotte and OECD category "South of Sahara, regional"; also excluding Comoros (2007), Eritrea (2011), Lesotho (2007–2008 & 2010), Somalia (2005, 2009 & 2011) and South Sudan (all years).
Source: OECD International Direct Investment Statistics (database) 2014, http://dx.doi.org/10.1787/data-00335-en (accessed on 20 February 2015).

FDI outflows from OECD countries reached a cumulative value of 3.26 billion USD in 2013 compared to 44.8 billion USD of FDI inflows reported by UNCTAD in the same year. These two statistical results for the same year show how blatantly different the data collection at FDI source is from data collection at the host country level. One hypothetical assump-

34 See: http://www.oecd.org/daf/inv/investmentfordevelopment/fdistatisticsanddata-frequentlyaskedquestions.htm#Q6 (accessed on 1st March 2015).

tion is that OECD outflows to SSA are identical to FDI inflows; the OECD share in FDI inflows would have been at a meagre 7.2 per cent in 2013 which is implausibly low despite the increasing emergence of non-OECD FDI engagements on the African continent. Generally, OECD outflows directed to single SSA economies are subject to high volatility and negative FDI outflows (i.e. a reverse investments) appear to be a common phenomenon; this has occurred at least once in Angola, Congo (Rep.), Mauritius, Nigeria and South Africa. Unlike FDI inflow statistics where SA or Nigeria alternated to attract the largest share of yearly FDI inflows, OECD outflow statistics show a different pattern as countries such as Mauritius in 2007 (9.87 billion USD) and Angola in 2009 (2.85 billion USD) and in 2013 (1.55 billion USD) featured among the most attractive destinations for OECD investors for a given year.

FDI outward positions of OECD countries in SSA are available but such data is sketchier than that of OECD outflow data.[35] Different OECD central banks report on their SSA outward FDI position at different levels of aggregation. The most detailed information is reported by France, Germany, Italy, Korea, UK and US in the sense that the FDI outward stock is reported for almost every SSA country and on a yearly basis. At the other end of the spectrum are, for example, Japan and Spain that are reporting their FDI stock in SA and otherwise any other stock under "unallocated Africa". Portugal is reporting its FDI outward stock for all Lusophone African countries plus Nigeria and SA. Central European DAC member countries have no widely dispersed FDI outward stock in SSA and they limit data reporting to a maximum of two or three SSA countries.

The overall FDI outward stock of OECD countries in SSA has nearly doubled from 88.5 billion USD in 2006 to 172.4 billion USD in 2012.[36] During the years 2007–2009 it remained almost constant at a total level of 114 billion USD. In 2010, outward stocks soared to 158.5 billion USD and

35 The OECD International Direct Investment Database is available under: http://stats.oecd.org (accessed on 1st March 2015).

36 Information based on own calculations and on individual reporting by 34 OECD member countries: Austria, Belgium, Canada, Chile, Czech Republic, Denmark, Estonia, Finland, France, Germany, Greece, Hungary, Iceland, Ireland, Israel, Italy, Japan, Korea, Luxembourg, Mexico, the Netherlands, New Zealand, Norway, Poland, Portugal, Slovak Republic, Slovenia, Spain, Sweden, Switzerland, Turkey, UK and US; In the case of Canada, category "Africa unallocated" has been interpreted to be SSA but may erroneously include Canadian outward FDI stock in Northern Africa.

remained relatively constant thereafter. The OECD outward stock of 172.4 billion USD for the year 2012 compares to a total FDI inward stock of 457.1 billion USD in the same year (UNCTAD 2014d). The share of OECD outward stocks in FDI inward stocks is hence 37 per cent and explains a larger portion than OECD outward flows in SSA´s FDI in flow data (7.2 per cent). Notwithstanding, it is still in glaring disharmony to a reported 91.6 per cent share of developed countries' inward stock compared to the total FDI inward stock in Africa (UNCTAD 2010a).

Figure 2.6: OECD countries outward FDI stock in selected SSA countries, 2006–2012

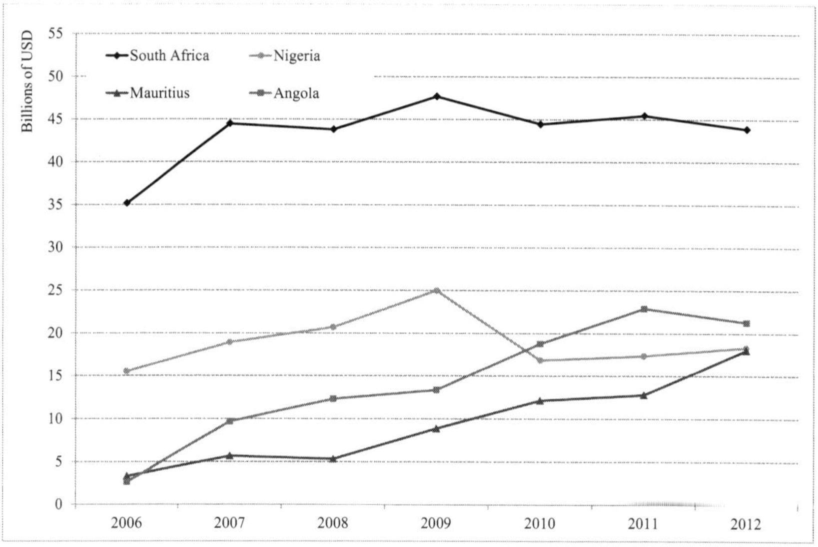

Source: OECD International Direct Investment Database

In Figure 2.6 above, FDI outward positions of OECD countries are reported for some selected SSA economies. An interpretation of results needs to factor in the many remaining data constraints that cannot be eliminated through statistical techniques.[37] In the light of these limitations, OECD

37 Data omissions for some years have not been replaced with FDI outward stock values of previous years; outward stocks to SA do not include the following OECD countries: Czech Republic, Luxembourg, Mexico, New Zealand and Slovak Republic; outward stocks to Nigeria do not include the following OECD coun-

FDI outward stock in SA remained quite stable at an average 45 billion USD over previous years. In 2012, the three countries, Angola, Mauritius and Nigeria had OECD outward stocks not too dissimilar from each other between 18 to 21 billion USD. It is noteworthy that, after a harsh decline of outward stocks dropping from 25 billion USD to 16.9 billion USD in 2010, Nigeria has lost its position as the second largest destination country of OECD outward stocks to Angola. Mauritius has seen a year-by-year increase from 3.3 billion USD in 2006 to 18 billion USD in 2012 primarily driven by UK and US outward stocks. This reveals a rare situation where the aggregated FDI outward stock of OECD countries to Mauritius is not significantly lower but considerably higher than the total FDI inward stock of the country which UNCTAD reported to be 3.2 billion USD in 2012 (UNCTAD 2014d).

Sub-Chapter 2.4.2 will focus once again on the issue of discrepancies between FDI flow and stock data depending on its measurement at origin- or source-level. FDI outward position statistics will be presented from the perspective of the OECD country of origin.

2.3.5 Comparison between World Bank, IMF, UNCTAD and OECD

This sub-chapter juxtaposes the FDI inflow statistics of the four main reporting IOs i.e. the IMF, the World Bank, UNCTAD and OECD from 2006 to 2013. Aggregated FDI inflow statistics of these different institutions are determined by the number of countries subsumable under the overall category of SSA. The largest omissions occur in FDI statistics reported by the IMF whereas the World Bank's and UNCTAD's databases cover all SSA countries, with the exception of South Sudan. It is not surprising therefore that, from 2006 and 2009, the World Bank and UNCTAD

---

tries: Australia, Austria, Canada, Chile, Estonia, Finland, Iceland, Ireland, Japan, Luxembourg, Mexico, New Zealand, Slovak Republic, Slovenia and Spain; outward stocks to Angola do not include the following OECD countries: Australia, Austria, Canada, Chile, Czech Republic, Estonia, Finland, Greece, Hungary, Iceland, Ireland, Israel, Japan, Luxembourg, Mexico, New Zealand, Slovak Republic, Slovenia, Spain, Sweden, Switzerland, Turkey and UK; outward stocks to Mauritius do not include the following OECD countries: Austria, Canada, Chile, Czech Republic, Estonia, Finland, Greece, Hungary, Ireland, Japan, Luxembourg, Mexico, New Zealand, Poland, Portugal, Slovak Republic, Slovenia, Spain, Sweden, Switzerland and Turkey.

FDI inflow statistics are up to 20 per cent above IMF statistics for the same year (see Table 2.9 below).

Table 2.9: FDI inflows to SSA from different sources, 2006–2013, maximum coverage of countries

Source	2006	2007	2008	2009	2010	2011	2012	2013
	In billions of USD							
IMF: Aggregation of BOP direct investment liability positions	15.84	26.15	34.38	31.27	56.40	92.12	53.75	48.34
World Bank: FDI inflows	16.50	30.17	39.65	36.95	32.38	42.95	39.90	44.37
UNCTAD: FDI inflows	15.97	29.77	38.72	39.64	33.35	42.21	41.04	44.84
OECD: Member country outflows to SSA	4.45	19.51	4.94	10.32	9.07	7.65	2.00	3.26

Source: IMF, World Bank, UNCTAD and OECD. Own calculations.
IMF: Excluded are Benin (2013), Burkina Faso (all years), Central African Republic (all years), Chad (all years), Comoros (all years), Congo, Rep.(2008–2013), Côte d'Ivoire (2011–2013), DRC (all years), Equatorial Guinea (all years), Eritrea (all years), Ethiopia (2013), Gabon (all years), Gambia (2013), Guinea-Bissau (2013), Kenya (2013), Madagascar (all years), Malawi (2013), Mali (2012–2013), Mauritania (all years), Niger (2013), Nigeria (2013), Senegal (2012–2013), Somalia (all years), South Sudan (all years), Togo (2011–2013) and Zimbabwe (all years).
World Bank and UNCTAD: Excluded is South Sudan (all years).
OECD: Excluded are Comoros (2007), Eritrea (2011), Lesotho (2007–2008, 2010), Somalia (2005, 2009 & 2011) and South Sudan (all years).

This trend takes a dramatic turn in 2010 which is when IMF FDI inflows reach 56.4 billion USD in SSA as opposed to 32.4 billion USD reported by the World Bank and 33.4 billion USD reported by UNCTAD. In spite of covering fewer countries, from 2010 until 2013, FDI inflow statistics of the IMF remain above all other FDI statistics reported by any other institution. Rather than a general trend, the former is however a result of major discrepancies of reported FDI inflows in the financial sector of Mauritius, as will be explained in greater detail in sub-Chapter 2.3.6. Once Mauritius is excluded from IMF inflow statistics, the pattern is reversed in the sense that UNCTAD and World Bank FDI inflow statistics remain considerably above IMF inflow statistics with a widening year-by-year gap. Excluding Mauritius, IMF reported FDI inflows for SSA were 21.1 billion USD in 2013, compared to 44.1 billion USD reported by World Bank and 44.6 billion USD reported by UNCTAD. In relation to these three data sources, OECD FDI outflow data is considerably lower, accounting for less than 30 per cent of reported FDI inflows of most years until 2011 and between 5 to 10 per cent of FDI inflows in 2012 and 2013.

Table 2.10: FDI inflows to SSA from different sources, 2006–2013, country coverage adjusted to BOP availability

Source	2006	2007	2008	2009	2010	2011	2012	2013
	In billions of USD							
IMF: Aggregation of BOP direct investment liability positions	15.73	25.81	34.00	31.02	22.15	32.12	26.58	21.08
World Bank: FDI inflows	14.48	24.90	31.73	32.75	22.81	30.92	27.09	24.85
UNCTAD: FDI inflows	14.97	25.63	32.79	31.05	22.05	32.31	26.37	24.38
OECD: Member country outflows to SSA	2.92	8.92	5.77	9.15	6.58	7.62	1.47	1.94

Sources: IMF, World Bank and UNCTAD. Own calculations.
Note: To ensure maximum comparability, following SSA countries and years are not included in the analysis due to non-availability of BOP statements displaying the direct IIPs: Benin (2013), Burkina Faso (all years), Central African Republic (all years), Chad (all years), Comoros (all years), Congo, Rep.(2008–2013), Côte d'Ivoire (2011–2013), DRC (all years), Equatorial Guinea (all years), Eritrea (all years), Ethiopia (2013), Gabon (all years), Gambia (2013), Guinea-Bissau (2013), Kenya (2013), Madagascar (all years), Malawi (2013), Mali (2012–2013), Mauritania (all years), Mauritius (all years), Niger (2013), Nigeria (2013), Senegal (2012–2013), Somalia (all years), South Sudan (all years), Togo (2011–2013) and Zimbabwe (all years); Despite having BOP statements, Mauritius has not been included to avoid data distortions.

A thorough conclusion on the extent of the discrepancy which stems from statistical practices rather than differences in country coverage can best be reached if aggregated yearly FDI inflows figures are related to a common number of SSA countries for which IMF BOP statements exist. Mauritius has been excluded once again to avoid distortions in this comparative analysis. Table 2.10 above presents again a comparison of FDI inflows reported by IMF, the World Bank, UNCTAD and OECD from 2006 to 2013 but within this new framework of applying the same SSA definition for all of them. The extreme differences in FDI inflow statistics have disappeared. World Bank and UNCTAD stay within a 10 per cent upper or lower bandwidth around IMF's results, except in 2013 where there is a positive difference of more than 3 billion USD between UNCTAD and the World Bank vs. IMF's results. All data sources show a drastic decline of FDI inflows in 2010 and a rapid increase in the subsequent year 2011 reaching approximately the same level as FDI inflows of the year 2009. For all years under observation, the distance between IMF results and UNCTAD's FDI inflow estimates is smaller than that between IMF results and that of the World Bank.

Annex Table 2 provides a meta-analysis of statistical discrepancies of FDI inflows reported by the IMF, the World Bank and UNCTAD for the years 2006 to 2012 and at individual SSA country level. Only in four SSA countries (Angola, Burundi, Malawi and Uganda) is there a perfect match between the three statistical sources from 2006 to 2012. In another ten SSA countries for which no BOP IIP data of the IMF exists, there is congruency between the World Bank's and UNCTAD's FDI inflow data (Central African Republic, Chad, Comoros, Equatorial Guinea, Eritrea, Gabon, Madagascar, Mauritania, Somalia, and Zimbabwe). A common observation is that World Bank data and IMF data are matching for a particular year and SSA host country while FDI inflows reported by UNCTAD remain different e.g. in Cape Verde, Gambia, Ghana, Liberia, Mozambique, Nigeria, South Africa, Swaziland, and Tanzania. Reported FDI inflows from 2006 to 2012 are different amongst all three sources in the case of Congo, DRC and Namibia.

A further comparison can be made between *net* FDI statistics between the IMF, the World Bank and UNCTAD. UNCTAD's FDI flow statistics were processed in such a manner that they become net figures, namely by subtracting outflow data from inflow data of the same year.[38] Table 2.11 on the next page reports FDI net statistics from 2006 to 2013.

The general observation is as expected in that statistics with the largest country and year-by-year coverage also report the highest net FDI deficit at SSA level. UNCTAD's country coverage is larger than that of the World Bank. In turn, the World Bank covers more countries in a particular reporting year than the IMF. As a consequence, UNCTAD's reported yearly net FDI deficit is the highest and the World Bank's net FDI is higher than that of the IMF.

The only exceptions occurred in 2006 when IMF reported the highest net FDI deficit compared to UNCTAD or World Bank and in 2010 when IMF's and World Bank's net FDI statistics exceeded UNCTAD's statistics. The previous Chapter 2.3.2 compared a reduced data set of FDI net statistics of the World Bank with available IMF data. Both datasets had shown minor discrepancies. This corroborates the conclusion that the main determinant for statistical deviations in net FDI between the different sources relates to differences in country coverage rather than different compilation techniques.

38 UNCTAD does not report net FDI directly.

Table 2.11: Net FDI flows to SSA from different sources, 2006–2013, maximum coverage of countries

Source	2006	2007	2008	2009	2010	2011	2012	2013
	In billions of USD							
IMF: Aggregation of BOP net direct investment positions	-9.34	-21.14	-32.56	-28.22	-32.15	-28.05	-25.86	-11.23
World Bank: Net FDI	-8.47	-23.13	-33.47	-28.03	-34.93	-29.67	-30.15	-14.05
UNCTAD: Net FDI (outflows minus inflows)	-9.21	-26.06	-42.43	-35.86	-31.47	-36.92	-32.14	-32.99

Sources: IMF, World Bank and UNCTAD. Own calculations.
IMF: Excluded are Benin (2013), Burkina Faso (all years), Central African Republic (all years), Chad (all years), Comoros (all years), Congo Rep. (2008–2013), Côte d'Ivoire (2011–2013), DRC (all years), Equatorial Guinea (all years), Eritrea (all years), Ethiopia (2013), Gabon (all years), Gambia (2013), Guinea-Bissau (2013), Kenya (2013), Madagascar (2006–2013), Malawi (2013), Mali (2012–2013), Mauritania (all years), Niger (2013), Nigeria (2013), Senegal (2012–2013), Somalia (all years), South Sudan (all years), Togo (2011–2013) and Zimbabwe (all years).
World Bank: Excluded are Benin (2013), Burkina Faso (2011–2013), Central African Republic (all years), Chad (all years), Comoros (2013), Congo Rep. (2008–2013), Côte d'Ivoire (2011–2013), Equatorial Guinea (all years), Eritrea (all years), Ethiopia (2013), Gabon (2006–2013), Gambia (2013), Guinea-Bissau (2013), Kenya (2013), Madagascar (2006–2013), Malawi (2013), Mali (2012–2013), Mauritania (2005–2011), Niger (2013), Nigeria (2013), Senegal (2012–2013), Somalia (all years), South Sudan (all years), Togo (2011–2013) and Zimbabwe (all years).
UNCTAD: Excluded are Djibouti (all years), Eritrea (all years), Ethiopia (all years), Gambia (all years), Somalia (all years) and South Sudan (all years).

A further comparison between available international providers of FDI statistics is possible at the level of FDI *inward stocks*. The most meaningful comparison can be undertaken between aggregated IIP direct investment liability positions published by the IMF, IMF's CDIS, UNCTAD data and OECD SSA outward stock data. The following Table 2.12 displays the results. The World Bank does not publish FDI stock statistics. In recent years, FDI stock figures based on the CDIS have been on par with FDI statistics of IMF's IIP direct investment liability positions although much fewer countries are covered. In 2013, FDI stock estimations based on IMF's CDIS were the largest of all institutions and reached a total of 562.3 billion USD for 19 SSA countries. Data obtained from the IMF CDIS incorporate the effect of reinvested earnings in FDI inward stock statistics and they cover "Own funds at book value" (OFBV) as an accepted proxy for asset valuation at market value (IMF 2010). Both factors may explain why CDIS-based FDI inward statistics have lately surpassed FDI statistics of UNCTAD and of IMF's IIP, since both base their data mostly on ITRSs that do not capture reinvested earnings or valuate direct investment assets at lower book values instead of market values (Quin et al.

2013). The extent of undervaluation of FDI stocks seems to be significant given that 2013 FDI inward stocks of 19 SSA countries that participated in the CDIS were almost 90 billion USD above the reported FDI inward stocks by UNCTAD (474.3 billion USD) for all SSA countries with the exception of South Sudan.

Table 2.12: FDI inward stocks in SSA from different sources, 2009–2013, maximum coverage of countries

Source	2009	2010	2011	2012	2013
	In billions of USD				
IMF: Aggregated IIP direct investment liability positions	494.22	558.18	669.50	696.83	527.05
IMF: Inward direct investment positions from CDIS Survey	349.16	454.57	591.46	656.45	562.33
UNCTAD: FDI inward stock	344.83	411.55	423.41	457.09	474.32
OECD: SSA outward stocks	113.91	158.54	164.06	172.44	not available

Sources: IMF, IMF-CDIS, UNCTAD and OECD. Own calculations.
IMF – IIP based reporting: Excluded are Benin (2013), Burkina Faso (all years), Cameroon (all years), Central African Republic (all years), Chad (all years), Comoros (all years), Congo, Rep.(all years), Côte d'Ivoire (2011–2013), Equatorial Guinea (all years), Eritrea (all years), Ethiopia (all years), Gabon (all years), Gambia (all years), Ghana (2013), DRC (all years), Guinea-Bissau (2012–2013), Kenya (all years), Lesotho (all years), Liberia (all years), Madagascar (all years), Mali (2012–2013), Mauritania (all years), Niger (2013), Nigeria (2013), São Tomé and Príncipe (all years), Senegal (2012–2013), Seychelles (all years), Somalia (all years), South Sudan (all years), Togo (2011–2013) and Zimbabwe (all years).
IMF – CDIS based reporting: Excluded are Angola (all years), Benin (2009–2010), Burkina Faso (2009–2011), Burundi (all years), Cape Verde (2009–2011), Cameroon (all years), Central African Republic (all years), Chad (all years), Comoros (all years), Congo, Rep.(all years), Côte d'Ivoire (all years), Djibouti (all years), DRC (all years), Equatorial Guinea (all years), Eritrea (all years), Ethiopia (all years), Gabon (all years), Gambia (all years), Guinea-Bissau (2009–2010), Kenya (all years), Lesotho (all years), Liberia (all years), Madagascar (all years), Malawi (all years), Mali (2009–2010), Mauritania (all years), Namibia (all years), Niger (2009–2011), Rwanda (2009–2010), São Tomé and Príncipe (all years), Senegal (2009–2010), Sierra Leone (all years), Somalia (all years), South Sudan (all years), Sudan (all years), Swaziland (all years), Tanzania (2009), Togo (2009–2010) and Zimbabwe (all years); In the case of Benin, Ghana, Guinea-Bissau, Mozambique, Niger, Rwanda, Senegal and Tanzania, the 2012 data was extrapolated to 2013; In the case of Togo, 2011 data was extrapolated to 2012.
UNCTAD: Excluded is South Sudan (all years).
OECD: Based on individual reporting of Austria, Belgium, Canada, Chile, Czech Republic, Denmark, Estonia, Finland, France, Germany, Greece, Hungary, Iceland, Ireland, Israel, Italy, Japan, Korea, Luxembourg, Mexico, the Netherlands, New Zealand, Norway, Poland, Portugal, Slovak Republic, Slovenia, Spain, Sweden, Switzerland, Turkey, UK and US; In the case of Canada, category "Africa unallocated" has been interpreted to be SSA but may erroneously include Canadian outward FDI stock in Northern Africa.

As mentioned in the previous sub-chapter, FDI outward stocks of OECD countries account on average for less than one third of FDI inward stocks. Moreover, there is a trend whereby OECD outward stocks explain an increasingly smaller proportion of FDI inward stocks between 2009 and 2013.

2.3.6 Factors influencing variations in FDI flow and stock statistics

Previous chapters highlighted the many gaps that exist in recording and reporting FDI data, which has led to the application of a variety of proxies by the different IOs that regularly report on FDI. These methods will be listed and their likely effect will be assessed as to whether they lead to an inflation of FDI inflows and inward stocks or result in an underestimation. Since these opposing effects are at play at the same time and at varying intensity depending on the accuracy of a country's reporting standard of its ITRS or its IIP, it is impossible to come to a terminal conclusion on what causes discrepancies in FDI statistics of different IOs for such a large and disperse group of countries in SSA.

The following factors are likely to cause an **underestimation** of FDI flows or stocks:

- **Non-recording of reinvested earnings**
  One major weakness which is reiterated frequently is that BOP statistics do not correctly capture reinvested earnings because they do not involve a cross-border financial flow and do thus not appear in records of exchange transactions (Cantwell 1992, Bame 1995, Zhan 2006, Fujita 2008, UNCTAD 2008b, UNCTAD 2009b). Such data can hence not be obtained without complementary FDI surveys. Being the opposite of profit repatriation, reinvested earnings can be significant whenever a foreign investor organizes its investments in an incremental fashion in order to assess the opportunity costs at each step of the expansion process (Lundan 2006, Financial Times 2012). Consequently, the likelihood of reinvestments increases in older foreign firms with longer investment tenures (Mudambi 1998). At a global scale, it is estimated that reinvested earnings account for up to 30 per cent of average yearly investment flows and that the proportion of reinvestment in FDI is rapidly increasing (UNCTAD 2007a). In 2011, the Financial Times reported that expansions accounted for 23 per cent of global capital investment from FDI during that year. 45 per cent of FDI in extractive

industries and 39 per cent in manufacturing are carried out through reinvestments (Financial Times 2012). In the UNIDO "Africa Investor Report 2011" it was found that an average 60 per cent of working capital and fixed assets financing comes from retained earnings (UNIDO 2012a). In SSA, 22 countries have never recorded the reinvested earnings component of FDI whereas others have many year-by-year omissions in their reporting (see Table 2.1).

– **Non-recording of small cash-transactions of FDI by small and medium-sized enterprises (SMEs)**
  The role of FDI by small and medium-sized enterprises (SMEs) is given increased attention in international literature and specific studies pointed to the rapid emergence of this type of FDI on the African continent (Kiggundu 2002, UNIDO 2007, UNCTAD 2011a, UNIDO 2012a). These largely entrepreneurial companies are involved in cross-border regional FDI and their cumulative impact in terms of sales and employment generation may be significant, but their relevance and volume in terms of capital flows remains outside of existing macro-level reporting systems (Biggs and Shah 2006). Formal but small FDI transactions made through post offices, exchange bureaus, and other agents of money transfer operators (MTOs) are usually not reflected in official FDI statistics. This is even more so in the case of informal cash-based transactions resulting from international remittances of migrant workers and informal lending systems through family networks and African diaspora (Buencamino and Gorbunov 2002, Kratzsch 2010). Pertinent examples are Indian-Asians in East Africa or Lebanese communities in West Africa but also the stratum of Chinese micro-FDI in Africa undertaken by Chinese migrant workers (Broadman 2008, Dobler 2009).
– **Valuation of FDI projects based on book values instead of market values**
  For the correct measurement of FDI data, IMF's BPM-6 recommends the use of estimates for market values for positions not listed on a stock exchange which is a situation that often arises for direct investment enterprises, private equity and others (IMF 2009). With the only exceptions of SDDS members Mauritius and SA, which valuate FDI stocks at market values, the only regular source for valuation of inward FDI stocks is shown as book values in the foreign companies' balance

sheets.[39] Although this is not the ideal scenario because the book value is not fully reflective and usually lower than the market value, it has been considered an acceptable approximation of FDI stocks due to lack of other alternatives (UNCTAD 2009b). In SSA, there has until recently been an absence of a timely valuation of FDI assets at source e.g. through regular enterprise surveys.[40] For instance, in 2013, only 18 SSA countries reported FDI liability positions (inward stocks).[41] Twenty-two SSA countries have not established an IIP and a further number of countries have had omissions in the year-by-year reporting of FDI stocks as part of their respective IIPs. This results in statistical techniques that approximate FDI inward stocks through accumulated FDI inflows from the BOP statistics. A year-by-year extrapolation of FDI inflows as nominal proxies to foreign inward assets is, however, problematic. The book values are confined to historical costs and disregard inflation effects, exchange rate effects, transaction of non-financial assets, FDI assets created through local borrowing and others, the sum of which is leading to a systematic underestimation of MNE activity (Cantwell 1992, Bellak 1998, Stephan and Pfaffmann 2001, Bellak and Cantwell 2004). Moreover, a change of FDI stocks can stem from other factors not related to new FDI transactions but reclassifications, depreciations, revaluations of patents, expropriations, etc., related to existing FDI inward stock (UNCTAD 2005d, Fujita 2008).

– **Locally financed FDI projects**
  Similar to reinvested earnings, BOP statistics fail to capture a scenario wherein a foreign subsidiary is borrowing from a local bank or raises capital from local minority shareholders. According to Bellak, it is estimated that domestically-financed projects by foreign investors or foreign entrepreneurs (FEs) may actually account for the same aggregated global value of FDI flows as flows formally recorded through the BOP statistics, or, in other words, official global FDI flow figures might be by about 50 per cent underestimated because they explicitly exclude

39 The valuation of yearly FDI *flows* from the balance sheet is in accordance with the requirement of BPM-6 to capture market values because the parties conclude the financial transaction at current values, except in some particular cases such as transfer pricing or M&As.

40 In particular before the introduction of IMF's CDIS in 2009.

41 See: http://elibrary-data.imf.org/DataReport.aspx?c=20303471&d=33061&e=170784 (accessed on 30 January 2015).

domestically-financed FDI projects (Bellak 1998). This effect is quite pronounced in the foreign real estate sector in which the raising of local debt capital such as mortgages, bonds and loans from local banks is quite common resulting in sizable real estate holdings but from a low FDI capital base (UNCTAD 2009b).

The following factors are likely to cause an **overestimation** of FDI flows or stocks:

- **Reporting of FDI data based on announcements**
  The review of meta-data related to BOP compilation and reporting presented in Chapter 2.2 revealed that most SSA countries that fall under IMF's General Data Dissemination System (GDDS) base their FDI inflow data on data collected during the approval or registration phase prior to the FDI implementation phase. In this case, FDI statistics constitute a form of by-product from the regular work by host country administrations such as investment promotion agencies (IPAs), registrar's offices or export promotion agencies. These approved investments represent "the amount of the proposed contribution or share of foreigners to various projects in the country" (UNCTAD 2009d, p. 21). Very often, there is a significant time span between the transmission of information about a foreseen foreign investment to a specialized authority (i.e. the approved investment) and the actual realization of the investment project. In other cases, the announced FDI project may not materialize at all because of changing corporate priorities or a re-assessment of the costs and risks associated with the proposed FDI project prompting the foreign investor to withdraw from its original plans. A case in point is natural-resource-seeking investment with long preparation times related to e.g. exploration drilling in the oil, gas and mining sector. During that time, originally positive feasibility studies might turn negative in view of unexpected quality changes of the commodity coupled with an unforeseen drop in global commodity prices. Due to the lack of consistent and exhaustive mechanisms applied by SSA's IPAs for the continuous tracking of foreign investors' activities, there exists no reliable information about the extent of the deviation between registered FDI and implemented FDI, let alone a sector-specific factor which would indicate the proportion of the realization rate compared to announced investment volumes at the FDI registration stage. Beyond that, in the case of a shared domestic-foreign investment project, the entire project volume may be reported instead of the financial equity contribution of only the foreign partner. Moreover, the granting of fi-

nancial or fiscal incentives by the host country is usually proportionally tied to the committed foreign investment and this may prompt foreign firms to record overly optimistic future investment volumes. In the majority of cases, the actual *implemented* investment levels are much lower provided the investment is realized at all (UNCTAD 2008b). In 2004, for instance, the realization rate of approved FDI inflows accounted for 70.2 per cent in the case of South Korea, 51.1 per cent in Singapore, 39.5 per cent in China and only 18.2 per cent in Indonesia (Fujita 2008).

- **Sketchy reporting of reverse investments (divestments)**
  Divestments or reverse investments i.e. a foreign affiliate investing in its parent firm, are rarely captured in BOP direct investment statistics. They are determined by a complex set of interrelated factors that by and large follow the reverse logic of Dunning's OLI paradigm for new FDI (Boddewyn 1983). Divestments are not always an expression of a project's failure such as dwindling market demand for the main subsidiary's product, mismanagement, overinvestment, etc., but can also be the outcome of a broader corporate strategy which is to consolidate the operations of MNE subsidiaries, including successful ones (UNCTAD 1998). As Table 2.1 has shown, reverse investments for the direct investment equity component are compiled and reported by only six SSA countries, namely Benin, Botswana, Mali, Mozambique, Senegal and Niger and, even for these six, reporting has not been without gaps.[42] As a result, FDI inflows are overestimated because the lack of data on reverse investment is statistically treated as if its value was zero (UNCTAD 2005d). As chapter 2.4.3 will show, M&A deals of one foreign investor selling its assets and operations to another national foreign investor, are quite frequent in SSA. In fact, the largest recent single M&A transaction was a 2.2 billion USD divestment in the oil sector of Equatorial Guinea undertaken by the US MNE Devon Energy Corporation. Smaller-scale divestments that attract less public fanfare are susceptible to double counting because the foreign assets of the previous foreign owner may not be eliminated from the FDI inward stock statistics whereas the value of the M&A sale to a new foreign in-

42 Reverse investment in the debt component of FDI is compiled and recorded by 10 African countries, namely Benin, Botswana, Cape Verde, Cameroon, Côte d'Ivoire, Mali, Mozambique, Niger, Senegal and Togo.

vestor is recorded as new FDI inflow thereby distending the country's FDI inward stock.

- **FDI in the financial sector and by multi-territory companies**
According to UNCTAD, the accurate measurement of FDI in the financial sectors is particularly challenging (UNCTAD 2008b). Equity capital and long-term liabilities such as long-term loans, bonds and debentures extended by the parent bank to its affiliated bank fulfil the criteria of the debt component of FDI (see Chapter 2.1) and are thus correctly classified as FDI in the financial sector (UNCTAD 2009b). In actual practice, however, it is difficult to delineate FDI from portfolio investments which occur whenever short-term transactions take place between the parent bank and the affiliate bank as part of the regular financial intermediation process. An increase in short-term deposits can be a reaction to interest-rate differentials, fiscal changes, political uncertainty or increased household borrowing in foreign currency but has nothing in common with the long-term investment motive underlying the FDI definition (Beugelsdijk et al. 2010). A case in point is the offshore financial sector that has thriven in Mauritius over the past decade and which has resulted in the creation of multiple special purpose entities (SPEs) as "flexible corporate structures with little or no physical presence" (IMF 2009, p. 58) with the purpose of exploiting a business climate offering favourably low tax rates, limited regulatory burden and high standards of confidentiality (IMF 2014a). The integration of offshore banking businesses in Mauritius' BOP and its validation through a series of enterprise surveys has contributed to an enormous inflation of "FDI" inflows in 2010 and 2011 of 34.2 billion USD and 60 billion USD respectively reported by IMF's aggregated BOP direct investment liability positions (Quin et al. 2013). In reality, these "FDI inflows" seem to mask an increase in short-term foreign currency deposits which rather fulfil the characteristic of portfolio investment instead of FDI. Many of such deposits are held by global business corporations that are not considered resident for Mauritius tax purposes (IMF 2014a). As a result, UNCTAD and the World Bank have adjusted their reported FDI inflows to much lower values of 430 million USD and 433.4 million USD in 2010 and 2011 respectively. The case of Mauritius has been receiving heightened public attention and has led the country to gradually abandon its status as one of the tax haven countries in SSA (OECD 2014c). Besides Mauritius, the "Global Forum on Transparency and Exchange of Information for Tax" attributes

only SA and Ghana as having large or full compliance with the Forum's mandate to establish and monitor international safeguards for tax transparency to achieve transparency and exchange of information for tax purposes (OECD 2015). Beyond that, Cameroon, Gabon, Nigeria, and Seychelles have signed the "Convention on Mutual Administrative Assistance in Tax Matters"[43] which, in turn, means that transparent standard-setting in SSA's foreign financial sector is still an exception and the likelihood of mistaking portfolio investment as FDI remains very high.

A further example of a bloated FDI sector is the shipping sector which has been particularly buoyant in Liberia. Liberia has the world's second largest fleet by flag of registration after Panama. In 2014, a total number of 3,126 ships have been registered under the Liberian flag by foreign owners with almost zero per cent of local co-ownership (UNCTAD 2014b). Germany, Greece and Japan are the most important investors in Liberia's shipping sector (Ampiah 1997, UNCTAD 2011a, UNCTAD 2013a). The second largest shipping sector in SSA is in Tanzania where a total of 163 large vessels are registered (UNCTAD 2014b). Most of these "flag of convenience" investments fulfil IMF's criteria of SPEs in that they are exempt from tax and that all assets and liabilities of the investment are with non-residents apart from any deposits or loans with resident banks (Sharife 2010, IMF 2014a). Since, according to the IMF "there is no internationally standard definition of SPEs" (IMF 2009, p.66) compounded with complexities associated with multi-territorial companies operating "seamlessly across multiple economies" (IMF 2014a, p. 120), there is a high probability that many of such "flag of convenience" investments are erroneously recorded as FDI. In 2010, for instance, a Greek shipping company owner concluded a 587 million USD M&A deal in Liberia (UNCTAD 2011a). Presumably in the aftermath of this mega deal in 2011, IMF reported a historical direct investment liability position of Liberia's BOP of 1.31 billion USD. In contrast, UNCTAD reported FDI inflows of only 508 million USD in 2011. This discrepancy is likely to stem from the fact that IMF reported unadjusted BOP data reported by its GDDS member

43 http://www.oecd.org/ctp/exchange-of-tax-information/Status_of_convention.pdf (accessed on 18 March 2015).

Liberia, whereas UNCTAD made a downward correction by not classifying this particular shipping M&A investment as FDI.
More generally, the correct compilation of investment data from multi-territorial companies would require a highly complex process of pro-rata splitting of foreign assets and transactions to the respective territories (IMF 2014c). This may overstrain the current capacities of SSA's institutions mandated to compile FDI data. As a consequence, a particular foreign asset which is either mobile or not clearly attributable to one single country (vessels of a shipping company, aircrafts pertaining to an airline, hydro-electrical schemes of border rivers, cross-border pipelines or infrastructure projects and others) may be counted several times thus inflating FDI inflows and stocks. Some authors argue that the concept of multi-territoriality goes beyond specific sectors but is a logical outcome of production networks becoming more intangible and fluid across well-defined geographical locations in a bid to harness tax advantages through convoluted corporate governance networks involving holding companies and SPEs (Lipsey 2007, Buckley 2014, UNCTAD 2016).

Despite a long list of methodological problems pertaining to macroeconomic FDI statistics in SSA and in developing countries more generally, a plethora of studies has extensively utilized such statistics as a dependent variable to a set of presupposed FDI determinants (Pigato 2000, Cotton and Ramachandran 2001, Pigato 2001, Asiedu 2002, Bende-Nabende 2002, Naudé and Krugell 2003, Asiedu 2004b, Onyeiwu and Shrestha 2004, Akinkugbe 2005, Lumbila 2005, Mlambo 2005, Anyanwu 2006, Asiedu 2006, Dupasquier and Osakwe 2006, UNECA 2006, Naudé and Krugell 2007, Adams 2009, Suliman and Mollick 2009, Gohou and Soumaré 2009, Kolstad and Wiig 2011, Sichei and Kinyondo 2012). Conversely, only a handful of authors have made an attempt to look behind the veil to denote and unearth the recurrent methodological problems in the compilation of FDI data which also brings into question the validity of many FDI-data based studies (Cantwell 1992, Bellak 1998, Stephan and Pfaffmann 2001, UNCTAD 2005d, Fujita 2008, Beugelsdijk et al. 2010). Noteworthy is the study of Kerner, which shows quite plainly how classical FDI determinant analyses can lead to different results depending on the chosen outcome variable.[44] This leads him to assert that "getting the measure right or wrong has significant implications for the sort of conclusions that we draw concerning the nature of FDI and the role of political forces in global finance" (Kerner 2014, p. 813).

Two studies have to date gone beyond the mere diagnosis of FDI compilation and reporting problems and sought to formulate a methodological foundation for the revaluation of international MNE activity with potential applicability in a cross-country context (Bellak and Cantwell 2004, Beugelsdijk et al. 2010). Bellak and Cantwell have found a systematic undervaluation of FDI stocks and have employed a perpetual inventory model to revalue FDI stocks to constant and current values (Bellak and Cantwell 2004). Beugelsdijk et al. also find a significant mismatch between FDI stock and actual MNE affiliate activity and assert that the mismatch is a function of FDI host country factors. In particular, FDI stocks are overestimating real MNE affiliate activities in case the host country is considered a tax haven. FDI is underestimated in countries with well-developed financial markets leading to increased local borrowing by foreign affiliates (Beugelsdijk et al. 2010). Notwithstanding these results, a holistic methodology for the quantification of the discrepancy between officially reported FDI statistics and the "real" unknown level of FDI flows or stocks does not exist to date. Such a methodology would require the inclusion of all possible predictors with influence on the extent of the mismatch between FDI data and actual MNE activity.

From the predictors listed in Figure 2.7 on the next page, previous studies have picked only three. Bellak and Cantwell's study can be referred to the predictor for FDI underestimation *"Extrapolation of FDI inflows at nominal values disregarding inflation, exchange rates, etc."* and Beugelsdijk et al. refer to *"FDI in tax haven countries"* as a factor of FDI overestimation and *"Domestic financing of FDI projects"* as a factor of FDI underestimation.

44 Kerner finds a positive and statistically insignificant relationship between democracy and FDI flows, a negative and statistically insignificant relationship between democracy and annual changes in FDI stock, and a positive and highly statistically significant relationship between democracy and the enterprise-level variable annual expenditures on fixed capital (Kerner 2014).

Figure 2.7: Determinants of over- under underestimation of FDI flow and stock statistics

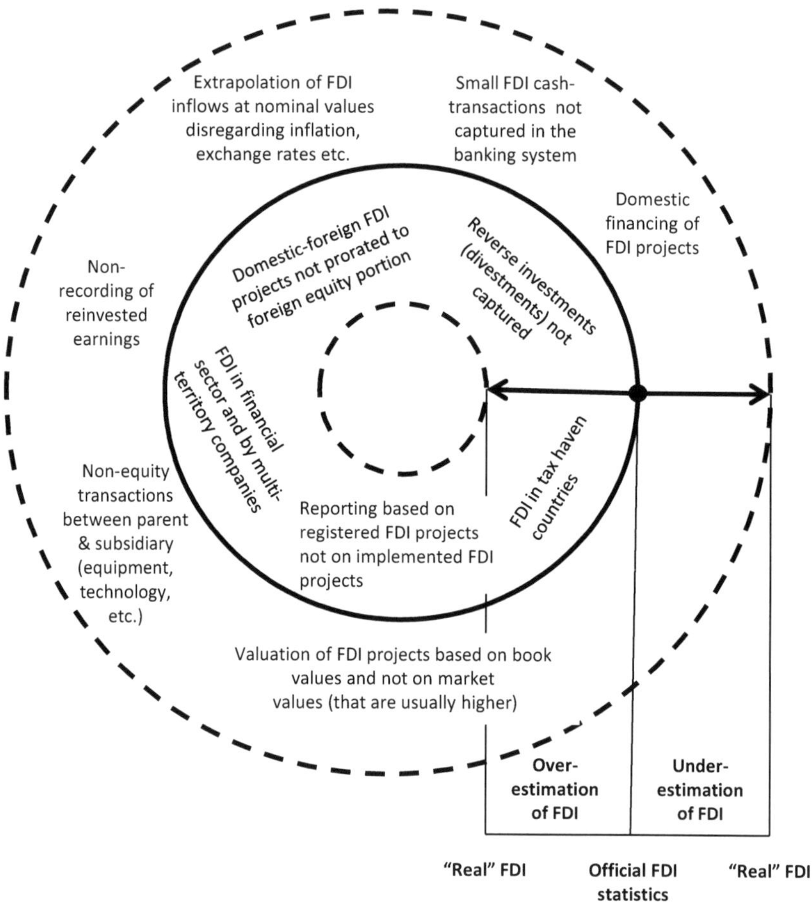

2.4 Disaggregated FDI statistics in SSA

2.4.1 Industry subsectors of FDI

Over many decades, the sector distribution of yearly FDI inflows have corroborated the established notion that FDI into SSA has primarily been driven by resource-seeking motives with a concentration in the primary sector, especially in oil and minerals (UNCTAD 2005c, UNCTAD 2008b). UNCTAD estimates that approximately 50 to 80 per cent of FDI stocks in Africa are related to natural-resource exploitation (UNCTAD 2004b). Between 1996 and 2000, cumulated outflows of seven large investor home countries indicated that 54.6 per cent were directed to the primary sector, 20.6 per cent were directed to the secondary sector and 24.8 per cent targeted the services sector (UNCTAD 2002). Reliable statistics on FDI flows or stocks by subsector are scant and exist for only a few SSA economies. Table 2.13 below shows estimates of FDI *stock* disaggregation into main sectors for twelve SSA countries and for different reporting years.

Table 2.13: Main sector disaggregation of FDI stocks in selected SSA countries, different reporting years

Country	Year	Primary	Secondary	Tertiary	Unspecified
		in per cent			
Botswana	2005	59.6	3.2	36.8	0.5
Cape Verde	1995	25.5	24.2	50.5	–
Gambia	2000	2.8	22.1	74.8	0.3
Madagascar	2006	48.9	22.8	28.3	–
Malawi	2001	13.2	41.8	44.6	0.4
Namibia	2006	37.6	7.0	55.4	–
Nigeria	2005	74.7	0.0	0.0	25.2
South Africa	2006	41.1	27.0	31.9	–
Swaziland	2005	20.2	62.0	17.8	–
Tanzania	2001	34.7	33.5	31.8	–
Uganda	2003	0.7	26.7	64.6	8.0
Zambia	2001	33.8	13.3	51.6	1.3
Source: UNCTAD 2008b					

Eleven SSA countries (Cape Verde, Ethiopia, Kenya, Madagascar, Mauritania, Mauritius, Mozambique, Nigeria, Tanzania, Uganda, and Zimbabwe) have reported sector-related breakdown of FDI *inflows* (UNCTAD 2008b). The data is quite outdated, similar to the sector-level breakdown of FDI inward stocks.

Due to the unreliability of disaggregated FDI data whenever it is compiled and reported directly by the respective central banks, UNCTAD has recently based the majority of its sector-based FDI reporting on the "fDi Markets" greenfield database of UK company "The Financial Time

Ltd."[45] In its 2014 WIR, UNCTAD reports FDI greenfield data for the 2004 to 2013 period and for different main sectors. The share of FDI in the extractive industry is no longer the prime driver of new FDI inflows and it accounted for a cumulative value of 26 per cent of the volume of all greenfield projects in Africa over the observed 10 year period. The share of new foreign greenfield projects in mining, quarrying and petroleum decreased further in 2012 (7.5 billion USD, 15.8 per cent of total) and 2013 (3.8 billion USD, 8 per cent of total) (UNCTAD 2014d). Despite the general decline, the majority of the most recent mega-greenfield projects are still related to the extractive industries sector (see Annex Table 4). Large-scale investments into oil extraction have focused on Sudan, Angola and Nigeria and were mainly driven by Chinese, Korean, Russian and Brazilian investors (Foster et al. 2008, De la Fontaine and Seifert 2009, UNCTAD 2010a, White 2010).

The recent spike of global commodity prices has triggered FDI flows into agriculture projects that often entail large-scale land acquisitions. A recent phenomenon in this regard are state-driven investments of Gulf countries into staple crops such as rice, wheat, barley, corn, sugar and also biofuels. These investments, except for investments into biofuels, play an important role in ensuring food security in the FDI country of origin (Woertz et al. 2008, Cotula and Vermeulen 2009, Cotula et al. 2009, UNCTAD 2009f). Especially Chinese investors are providing sizeable lines of concessional credit that trigger complementary investments into infrastructure projects that facilitate the swift export of primary commodities to international markets (Foster et al. 2008, Bräutigam 2010).

FDI into the manufacturing sector has slowed down in many SSA economies. In SA, for instance, the share of FDI in the manufacturing sector went down from 41 per cent in 1996 to 28 per cent in 2006. A similar downward trend is visible in Botswana, Madagascar and Uganda (UNCTAD 2008b). The share of FDI in manufacturing in Africa rarely exceeds 30 per cent in terms of overall investment value. For example, announced manufacturing greenfield projects in Africa accounted for 13.8 billion USD in 2013 which was 25.8 per cent of the total value of all announced greenfield projects for that year (UNCTAD 2014d). In terms of *number* of greenfield investment projects, however, the share of manufacturing is somewhat higher and accounted for 41 per cent of all greenfield

45 See: http://www.fdimarkets.com/ (accessed on 12 June 2016).

projects between 2003-2009 including metals (9 per cent), transport equipment (7 per cent) and food and beverages (6 per cent) (UNCTAD 2010b). Over the period 2004–2013, the share of the manufacturing sector was 38 per cent in terms of number of greenfield investment projects (UNCTAD 2014d).

The majority of African countries are eligible for the generalized system of preferences (GSP) under the European Union's "Everything but Arms" (EBA) Agreement and the "African Growth and Opportunity Act" (AGOA) of the US (UNCTAD 2015a). The prospect of exporting duty-free to the EU and US markets has attracted some FDI inflows in export-oriented manufacturing industries, particularly in textiles, apparel and horticulture and has contributed to positive export growth effects (Brenton 2003, UNCTAD 2003a, UNIDO 2007, McLure 2008, Phelps et al. 2008, Staritz 2011). Studies in Kenya and Lesotho indicate a rapid accumulation of FDI due to AGOA. This changed after the expiry of the Multi-Fibre Arrangement in 2005, which eliminated garment and textiles quotas on a global scale and diluted the specific privileges granted to Africa through AGOA and EBA. As a result, many foreign investors relocated production into lower-wage host countries in Asia. The attempt by African governments to retain AGOA/EBA investors through the granting of incentives and tax holidays was overall not very successful in reversing this general trend. Textiles and garment FDI in Africa hence remains under severe pressure (Lall 2005, Kaplinsky and Morris 2008, Phelps et al. 2008, Staritz 2011).

The tertiary sector has shown a noticeable increase and accounted for a sizable share of cross-border M&As and the largest share of greenfield projects in Africa. In 2013, foreign investors announced an FDI greenfield volume in the African services sector of 34 billion USD which equals 63.5 per cent of the total volume of greenfield projects in that year (UNCTAD 2014d). Within the tertiary sector, the leading sector was the electricity, gas and water supplies sector with an announced 2013 greenfield investment volume of 11.8 billion USD, followed by 7.7 billion USD in the transport, storage and communications sector, 7.1 billion USD in the business services sector and 3.5 billion USD in the construction sector (UNCTAD 2014d). Most of the recent M&A mega-deals in the financial and telecommunication sector were undertaken by multinationals from developing countries which appear to be more resilient than developed country MNEs in the aftermath of the financial crisis and which take advantage of the liberalization trend of former state-owned monopoly operators in the fixed and mobile communication segments (Djiofack-Zebaze and Keck 2009). These mega-deals comprised, for instance, the acquisition of the mobile phone network of Kuwait's Zain by India's Bharti Airtel for 10.7 billion USD or the acquisition of a 20 per cent share in SA's Standard Bank Group for 5.6 billion USD by Chinese investors (UNCTAD 2010b). The FDI Global Outlook Report 2011 indicates financial services to be the top sector of African FDI inflows in 2010 (Financial Times 2011). In 2014, the financial services sector was ranked the second most important FDI sector attracting 18.1 per cent of all new FDI projects of which 40 per cent were launched by African enterprises (Ernest and Young 2015). On a global scale, multinational companies in the services sector are relatively more bullish with regard to future internationalization plans than manufacturing companies because the local demand structure for financial services, telecommunications and business services exhibits smaller fluctuations and shows solid future growth potential in African markets (UNCTAD 2014c).

2.4.2 FDI countries of origin

The breakdown of FDI inflows by the foreign investor's country of origin should under normal circumstances add up to match with the total FDI inflows for a particular SSA country in a particular year. This is not the case because UNCTAD often approximates FDI outflows from the most prominent capital exporting countries to become FDI inflows at the FDI host country level. In theory, outward FDI flows and stocks recorded by the economy of the direct investor should indeed match with the corresponding FDI inflows and inward stocks in the statistics compiled by the respective SSA host economy. In practice, different classification systems and accounting practices have however contributed towards a widening of reporting discrepancies and this "has been a cause of concern to the IMF in connection with the analytical implications for the IMF's surveillance of its members' economies" (Patterson et al. 2004, p. 14). For example, the US FDI inflows in 2004 reported by the National Bank of Ethiopia accounted for 123.1 million USD, whereas the FDI outflows from the US into Ethiopia accounted for a meagre 3 million USD in the same year (UNCTAD 2008b).

Table 2.14 below gives a sample of the most extreme discrepancies for selected economies. The reported yearly FDI inflows reflect by no means the amounts reported by the largest capital-exporting countries.

Table 2.14: Discrepancies between 2006 FDI inflows for selected SSA countries, reported at aggregated levels and according to country of origin

Country	Aggregated FDI inflows, 2006 (in USD million)	FDI inflows, by country of origin, reported by investor economies, 2006 (in USD million)		Unspecified portion of FDI inflows, according to country of origin (in USD million)
Botswana	274.1	Sweden: US:	-1.9 5	271 (98.87%)
Ethiopia	364.4	France: US:	1.3 6	357.1 (98.00%)
Ghana	434.5	Denmark: France: Germany: Sweden: US:	4 2.5 -2.5 0.6 -1	430.9 (99.17%)
Guinea	108	Denmark: France:	0.3 7.5	100.2 (92.78%)
Senegal	58	Denmark: France: Germany: US:	-0.3 22.6 -12.5 -60	108.2 (>100%)
Sudan	3,541.4	France: Germany: US:	13.8 1.3 1	3,525.3 (99.55%)
Uganda	306.7	Denmark: France:	-0.8 1.3	306.2 (99.84%)
Zambia	350.4	Germany: Sweden: US	11.2 14.4 -8	598.3 (97.14%)

Source: Author's own calculations based on UNCTAD 2008b.

The breakdown according to country of origin explains only a fraction of the total FDI inflows for most SSA economies in 2006, with the exceptions of Mauritania (12.9 per cent), Central African Republic (15.6 per cent), Cape Verde (16.7 per cent), Benin (25.4 per cent), Côte d'Ivoire (37.5 per cent), Gabon (46 per cent), Cameroon (70.9 per cent), Burkina Faso (87.3 per cent) and Mozambique (100 per cent). Another type of discrepancy can be observed for Equatorial Guinea and Togo, whose total FDI inflows in 2006 are far less than what France and the US reported as FDI outflows for the same year. The same effect applies to the Republic of

Congo which displayed inflows of 344.1 million USD in 2006 whereas French outflows to the Republic of Congo accounted for 421.5 million USD and US outflows accounted for 128 million USD for the same year (UNCTAD 2008b).

An attempt to mirror FDI inflow and outflow data in order to unearth potential discrepancies has also been made on the basis of IMF´s CDIS data. The results for SSA are shown in Box 1.

Box 1: Mirror data analysis between inflow and outflow data, 2009–2011

Being aware of the need to highlight data gaps and errors, the IMF has started to present "mirror" data through its Coordinated Direct Investment Survey (CDIS) Programme. Data from the reporting economy are shown side-by-side with the data obtained from all other counterpart reporting economies. Box Table 1 below shows the results of SSA countries that have participated in the CDIS over the 2009 to 2011 period.

Box Table 1: Mirroring inward and outward FDI stock in selected SSA countries, 2009–2011

Country	2009		2010		2011	
	Inward FDI stock	Outward FDI stocks reported by respective SSA country counterpart economies	Inward FDI stock	Outward FDI stocks reported by respective SSA country counterpart economies	Inward FDI stock	Outward FDI stocks reported by respective SSA country counterpart economies
	in USD million					
Benin					563	2
Botswana	1,849	396	2,292	571	3,282	833
Ghana	4,689	3,502	5,962	6,948		
Mali					1,672	4
Mauritius	179,265	22,936	185,784	39,575		
Mozambique	3,748	1,963	4,379	2,014		
Nigeria	11,156	35,762	34,543	34,600	48,614	39,172
Rwanda			343	1		
Seychelles	1,049	480	1,081	788	1,029	602
South Africa	117,434	46,148	153,133	74,540	134,391	85,130
Uganda	3,905	423	4,523	530		
Zambia	6,288	405	9,029	474	7,727	833
Total	**329,384**	**112,015**	**401,070**	**160,041**	**197,279**	**126,576**

Source: http://cdis.imf.org (accessed on 29 March 2015).

In 2011, there is an unattributed gap of more than 70 billion USD for the seven CDIS participating SSA economies, namely Benin, Botswana, Mali, Nigeria, SA, Seychelles and Zambia. If mirror data of SSA countries that did not participate in the 2011 CDIS Survey but participated in the 2010 CDIS Survey is included, the discrepancy reaches figures more than threefold, i.e. 222.6 billion USD.

These deviations contribute to asymmetries in FDI aggregations and make meaningful cross-country comparisons extremely difficult (UNCTAD 2005c). In spite of these problems and in an attempt to overcome the general paucity of FDI data in Africa, the majority of FDI inflows and stocks continue to be approximated by outflows from the largest capital-exporting countries (UNCTAD 2008b). This practice neglects the increasing role of transition and developing countries as new sources of FDI into Africa, mainly because they do not record FDI outflow statistics that are broken down by SSA destination countries.

A breakdown of FDI *inflows* by geographical origin is reported in UNCTAD's 2008 "World Investment Directory Volume X – Africa" and includes data from most African countries with the latest reporting year being 2004 or 2006 (UNCTAD 2008b). In 2004, the total FDI inflows from ten investor countries (China, France, Germany, India, Korea, Malaysia, Pakistan, SA, UK and US) accounted for 14.3 billion USD (see following Table 2.15) whereas the total FDI flows of that year into Africa were 21.7 billion USD, leaving approximately 34 per cent of the flows unspecified. In terms of volume, the UK remains by far the most important investor country with cumulated FDI inflows of 28.2 billion USD between 1995 and 2004.

A breakdown of FDI *stocks* in Africa by geographical origin appears more reliable than FDI *flows* because it is less sensitive to year-by-year variations and it includes more recent and additional data sources, in particular OECD related data and data from the IMF CDIS. According to the author's own calculations based on OECD data[46], presented in Table 2.16, the largest FDI stock holder in Africa amongst the OECD countries is the UK with 45.7 billion USD (of which 21.2 billion USD are stocks in SA and 9 billion USD are stocks in Mauritius).

46 International Direct Investment Statistics (database) 2014, available at http://dx.doi.org/10.1787/data-00335-en (accessed on 20 February 2015).

Table 2.15: FDI inflows to Africa 1995–2006, country of origin perspective

Country	1995	1996	1997	1998	1999	2000	2001	2002	2003	2004	2005	2006
	in USD million											
China	18				42	85	25	30	61	317[a]	392[a]	520[a]
France	259	740	596		901	1,301	1,796	855	1,096	1,028		
Germany	319	315	802	1,363	463	651	-260	-328	-319	181		
India						243	185	883	338	22		
Korea	38	8	88	81	20	24	14	7	2[b]	51[b]	249[b]	
Malaysia	72	496	148	78	222	78	49	340		411	176	
Pakistan	7	6	6	4	4	4	4	2	0.1	-0.1		
South Africa[c]	214	97	1,062	1,988	114	281	1,585	1,884	932	597[d]		
Taiwan	29	21		36	41	7	6	17				
UK	1,116	875	1,020	-41	1,901	2,120	1,658	3,291	5,639	10,588		
US	352	1,678	3,436	3,075	596	716	2,438	-578	2,697	1,325		

Compiled from UNCTAD 2005b, UNCTAD 2006b, UNCTAD and UNDP 2007 and UNOSAA 2010.
[a] Chinese Statistical Bulletin;
[b] Korea Export Import Bank;
[c] Business Map Foundation Database of Announced FDI reported in UNCTAD 2005b; only Southern African Development Community (SADC) countries;
[d] 1st half of 2004.

The UK is the largest investor in SA, Madagascar and Zambia. For instance, affiliates of UK's HSBC Bank, Barclays Bank or Unilever are present in many SSA economies (UNCTAD 2008b). US investors are most active in the natural extraction sector and hold a total FDI stock of 35 billion USD in Africa (of which 8.2 billion USD are stocks in Nigeria and 7.1 billion USD are stocks in Mauritius). French investors are ranked third with a total FDI stock of 26.2 billion USD (of which 6.9 billion USD are stocks in Angola and 5.6 billion USD in Nigeria) and with a focus on telecommunications, banking and transportation. Further important OECD investor countries in Africa are the Netherlands (wholesale, food and beverage), Norway (wholesale, non-metallic mineral products, mining and quarrying), Germany (wholesale, transport, chemical industry), Belgium (wholesale, construction), Switzerland (food and beverages, utilities), Japan (water transport, utilities) and Portugal. There is an obvious preference of Portuguese investors for Portuguese-speaking African countries, namely Angola, Mozambique and Cape Verde. In these countries, Portuguese investors are present in multiple sectors, ranging from non-metallic mineral products, construction, telecommunications, wholesale, utilities and financial intermediation.

Table 2.16: Top ten FDI stock owners in Africa from OECD countries

Investor country	FDI stocks (in billions of USD)	SSA 3 top destinations	Base year	Category
UK	45.7	21.2 billion USD in SA	2012	"Other African countries (excluding North Africa)"
		9 billion USD in Mauritius		
		3.1 billion USD in Nigeria		
US	35.0	8.2 billion USD in Nigeria	2012	"Other African countries (excluding North Africa)"
		7.1 billion USD in Mauritius		
		5.5 billion USD in SA		
France	26.2	6.9 billion USD in Angola	2012	"Other African countries (excluding North Africa)"
		5.6 billion USD in Nigeria		
		3 billion USD in Congo (Rep.)		
Netherlands	18.1	1.7 billion USD in SA	2012	"Other African countries (excluding North Africa)"
		1.6 billion USD in Gabon		
		757 million USD in Mauritius		
Norway	9.3	7.3 billion USD in Angola	2012	"Other African countries (excluding North Africa)"
		1.2 billion USD in Liberia		
		174 million USD in Tanzania		
Germany	7.5	6.2 billion USD in SA	2011	"Other African countries (excluding North Africa)"
		692 million USD in Mauritius		
		127 million USD in Namibia		
Belgium	7.2	537 million USD in SA	2012	Sum of "Africa unallocated" and "Other African countries (excluding North Africa)"
		314 million USD in DRC		
		273 million USD in Gabon		
Switzerland	7.2	2.5 billion USD in SA	2012	"Africa unallocated"
		464 million USD in Nigeria		
		370 million USD in Côte d'Ivoire		
Japan	6.9	2.4 billion USD in SA	2012	"Africa unallocated"
Portugal	6.7	5.2 billion USD in Angola	2012	"Other African countries (excluding North Africa)"
		660 million USD in Mozambique		
		319 million USD in Cape Verde		
Other	16.3		mostly 2012	Varying "Other African countries (excluding North Africa)"

Note: OECD International Direct Investment Statistics (database) 2014, available at http://dx.doi.org/10.1787/data-00335-en (accessed on 20 February 2015).

Many of these OECD firms were founded during colonial times and dominate the domestic market in terms of services or branded fast-moving consumer goods. As a consequence, more than 90 per cent of the estimated cumulative inward FDI stock in Africa is controlled by developed countries' investors (UNCTAD 2010a). A recent trend is that of divestments by developed countries' investors in the manufacturing sector; this had already started before the financial crisis and is likely to continue. Large multinational firms attempt to consolidate capital commitments in a smaller number of locations and focus on a few production hubs in Africa in e.g. Kenya or SA with regional distribution outlets (UNIDO 2007).

Some authors such as Broadman criticize the complacent "wait and see" approach of established European and US investors about their traditional first mover advantage whereas investors from developing and emerging economies are versatile and quicker in taking advantage of new business opportunities in Africa (Broadman 2009). The most visible engagement of emerging country FDI is in the natural resources sectors through state-owned investors like Brazil's Petrobras, the China National Offshore Oil Corporation, India's Oil and Natural Gas Corporation or Malaysia-based Petronas (UNCTAD and UNDP 2007). Available data shows increasing shares of developing countries' FDI inflows to Africa from 17.7 per cent over the period 1995–1999 to 20.8 per cent over the period 2000-2008 (UNCTAD 2010a). This has led to an increase of FDI inward stock attributable to South investors from 6.9 per cent in 1999 to 7.5 per cent in 2008 (UNCTAD 2010a). The emergence of developing country investors is even more evident when referring to the number of investment projects as opposed to FDI volumes. There has been a steady increase of greenfield investments owned by South investors from 29 per cent in 2003 to 39 per cent in 2008. These investment projects exhibit a certain level of diversification beyond natural resource exploitation and increasingly comprise infrastructure, finance, agriculture or light manufacturing. Of 2,720 greenfield investment projects carried out between 2003–2008, 931 (32.2 per cent) were attributable to developing country investors and, more specifically, to Asian investors (576 projects, 21.2 per cent), African investors (275 projects, 10.1 per cent) and investors from Latin America (21 projects, 1 per cent) (UNCTAD 2010a).

Besides OECD stock data, the CDIS initiative of the IMF provides a valuable and updated new data source on FDI inward stock disaggregation by investor origin for currently 19 participating SSA countries.[47] Figure 2.8 below underpins the dominant role of the three OECD countries, the UK, the US and the Netherlands which sum up to 244.7 billion USD and account for 43 per cent of FDI inward stock.

Figure 2.8: Breakdown of inward FDI stocks by country of origin, 2012/2013

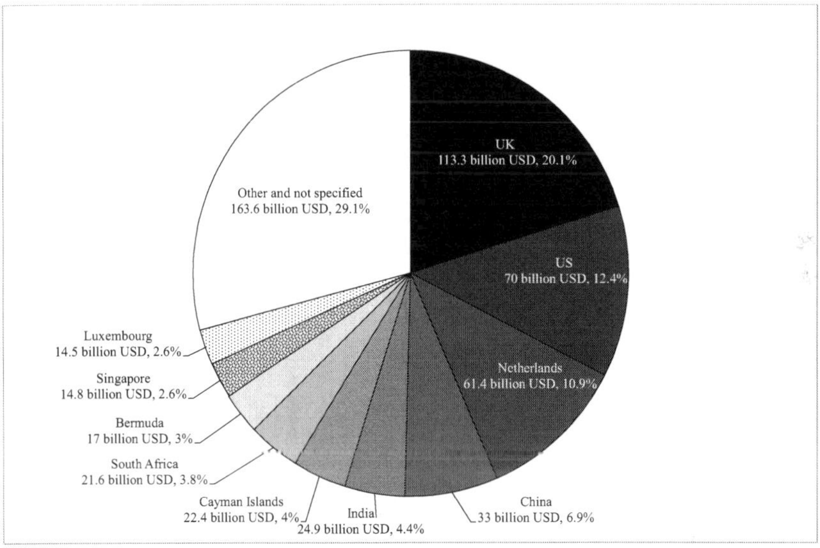

Source: IMF-CDIS

The results of CDIS also underscore more clearly than any other statistical source that the extent of presence of developing country FDI in Africa is already much larger than what had emerged from previous UNCTAD reports. It also pinpoints difficulties that arise in terms of the traceability of the ultimate beneficial ownership (UBO) as opposed to the first-level foreign ownership. For example, an FDI project may often be clouded due to the prevalence of SPEs or holding companies owned by a foreign investor in a third country (IMF 2003, OECD 2008, UNCTAD 2009c, UNCTAD 2016). In the specific case of "round-tripping", the UBO might remain in the ultimate FDI destination country because the direct investor is pursu-

47 See: http://cdis.imf.org (accessed on 29 March 2015).

ing tax-induced regulatory arbitrage and channels local funds abroad with the sole objective of returning these funds to the local economy in the form of FDI (OECD 2008, Buckley et al. 2015). In consequence, foreign investment in or from financial centres or tax-haven countries is often inflated and disguises not only the ultimate origin of the foreign investment but also the main intention of the investment (Haberly and Wójcik 2015, UNCTAD 2015b). FDI from such financial centres and tax-haven countries is a phenomenon that has not spared SSA and has reached a very considerable magnitude. Luxembourg, Cyprus, Gibraltar, the Cayman Islands and British Virgin Islands are preferred developed host countries for SPEs whose target is SSA although the unknown UBO might very well remain in a developing country. For example, the largest FDI stocks in Botswana (43.9 per cent of all FDI stocks, 2.1 billion USD) and Guinea-Bissau (42.9 per cent of all FDI stocks, 65 million USD) are owned by Luxembourg.[48] An amount of 1.5 billion USD and 1.2 billion USD of FDI inward stock in Ghana is attributable to investors from the Cayman Islands and the British Virgin Islands respectively.

Chinese FDI flows to SSA climbed from less than 1 per cent in 2003 to 16 per cent by 2008 (IMF 2011b). From an FDI inward stock perspective, the 19 CDIS participating countries reported a total cumulative Chinese FDI inward stock of almost 39 billion USD.[49] The largest Chinese inward stocks are located in Mauritius (16.7 billion USD), Nigeria (13.5 billion USD) and SA (6 billion USD) which is a multiple of the summated year-by-year Chinese FDI outflows as per previously shown Table 2.15. Within a relatively short time, Chinese FDI stocks have become the second largest in Botswana, Niger, Nigeria and Zambia and fifth largest in Mauritius (see Annex Table 5). There is a wide array of studies that have focused on Chinese FDI in Africa (Broadman 2007, Wang 2007, Zafar 2007, Besada et al. 2008, Foster et al. 2008, GTZ 2008, Bräutigam 2009, Kolstad and Wiig 2011). Chinese FDI in Africa very often takes the form of M&As in natural-resource-seeking and infrastructure investments carried out by medium and large state-controlled enterprises and closely bundled with aid and trade (Broadman 2007, Corkin 2007, Konings 2007, Broadman 2008, Foster et al. 2008, Ajakaiye and Kaplinsky 2009, Kaplinsky

48 Based on 2013 data in Botswana and 2012 data in Guinea-Bissau from http://cdis.imf.org (accessed on 29 March 2015) see Annex Table 5.

49 Own calculations based on 2012 or 2013 data from http://cdis.imf.org (accessed on 29 March 2015).

and Morris 2009, Bräutigam 2010, UNOSAA 2010). A prominent actor is the China National Petroleum Corporation (CNPC) which has planned or has current operations in Chad, Guinea, Mauritania, Niger, Nigeria and Sudan (UNCTAD 2011b). In terms of value, resource-seeking and infrastructure investments are by far the largest, with one major exception being the acquisition of a 20 per cent share of the Chinese Industrial and Commercial Bank into South Africa's Standard Bank for 5.5 billion USD in 2007. Far less attention is given to the fast-growing group of small and entrepreneurial private Chinese investors in Africa that invest in different service and manufacturing sectors to serve mainly local markets (UNIDO 2007, Wang 2007, Wang and Bio-Tchané 2008, Gu 2009, Shen 2013). IMF estimates that there are more than 2,000 of such private projects already established in SSA and further growth seems very likely (IMF 2011b). Manufacturing investments by Chinese investors are clearly on the rise and they account for nearly one third of registered projects in Ghana and Nigeria and 65 per cent of active projects in Ethiopia, most of which are undertaken by private investors (World Bank 2012, Clarke 2014). China is currently building five special economic zones in SSA (Ethiopia, Mauritius, Nigeria (two), and Zambia) that will prioritize Chinese private foreign investors without, however, being limited to only Chinese companies (Bräutigam and Xiaoyang 2011). Chinese direct investments in Africa are characterized by a large proportion of Chinese employees among the company's workforce and a relatively shallow integration with other indigenous business actors (UNIDO 2007, Wang 2007, Wang and Bio-Tchané 2008, Gu 2009). The promotion of Chinese direct investments into special economic zones in Africa may not turn back this tendency unless the zone establishment is accompanied by streamlined incentives and policy reforms that reward linkage creation, local employment and skills development (FIAS 2008, Bräutigam and Xiaoyang 2011). The preferred mode of entry of private foreign investors from China is that of greenfield investment. While these firms are usually incorporated in China, there is yet another category of "foreign investment" that operates at the borderline to informality and that is usually run by independent Chinese migrants (Ajakaiye and Kaplinsky 2009, Dobler 2009, Mohan and Lampert 2013). This group of Chinese investors is active in the retail and small-scale construction sectors and has partially crowded out African entrepreneurs or SMEs in the same sectors. This has led to an increased anti-Chinese sentiment and in some cases violent protests e.g. in Zambia or Namibia (Dobler 2009, Kragelund 2009).

India is another very important source country of foreign investments in Africa. The results of the CDIS presented in Figure 2.8 suggest that inward stocks from India reached a minimum of 24.9 billion USD in 2012/13 making it the fifth most important investor in terms of volume and the second most important developing country investor after China. Its evolution is however somewhat different from Chinese FDI, in that the relations between India and Africa have grown over many decades. FDI has been primarily carried out by the well-integrated Indian diaspora in Mauritius and further expanded into other East African economies, sometimes directly as Indian FDI or via holding companies based in Mauritius and owned by Indians (Das and Banik 2015). Indian investments are concentrated in the chemical, wholesale, food and beverages sectors (UNCTAD 2005a, Henley et al. 2008, Prabhakar 2008). Indian investors are relatively better integrated than Chinese investors. This is reflected in higher levels of local content and a higher proportion of mixed Indian-African JVs with a strong entrepreneurial orientation (UNIDO 2007, Broadman 2008, Prabhakar 2008). Recently, there have been signs of a more overt strategy to secure India's access to Africa's natural resources and commodities, which converges with that of Chinese state-driven FDI in Africa. The Indian government nowadays offers a wider array of mechanisms (e.g. through greater activities of the Indian Export-Import Bank) to bundle together the objectives of FDI, trade and aid (UNOSAA 2010). A case in point are greenfield investments like horticulture in Kenya and farming in Ethiopia by the Indian MNE Karuturi Global Limited or the successful acquisition of a large share in the Greater Nile Petroleum Operating Co. in Sudan by the Indian state-owned multinational ONGC Videsh Limited (UNCTAD and UNDP 2007, UNCTAD 2009f, UNCTAD 2010b). ONGC has further operations in South Sudan and in 2014 acquired a 2.6 billion USD stake in an offshore gas field in Mozambique.[50]

South Africa has become another important source country of FDI in Africa, and particularly in Southern Africa. Reliable statistics on FDI flows and stocks are difficult to obtain and the discrepancy between different data sources is sizable. In comparison to other sources, results from CDIS appear most reliable and indicate a cumulative FDI inward stock from SA of 21.6 billion USD in 2012/13 (see Figure 2.8). Estimates for

50 See: http://www.reuters.com/article/us-anadarko-ongc-mozambique-idUSBRE97P08520130826 (accessed on 14 May 2016).

the period 1994 to 2003 suggest that SA's FDI accounted for an average of 25 per cent of all FDI flowing into the Southern African Development Community (SADC) region. During that period, SA was the top investor in Lesotho with 86 per cent of cumulated FDI inflows, Malawi (80 per cent), Swaziland (71 per cent), DRC (71 per cent) and Botswana with 58 per cent (Rumney and Pingo 2004, Saunders 2008). Different data indicates that cumulated FDI inflows from SA companies into SADC were 12.3 billion USD between 2003 and 2007 (Draper et al. 2010). From an outward stock perspective, it is estimated that, in 2004, SA assets accounted for close to 9 billion USD in the SADC region (UNCTAD 2005b) and, in 2007, already 16.6 billion USD (Draper et al. 2010). SA firms prefer JVs or M&As over WOS or greenfield investments as the mode of entry (Bhaumik and Gelb 2005, Henley et al. 2008). Privatization programmes and financial liberalization boosted SA's FDI through their state-owned companies Eskom (energy generation), Transnet (transportation) and the Industrial Development Corporation (infrastructure) in countries like Mozambique, Zambia and Tanzania. Private firms have heavily invested into the services sector ranging from banking, telecommunications, retail, tourism and other areas (Naidu and Lutchman 2004, Henley et al. 2008, Saunders 2008, UNCTAD 2008a, Basdevant et al. 2014). A visible example of South African FDI are first-mover retail outlets like Pick 'n Pay and Shoprite which hedge against a volatile domestic market and follow an aggressive investment strategy in the Southern African region which is financed primarily through retained earnings (Okeahalam and Wood 2009, The Economist 2013b). Manufacturing FDI from South Africa is concentrated in packaging (Nampak) and in beverages (South African Breweries now SABMiller) (IMF 2012). South African multinational firms such as MTN (telecommunications) or Stanbic (Financial services) have lately expanded their investment portfolio also towards Western African economies (Games 2004, UNCTAD 2005b, IMF 2012). The share of African countries outside SADC has nearly reached 50 per cent of the entire SA FDI stock in Africa (Draper et al. 2010).

Other than South African FDI in SSA, there is also increasing evidence of intra-African FDI, which is more diverse across different economic sectors, especially in sectors with less capital and technology intensity. The majority of new greenfield projects by African direct investors are geared towards the manufacturing and service sector and not in extractive industries. African direct investors owned 18 per cent of greenfield projects in 2012, compared to 7 per cent in 2007 (AFDB et al. 2014). In the Economic Community of West African States (ECOWAS) and the EAC region, intra-African FDI in the manufacturing and services sectors represented about 36 per cent of the cumulative value of FDI greenfield projects between 2009 and 2013 (UNCTAD 2014d). In the manufacturing sector, intra-African investments focus on agricultural processing, building materials, electronic equipment and textiles. Telecommunications, retail, business services and banking are important service sectors for inner-African FDI. An interesting example is the expanding cross-border activity of Nigerian-based banks especially in Anglophone Western African countries such as Ghana, Sierra Leone or the Gambia. There is however no noteworthy Nigerian non-bank corporate presence across SSA (IMF 2012). An exception might be Nigeria´s Dangote Group (cement and other sectors) which is planning future investments of 3 billion USD or more across the African continent (The Economist 2014).

With regard to intra-African FDI, the role of Mauritius deserves special attention because it contributes to inflating total FDI inward stocks and flows to SSA (see e.g. Chapter 2.3.6) in a dual fashion: On the one hand, there is a large influx of FDI into Mauritius from investors whose motive is to structure investments in the form of "funds of funds" whereby US, UK and Indian based private equity funds set up a fund or a holding company with tax residency in Mauritius and the legal status of a so-called "Type 1, Global Business Company in Mauritius" (IMF 2014a). Nearly 100 billion USD of Mauritius' inward FDI stock have their origins in the UK, US and India, followed by the Cayman Islands (20.5 billion USD)[51], China (16.7 billion USD) and Singapore (13.5 billion USD). On the other hand, a sizable portion of Mauritius' inward stock does not remain in the country but translates into FDI outflows from Mauritius to the rest of the African continent often with the purpose of subsequent profit repatriation under the legal cover of currently 15 double taxation treaties that Mauritius had concluded with other SSA economies.[52] In 2013, companies with tax residency in Mauritius owned a total outward stock in other SSA coun-

---

51 The Cayman Islands–Mauritius–SSA route is touted as a particularly efficient vehicle for tax avoidance in the case of profit repatriation from SSA, http://www.ifcreview.com/restricted.aspx?articleId=2753&areaId=32 (accessed on 8th May 2015).

52 See http://unctad.org/Sections/dite_pcbb/docs/dtt_Mauritius.PDF (accessed on 8th May 2015).

tries of 14.2 billion USD.[53] From an inward perspective, this results in Mauritius being the largest owner of FDI assets in Rwanda and the Seychelles and the fifth largest investor in Botswana, Mozambique and Uganda (see Annex Table 5). Besides, the lion's share of Mauritius' outward investment position is with its main foreign investor countries in the form of round-tripping investments which explains the huge outward stock of 108.1 billion USD in India, 20.4 billion USD in China and 10.8 billion USD in Singapore.

Another important host country to inner-SSA FDI is Kenya. Kenyan investors have traditionally focused their FDI activities in other EAC member countries, in particular Uganda and Tanzania (UNIDO 2007). Results from the 2012/2013 CDIS illustrate that Kenya has become the third largest owner of FDI stocks in Uganda (386 million USD) and the fourth largest FDI stock holder in Tanzania (622 million USD). Related to Kenyan investment outside the EAC region, Nigeria appears to be the main FDI destination country and currently hosts 590 million USD of Kenyan FDI stocks. In Francophone Western Africa, Côte d'Ivoire and Senegal have achieved certain relevance as outward investors however maintaining a narrow geographical focus on neighbouring countries. Investors from Côte d'Ivoire have businesses mostly in Togo, Benin, Niger and Burkina Faso. Investors from Senegal have presence in Guinea-Bissau, the Gambia and Mali.

2.4.3 Entry mode of FDI

Besides FDI flow and stock statistics, UNCTAD is the only provider of aggregated data on the entry modes[54] of FDI, namely mergers & acquisitions (M&As) and greenfield investments. UNCTAD bases its M&A database on "Thomson ONE database" provided by the American company, the Thomson Reuter Corporation (UNCTAD 2014d). The data about

53 Based on own calculations with 2013 data from http://cdis.imf.org (accessed on 29 March 2015).

54 A detailed discussion on different FDI entry modes is presented in Chapter 4.1.1. Accordingly, the term of *establishment mode* is most accurate to describe the FDI entry mode choice between an M&A vs. greenfield FDI while delineating it from the *ownership mode* choice of a JVs vs. WOS. In the context of this Chapter 2.4.3, however, the broader term of entry mode will be employed.

greenfield investments originates from the "fDi Markets" database of the UK company "The Financial Time Ltd.".[55]

In this context, UNCTAD defines an M&A as "the taking over or merging of capital, assets and liabilities of existing enterprises" (UNCTAD 2009b, p. 98). The M&A transaction appears in the financial account of the BOP to capture additions or reductions in the foreign stock of the M&A target company. Privatization programmes of state-owned enterprise constitute a special form of an M&A that becomes FDI whenever the purchaser can be identified as foreign enterprise (UNCTAD 2000).

Although the M&A database conforms to the FDI definition as far as the minimum 10 per cent foreign equity share is concerned, it also includes financial forms such as syndicated loans, corporate bonds or venture capital that may not necessarily indicate the lasting interest by the direct investor in the direct enterprise which is in non-conformity to the official FDI definition (UNCTAD 2000, UNCTAD 2011a). Furthermore, there is no common definition of an M&A and available data is not collected uniformly and is sometimes based on an announcement basis (recorded when the deals are announced) or on completion basis (UNCTAD 2000). UNCTAD asserts that the cross-border M&A database "contains information on ultimate and immediate target and acquiring countries" (UNCTAD 2011a, p. 64) and that it does "not include pending deals that may be withdrawn later or withdrawn deals for which no value is available" (UNCTAD 2013b, p. 117). In actual practice, however, it is not clear whether validation mechanisms exist in the course of which the main three parties of the M&A deal i.e. the purchaser, the seller and the management of the target enterprise are being contacted to provide further information on the date of closing, the real value of the acquisition, countries of residence of the buyer/seller, spread of payment over several years, etc. By the same token, the M&A database may considerably overstate cross-border capital flows associated with M&A deals because "they include, inter alia, domestically-financed transactions, and in some cases include M&A deals between foreign affiliates and firms resident in the same host economy, neither of which are FDI transactions recorded in balance of payments statistics" (Patterson et al. 2004, p. 5). In the latter case, the foreign subsidiary may follow a closed system of governance by using retained earnings generated from its original FDI investment to pursue domestic M&A

55 See: http://www.fDimarkets.com (accessed on 12 June 2016).

expansion goals in the SSA host country. A good example for such an expansion strategy, mentioned in the previous Chapter 2.4.2, are SA retail chains such as Shoprite or Pick 'n Pay in Southern Africa (Okeahalam and Wood 2009, The Economist 2013b). Although this form of FDI belongs to the category of FDI through reinvested earnings, it remains in most cases unrecorded unless macro-level reporting systems are systematically complemented by FDI establishment surveys.

Table 2.17: Net cumulative M&A transaction volumes in SSA, 2006–2013

Year	Net[1] cumulative M&A transaction volumes (in million USD) in SSA[2]	Selected three largest transactions in million USD [no. of transactions]
2006	5,742	4,883m USD [5] in Nigeria; 1,332m USD [2] in Sudan[3]; -1336m USD [34] in SA;
2007	3,060	1,374m USD [41] in SA; 485m USD [1] in Nigeria; 396m USD [2] in Kenya;
2008	5,048	6,815m USD [37] in SA; -2,200m USD [1] in Equatorial Guinea[3]; 900m USD [3] in Ghana;
2009	3,382	3,860m USD [22] in SA; -471m USD [2] in Angola; -197m USD [2] in Nigeria;
2010	6,342	3,570m USD [27] in SA; 1,300m USD [1] in Angola[3]; 587m USD [1] in Liberia[3];
2011	7,275	6,673m USD [58] in SA; 539m USD [9] in Nigeria; -254m USD [1] in Eritrea;
2012	-866	-986m USD [n/avail.] in SA; 366m USD [n/avail.] in Ethiopia; -296m USD [n/avail.] in Zimbabwe;
2013	879	537m USD [n/avail.] in Nigeria; 214m USD [n/avail.] in SA; 103m USD [n/avail.] in Kenya;

Sources: UNCTAD 2011a, UNCTAD 2012b, UNCTAD 2013b and UNCTAD 2014d; based on Thomson Reuters Financial.
[1] M&A data is on a net basis, i.e. expressed as differences between gross cross-border acquisitions and divestments by firms in/from a particular SSA country.
[2] No data is available for Benin, Burundi, Central African Republic, Chad, Comoros, Djibouti, Gambia, Guinea-Bissau, Lesotho, São Tomé and Príncipe, Somalia, South Sudan, Swaziland and Togo.
[3] More details about the M&A transaction are available in the following Table 2.18.

M&A data for SSA is extremely sketchy. For the time period 2001–2014, there are 14 SSA countries which do not display any sizable M&A investment above 1m USD (UNCTAD 2014d). An additional six countries in SSA, namely Cape Verde, Côte d'Ivoire, Gabon, Guinea, Liberia and Niger have had only one single M&A entry since 2001. For most other countries, the aggregated M&A sales for a particular year are on average based on only one or two major yearly M&A deals. As Table 2.17 above shows, the net cumulative M&A transaction volume peaked at 7.28 billion USD in 2011.

Table 2.18: The largest cross-border M&A deals in SSA LDCs, 2002–2010

Acquired company	Industry of the acquired company	Host country	Ultimate acquiring company	Ultimate home country	Value in million USD	Year
Devon Energy Corp. (US-owned)	Crude petroleum and natural gas	Equatorial Guinea	GEPetrol	Equatorial Guinea	-2,200 (divest.)	2008
Heritage Oil Ltd.	Crude petroleum and natural gas	Uganda	Tullow Oil PLC	UK	1,500	2010
MobiTel	Radiotelephone communications	Sudan	MTC Kuwait	Kuwait	1,332	2006
Block 32 Offshore	Crude petroleum and natural gas	Angola	Pride Int. Inc.	US	1,300	2010
CMS Energy Corp	Crude petroleum and natural gas	Equatorial Guinea	Marathon Oil Co.	US	993	2002
Bashair Telecom Co Ltd.	Telephone communications	Sudan	Investcom	Lebanon	806	2006
Greater Nile Petroleum Operating Co.	Crude petroleum and natural gas	Sudan	Oil & Natural Gas Corp	India	768	2003
DRC Resources Holdings Ltd.	Ferroalloy ores, except vanadium	DRC	Central African Mining & Expl.	UK	732	2008
Vanship Holdings Ltd.	Deep sea foreign transport	Liberia	Navios Maritime Holdings	Greece	587	2010
Source: UNCTAD 2011a						

The relatively low net cumulative M&A transaction volumes of 2012 and 2013 are likely to be related to staggered M&A payment modalities that might upon their final disbursement increase the net M&A volumes *ex post* for 2012/13. The highest frequencies of M&A deals were observable in SA and Nigeria. The largest single divestment occurred in 2008 in Equatorial Guinea when the US multinational Devon Energy Corporation sold its oil and gas business to GEPetrol, Equatorial Guinea's national oil company.[56] The most sizable M&A deals from 2002 and 2010 in SSA

56 See: http://www.devonenergy.com/news/2008/Devon-Energy-Completes-22-Billion-Sale-of-Assets-in-Equatorial-Guinea (accessed 15 May 2016).

LDCs are reported in Table 2.18 on the previous page. Most of these M&A deals occurred in the crude petroleum and natural gas sector with the exception of two giant M&A deals related to Sudan's telecommunications sector and an M&A deal in Liberia's shipping industry in 2010. US and UK based multinationals dominated the scene of M&A mega deals over the observed period. It is noteworthy that all mega M&A deals in Sudan were carried out by TNCs from non-OECD countries, namely Kuwait, Lebanon and India.

The dearth of available data from SSA, compounded with the inherent "complexity, uniqueness, sensitive and dynamic nature" (UNCTAD 2009b, p. 102) of M&A deals, makes the M&A database of no or very limited use to adjust BOP based FDI inflow or FDI stock statistics. The share of cross border M&As in FDI inflows to Africa is one of the lowest of all world regions and oscillates between 25 to 45 per cent of yearly FDI inflows. This coincides with the thinking that greenfield investments are the preferred alternative entry mode to M&As in countries where investment risk and growth potential is perceived to be higher than elsewhere (Tatoglu and Glaister 1998, UNCTAD 2000). In a survey among IPAs in Africa, nearly half of the respondents confirmed that greenfield was the preferred FDI entry mode (UNCTAD 2004a). UNCTAD defines the alternative entry mode to an M&A, namely greenfield FDI as "investment projects that entail the establishment of new entities and the setting up of offices, buildings, plants and factories from scratch" (UNCTAD 2009b, p. 97). The value of greenfield investment projects indicates planned capital expenditures by the investor at the time of the announcement. Its information is normally recorded from media, industry associations, IPAs or market research companies (Fujita 2008, UNCTAD 2014d). Greenfield investment projects usually require a longer establishment period in terms of physical assets, human resources and development of business networks than M&As where these are already in place and whose expedited internalization constitutes one of the fundamental motives for choosing an M&A over a greenfield entry mode. Greenfield projects entail implicit opportunity costs of delayed entry and start of production which could even lead to a cancellation of the project in changing commercial and economic scenarios (Hennart and Park 1993, Dikova and van Witteloostuijn 2007). This characteristic poses a challenge for the accurate valuation of greenfield FDI because the time lapse between the announced value of the project and its actual value upon completion will on average be longer than that of an M&A. That makes any attempt to calculate values of announced greenfield investments at one particular point in time very prone to mistakes. Moreover, the greenfield investment database does not capture information on the extent of foreign equity participation and is inflexible in scenarios of local project financing by foreign investors (UNCTAD 2011a). In sum, the same set of existing methodological caveats of M&As also apply for greenfield investments and thus disqualifies them as a credible source for adjustments to official BOP FDI flow or stock statistics (UNCTAD 2005d, Fujita 2008).

The "fDi Markets" database which is used as the basis for UNCTAD greenfield project statistics, contains on average 400 yearly greenfield investment projects for 46 SSA countries.[57] From a total number of 2,803 greenfield projects that were announced between 2005 to 2011, 711 projects concerned SA (25.4 per cent) which results into an average number of 100 announced projects per year. A large number of greenfield projects were announced in Nigeria, namely 259 projects (9.2 per cent), followed by 247 projects in Angola (8.8 per cent), and 178 projects in Kenya (6.4 per cent). Uganda, Tanzania and Zambia also had more than 100 announced projects within the 2005 to 2011 period (UNCTAD 2012b). A combined review of UNCTAD's 2013 and 2014 WIRs also allows the calculation of announced cumulative values of greenfield projects in SSA for the period 2006 to 2013 (UNCTAD 2013b, UNCTAD 2014d). On the assumption that no greenfield projects have been double-counted within different consecutive years, the overall cumulative value from 2006-2013 has been close to 416 billion USD. Apart from the unknown real impact of these greenfield projects on FDI inflows, a sizable proportion should have materialized as newly created foreign assets as reflected in the respective liability positions of SSA's IIP (FDI stock). The average foreign equity participation in these greenfield projects is however unknown but will surely not be 100 per cent foreign-owned for all of them. It would hence be a fallacy to conclude that FDI inflows or FDI inward stocks had also increased by the same amount. As shown in Annex Figure 1, the year-by-year cumulative volumes of FDI greenfield projects in SSA have been significantly above the reported SSA FDI inflows for all years from 2006 until 2011. In 2012, however, the combined volume of FDI M&A and greenfield projects fell about 10 billion USD below SSA's 2012

57 Based on the number of greenfield projects reported during the period of 2005 to 2011; Source: UNCTAD 2012b.

FDI inflows. In 2013, the volume of FDI M&A and greenfield projects converged to SSA's 2013 FDI inflows and the difference accounted for less than 1 billion USD.

Figure 2.9: SSA host country breakdown of cumulative announced greenfield project volume for the period 2006–2013

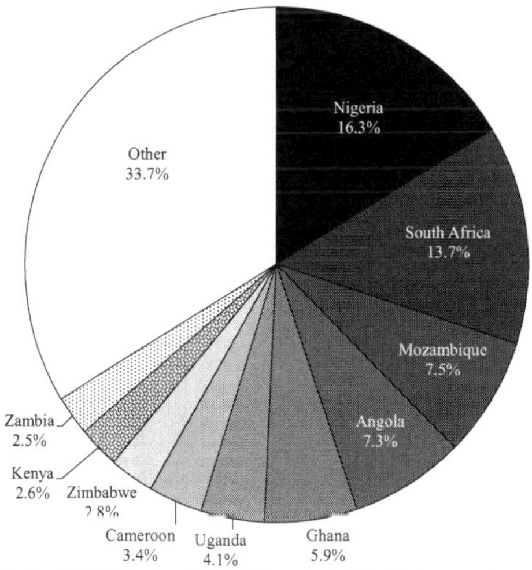

Source: UNCTAD 2013b and UNCTAD 2014d based on "fDi Markets" database.

Figure 2.9 above provides a breakdown of cumulative announced greenfield projects in different SSA host countries for the period 2006–2013. Accordingly, Nigeria had the largest value of 72.6 billion USD (16.3 per cent), followed by 61.2 billion USD (13.7 per cent) in SA, 33.7 billion USD in Mozambique (7.5 per cent) and Angola with 32.6 billion USD (7.3 per cent).

When the volume of greenfield projects is contrasted with the number of greenfield projects in specific SSA countries, there emerges a tendency towards large volume greenfield projects in Angola, Ghana, Uganda, Nigeria and Mozambique and smaller greenfield projects in SA and Kenya. With regard to Angola, multinationals such as Total (France), Chevron (US) and Exxon Mobil (US) have announced gigantic greenfield projects each of which is supposed to have a value of at least 3 billion USD and a promulgated employment creation impact of 800 or more new jobs (UNCTAD 2011a). Besides Angola, the energy sector has been the leading sector of greenfield investments in Uganda with 95 per cent of value, Mozambique with 54 per cent of value and Ghana with 48 per cent of value of all cumulative greenfield projects between 2009-2013 (World Bank 2014). In Nigeria, the electronics/ICT sector has outstripped the energy sector and attracted more than double of new greenfield investment flows between 2009–2013 amounting to 4.7 billion USD. Greenfield investments in SA have been more diversified and are concentrated in the manufacturing sector such as environmental technologies, metal fabrication, chemicals and transport equipment. The construction sector was particular attractive for greenfield investors targeting Angola, Kenya and Mozambique (World Bank 2014). In this connection, in 2008, one of the largest greenfield engagements of China in Africa was launched between the state-owned CITIC Group and the Angolan government for a total anticipated investment volume of 3.5 billion USD in large-scale housing and public infrastructure construction (UNCTAD 2011a, Corkin 2012, Power and Alves 2012, Mohan and Lampert 2013).

There is a usually a strong correlation between the size of greenfield investments and the economic sectors in which they take place. For example, greenfield investments into the energy sector (including oil and gas) tend to be among the largest. Between 2003–2010, eight out of the ten largest greenfield investment projects in African LDCs occurred in this sector (see Annex Table 4). This is an interesting new trend which supersedes a pattern that has been quite pronounced for many decades, namely that large investments into mining, quarrying and petroleum in SSA have traditionally taken the form of M&As and were the result of large-scale privatization programmes in the 1990's and the beginning of 2000's (UNCTAD 2000). Under normal circumstances, M&As are the expression of an active strategy by MNEs to secure access to strategic assets to expand or secure market power (Hennart and Park 1993). In the case of SSA, however, the availability of newly created corporate assets in capital-intensive subsectors such as mining and oil and gas extraction is limited and the scenario in which the foreign investor has the actual choice between the two entry modes of greenfield vs. M&A may be an exception rather than the rule. Unless corporate assets have been created *a priori*, for example, by state-owned companies of the SSA host economy open for acquisition by a foreign investor, the foreign investor has no other choice than that of a greenfield investment to establish its operations from scratch.

2.4.4 Size of FDI

The limitations of macro-economic data on FDI stocks and flows become particularly blatant when foreign investors are classified according to their size of operations. The compilation of macro-economic data according to FDI size poses serious caveats and is skewed towards reporting of mainly larger investments, which may be announced with some public fanfare but which are subsequently not realized or are only realized in parts. The most referred to databases are UNCTAD's cross border M&A database or the "fDi Markets" database of the Financial Times. There can be some doubt whether enough justice is done to the many small-scale investments that are carried out by foreign investors in SSA and that, in most cases, are not captured by the host country's registration offices, IPAs or private sector associations. The pertinent literature has recently recognized the relevance and contribution of rapidly internationalizing SMEs, so called "born-global" or international new ventures (INV) firms, which challenge the established notion that FDI is the prerogative of larger and well-experienced multinational enterprises (Oviatt and McDougall 1994, Coviello and McAuley 1999, Lu and Beamish 2001, Beamish and Lee 2003, Zahra 2004, Knight and Cavusgil 2005, Lu and Beamish 2006). In one of its recent Reports, UNCTAD refers to FDI by small TNCs and entrepreneurs as the frequently overlooked "middle ground" (UNCTAD 2011a, p. 23) foreign investors in LDCs although "they have also proved to be a good match for LDCs in the sense that they tend to be nimble and able to operate in challenging environments" (UNCTAD 2011a, p. 23). More particularly, intra-African FDI is undertaken by mostly small enterprises, with the exceptions of a few large MNEs that are based in Egypt, Kenya, Morocco, Nigeria, and SA (UNCTAD 2008b). For example, there are prominent signs of an increasing relevance of small and entrepreneurial businesses, many of which emanated from non-indigenous family businesses like Indians in Eastern Africa, Europeans in SA or Lebanese or Syrians in Western Africa (Ramachandran and Shah 1999, UNIDO 2007, Prabhakar 2008, Bewayo 2009).

Some foreign investors may be returning members of the Africa diaspora holding foreign passports (African Courir 2010, Nanda and Khanna 2010, Chacko and Gebre 2013, Boly et al. 2014). Not all would be recorded as FDI because they are unlikely to register as subsidiaries of a company with headquarters in another country. They may have a competitive edge over larger foreign investors since they are not facing the "costs of foreignness" that are incurred by non-diaspora investors while, at the same time, being able to tap into formal and informal cross-border networks that may not be open to purely domestic entrepreneurs (Buckley and Casson 1976, Hymer 1976, African Courir 2010, Nanda and Khanna 2010). These entrepreneurial enterprises often seek to diversify their sources of revenue through an involvement in a range of unrelated and disparate enterprises that are solely linked by the company owner and that can take the organizational form of an "octopus" with capital flows that are often convoluted and non-transparent (Kiggundu 2002). The Economist Magazine labels these firms as run by "parallel entrepreneurs" whereby the company owner adjusts swiftly to changing market and tax conditions in SSA and sets up a network of several firms across a number of different sectors of the economy in order to hedge against risks that stem from being involved in only one large operation and in one particular economic sector (The Economist 2012).

In its 2005 Africa Foreign Investor Survey, UNIDO undertook a classification of large TNCs which have global group sales of over 200 million USD, subsidiaries of small TNCs with global group sales below 200 million USD, and foreign-owned and operated firms that are not subsidiaries of a foreign-based enterprise but are owned and operated by an FE (UNIDO 2007). Generally, the extent of a firm's overall conglomerate says relatively little about the size of the subsidiary e.g. a large multinational firm can have small distribution outlets with relatively few employees. In the case of SSA, however, large TNCs operate larger subsidiaries than smaller TNCs or FEs regardless of whether the size is measured in terms of annual sales, average employment or invested capital. Only 25 per cent of surveyed subsidiaries belonged to such large multinationals but the cumulative contribution in terms of employment (43 per cent of total sample) and sales (62 per cent of the total sample) was proportionally larger than for smaller foreign investor types. More than two thirds of these large TNCs are currently headquartered in developed countries, in particular in the former colonial powers UK and France. The recent emergence of large multinationals from developing countries is also confirmed. Fifty per cent of FDI projects carried out after the year 2000 pertained to large multinationals from developing countries (UNIDO 2007). The firm-level data that has been generated for the compilation of UNIDO's "Africa Investor Report 2011" (UNIDO 2012a), will, in the following main Chapter 3, form the basis for a more granular analysis on both the size and governance patters of FDI in SSA.

2.5 Summary of findings and Chapter 2 conclusions

Chapter 2 has shed light on the status and underlying trends of FDI in SSA from a strictly macro-economic perspective. It drew attention to the definition of FDI and the ensuing emphasis on the cross-border nature of FDI whereby a parent company provides a financial input to its international affiliate either in the form of equity capital or as an intercompany loan. The chapter revealed that the crux of SSA's FDI BOP statistics is less about the absence of definitional guidelines for the collection and compilation of FDI data as per BPM-5 and BPM-6, but rather on the side of capacity building and effective implementation of these guidelines. Only two countries, SA and Mauritius, have upgraded their statistical systems to comply with the rigid criteria of IMF's SDDS. By virtue of membership in IMF's GDDS, most other SSA countries have in principle committed themselves to BPM-5 being the predecessor of BPM-6. Despite GDDS membership, more than a dozen SSA did not publicize a BOP. For those SSA countries publishing a BOP, reporting on all FDI components especially on reinvested earnings, intercompany loans (within which reverse intercompany loans and loans amongst fellow enterprises also play a role) remains the exception as they may be recorded in one particular year but not subsequent years. The majority of SSA countries do not divulge metadata on data collection and approximation methods.

Against this background, it was not surprising that the comparison of the four main sources of SSA FDI statistics i.e. the IMF, the World Bank, UNCTAD and OECD led to inconsistent results given that each IO valuates FDI flows differently in an attempt to minimize the statistical error of FDI over- or underestimation. On the one hand, FDI flows may be underestimated whenever sequential investments from the foreign affiliates' reinvested earnings or locally-financed FDI expansion projects do not translate in a cross-border financial transfer and happen under the radar of the respective central banks' ITRSs. Moreover, FDI statistics are skewed towards the recording of "mega-deals" whereas small and sometimes cash-based foreign transactions are not captured by the local banking system in spite of their assumed large total cumulative effect. As for FDI inward stocks, they are mostly valuated based on book values and not on usually higher market values. On the other hand, FDI is systematically overestimated if it is compiled from foreign investors' announcements about a future FDI project which may not be realized or realized only partially during the subsequent FDI implementation phase. Likewise, reverse investments or divestments whereby the parent company siphons off financial liquidity from its subsidiary in most cases go unnoticed and contribute to the bloating of FDI stocks and flows. FDI in the financial sector and in SSA tax haven countries, in particular in Mauritius and the Seychelles, cast doubts about the longevity of the FDI motive and should in many cases instead be classified as short-term portfolio investments.

Disaggregated macro-level FDI statistics like those presented in Chapter 2.4 can at best give an inkling about some underlying FDI trends with regards to the industry sector composition, the origin of the investment, market entry and subsidiary size. Notwithstanding statistical bottlenecks, the macro-level analysis confirmed that the lion's share in new FDI inflows continues to be attributable to extractive industries boosted by the fact that countries like Ghana, Mozambique or Uganda have newly entered the circle of SSA's resource-rich countries. FDI into SSA's service sector, particularly in financial intermediation and telecommunications, has picked up momentum whereas the share of manufacturing FDI has been falling or stagnating in the majority of SSA countries. The rapid emergence of South-South FDI is still barely visible in SSA's BOP statistics whereas it becomes glaring in IMF's CDIS database. Accordingly, China already holds the fourth largest FDI stocks in SSA, followed by India in the fifth rank and South Africa in the seventh rank. In terms of FDI entry mode, greenfield FDI has during recent years exceeded M&A FDI by a factor of 10 or even more (see Annex Figure 1). There is often no other choice for the foreign direct investor than to establish its operations from scratch because existing local assets in SSA are either absent or not attractive enough for a profitable M&A investment.

In conclusion, it is evident that the statistical problems associated with macro-economic FDI statistics militate against the aspiration of industrial policy makers in SSA to get a real and better picture of FDI in order to enable the formulation of evidence-based and sector-specific investment promotion policies that cut across issues of pro-active FDI targeting, the granting of incentives, the granting of land, the granting of licenses, labour issues, taxation and others. Unless these statistical problems are swiftly addressed and eventually overcome, there remains a risk that SSA policy makers would return to the original point-of-departure when extensive deregulation combined with a myopia on "Doing Business" scores were regarded as sufficient ingredients to attract "quality" FDI inflows. There is thus a need for a harmonized approach of measuring FDI data in SSA which should include, among others, the execution of frequent enterprise-level FDI surveys to test the validity of macro-economic estimates and to add an enterprise-level perspective to the discussions on emerging FDI trends and their ensuing impact. The next main Chapter 3 will show how such enterprise-level FDI data can be harnessed for the categorization of different FDI types in SSA.

3. A firm-level perspective of different FDI forms in SSA

3.1 Available resources and foreign firm-level samples

Two multilateral institutions, namely the World Bank and UNIDO, have in the past implemented SSA-wide enterprise-level surveys in an attempt to complement macro-economic FDI statistics and to overcome some of the identified shortcomings (UNIDO 2007, UNIDO 2012a, World Bank 2016).

In the early 1990s, the World Bank started to carry out firm-level surveys in Africa within the framework of its Regional Programme for Enterprise Development (RPED). The first round of surveys, conducted during the consecutive years 1992 to 1995, generated panel data on a range of performance and competitiveness variables from manufacturing companies in a total of eight SSA economies. The second survey round was conducted in the early 2000s and shifted focus towards firm perceptions of the regulatory business environment (costs of doing business, level of institutional and government support, red tape, etc.) in about 10 to 15 SSA economies (Bigsten and Söderbom 2006). In 2006, the World Bank standardized its global methodology for conducting enterprise-level surveys which resulted in the design of one core questionnaire and a sampling strategy that is representative of each country's private sector, including the services sector.[58] This greatly facilitated cross-country comparisons between SSA countries but reduced the ability of performing time series analysis for the data collected before and after 2006. The sample is usually stratified according to the sector of activity, firm size, and geographical location.

As presented in Annex Table 6, the World Bank Enterprise Surveys covered 44 SSA economies from 2006 to 2014 and the total sample comprises 15,629 companies with country samples varying from 150 companies in small SSA economies (Benin, Chad, Central African Republic, Liberia, Mauritania, Niger, Sierra Leone) to 2,162 companies in Nigeria as the largest economy in SSA. Panel data for three years (2006, 2010, 2013)

58 See: http://www.enterprisesurveys.org/methodology (accessed on 15 May 2016).

exists for the DRC and for two years in Angola, Botswana, Burundi, Ghana, Kenya, Madagascar, Malawi, Mali, Mauritania, Namibia, Nigeria, Rwanda, Senegal, Tanzania, Uganda and Zambia. The World Bank data is not stratified according to investor ownership. The proportion of foreign subsidiaries cannot therefore be regarded as representative of the FDI populations in the respective SSA economies and a non-response bias cannot be ruled out. For the period under observation, there are 3,316 firms with more than 10 per cent foreign ownership which equals a proportion of 17.5 per cent of FDI firms among all surveyed firms in SSA. The country-by-country variations of the FDI share are quite significant with some SSA countries having a comparably large sample share of foreign firms such as Gabon (61.5 per cent), Botswana (48.5 per cent), Central African Republic (42.7 per cent) or South Sudan (40 per cent) whereas others have very low sample proportion of foreign firms, such as Sudan (1.4 per cent), Eritrea (3.4 per cent), Tanzania (5.8 per cent) or Namibia (6.7 per cent).

In 2001, UNIDO started to carry out its first pilot survey of foreign subsidiaries in four SSA countries (Ethiopia, Nigeria, Tanzania and Uganda) with the objective of gaining new insights into determinants, motives and performance of FDI and to help SSA's IPAs in the enhanced execution of their mandates (UNIDO 2002a). UNIDO's second FDI Survey in 2003 comprised a sample of 758 foreign subsidiaries with more than 30 per cent foreign equity in ten SSA countries (UNIDO 2003). UNIDO's 2005 FDI Survey expanded the country coverage to 15 SSA countries and produced 1,216 valid observations (UNIDO 2007). The analyses in this Chapter will be based on the raw data generated from the UNIDO 2010/11 Investor Survey which covered 2,692 foreign subsidiaries with operations in 20 SSA countries (UNIDO 2012a).[59] Foreign subsidiaries in Kenya and Uganda make up more than one third of the sample.[60] Furthermore, the sample comprises 184 (6.8 per cent) foreign firms in Ghana, 156 firms (5.8 per cent) in Tanzania, 151 firms (5.6 per cent) in Nigeria, 133 firms (4.9 per cent) in Cameroon and Ethiopia, 131 firms (4.9 per cent) in Mozambique, 124 firms (4.6 per cent) in Madagascar, 110 firms (4.1 per cent) in Senegal, 107 firms (4 per cent) in Cape Verde and 105 firms (3.9 per cent) in Zambia. The respective sample sizes of Lesotho, Malawi,

59 In the following, reference will be made to the UNIDO 2010/11 Investor Survey database.

60 There are 510 responses (18.9 per cent) of foreign subsidiaries based in Kenya and 420 responses (15.6 per cent) based in Uganda.

Mali and Rwanda range between 50 and 100 foreign firms. Burkina Faso, Burundi, Côte d'Ivoire and Niger have even smaller samples of less than 50 foreign firms with a cumulative sample representation of 5 per cent.

Information on the approach of the survey implementation as well as mechanisms for data quality assurance is provided in Annex 2 of UNIDO's "Africa Investor Report 2011: Towards Evidence-Based Investment Promotion Strategies" (UNIDO 2012a, p. 185–187). UNIDO ascertains that the Survey has met rigorous standards and that it can thus be regarded as an internationally recognized and authoritative reference survey of domestic and foreign investments in SSA (UNIDO 2012a). The survey strategy involved sampling techniques based on business directories that UNIDO had to specifically compile for this purpose. Whenever possible, the stratification of the sample was undertaken according to economic subsector, size (number of employees), and ownership status (foreign- vs. domestically-owned). A mixed sampling procedure was applied, involving direct and random selection of companies from the sampling frame. Direct or non-random sampling was chosen in the case of medium to large foreign companies with more than 50 employees and some economic sectors which comprise a low number of companies in a specific SSA host country. Otherwise probability proportional to size (PPS) sampling has been applied for the middle-range size groups and random sampling for the largest group of small firms.[61] Over and above sampling, UNIDO has established multi-layered quality assurance systems. Skilled survey enumerators have been identified and trained prior to data collection. Without exception, the interviews have been carried out as face-to-face interviews. The large majority of interviews were conducted with the most senior decision maker i.e. the Chief Executive Officer (CEO) or the General Manager of the foreign subsidiary and were usually complemented by data provided by specific Department Managers, particularly the Chief Financial Officer (CFO) for financial accounting data. Computer software was locally deployed to ascertain internal data consistency at the time of data entry and to re-launch a company visit to validate specific elements of the data in the case of inconsistencies or a large number of missing values. In addition, each questionnaire was subject to review by a local survey super-

61 In the course of the survey implementation, UNIDO has prepared a range of unpublished documents such as the "Supervisor Handbook", the "Enumerator Handbook" and the "Sampling Manual" which have been made available to the author.

visor as well as further reviews directly made by an expert team at UNIDO headquarters.

Firm-level data presented in the subsequent sub-chapters will be based on the UNIDO 2010/11 Investor Survey sample, and more specifically, the sample comprising foreign firms.[62]

3.2 Industry subsectors of FDI

The UNIDO 2010/11 Investor Survey covered responses from 2,692 foreign firms of which 208 are operating in agriculture or mining[63] (7.7 per cent), 1,340 in manufacturing[64] (49.7 per cent), 155 in non-manufacturing industries such as construction and electricity supply[65] (5.9 per cent) and 985 in services[66] (36.6 per cent). The following Table 3.1 provides the sample breakdown for different industrial subsectors. Manufacturing can be further divided into low-tech, medium-tech and high-tech manufacturing, which follows the structure suggested by OECD but introduces three categories instead of the original four suggested by OECD (OECD 2005a).[67]

---

62 Unless otherwise indicated, the source of all graphs and tables of Chapter 3 will be the FDI sub-sample derived from the UNIDO 2010/11 Investor Survey sample. It may sometimes be referred to as "UNIDO FDI Survey sample".

63 Corresponding to International Standard Industrial Classification (ISIC) Rev. 3.1 Sections A, B and C.

64 Corresponding to ISIC Rev. 3.1 Section D.

65 Corresponding to ISIC Rev. 3.1 Sections E and F.

66 Corresponding to ISIC Rev. 3.1 Sections G to Q.

67 Annex 1.1 of the OECD Science, Technology and Industry Scoreboard 2005 (OECD 2005a) suggests four categories i.e. high-technology, medium-high technology, medium-low technology and low-technology and is based on aggregate sectoral R&D intensities in 12 OECD countries (Canada, Denmark, Finland, France, Germany, Ireland, Italy, Japan, Spain, Sweden, UK and US) over the 1991 to 1999 period. The suggested three groups are subdivided as follows: "Low-tech manufacturing" subsumes food and beverages (15), tobacco (16), textiles (17), wearing apparel (18), leather and related products (19), wood products except furniture (20), paper and paper products (21), publishing and printing (22), manufacturing of furniture and n.e.c. (36) and recycling (37). "Medium-tech manufacturing" covers coke and refined petroleum products (23), rubber and plastics (25), other non-metallic mineral products (26), basic metals (27), fabricated metal products, except machinery and equipment (28). "High-tech manufacturing" groups together chemical and chemical products (including pharmaceutical products) (24),

Table 3.1: UNIDO FDI survey sample breakdown by subsector

Subsectors	Count	Per cent
Agriculture and fishing	152	5.6
Mining and quarrying	56	2.1
Primary sector, TOTAL	**208**	**7.7**
Manufacturing (Low-tech)	635	23.6
Manufacturing (Medium-tech)	416	15.4
Manufacturing (High-tech)	289	10.7
Manufacturing TOTAL	**1,340**	**49.7**
Electricity, gas and water supply	18	0.7
Construction	141	5.2
Non-manufacturing industry TOTAL	**159**	**5.9**
Wholesale trade and Vehicle trade	251	9.3
Retail trade	132	4.9
Hotels and restaurants	99	3.7
Transport	105	3.9
Post and telecommunications	53	2.0
Financial institutions	147	5.5
Real estate, consulting, IT	170	6.3
Public admin, education, health, etc.	28	1.0
Services TOTAL	**985**	**36.6**
TOTAL	**2,692**	**100**

UNIDO also adopted this three-level classification (UNIDO 2015a). Amongst foreign investors operating in SSA's services sector, there is an orientation towards wholesale, vehicle and retail trade. By the same token, a large number of foreign investors concentrate on the real estate, consulting, IT and financial services sectors.

Amongst the manufacturing sector, Table 3.2 below indicates that foreign firms are mostly concentrated in food and beverages (258 firms), rubber and plastic (179 firms) chemical products (169 firms) and fabricated metal products (118 firms). Nearly 50 per cent of manufacturing FDI in SSA is low in technology content.

machinery and equipment (29), office, accounting and computing machinery (30), electrical machinery and apparatus (31), radio, TV and communications equipment (32), medical, precision and optical instruments (33), motor vehicles, trailers and semi-trailers (34) and other transport equipment (35).

Table 3.2: UNIDO FDI Survey sample breakdown by manufacturing sub-sector

Manufacturing subsectors based on ISIC Rev. 3.1	Count	Per cent
Food and beverages (15)	258	19.3
Tobacco (16)	17	1.3
Textiles (17)	52	3.9
Wearing apparel (18)	87	6.5
Leather and related products (19)	29	2.2
Wood products except furniture (20)	40	3.0
Paper and paper products (21)	43	3.2
Publishing and printing (22)	44	3.3
Furniture and n.e.c. (36)	59	4.4
Recycling (37)	6	0.4
Low-tech manufacturing TOTAL	**635**	**47.4**
Coke and refined petroleum products (23)	14	1.0
Rubber and plastics (25)	179	13.4
Other non-metallic mineral products (26)	59	4.4
Basic metals (27)	46	3.4
Fabricated metal products, except machinery and equipment (28)	118	8.8
Medium-tech manufacturing TOTAL	**416**	**31.0**
Chemical and chemical prods. (incl. pharmaceutical products) (24)	169	12.6
Machinery and equipment n.e.c. (29)	39	2.9
Office, accounting and computing machinery (30)	3	0.2
Electrical machinery and apparatus (31)	33	2.5
Radio, TV and communications equipment (32)	12	0.9
Medical, precision and optical instruments (33)	9	0.7
Motor vehicles, trailers and semi-trailers (34)	18	1.3
Other transport equipment (35)	6	0.4
High-tech manufacturing TOTAL	**289**	**21.6**
TOTAL	**1,340**	**100**

Relatively larger foreign firms i.e. firms that employ more than 100 workers, tend to concentrate in the financial sector, in electricity, gas and water supply, in low-tech manufacturing and mining. Foreign subsidiaries that are active in trade, real estate and consulting are usually small and employ less than 50 employees. In terms of capital intensity, the proportion of large firms holding more than 1m USD assets is above 50 per cent in the primary sector and in the manufacturing sector, where the proportion of capital-intensive firms is expectedly higher in high-tech manufacturing compared to medium-tech and low-tech manufacturing. Manufacturing foreign investors in SSA are on average older than foreign investors in the primary or tertiary sectors. Two thirds of investors that started operations more than 20 years ago are investors with operations in the manufacturing sector. The share of manufacturing investment, measured in terms of numbers of firms, has decreased constantly and represents around half of the investors of the young age cohort.

Figure 3.1: Proportion of selected subsectors in different FDI age cohorts

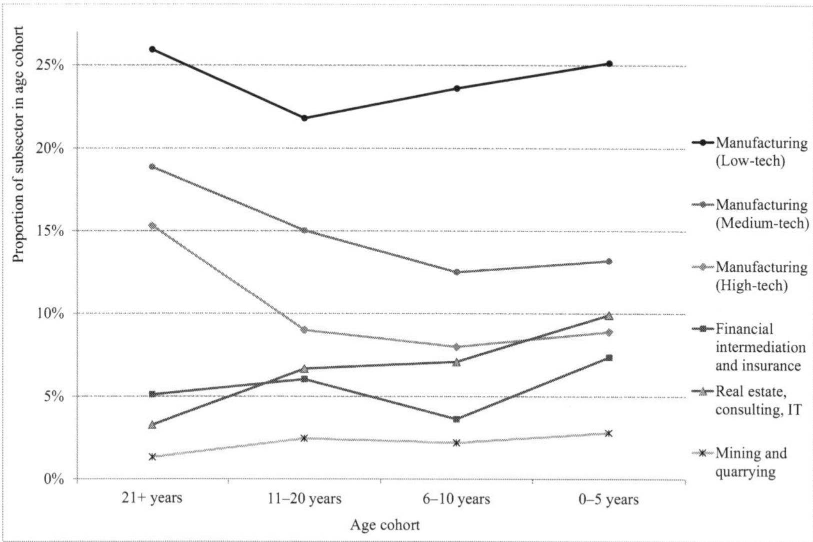

As shown in Figure 3.1 above, manufacturing in the medium-tech and high-tech sectors has particularly sharply declined. For instance, the rubber and plastic sector, which is part of medium-tech manufacturing, represents 7.5 per cent of FDI firms that were established more than 20 years ago but only 4.3 per cent of young firms with less than five years of operations. Low-tech manufacturing, as an aggregate group, has not changed significantly within the different age groups even though there were variations at the subsector-level. For example, the share of low-tech wearing apparel production tripled between the oldest and the youngest age group whereas food and beverages, tobacco and paper saw a decline. A similar trend can be observed for investors in the chemical (including pharmaceutical) sector which represent a small share of 3.6 per cent among young firms from previously 4.4 per cent (6–10 years old), 5.0 per cent (11–20 years old) and 10.3 per cent (>20 years old). Service sectors that have increased their representative share in the cohort of young firms are related to real estate, consulting and IT, financial intermediation as well as hotels and restaurants.

3.3 FDI origin

The majority of investors in the UNIDO sample have their origins in a developing country namely 53.6 per cent vs. 46.4 per cent from a developed country.[68] The largest group of foreign investors in the sample is from India (344 firms, 13.4 per cent), followed by investors from the UK (244 firms, 9.7 per cent), France (234 firms, 9.3 per cent), SA (180 firms, 7.2 per cent), China (154 firms, 6.1 per cent), and Kenya (144 firms, 5.7 per cent). Investors from Germany, Italy, Lebanon, the Netherlands, Portugal and the US have respective sample shares of between 2 and 4 per cent. The increasing role of Brazil as investor in Africa (De la Fontaine and Seifert 2009, White 2010) is not confirmed in the sample which may also be a result of the country distribution which included only two Lusophone countries, namely Cape Verde and Mozambique but excluded Angola, the prime target country for Brazilian FDI in SSA (Rundell 2010).

Moreover, there is also a pattern in terms of the age of the investment and whether the firm originated in a developing or developed country. Nearly 42 per cent of investors from developing countries are less than 10 years old, compared to 30 per cent of investors from developed countries. In contrast, 36.5 per cent of investors from developed countries made their investment more than 21 years ago, compared to only 20.6 per cent of investors from developing countries. Investors from the former colonial powers UK and France are mostly longstanding investors. 46.1 per cent of UK investors and 41.9 per cent of French investors have been in operation for more than 21 years. Investors from African countries and Asian countries, particularly Chinese investors, are proportionally overrepresented

68 The definition is based on UNIDO 2010. Accordingly, investors from China, India or SA are classified as investors from developing countries. In the following, the term *South* FDI may be employed as a synonym for *developing* country FDI and the term *North* FDI may be employed as synonym for FDI from a *developed* country.

within the group of young foreign firms as compared to the rest of the sample.

Figure 3.2: Proportion of foreign investors from different countries of origin in different age cohorts

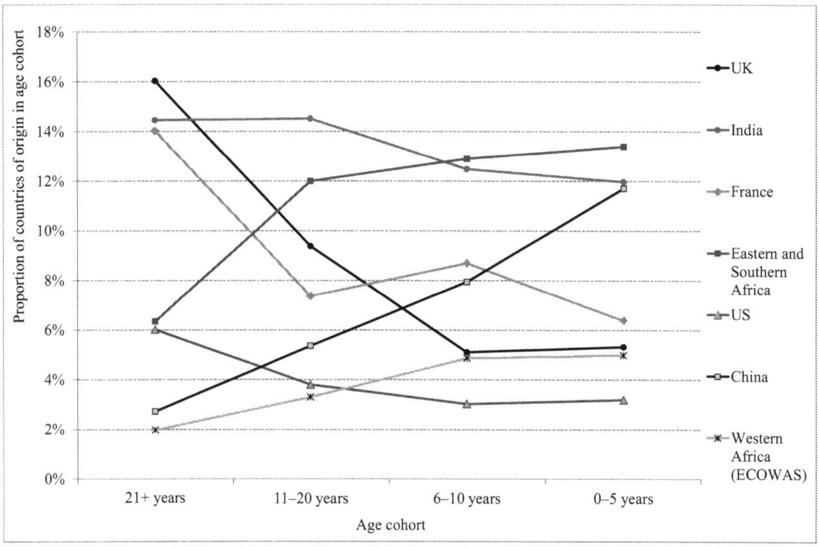

Figure 3.2 above shows the proportions of the main groups of investor origin in the four age cohorts. Based on the assumption that the country of origin of the surveyed foreign company has not changed over the years, it becomes evident that Chinese investors and investors from within Africa are rapidly increasing their share in the youngest age cohort at the expense of Indian, UK, French and US investors whose share in the youngest age cohort has been declining.

A further remarkable relationship exists between the country of origin and the size of foreign operations.[69] There is a strong positive link between subsidiary age and its size measured along the three dimensions of total full-time employees, total fixed assets and the yearly output of the firm. It is no surprise that older investors from developed countries with continuous business operations for many years are also overrepresented in

69 Chapter 3.6 provides a detailed classification of size categories.

the group of large investors. Around two thirds of these old firms from developed countries employ more than 100 workers on average, they own fixed assets above 1 million USD and they generate outputs of more than 10 million USD per year. It appears that investors from developed countries required several years to adjust operations to prevailing market conditions before they grew into large foreign subsidiaries. In contrast to that, there is a sizable subgroup of investors with South origins that have, right from the outset, set up large subsidiaries in SSA. However, the size of young Southern foreign subsidiaries is mostly determined in terms of employment creation and less in terms of total yearly output or fixed assets. 23.7 per cent of developing country FDI that arrived in SSA within the past 5 years has created 100 or more jobs.

Table 3.3: Size structure of subsidiaries owned by foreign investors from different countries of origin

Country	Median no. of employees	Median, fixed assets (USD)	Median, yearly output (USD)
China	48	453,140	972,000
France	63	739,673	3,155,447
Germany	83	1,636,944	5,023,017
India	50	778,762	1,668,675
Italy	51	685,980	1,068,777
Kenya	42	400,628	1,408,093
Lebanon	40	544,984	1,676,989
Netherlands	55	1,134,309	2,203,433
Portugal	44	444,558	2,276,242
South Africa	70	753,362	3,313,926
UK	92	1,619,735	4,101,482
US	83	1,000,426	3,906,791
Other	57	956,022	2,405,125
Total	**59**	**817,395**	**2,295,223**

As Table 3.3 above shows, foreign investors from the UK, the US and Germany stand out as the largest investors in all three size categories. The median firm creates between 83 and 92 jobs, fixed assets are above 1m USD and total yearly output is close to or above 4m USD. At the other end of the spectrum are Chinese, Kenyan and Lebanese investors in which case the median firm employs less than 50 employees, owns fixed assets between 400,000 USD and 550,000 USD and generates a yearly output of between 1 to 2 million USD. The size patterns of Italian and Portuguese investors follow more closely that of the group of China-Kenya-Lebanon with a large number of smaller businesses in terms of employment, fixed assets and total outputs. SA investors bear more resemblance to the larger investors from the UK, US and Germany except for their considerably lower median in fixed assets which is an early indication of their preference for the service sector or low-tech manufacturing sectors.

Investors from developing countries show a higher propensity to engage in manufacturing activities compared to investors from developed countries. For example, 71 per cent of the Chinese investors and 68 per cent of Indian investors are manufacturers compared to only 43 per cent of the French or 54 per cent of Italian investors. UK and German investors constitute an exception within the group of developed country investors since more than 60 per cent are manufacturers.

Annex Table 7 provides an overview of the top five sector preferences of the main investor countries in SSA. The numerically largest investor group is made up of Indian investors who focus on food and beverages, wholesales and rubber and plastics. The sector focus is relatively similar to that of investors from the UK which means that competition for domestic market shares might be fiercer between these two investor groups than between other groups. French investors have a particular focus on real estate, consulting and IT services followed by wholesale trade and construction. Italian and Portuguese FDI resembles the sector patterns of French FDI in SSA, with the exception that the two place a relatively higher emphasis on the construction sector as well as on hotels and restaurants. SA investors are relatively more diversified as their priority five sectors account for only 40 per cent. Their sector preference is less clear than that of other countries of origin and covers both manufacturing and service sectors. At the other end of the spectrum are Dutch, Lebanese and US investors which show preference for one particular sector that is then followed by other sectors. For example, 31 per cent of Dutch investors have invested in the agricultural sector which is remarkably high compared to other investor groups. The strong orientation of Lebanese investors towards wholesales and trade is also confirmed from the dataset.[70]

70 See: http://www.economist.com/blogs/baobab/2011/05/lebanese_west_africa (accessed on 16 May 2016).

3.4 FDI establishment and ownership mode

Another important feature of the structure of FDI in SSA is the choice of the entry mode. In line with the definitions to be provided in Chapter 4.1.1, the entry mode subdivides into two separate choices. One choice relates to the *establishment* mode which can take the form of a merger & acquisition (M&A) or a greenfield investment (Brouthers and Brouthers 2000, Slangen and Hennart 2007). The other choice concerns the foreign ownership mode. The foreign investor can opt to own a partial foreign equity share through a JV arrangement with another partner or it can run a WOS.

The overarching majority of foreign investors (85.2 per cent, 2,222 firms) in the UNIDO 2010/11 Investor Survey sample prefer the establishment mode of greenfield investment. Conversely, 386 firms (14.8 per cent) chose the M&A establishment mode. Within the M&A establishment mode, 38.3 per cent of firms (148 firms) purchased existing assets from local private owners, 39.1 per cent (151 firms) purchased existing assets from other foreign owners and 22.6 per cent (87 firms) took advantage of privatization programmes of formerly state-owned enterprises.

In terms of current ownership, foreign investors prefer to control their operations through a wholly-owned ownership mode. 71.8 per cent of (1,859 firms) have chosen the former mode as opposed to 28.2 per cent of firms (729 firms) that operate under a JV. The share of WOSs in the UNIDO 2010/11 Investor Survey sample is considerably higher than in UNIDO′s 2005 FDI sample where the share of the wholly-owned ownership mode was at 60.7 per cent (UNIDO 2007). Within the group of domestic-foreign JV firms, more than half of the firms are majority-owned by the foreign partner, 13.4 per cent are co-owned by both partners each holding a share of 50 per cent and in 36.4 per cent of JVs the indigenous partner holds the majority in equity ownership. On average and without applying weighting in terms of the amount of invested equity, each foreign firm owns approximately 86 per cent of equity in the respective JV or foreign subsidiary whereas, consistent with the official definition of FDI, the classification as foreign investor requires a minimum foreign ownership of at least 10 per cent (IMF 2009). This compares to 81 per cent average foreign equity in UNIDO's 2005 FDI sample and 74 per cent based on the World Bank Enterprise Survey data.[71]

The cross-tabulation of the two main establishment modes and two main ownership modes, presented in Table 3.4, clearly underpins the dominance of the combined greenfield-WOS entry mode.

Table 3.4: Distribution of FDI entry modes in SSA

		Establishment mode	
		Greenfield	Acquisition
Ownership mode	JV	22.9% (584 cases)	5.0% (128 cases)
	WOS	62.2% (1,584 cases)	9.8% (249 cases)

62.2 per cent of FDI investors have entered through this mode. Foreign investors exhibit a clear preference for the combination of greenfield/full ownership in the case of textiles, garments, wood, construction, wholesale and distribution. More specifically, 73.1 per cent of greenfield establishment modes are also WOSs and 86.4 per cent of all WOSs have been established as greenfield firms. In terms of JV preference, 34 per cent of M&A establishment modes coincide with a JV ownership mode compared to 26.9 per cent of JVs within the greenfield establishment mode.[72]

In the following section, the JV ownership mode choice will be reviewed from the perspective of main investor categories. Starting with main sectors, there are some variations of foreign ownership with moderate statistical significance. As shown in the following Table 3.5, 27.5 per cent of agriculture and mining firms prefer a JV arrangement, compared to 30.3 per cent in the secondary sector (combining manufacturing, utilities and construction) and 25.1 per cent in the services sector.

This indicates a slight preference of JVs as ownership modes in foreign manufacturing. Within the manufacturing sector, JVs are more attractive ownership modes when foreign operations become more technology-intensive. This observation is counter-intuitive to transaction cost-based considerations which assume that the high knowledge content of the pro-

71 Based on Annex Table 6 and the dataset from http://www.enterprisesurveys.org (downloaded 9 January 2016), comprising 3,316 foreign subsidiaries with more than 10 per cent foreign equity ownership.

72 Chi (1, 2575)=19.795; $p<0.001$.

cesses and products make the transfer to a JV partner and the protection of proprietary assets particularly difficult and costly from the perspective of the foreign subsidiary (Anderson and Gatignon 1986, Gatignon and Anderson 1988, Erramilli and Rao 1993, Shrader 2001, Brouthers 2002, Zhao et al. 2004). The latter would prompt the foreign firm to prefer full internalization which is achieved through a WOS.

Table 3.5: Ownership mode choice in different FDI categories

Main category		JV occurrence		WOS occurrence		Significance
		N	Per cent	N	Per cent	
Main sectors	Agriculture and mining	56	27.5	148	72.5	Chi (3, 2588) =8.186; p=0.042
	Manufacturing	392	30.6	890	69.4	
	Electricity, water and construction	44	28.0	113	72.0	
	Services	237	25.1	708	74.9	
Investor origin (North/South)	North	383	33.0	778	67.0	Chi (1, 2496) =33.517; p<0.001
	South	302	22.6	1,033	77.4	
Investor origin, detailed	Investor from last colonial power	163	37.0	278	63.0	Chi (1, 2496) =44.397; p<0.001
	North investor with no (recent) colonial ties	220	30.6	500	69.4	
	Investor from SSA	91	27.5	240	72.5	
	South investor (non-SSA)	211	21.0	793	79.0	
Organizational structure	TNC	202	22.6	693	77.4	Chi (1, 2545) =8.843; p=0.005
	FE	518	30.8	1,162	69.2	

More specifically, more than 50 per cent of foreign investors in motor vehicles manufacturing in SSA prefer JVs. By the same token, the majority of foreign firms (52.5 per cent) form JVs in the area of financial intermediation which might be the result of prevailing foreign ownership restrictions that prohibit the creation of WOSs in this particular sector (Ahmed and Islam 2010, World Bank et al. 2010). The average proportion of foreign equity in this sector is 76 per cent which indicates that foreign equity majority is very common in the case of JVs in the financial sector. In contrast, WOEs are largely preferred by foreign investors in the garment sector as well as in leather and footwear production. Only 16 per cent and 10 per cent of foreign firms respectively share equity with another domestic or foreign partner. Likewise, in the services sector, foreign firms running operations in hoteling, restaurants, trade and wholesales also prefer WOSs.

The "cultural distance" theory posits that investors from culturally distant economies avoid establishment modes of M&As where they would have to accommodate the target firm's national and corporate culture into their own specific and presumably more distant firm culture (Kogut and Singh 1988, Padmanabhan and Cho 1995, Barkema and Vermeulen 1998, Chang and Rosenzweig 2001, Shenkar 2001). The impact of cultural distance on the choice of ownership mode is more mixed (Zhao and Zhu 1998, Brouthers and Brouthers 2001, Mayrhofer 2004). A positive link has been found between large cultural distance and the selection of wholly-owned entry modes in the case of Japanese outward investments (Padmanabhan and Cho 1996, Anand and Delios 1997). US investors, again, seem to choose JVs as a means to offset large cultural distance (Kogut and Singh 1988). The sample at hand does not support the idea that culturally distant investors prefer a specific establishment mode. For example, Asian investors which supposedly exhibit high levels of cultural distance do not show a clear pattern in terms of preferring greenfield establishment modes when compared to allegedly culturally closer investors, such as those from within Africa or also those with former colonial ties. 89 per cent of Asian investors establish their operations as greenfield operations compared to 86 per cent of Kenyan investors, 83 per cent of SA investors, 84 per cent of investors from the UK and 83 per cent of French investors. The differences are thus marginal and by no means statistically significant. There are some differences between the samples of the UNIDO 2010/11 Investor Survey and UNIDO′s 2005 FDI sample that formed the basis for UNIDO's 2007 FDI Survey Report. The latter confirmed that 25 per cent of the responding foreign investors entered through an M&A and SA investors showed a significantly higher propensity to enter through an M&A (UNIDO 2007, Henley et al. 2008). Both findings can now no longer be confirmed from the UNIDO 2010/11 Investor Survey sample.

Unlike the effect on establishment mode, there are signs that cultural distance might play a role in the selection of the ownership mode. As Table 3.5 above indicated, there exists a significantly larger proportion of foreign investors from developed countries (denoted as *North*) forming JVs compared to foreign investors from developing countries (denoted as *South*). One third of North investors operate under a JV arrangement as opposed to 22.6 per cent of South investors. Among the FDI groups of North vs. South FDI exist subgroups with supposedly lower levels of cultural distance: On the one hand, a developed country foreign investor whose country of origin represents a former colonial power of the SSA host country (e.g. Belgian FDI in Burundi and Rwanda, Portuguese FDI in Cape Verde and Mozambique, UK FDI in Eastern and Southern Africa, French FDI in Western Africa) may be more familiar with the host country environment and can operate without any language barriers. In fact, 37 per cent of FDI investors from the former colonial power operate as JVs, compared to 30.6 per cent of developed country investors without such historical ties. For example, the overarching majority of UK investors focus their investments in UK's former SSA colonies (87 per cent of UK investments in the sample). More than 40 per cent of UK investors with a historical connection to a particular SSA host country prefer JV ownership modes. Within the group of JVs, a relatively larger percentage of UK firms even accept minority shareholding (40 firms representing 40 per cent of UK-domestic JVs). On the other hand, amongst developing country investors, investors from within SSA are subject to lower cultural barriers especially if they invest within a geographically confined area and in regions of common language. Kenyan FDI in Uganda and Tanzania or SA investments in Southern Africa are examples. 27.5 per cent of investors from within SSA choose JVs compared to 21 per cent of developing country investors from outside SSA. Being part of the latter category, only 12 per cent of Chinese and Lebanese investors form a JV. The largest group of foreign investors, namely Indian investors, are also fairly reluctant to form JVs as indicated by a relatively low JV proportion of 19.6 per cent. In the case that a JV had been formed, Indian investors are however more willing to take minority shareholding than peers from other countries of origin. Overall, the observations seem to confirm previous findings in the literature of a positive link between high (low) cultural distance and higher (lower) foreign equity entry modes (Padmanabhan and Cho 1996, Anand and Delios 1997).

The preference of a particular ownership mode also depends on the organizational structure of FDI. The survey data confirms that FEs have a greater tendency to form JVs compared to TNCs.[73] Table 3.5 has shown that more than 30 per cent of FEs formed JV agreements as opposed to 22.6 per cent of the TNCs. The average foreign equity ownership of TNCs

73 Sub-Chapter 3.7 provides a detailed explanation for the distinction between FEs and TNCs.

is 90.6 per cent and 83.9 per cent of FEs. This observation is in keeping with transaction cost theory which posits that resource-constrained and smaller firms are better off in internationalizing through mixed FDI entry modes as opposed to full internalization through WOSs (Zacharakis 1997, Lu and Beamish 2001, Lu and Beamish 2006). It also follows the argumentation that smaller international firms follow a prudent approach of risk and set-up cost minimization (Mutinelli and Piscitello 1998b). Conversely, firms which command a larger international network of subsidiaries are more prone to prefer high control options (Taylor et al. 1998). When FEs enter into a JV agreement they are more often ready to relinquish majority ownership in favour of the indigenous partner (58.1 per cent) unlike TNCs that prefer to hold majority equity ownership in order to maintain managerial control over the JV.

Table 3.6: Mean foreign equity share in FDI subsidiaries of varying sizes

Size category	Foreign equity ownership in per cent		
	Small	Medium	Large
Output	89.4	85.0	82.7
Fixed assets	89.7	88.9	82.6
Employment	88.1	86.1	82.8

The average foreign equity share is inversely related to the size of operations, irrespective of whether size is measured in terms of output, fixed assets or the number of employees (see Table 3.6 above). In all cases, there is a statistically significant difference of 5 to 7 per cent between small FDI projects and large FDI projects. The latter have mean foreign equity shares of between 82.6 and 82.8 per cent depending on the classification of firm size.

The relationship between the ownership mode and the size of foreign operations is further corroborated by the median values of output, fixed assets and employment. Accordingly, the median JV firm employs 80 employees (WOS: 50 employees), it generates an annual output of approximately 3.7 million USD (WOS: 2 million USD) and owns fixed assets of 1.7 million USD (WOS: 660,000 USD). The cross-tabulation of different categories of FDI size and the selected ownership mode shows the same clear trend towards the selection of shared equity modes in larger business operations in the SSA host country. Figure 3.3 on the next page illustrates that the proportion of JVs increases between small to medium subsidiaries and medium to large subsidiaries, regardless of the three different measurements of subsidiary size. The differences within each size category are highly statistically significant.[74]

Figure 3.3: Occurrence of JV ownership mode in different subsidiary size groups

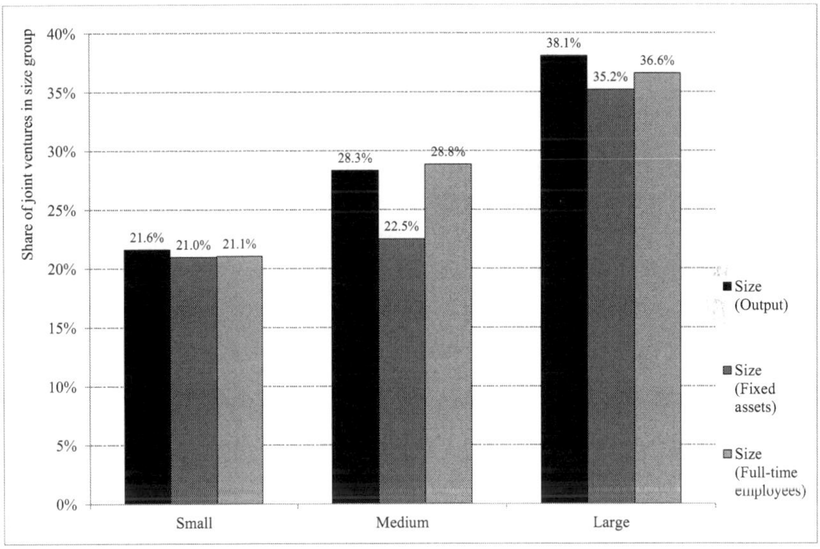

For example, the share of JVs soars from 21 per cent to 35.2 per cent from lower to higher nominal values of fixed assets which means that the share of WOSs in these groups develops inversely and thus decreases. This finding conforms to the established notion in transaction cost literature that foreign firms prefer to share the risks of asset-intensive investments with a local equity partner. Consequently, FDI entails lower levels of equity ownership the higher is the required investment into fixed assets (Gatignon and Anderson 1988, Kogut and Singh 1988, Shan 1991, Pan 1996, Makino and Neupert 2000). For instance, Gomes-Casseres finds a positive and significant relationship between the probability of forming a JV and owning physical assets above 10 million USD (Gomes-Casseres 1990).

74 Size (employment-related) produces Chi (2, 2587)=60.747; $p<0.001$; size (output-related) produces Chi (2, 2488)=42.979; $p<0.001$, and size (asset-related) produces Chi (2, 2479)=53.447; $p<0.001$.

Although large investments may more often be structured through a JV instead of a WOS, it does not mean that the foreign firms would be content with minority or equal foreign ownership after JV formation. On the contrary, foreign investors wish to retain majority shareholding inside the JV when the operations are large, especially when the size is measured in terms of employment and annual total output. In that sense, empirical findings such as those by Yigang Pan may have explanatory value in determining FDI preference of JVs over WOSs but the assumption that large FDI projects prompt foreign firms to unreservedly decrease foreign equity cannot be validated by the data set at hand (Pan 1996). For example, the foreign investor has majority shareholding in almost 60 per cent of JVs with more than 10 million USD of annual output contrasted with only 40 per cent in JVs with an annual output of below 1 million USD. Concerning total fixed assets, foreign direct investors show no propensity to increase foreign majority shareholding in JVs if fixed assets are larger.

The relationship between the age of the investing firm and the ownership mode also provides interesting findings. The highest share of the JV mode can be found amongst firms that have been in operation for more than 20 years. In this age group, 41 per cent of foreign firms are engaged in JVs compared to only 23.3 per cent in the youngest FDI cohort where WOS ownership modes are clearly preferred. The middle aged cohorts, such as investors between 6-10 and 11-20 years, exhibit JV preference in 19.9 per cent and 24.9 per cent of the cases. It is possible that this reflects a trend whereby older foreign investors had originally entered SSA as WOSs early in their investment cycle and had carried out a switch towards shared equity ownership modes at a later stage of the cycle after having gained sufficient confidence in the local market and having mapped potential local candidate firms with whom a JV formation would augur success. The longer the subsidiary is operating abroad the more it would adjust to the SSA host country's environment. It may open up to new opportunities for local partnerships that it would not have dared to conclude during the early stages of operations when the perceived cultural distance was still high (Chang and Rosenzweig 2001, Wilkinson et al. 2008).

Related to the time frame of the most recent five years of the foreign investment, the following Table 3.7 indicates that the large majority of foreign investors (86.1 per cent, 2,193 cases) have not implemented any ownership changes.[75]

Table 3.7: Ownership changes in FDI firms in SSA within the past 5 years

Ownership change within the past 5 years			No. of cases	Per cent
No ownership change			**2,193**	**86.1**
Ownership change			**355**	**13.9**
	of which:			
	Ownership decrease		119	4.7
		of which:		
		WOS to JV switch	45	1.8
	Ownership increase		236	9.3
		of which:		
		JV to WOS switch	114	4.5
Total			**2,548**	**100**

As for the rest, 119 investors (4.7 per cent) decreased their foreign equity share whereas 236 investors (9.3 per cent) increased their foreign equity share. In a total of 159 cases (6.3 per cent), the foreign equity change resulted in a switch from one ownership mode to another. The switch from a previous collaborative agreement to a WOS is more common than the switch from a former WOS towards a collaborative JV agreement. This provides some support to the presence and use of the real options approach in international JV partnerships. Real options enable the foreign investor to monitor the evolution of the JV and to buy out the local partner at some stage during the partnership (Kogut 1991, Chi 2000, Kumar 2005, Brouthers et al. 2008a, Puck et al. 2009). Interestingly, the occurrence of a foreign equity change within the past five years is significantly larger in M&A establishment modes compared to greenfield establishment modes, namely 21.4 per cent in M&As vs. 12.6 per cent in greenfield investments.

75 Detailed information about the construction of this variable is provided in Chapter 5.2.2.

3.5 Perceived partner contributions to joint venture success

The UNIDO 2010/11 Investor Survey also sought to gain a better understanding of the rationale of foreign investors to form a JV. To this end, foreign investors were asked to rate the importance of their own contribution as well as the contribution of the indigenous partner to the success of the JV.[76] Following the suggested approach of Labovitz, numerical values can be assigned to rank categories to reach better statistical results and greater versatility in statistical manipulation (Labovitz 1970). The results indicate that the motives for JV creation are grounded in a complementary mix of resource-based and transaction cost-based theories. In a wider sense, the first three factors are attributable to the JV's pools of available resources. The first one, *"Use of patents/trademarks/brand names"* is an expression of knowledge superiority in a specific and inimitable product category of an industrial sector and constitutes the successful result of the MNE's efforts in product design, production and marketing (Wernerfelt 1984, Dierickx and Cool 1989, Dunning 1993). Closely related to the first factor are firm resources related to the second factor of *"technology and know-how"* which help to secure and expand the ownership advantage that the multinational firm has acquired over its competitors (Barney 1991). The third factor *"Upgrading quality of staff"* represents the multinational firm's human capital as a resource that is complex, often tacit and difficult to be imitated or substituted by a competitor firm (Hatch and Dyer 2004). Besides, it is the most commonly studied resource within the plethora of resource-based literature (Newbert 2007). The importance placed on human capital is also a proxy for the MNE's willingness to expand its competitive position through learning. This learning process may result in the codification of hitherto unknown or tacit knowledge elements of the firm's human resource in order to apply it more widely inside the JV or at the level of the multinational parent (Hamel 1991, Kogut and Zander 1992, Lyles and Salk 1996, Hatch and Dyer 2004). The fourth factor *"access to finance"* confirms one of the basic transaction costs motives for the creation of international partnerships, namely to spread the risks of injected equity capital between one or more partners (Contractor and Lorange 1988, Zhao et

76 Importance has been measured on a 5-point Likert scale. "Not important" has been ranked as "1", "Slightly important" has been ranked as "2", "Important" has been ranked as "3", "Very important" has been ranked as "4", "Crucial" has been ranked as "5".

al. 2004, Dong and Glaister 2006). Factors five and six relate to the extent of vertical forward or backward linkages that could be harnessed through a cooperative arrangement between the foreign and the local investor (UNCTAD 1993, Glaister and Buckley 1996, UNCTAD 2013b).

As Figure 3.4 below shows, the foreign investor perceives superiority in five of six determinants, especially related to technology and know-how, global upstream supplier networks (*"Access to foreign supplier network"*) and international downstream customer networks (*"Global market access"*). Accordingly, the foreign investor has limited expectations with regard to the vertical linkages offered by the SSA partner, especially related to backward linkages and international forward linkages. Relatively more importance is placed on the existence of existing patents, trademarks or brand names of the local partner (score: 3.35) since the latter could stimulate greater market acceptance and external legitimacy of the JV's main services or products while reducing costs through the re-utilization of locally available distribution and marketing channels (Lu and Xu 2006).

Figure 3.4: The importance of foreign and local partner's contribution to JV success

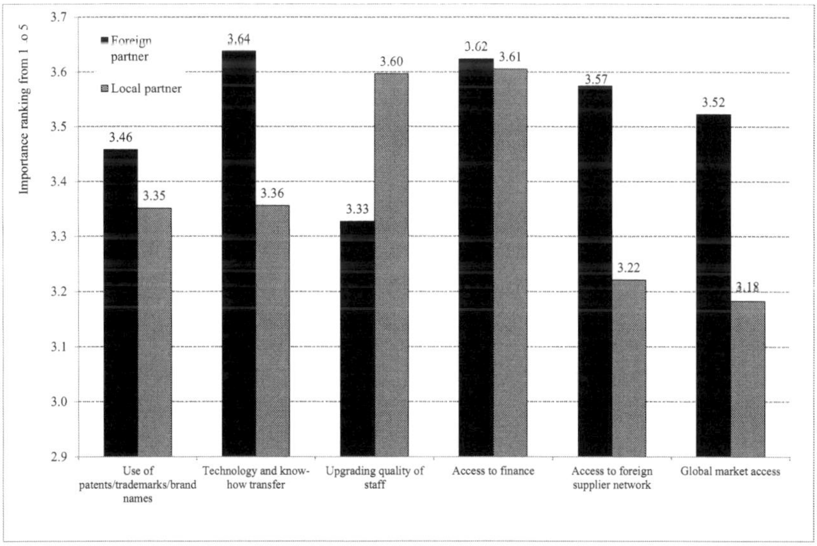

As expected, the importance of local patents or brands varies according to the market orientation of the foreign investor and becomes more important for local market-seeking investors and less important for export-oriented and efficiency-seeking investors (score: 3.25). The importance of the local partner's brands shows a strong increase if the foreign investor has plans to expand into regional SSA markets (score 3.69) which coincides with the finding that regional market orientation is an important factor tilting the foreign investor's preference towards JVs as opposed to a WOS.[77]

Concerning the expected technology and know-how transfer, the foreign investor appears confident about the paramount superiority of its process and product know how vs. that of the SSA partner. In spite of the technology gap between the foreign and local partner, there is the perception of a sufficient inter-partner "fit" which makes both partners confident to overcome the initial technology gaps by means of internal learning and exchange of know-how (Lyles 1994, Luo 1997, Lane et al. 2001). Unless the existing skills and technology threshold of the local partner is deemed sufficient for such a synergistic process to materialize during the initial stages of the JV, the foreign investor would prefer full internalization through a WOS or rather cancel the FDI plans altogether. The perceived technology gap may be offset by the critical role that the local partner is expected to assume in the financing of the JV and the upgrading of its staff. With importance scores of 3.62 for the foreign partner and 3.61 for the local partner respectively, access to finance is the main preoccupation of the foreign investor for the success of the JV. This is a rather pragmatic approach and underscores the risk-sharing rationale of the JV ownership mode which is meant to reduce the overall transaction costs of internationalization. The local partner's ability to subscribe the required capital for the JV also lowers FDI entry barriers for less internationalized and small FEs which dispose of a limited budget for internationalization purposes and have fewer options to borrow from international capital markets compared to large MNEs (Zacharakis 1997, Lu and Beamish 2001, Lu and Beamish 2006). Unsurprisingly, FEs place a higher importance than established TNCs on the ability of the local partner to make a significant financial contribution to the JV (score: 3.64 vs. 3.49).

The factor *"Upgrading quality of staff"* is the only factor wherein the foreign partner perceives the local partner's contribution to the JV as be-

77 27.8 per cent of local market-seeking investors establish a JV, 26 per cent of global market-seeking investors but 34.3 per cent of regional market-seeking investors, Chi (2, 2484)=6.041, p=0.49. The classification according to market orientation is explained in greater detail in Chapter 3.9.

ing more important than its own contribution. It may imply that the indigenous JV partner disposes of codified and tacit knowledge amongst its work force that the foreign partner considers worth internalizing and standardizing through inter-partner learning in a bid to propel the overall competitiveness of the JV. Other more pragmatic reasons could however also be at play, namely to circumvent a costly screening of and recruitment process from the local labour market as would be the case for the greenfield-WOS FDI entry mode. Hamel argues that "the alliance is viewed not as an alternative to market-based transaction or full ownership, but as an alternative to other modes of skill acquisition. [...] Alliances may be seen as a way of short-circuiting the process of skills acquisition and thus avoiding the opportunity cost of being a perpetual follower" (Hamel 1991, p.99). In this line of argumentation, the JV entry mode offers the foreign partner relatively quick access to the existing human resource pool of the local partner instead of building the human resource structure from scratch and being confronted with the risks and complexities associated with the organizational integration of newly recruited workforce.

Figure 3.5 on the next page illustrates how the perceived importance of the local partner's contribution to human resource skills development alternates depending on the category of the foreign investor.

For FDI firms in the primary and services sector, the role of the local JV partner for internal skills development is perceived to be considerably more important than that of the foreign partner. In the primary sector, this might seem plausible in JVs where the local partner assumes responsibility for the agricultural value chain and the management and skills development of smallholder farmers aimed at adopting cultivation methods introduced by the foreign partner in the framework of outgrower schemes or contract farming arrangements (Cotula and Vermeulen 2009, Oya 2012). In the service sector, especially those related to wholesale and distribution, the SSA partner is expected to ensure that the local staff stays abreast of product or service improvements and innovations introduced through the JV in order to effectively communicate and promote those via established local marketing channels. For similar reasons, local market-seeking FDI investors value the importance of the local partner for skills development by 0.3 points higher, compared to 0.27 points for regional market-seeking investors and 0.08 points for global market-seeking investors. TNCs find that both partners play an equally important role in the upgrading of staff quality. Conversely, FEs perceive the onus for staff development to be oriented towards the local partner.

Figure 3.5: Perceived importance gap of foreign vs. local partner contributions for JV's upgrading of staff quality

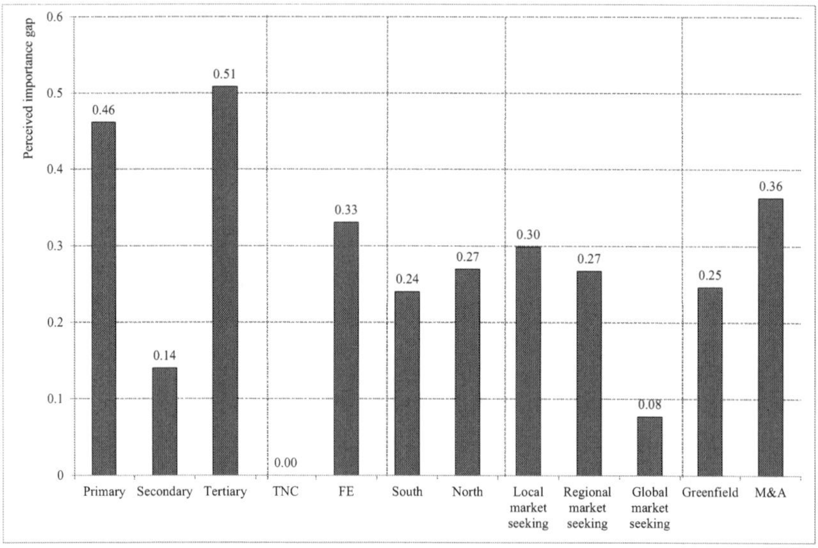

If the factor *"Upgrading quality of staff"* is assessed in conjunction with the first two factors related to technology, trademark and brand name, some similarities in perception could be found with the study of Yan and Gray which quotes a US manager in a US-Chinese JV: "We have the technology and certain know-how. The Chinese partner knows how to make things happen in China. You put the two together right, it works" (Yan and Gray 1994, p. 1492). Apart from the capital injection that both partners provide to the JV and whose importance was perceived to be nearly similar, the underlying bargaining position of both partners remains stable as long as the foreign partner fulfils its role as provider of technology, expertise in production management, networks and global market access whereas the SSA partner assumes leadership in human resource management, training and learning. An intended or unintended change in previously stable bargaining positions has been identified as an important cause of JV instability at later stages (Inkpen and Beamish 1997, Chung and Beamish 2010). In this sense, some FDI investors may regard JVs as transitional learning devices where the primary objective is to gradually appropriate the local partner's skills in order for the foreign partner to effectively navigate through a complex and multifaceted business environment like that of

SSA (Larsson et al. 1998). Once this goal is accomplished the foreign partner may come to a new conclusion about the value-added of the partner and may find it more profitable to run operations independently, thereby turning previous collaborators into potential future competitors.

3.6 Size of FDI

The size of foreign subsidiaries or FE operations in SSA will be measured in three dimensions: total full-time employment, the current total value of the firm's assets (book value) and total annual output.[78] The distribution of the three subsidiary size categories is shown in Figure 3.6.

The distribution of subsidiary size categories can vary significantly depending on how a small, medium or large subsidiary is defined. The definition of UNIDO is applied for the employment-related subsidiary size measure (UNIDO 2012a). There are 1,180 foreign investors (44 per cent) operating small subsidiaries with less than 50 full-time employees whereas 951 foreign investors (35.5 per cent) run large subsidiaries employing more than 100 full-time employees. In terms of assets, 1,208 foreign firms (47.3 per cent) own or, in the case of a JV, co-own assets of more than 1 million USD, hence meeting the definition of large investors. In terms of total annual output, the largest proportion of foreign investors (45.4 per cent) has yearly outputs in the medium category between 1 million and 10 million USD.

78 If subsidiary size is measured according to the number of full-time employees, a small subsidiary has between 1–50 employees, a medium-sized subsidiary has between 51–100 employees and a large subsidiary has more than 100 employees. If subsidiary size is measured according to the total value of fixed assets, a small subsidiary owns fixed assets of less than 100,000 USD, a medium-sized subsidiary owns fixed assets between 100,000 USD and 1 million USD and a large subsidiary owns fixed assets equal or above 1 million USD. If size is measured in terms of total annual output (i.e. sales plus changes in stock of final goods minus sales of goods bought for resale) of the subsidiary, a small subsidiary has an annual output of less than 1 million USD, a medium-sized subsidiary has a total annual output of between 1 to 10 million USD and a large firm has a total annual output of 10 million USD or more.

Figure 3.6: Size distribution of foreign subsidiaries in SSA

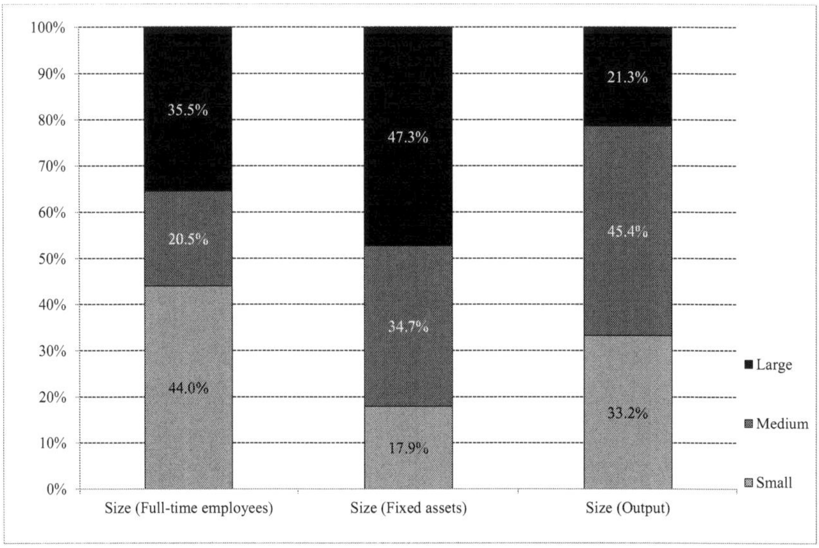

As mentioned in Chapter 3.2, large foreign subsidiaries or FEs, as measured by the number of employees (>100 workers), can be found relatively more often in sectors such as financial intermediation, electricity, gas and water supply, low-tech manufacturing and mining. Small subsidiaries with less than 50 employees are dominant in a range of service sectors such as real estate (82.1 per cent are small), computer and IT related services (73.7 per cent are small), wholesale trade (73.3 per cent are small) and retail trade (69.7 per cent are small). This pattern is confirmed by median values of the number of full-time employees as displayed in the following Table 3.8.

The median foreign investor in the electricity, gas and water supply sector employs 130 workers, followed by financial intermediation with 104 workers and low-tech manufacturing with 78 workers. Within the low-tech manufacturing sector, the garments sector has the largest median employment of 519 workers, followed by the tobacco and textiles sector within which a median of 157 workers and 165 workers are employed respectively.

Table 3.8: Median size (employment, fixed assets and annual output) of different FDI subsectors in SSA

Subsector	Median # of employees	Median, fixed assets (USD)	Median, annual output (USD)	Summary
Agriculture and fishing	76	1,600,000	2,293,290	High employment and assets, medium output
Mining and quarrying	68	1,935,092	5,392,160	Medium employment, high assets and output
Manufacturing (Low-tech)	78	1,128,073	2,455,975	High employment, medium assets and output
Manufacturing (Medium-tech)	70	1,328,769	2,582,020	High employment, medium assets and output
Manufacturing (High-tech)	67	1,636,814	3,044,429	Medium employment, high assets and output
Electricity, gas and water supply	130	12,925,864	19,339,266	High employment, assets and output
Construction	66	590,504	2,408,860	Medium employment, assets and output
Wholesale trade and vehicle trade	25	281,162	2,029,122	Low employment, assets and output
Retail trade	22	129,558	1,314,376	Low employment, assets and output
Hotels and restaurants	45	270,986	498,453	Medium employment, low assets and output
Transport	37	778,762	2,268,016	Low employment, medium assets and output
Post and telecommunications	55	441,503	3,447,716	Medium employment and assets, high output
Financial institutions	104	1,666,179	9,200,715	High employment, assets and output
Real estate, consulting, IT	22	157,745	759,473	Low employment, assets and output
Public admin, education, health, etc.	22	271,201	779,323	Low employment, assets and output
Total	**60**	**817,701**	**2,327,694**	

In terms of fixed assets owned by foreign subsidiaries, the largest median assets of close to 13 million USD belong to the utilities sector. FDI in the primary, secondary and financial sectors shows median fixed assets of between 1 million to 2 million USD. In terms of manufacturing FDI, the largest fixed assets are owned by foreign investors in the tobacco and basic metals sector. As expected, the mining and quarrying sector operates from a large fixed asset base and the median in the sector is close to 2 million USD. In terms of median annual outputs, utilities, financial intermediation, mining and quarrying as well as telecommunications display comparatively large median values. The majority of service sector FDI (wholesale trade, retail trade, real estate, public administration) is small in all respects. It has a limited employment effect, operates from a low fixed capital base and generates relatively meagre outputs.

3.7 Organizational structure of FDI

Until the early 1990's, there was a persistent notion that FDI was the prerogative of large MNEs that must have gone through an extended and incremental process of learning and market adaptation as a mechanism to preserve the MNE's ownership advantage whilst operating in a foreign market. The influential "Uppsala-Model" was based on the tenet that the establishment of international operations is an incremental process starting with no regular export activities of the MNE, then followed by regular export activities via independent representatives in the target country, then followed by the establishment of sales subsidiaries and finally leading over to FDI (Johanson and Wiedersheim-Paul 1975, Johanson and Vahlne 1977, Johanson and Vahlne 1990). The majority of cases of business internationalisation was adequately described by the "Uppsala-Model" until the advent of an increasing number of small and aggressively internationalizing firms that have since then been classified as born global firms or INVs. Oviatt and McDougall define an INV as "a business organization that, from inception, seeks to derive significant competitive advantage from the use of resources and the sale of outputs in multiple countries" (Oviatt and McDougall 1994, p. 49). INVs seem to have a greater potential to leapfrog several stages of the internationalization process and they enter international new markets at a much faster pace than traditional international investors (Knight and Cavusgil 2004). The focus was initially on innovative and technology-intensive firms as an essential condition for becoming a born-global or INV (Coviello and Munro 1997, Autio et al. 2000, Burgel and Murray 2000, Crick and Jones 2000, Yli-Renko et al. 2002, Mahnke and Venzin 2003). More recently, the conception of a born-global firm as an alternative form to a traditional TNC has been enriched with elements from the international entrepreneurship literature which puts supplementary emphasis on how the entrepreneur harnesses its experience and existing personal networks for the internationalization process

(Coviello 2006). As Oviatt and McDougall state: "in contrast to multinational firms, knowledge in the entrepreneurial firm tends to be more individualized to the founder or entrepreneurial team" (Oviatt and McDougall 2005, p. 547) and in small businesses it is often an internationally-minded entrepreneur who discovers, enacts, evaluates and exploits cross-border opportunities to create future goods and services (Oviatt and McDougall 2005). At the same time, an increasing number of studies have invalidated the original argument that entrepreneurially-driven FDI through INVs or born global firms can only exist in specific niche sectors such as high-tech or specialized ICT service sectors (Loane and Bell 2006, Fernhaber et al. 2007, Andersson et al. 2014). In fact, an increasing number of studies recognize the role of INVs in low-technology and traditional manufacturing sectors (Ibeh 2005, Evers 2011, Puig et al. 2014).

The increased relevance of the international entrepreneurship literature has prompted UNIDO to distinguish between two organizational types of FDI in the context of SSA, namely a TNC vs. an FE (UNIDO 2007, UNIDO 2012a). The first type describes a scenario where the SSA subsidiary belongs to a transnational parent company with headquarters in another country and thus represents the most classical form of a multinational corporation. The second type is where the foreign investor is a foreign national or family which acts as an owner of a company or venture which can, however, not be strictly classified as a subsidiary of an enterprise based in another country. This classification is not too different to that of Li and Guisinger who identified three organizational categories: a multinational corporation (MNC), an individual foreign investor and a government-owned enterprise. They found that MNCs display lower failure rates than foreign individuals (Li and Guisinger 1991).[79]

The FDI category of an FE has strong similarities to the "heterarchical" way (Hedlund 1986, Williams and Lee 2011) of organizing an internationally-minded entrepreneurial firm where the founder of the firm is not physically tied to a specific parent but is more elusively and flexibly coordinating an otherwise dispersed and autonomous network of subsidiaries in either the same or different business sectors (Lee and Williams 2007, Williams and Lee 2009). The Economist has labelled these firms "parallel entrepreneurs" (The Economist 2012). Such firms can operate at local lev-

79 Yet, Li and Guisinger fail to provide a clear demarcation between the three categories particularly between the foreign MNC category and the foreign individual.

el or at cross-border level. In the latter case they incorporate characteristics of INVs in the context of traditional service and low-technology manufacturing sectors.

In its 2010/11 Investor Survey sample, UNIDO identifies 924 TNCs (34.8 per cent) and 1,734 FEs (65.2 per cent) as operating in SSA. A large percentage of 72.9 per cent of FEs have indicated to have established their business in a stand-alone fashion whereas 27.1 per cent consider the firm to be part of a family or group of companies. Foreign investors from developing countries are more likely to be private FEs than investors that have their origins in developed countries.[80] A large majority of Asian investors (81.2 per cent) are entrepreneurial firms and, among those, Chinese and Indian firms stand out as being even more entrepreneurial than the average Asian foreign investor. A recent IMF study confirms the growing trend of Chinese individuals as investors in Africa in different sectors of the economy ranging from construction, logistics, and manufacturing. These Chinese entrepreneurs are often tied as first or second tier suppliers to larger Chinese state-owned investments in Africa's natural resource, construction or infrastructure sector (Mlachila and Takebe 2011). In the majority of cases, however, private Chinese investors are solely oriented towards SSA's local or regional markets (Gu 2009, Shen 2013). Flexibility and adaptability are important attributes of these entrepreneurial foreign firms although they are geared towards maintaining cost advantages rather than advantages that stem from differentiation and innovation (Elango and Pattnaik 2007, AFDB 2011a).

Another group that is highly entrepreneurial are Lebanese investors in Western Africa. A very large majority of Lebanese FDI is carried out by Lebanese individuals or families (91.8 per cent). Lebanese investors often take advantage of informal financial and trade networks and they simultaneously operate in several sectors especially in wholesale, construction and telecommunications.[81]

The organizational form of a TNC is generally preferred by investors from developed countries and, among those, particularly from Switzerland (68.8 per cent), the US (58.7 per cent) and SA (51.1 per cent). An excep-

80 67.6 per cent of FDI from developing countries in SSA is carried out by an FE compared to 60.7 per cent of FDI from developed countries; Chi (1, 2549)=13.142, $p<0.001$.

81 See http://www.economist.com/blogs/baobab/2011/05/lebanese_west_africa (accessed on 16 May 2016).

tion are Italian investors, of which almost 90 per cent are private entrepreneurs who have an investment focus on Cape Verde, Ethiopia, Cameroon and Nigeria.

There is generally no clearly observable trend as to whether different age cohorts of foreign direct investors would prefer a particular organizational structure. The share of FEs fluctuates only slightly between the four pre-defined age categories and remains close to the average value of 65.2 per cent of the total sample. Foreign investors of an age of 2 years and 18 years respectively show a percentage of FEs of more than 80 per cent. This observation falls in the category of statistical outliers because FDI age does otherwise not appear to determine the selection of organizational structure. Likewise, there is no indication that FEs with stand-alone businesses would be particularly young or old compared to FEs with existing family networks. It shows that FEs had already been a prominent form of FDI in SSA long before the international business literature introduced the methodological concept of born-global FDI or INVs starting from the mid-1990s.

Table 3.9: Subsectors in SSA with dominance of TNCs vs. FEs

Subsectors with high share of FEs (low share of TNCs)	Count	Per cent FEs
Publishing and printing	38	88.4
Wood products except furniture	32	82.1
Rubber and plastics	147	82.1
Manufacture of furniture and n.e.c.	47	79.7
Fabricated metal prods., except machinery & equipment	94	79.7
Basic metals	34	75.6
Textiles	37	74.0
Subsectors with high share of TNCs (low share of FEs)	**Count**	**Per cent TNCs**
Financial institutions	95	67.4
Tobacco	10	58.8
Post and telecommunications	29	55.8
Electricity, gas and water supply	10	55.6
Transport	56	53.8
Coke and refined petroleum products	7	50.0
Mining and quarrying	26	46.4

There is clear evidence that FEs are more active in specific subsectors whereas TNCs are dominant in others. FEs operate in manufacturing sectors more than their TNC counterparts. Close to 56 per cent of FEs are manufacturers compared to only 39 per cent of TNCs. As Table 3.9 above shows, the seven subsectors with the highest share of FEs are attributable to low- or medium-tech manufacturing and cover, among others, publishing and printing, rubber and plastics as well as fabricated metal products. Overall, 78 per cent of FDI (322 firms) in medium-tech manufacturing and 72.1 per cent (452 firms) in low-tech manufacturing are carried out by FEs and not TNCs. This specific subgroup has a particularly large proportion of developing country investors (61.8 per cent) in which Indian and Chinese entrepreneurs are overrepresented with respective shares of 20.4 and 9.4 per cent.[82] On the other hand, TNCs represent a considerable proportion in the service sector. More than half of FDI in financial intermediation, tobacco, telecommunications, electricity, gas and water supply, transport and refinery industries belongs to TNCs. The few FEs who have ventured into sectors that are otherwise dominated by TNCs rely more than others on family support and networks, in particular in financial intermediation and electricity, gas and water supply.

The size of operations by a particular foreign direct investor in a given country can be put in relation to the global level of FDI internationalization. Several studies made an important distinction between the two and introduced a hybrid variable that measures the *relative* size of the FDI project vs. the overall size of the foreign firm as an entry mode determinant (Caves and Mehra 1986, Kogut and Singh 1988, Hennart and Park 1993, Padmanabhan and Cho 1995, Brouthers et al. 2000, Makino and Neupert 2000, Harzing 2002). On the one hand, a large TNC with a global network of subsidiaries can indeed have reasons to run a small FDI subsidiary in SSA. On the other hand, a private FE may not need to be experienced in running a global network of business operations prior to starting a new and large FDI project in SSA. The data confirms that TNCs are larger and significantly more internationalized than FEs based on the number of subsidiaries or investment projects that they manage in different lo-

82 Respective total sample share of Indian FDI is 13.4 per cent and 6.1 per cent in the case of Chinese FDI.

cations in addition to the FDI operation in the respective SSA country.[83] The median TNC owns four additional subsidiaries whereas the median FE owns only one additional FDI project. The 75-percentile TNC owns an additional 15 subsidiaries while the 75-percentile FE owns only three additional FDI projects which is still less than the TNC median. The results further indicate a relationship between TNCs with large global operations and the respective sizes of subsidiaries in SSA. The group of TNCs in the sub-sample of large FDI projects in SSA is overrepresented and is consistently higher than the 34.8 per cent share of TNCs in the total sample. Accordingly, TNCs represent 39.7 per cent of FDI projects with total fixed assets of above 1 million USD. They also represent 46 per cent of FDI projects with more than 100 employees and 56.2 per cent of FDI projects generating more than 10 million USD of annual output. The median values related to total employment, fixed assets and annual output confirm this pattern. TNC subsidiaries have median annual output figures of 4.8 million USD which is about three times higher than the median annual output of FEs. The median value of fixed assets owned by TNC subsidiaries is more than twice as high than that of FEs and the median employment levels of TNCs are 60 per cent above that of FEs (80 employees vs. 50 employees). Below Table 3.10 gives a more granular distinction based on the degree of internationalization of a TNC vs. an FE. It confirms that a higher degree of internationalization endows the firm with sufficient internal resources to run larger subsidiaries in terms of median employment and median fixed assets and that both result in larger median yearly output levels.

Foreign firms that are less extensively internationalized may have fewer resource options to be able to choose full equity modes, especially in the event that the envisaged FDI project is considered to be large relative to the size of the firm (Makino and Neupert 2000, Lu and Beamish 2001). Following similar considerations, numerous studies have also confirmed

83 A methodological caveat is that the level of global firm size would be more accurately measured through global sales or the total number of employees of the foreign investor. Such data was not available. Even if it was available, its reliability would be questionable given that the respondent, in most cases the CEO of the SSA subsidiary, would probably not accurately report such global figures. From a methodological point of view, it is however safe enough to assume that foreign investors with a greater number of global subsidiaries are also larger and more internationalized.

that resource-intensive greenfield entry modes are less often chosen than M&As when the relative size of the FDI project is large compared to the overall size of the firm (Caves and Mehra 1986, Hennart and Park 1993, Padmanabhan and Cho 1995, Brouthers and Brouthers 2000, Harzing 2002).

Table 3.10: Degree of FDI internationalization and subsidiary sizes in SSA

Internationalization degree	Median no. of employees	Median, fixed assets (USD)	Median, annual output (USD)
FE with no other operation	33	300,000	928,601
FE with at least one more operation	56	934,231	2,117,379
TNC with less than 4 additional subsidiaries	70	996,945	2,904,214
TNC with ≥ 4 additional subsidiaries	104	1,856,050	7,098,886

The findings from the sample confirm the findings from Makino and Neupert in that less internationalized FEs hold significantly smaller foreign shares in large FDI projects compared to TNCs (Makino and Neupert 2000). The foreign equity share of FEs ranges between 76 and 78 per cent in projects with respectively more than 100 employees, with more than 1 million USD fixed assets and more than 10 million USD of annual output. TNCs own between 87 to 89 per cent foreign equity in the same size categories. By the same token and as shown earlier in Figure 3.3 in Chapter 3.4, the share of JVs in the category of large FDI projects increases significantly and this is even more the case for FEs compared to TNCs. Relative to the mean percentage of JVs in the total sample, TNCs conclude 5.4 per cent more JVs in in very labour-intensive FDI projects compared to FEs entering 12.9 per cent more often into JVs (see Figure 3.7 on the next page). The pattern is the same for the other two size categories. It underpins that FEs have less managerial options than TNCs and are therefore compelled to choose JVs more often. This appears to be a well-established coping strategy to overcome resource constraints within entrepreneurially-oriented foreign firms in SSA.

Figure 3.7: Proportion of JV formation in large SSA subsidiaries of TNCs and FEs

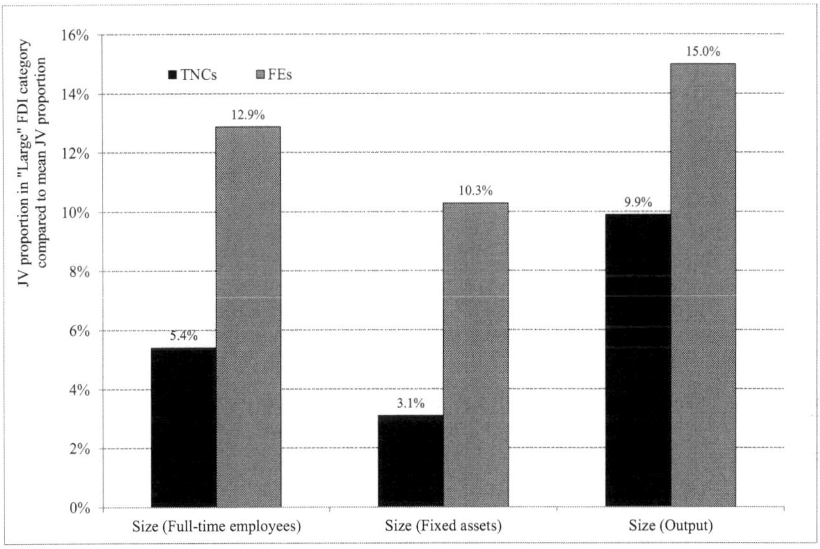

3.8 Age of FDI

The age of FDI is in the following defined as the difference between the year of first market entry into the SSA host country and the year in which the survey was undertaken (2010/11). The four major age categories can be divided as follows: 14.5 per cent of foreign investors are relatively young (0–5 years), 20.8 per cent are between 6 to 10 years, 35.6 per cent are between 11 to 20 years and 28.8 per cent are 21 years or older.

The two recent UNIDO Africa Investor Survey Reports have already highlighted that the age of the foreign direct investor in SSA is closely linked to the size of its operations. There is a survivor bias in the sense that older firms are usually also larger firms (UNIDO 2007, UNIDO 2012a). Table 3.11 below illustrates that the different size measures coincide with the age cohort of the foreign firm. As a result, the median size spread between the youngest and the oldest foreign firms in the sample is considerable.

Table 3.11: Median subsidiary size (employment, fixed assets, annual output) in different FDI age cohorts

Age cohort	Median no. of employees	Median, fixed assets (USD)	Median, annual output (USD)
0–5 years old	29	310,413	838,090
6–10 years old	39	445,729	1,369,329
11–20 years old	58	778,762	2,319,959
21+ years old	100	2,469,040	5,507,939

Further analyses, not reported here in detail, support the strong relationship between the size of operations and the FDI governance structure within each of the four age groups. More specifically, FEs run smaller operations than TNCs in similar age groups regardless of whether the firm is young or old. From a resource-based reasoning this indicates that an entrepreneurial-oriented international firm needs to first mobilize and create the necessary resources for the expansion of its subsidiary (e.g. through reinvested earnings or cooperative agreements), whereas a subsidiary of an established multinational firm can relatively more easily resort to equity injection, inter-company loans, human resources, etc. to be provided by its parent firm.

Previous sub-chapters have already unearthed several patterns related to the different FDI age cohorts. The most striking finding has been that the proportion of medium-tech and high-tech manufacturing is underrepresented in young age cohorts. The effect of South-South FDI in SSA was also observable from the dataset and explained why African and Asian investors are generally younger than more traditional investors e.g. from France or the UK. WOSs are the preferred ownership mode of young FDI in SSA.

3.9 Market orientation of FDI

The classification of FDI according to its market orientation leads to three subgroups and replicates the classification of UNIDO (UNIDO 2007). The first subgroup is defined as *"local market-seeking"* FDI in which case equal to or above 90 per cent of the foreign firm's outputs are sold locally. The second category is defined as *"regional market-seeking"* in which case the foreign direct investor exports more than 10 per cent of its outputs, out of which more than half is destined for other SSA countries.

"Global market-seeking" foreign investors export at least 10 per cent of their total output of which more than half targets markets outside SSA.

Investors were also asked to indicate the dominant initial investment motive for their engagement in SSA on the basis of a simplified version of Dunning's investment motive classification (Dunning 1993, UNCTAD 1998).[84] The triangulation of the original motive and the eventual output destinations indicate that firms with the original intention of exploiting market opportunities also succeeded in doing so either locally or regionally within SSA. FDI following resource-seeking and efficiency-seeking motives is also closely connected to FDI with larger shares of global exports (Kumar 1994, UNCTAD 2013b). Unsurprisingly, almost half of all global market-seeking foreign investors in the sample responded that their primary FDI investment was to access natural resources or to realize efficiency gains by lowering factor costs, in particular wage costs.

Table 3.12: FDI market orientation in different subsectors

Attractive sectors for local market-seeking FDI	Count	Per cent local market-seeking
Services (aggregated)	893	96.3
Electricity, water and construction (aggregated)	147	94.2
Basic metals	36	81.8
Machinery and equipment n.e.c.	31	81.6
Other non-metallic mineral products	44	80.0
Attractive sectors for regional market-seeking FDI	**Count**	**Per cent regional market-seeking**
Motor vehicles, trailers and semi-trailers	5	29.4
Tobacco	5	29.4
Rubber and plastics	45	26.8
Chemical products (incl. pharmaceutical products)	40	24.8
Paper and paper products	9	22.0
Attractive sectors for global market-seeking FDI	**Count**	**Per cent global market-seeking**
Wearing apparel	64	74.4
Agriculture, forestry and fishing	101	69.7
Leather and related products	17	58.6
Mining and quarrying	19	39.6
Wood products except furniture	14	35.0

84 The strategic asset-seeking category was subsumed under "other motives".

Three quarters of all FDI firms in the sample belong to the category of local market-seeking foreign investors, 10.8 per cent are regional market-seeking and 14 per cent are global market-seeking foreign investors. As expected, the tertiary and the combined sector of electricity, water and construction are incompatible with large shares of regional and global exports and attract primarily local market-seeking FDI (see Table 3.12 above). Regional market-seeking investors appear with relatively higher percentages in sectors classified as high-tech manufacturing (22.1 per cent) and medium-tech manufacturing (20.9 per cent). For example, around one quarter of FDI investors in motor vehicles, rubber, plastics and the chemical sector exhibit sizable intra-SSA export volumes.

At the other end of the spectrum are global market-seeking investors that are particularly prominent in the wearing apparel sector, in the agricultural sector and in leather, mining and wood products.

The FDI orientation towards global markets in the primary sector and in the low-tech manufacturing sector is reflected by the median number of full-time employees. The median employment in this category is 150 employees, compared to a median employment of 104 in regional market-seekers and 45 in local market-seekers. Global market-seeking foreign investors are usually labour-intensive as they organize their international production networks in a vertical manner and offshore labour-intensive production steps to countries with an abundance of relatively cheap and low-skilled labour (UNCTAD 1998). The high prevalence of global market-seeking foreign investors in the primary sector corroborates the known link between natural resource-seeking FDI and international trade (UNCTAD 1996, UNCTAD 2007b). Non-renewable resources like oil, gas, copper, iron ore and others are by their very nature location-bound, whereas the markets for these commodities are highly international. In most cases, the output of the extracted commodity greatly exceeds the demand within the host country. As a result, the home country of the FDI parent firm or third countries are served through exports. Occasionally, out of the need to ensure a constant and reliable supply of raw materials, FDI replaces a trade contract between a previously independent raw materials supplier in a resource-rich SSA country and the major producer in the importing country. The MNE then incorporates both extracting and processing activities through vertical insourcing.

In terms of median fixed assets and outputs, regional market-seeking FDI firms outperform both other groups. The median regional market-seeking foreign investor owns fixed assets of 3.1 million USD and has an annual output worth 5.9 million USD. In contrast, local market-seeking FDI investors not only have the lowest median employment and lowest median fixed assets but also the lowest annual outputs amongst the three market orientation categories. The results underpin the dominance of the tertiary sector in the local market-seeking category and are consistent with the findings in Table 3.8 of Chapter 3.6 which indicate that the majority of FDI in the service sector creates moderate employment effects, owns low fixed assets and generates low annual outputs.

There is no clear and significant pattern in that FDI investors from developing countries would have fundamentally different FDI market orientations compared to investors from developed countries. The share of local market-seeking investors is nearly identical between FDI from the South vs. from the North. Noticeable differences exist, however, between foreign firms from individual home countries. For example, Dutch, Italian, UK, and US investors have a remarkably higher propensity to export globally than the average investor in the sample. This is an outcome of intensive engagements in the primary sector by these FDI groups (see also Annex Table 7).[85] Conversely, service-driven FDI carried out by Portuguese, French and Kenyan investors is primarily oriented towards the local market and tends to be smaller in size. FDI investors from the UK, India and Germany show the largest propensity to intra-African exports relative to other foreign investors.

The cross-tabulation between investor age and its market orientation shows an almost equal proportion of global market-seeking investment in all four age groups. Between 14 to 16 per cent of investors are global market-seeking regardless of whether the investor is relatively young (0–5 years), between 6–10 years, between 11–20 years or 21 years or older. Signs of endogeneity can be observed for the proportion of regional market-seeking FDI in the different age cohorts because the likelihood of a swap between a formerly purely local market-oriented investor to a regional market-oriented investor plausibly increases with FDI tenure.[86] A similar bias was found for the size of FDI operations and the age cohort of the firm. Both indicate that regionalization of FDI in SSA is not instanta-

85 31.3 per cent of Dutch investors, 21.7 per cent of UK investors, 21.3 per cent of Italian investors and 20.6 per cent of US investors are global market-seeking.

86 4.1 per cent of young foreign investors are regional market-seeking, 6.9 per cent of foreign investors between 6–10 years, 10.9 per cent between 11–20 years and 17 per cent of foreign investors above 21 years.

neous, as posited in the literature on INVs, but presupposes a solid growth trajectory of the foreign investment based on local market sales in the first SSA host economy.

As concerns the two main organizational forms of TNC and FE, the proportion of local market-seeking investors is almost the same and accounts for 75 per cent of firms in each group. There is nonetheless a statistically significant difference[87] which stems from the fact that TNCs display a more pronounced global market orientation (16.9 per cent) than FEs (12.5 per cent). Conversely, FEs put more weight on regional markets compared to TNCs (12. 1 per cent vs. 8.4 per cent).

Related to the preferred ownership mode, there is only a weak statistical link between FDI market orientation and the selected ownership mode.[88] The proportion of WOSs in local market-seeking foreign investors is 72.2 per cent, a result that is nearly perfectly congruent with the share of WOSs of 71.8 per cent in the total sample. The results therefore neither corroborate nor refute the findings of studies that found a performance-enhancing link between a foreign firm's local market-seeking strategy and the tendency towards operational autonomy and profit monopolization of a WOS (Aulakh and Kotabe 1997, Gil et al. 2006, He et al. 2015). A prior export relation may have helped the foreign investor to get acquainted with the product preferences and demand patterns in the FDI target country and a local JV partner may therefore no longer be necessary. As opposed to that, investors with an orientation towards regional markets show more openness to strategic alliances as indicated by a higher share of 34.3 per cent of JVs. Following the argumentation of Erramilli and Rao, the selection of JVs might be an attempt to offset the foreign investor's knowledge deficiencies about regional distribution channels and regional customer preferences (Erramilli and Rao 1990). Further support for this hypothesis comes from an analysis of perceived local and foreign partner contributions as presented in Chapter 3.5. Foreign investors with regional market orientation perceive the contribution of the local partner for patents, trademarks and brand names as being more valuable than their own. Such brands may already have regional recognition and legitimacy and can therefore act as door opener in boosting regional exports of the mixed foreign-local JV.

---

87 Chi (2, 2538)=15.036; $p<0.001$.

88 Chi (2, 2484)=6.041 $p=0.49$.

No statistical significance was found between the market orientation of the investor and the propensity to select a specific establishment mode of greenfield or M&A.

3.10 Summary of findings and Chapter 3 conclusions

Chapter 3 has provided a typology of FDI in SSA on the basis of UNIDO's 2010/11 Investor Survey dataset comprising 2,692 foreign firms. Its focus has been to reveal distinctive features of different FDI groupings with regard to subsector distribution, origin of the investment, ownership and establishment mode, subsidiary size, organizational structure, FDI age and market orientation. Nearly half of all FDI belongs to manufacturing within which food and beverage, rubber and plastics and the chemical sector are most common. Medium-tech and high-tech manufacturing is attributable to foreign subsidiaries that have been operational for many years whereas younger and often South FDI firms are very numerous in lower-tech manufacturing e.g. in textiles and garments. In the service sector, over-proportionally many new FDI projects have started in the real estate sector, consulting and IT, financial intermediation and hotels and restaurants. Despite this recent trend, wholesale and retail trade remain by far the most prominent FDI service sectors in the survey sample.

The market orientation is usually endogenous to the chosen line of business of the foreign investment in SSA. Local market-seeking FDI is the dominant investment motive for three quarters of all FDI firms. Efficiency- and global market seeking is most prominent in labour-intensive manufacturing and it is therefore not surprising that the export proportions of FDI projects in wearing apparel, agriculture, mining, leather and wood products are considerably larger than in other manufacturing sectors, let alone the service sectors.

FDI tenure determines whether a foreign subsidiary is large and whether it sells not only to domestic but also to regional SSA markets. Many of the early FDI arrivals in SSA came from developed countries and many seem to root back into a common colonial past. For example, 46.1 per cent of UK investors and 41.9 per cent of French investors have been in operation for more than 21 years. These established TNC firms emerge as being the largest in terms of employment, fixed asset ownership and annual outputs and impact largely on the SSA host country given their sheer size of operations and resulting domestic market dominance. Strategic alliances such as JVs are significantly more frequent among old-established and large foreign firms than in their younger and more entrepreneurial counterparts which demonstrate preference for WOSs. The propensity to form a strategic alliance with a local partner appears to be the outcome of a gradual familiarization and adjustment process with regard to the business conditions in the SSA host economy. In this context, Chapter 3.5 has shown that foreign investors attach particular importance to the ability of the African JV partner to contribute and develop the required skills of the JV staff besides other factors such as access to finance, technology, patents and trademarks. The lack of a sufficiently large pool of potential local JV partners combined with a general absence of strategic assets ready for foreign purchase, may at least partially explain why the overarching majority of FDI in SSA is wholly foreign-owned (71.8 per cent) and greenfield (85.5 per cent).

FEs outnumber TNCs by far. Two of three firms in the sample are FEs. The large majority of Chinese and Indian investors are FEs and they display a distinct interest in undertaking low or medium-tech manufacturing in SSA. This calls into question a good number of studies that narrowly describe Chinese FDI, spearheaded by its state-owned enterprises in the natural extraction sector, as a means of re-colonializing the African continent. This and other observations of Chapter 3 carry relevance from an industrial policy angle which calls for a coordinated and tailored mix of interventions by SSA's political and private stakeholders in order to increase and diversify the level of manufacturing value added of currently 15 per cent of SSA's GDP (Asche et al. 2012). In this regard, FDI in the low and medium-tech manufacturing sectors undertaken by non-traditional FEs may deserve specific attention in SSA's investment promotion strategies and policies (UNIDO 2007, UNIDO 2012a). FEs and domestic firms may constitute an industrialization springboard to usher in a structural change in SSA's economies in favour of higher manufacturing value-added activities and a gradual increase of the technology and innovation content in domestic or foreign production (UNIDO 2009).

4. The theoretical underpinnings of FDI performance

Firm-level characteristics, such as those described in the previous chapter, are critical determinants for the growth and performance of FDI in SSA. Foreign firms operating in different industry subsectors (see Chapter 3.2) and with different market orientations (see Chapter 3.9) will be confronted with varying market dynamics at the local, regional or global level. The ability of the foreign investor to effectively master and react to these dynamics will have a bearing on its performance. A further example of the influence of FDI characteristics on performance is the intensive debate about the role of the "right" FDI entry mode, extensively analysed at the level of SSA in Chapter 3.4, striking a balance between the foreign investor's preoccupation with preserving its ownership advantages vs. an objective of knowledge accumulation and learning within a strategic alliance. The entry mode choice is largely influenced by expected costs and its associated risk-adjusted returns and reflects the overriding perspective of transaction cost economics in the extant literature (Anderson and Gatignon 1986, Contractor and Lorange 1988, Gatignon and Anderson 1988, Gomes-Casseres 1989, Hennart 1991, Taylor et al. 1998, Barbosa and Louri 2002), a finding that has further been confirmed by two recent meta-analyses on entry mode selection (Zhao et al. 2004, Brouthers and Hennart 2007).

There is growing recognition that the FDI entry mode is of paramount importance in explaining subsequent FDI performance. Unfortunately, the measurement of the isolated impact of FDI entry mode on firm performance is largely complicated by an endogeneity effect (Shaver 1998, Brouthers 2002). It stems from the fact that the same set of FDI entry mode determinants (i.e. the internationalization of the MNE, its available resources, its learning experiences from previous entries, external requirements imposed by host country governments, natural endowments and domestic market conditions of the host country, etc.) will eventually also impact on FDI performance. As a result, the earlier focus on FDI entry mode determinants dovetailed into a more comprehensive array of FDI performance literature which considerably widened its initially narrow focus on transaction costs to also include other theoretical strands. Nowadays, the literature on FDI performance cuts across theoretical topics of host country effects on firm performance (Makino et al. 2004, Chan et al. 2008), industry and corporate effects (Rumelt 1991, McGahan and Porter 1997), home country and cultural distance effects (Schroath et al. 1993, Barkema et al. 1997, Gomez-Mejia and Palich 1997, Park and Ungson 1997, Morosini et al. 1998, Hawawini et al. 2004, Tihanyi et al. 2005), the extent of the firm's diversification and internationalization (Kim et al. 1993, Fujita 1995b, Fujita 1995a, Hitt et al. 1997, Gomes and Ramaswamy 1999, Zahra et al. 2000) and others.

The objective of Chapter 4 will be to review the various theoretical underpinnings of FDI performance in greater detail and derive a sequence of hypotheses for further testing in the subsequent Chapter 5.

4.1 FDI entry mode

Buckley and Casson accurately summarized that "location costs, internalization factors, financial variables, cultural factors, such as trust and psychic distance, market structure and competitive strategy, adaptation costs (to the local environment), and the costs of doing business abroad are all identified in the literature as playing a role in determining firms' foreign market entry decisions" (Buckley and Casson 1998, p. 543). The decision to undertake FDI and to select a particular mode of entry, relates back to resource-based and transaction costs theories and, once combined with factors that describe the local business environment and host country's factor endowments, constitute a holistic set of determinants for firm performance (Dunning 1993). Dunning's eclectic paradigm provides an accurate yardstick for predicting the MNE´s optimal entry mode because it encompasses more contingency factors than, for example, entry mode predictions based on only transaction cost variables (Agarwal and Ramaswami 1992, Brouthers et al. 1999). The eclectic paradigm does not give an absolute prescription as to which entry mode is to be preferred but rather it outlines benign conditions in which a particular entry mode would best meet foreign investors' performance expectations. Brouthers et al. found that entry modes that were predicted by Dunning's eclectic OLI theory led to significantly better performance levels than firms whose entry mode choice did not conform to the OLI framework, and this similarly when controlling for other variables with influence on varying performance levels (Brouthers et al. 1999). In line with Brouthers et al.'s study, Aulakh and Kotabe developed a holistic contingency model to assess the performance outcome of different degrees of distribution channel integration and concluded that "firms conforming to the theoretical prescriptions of the eclectic conceptual model in making channel integration choice in foreign markets perform better than firms that deviate from the model's prescriptions. Choosing a wrong channel is not only detrimental to the firm in terms of switching costs, but also leads to suboptimal performance on indicators such as market share and sales growth. Thus, managers need to carefully make the channel integration decision through the balancing of efficiency, resource commitment requirements and strategic goals" (Aulakh and Kotabe 1997, p. 167–168). Chung and Beamish argue similarly, albeit from an institution-based perspective, that "foreign firms that select an 'appropriate' mode of entry [...] can seize the opportunities created by uncertain competitive conditions in the post-crisis institutional environments of emerging economies. On the other hand, foreign firms that overlook those opportunities may place their long-term profitability and growth at risk in emerging economies" (Chung and Beamish 2005a, p. 59).

Following the basic notion of real option theory in FDI, ownership modes can be changed throughout the lifetime of the FDI project because the foreign investor has a perennial choice to increase the foreign equity share (i.e. by switching from a JV to a WOS) or to decrease it (switching from a former WOS to a JV). Likewise, the establishment mode can change when a former greenfield project is sold to a new partner, transforming it into an acquisition either co-owned by two JV partners or owned by a single firm. The following sub-chapter will delve deeper into issues of terminology of ownership mode and establishment mode while comparing the suitability of both modes in a dynamic framework of mode change and mode switch.

4.1.1 Definitional issues

Before reviewing the extant entry mode literature, it is important to overcome certain ambiguities regarding the definition of the foreign firm's *entry mode*. Many researchers use the term entry mode to describe the foreign investor's decision to establish its international business as a JV with another partner, in most cases an indigenous partner, versus establishing the business as a WOS (Gatignon and Anderson 1988, Chowdhury 1992, Makino and Beamish 1998, Mutinelli and Piscitello 1998a, Luo 2001,

Brouthers 2002, Brouthers et al. 2003, Zhao and Decker 2005, Dikova and van Witteloostuijn 2007, Gaur and Lu 2007, Cui and Jiang 2009). Strictly speaking, the former refers to foreign *equity* entry modes, which are defined by a foreign equity share of more than 10 per cent and which exclude non-equity forms of international market entry in particular direct or indirect exporting, licensing, franchising, etc. A further group of researchers have therefore specifically included one or more forms of non-equity entry modes into their empirical models (Kim and Hwang 1992, Taylor et al. 1998, Pan and Chi 1999, Pan et al. 1999, Shrader 2001, Chen and Hu 2002, Brouthers et al. 2008a). Yet another group of researchers refer to the entry mode as the foreign investor's choice between a greenfield investment and an M&A (Hennart and Park 1993, Shaver 1998, Slangen and Hennart 2008, Georgopoulos and Preusse 2009, Tan 2009, UNCTAD 2009b).

To achieve an unambiguous definition of entry mode for the purpose of the forthcoming model building, entry mode will be separated between *ownership* mode and *establishment* mode. *Ownership* mode is thereby defined by the level of foreign ownership which can range from non-equity i.e. contractual entry modes, JVs to wholly-owned entry modes (Gomes-Casseres 1990, Zhao and Zhu 1998, Kaynak et al. 2007). The *establishment* mode describes the choice between a greenfield subsidiary vs. an M&A (Padmanabhan and Cho 1995, Barkema et al. 1996, Padmanabhan and Cho 1996). Recent entry mode literature has introduced taxonomies treating ownership and establishment mode as two separate decisions that the multinational firm must take (Brouthers and Hennart 2007, Dikova and van Witteloostuijn 2007). On the one hand, the MNE parent has a choice on the extent of integration of already existing local or foreign assets available in the target investment location, which is a choice in terms of the establishment mode. On the other hand, there is a choice on the extent of control over the MNE's subsidiary operations that is lower in the case of a JV and highest in the case of a WOS. While there is controversy as to whether such choices occur simultaneously or sequentially, there appears to be consensus on the fact that both choices are determined by a largely similar set of transaction cost, industry-related and institutional factors (Padmanabhan and Cho 1999, Brouthers and Hennart 2007, Dikova and van Witteloostuijn 2007). The taxonomy in Table 4.1 encompasses the four occurrences of JV-greenfield, JV-acquisition, WOS-greenfield, WOS-acquisition as per Brouthers' and Hennart's definition (Brouthers and Hennart 2007).[89] Depending on the timing of each choice i.e. whether the establishment mode choice precedes the ownership mode choice or vice versa, the selection process would take the structure of a tree with four branches.

Table 4.1: Configurations of establishment and ownership modes

		Establishment mode	
		Greenfield	**Acquisition**
Ownership mode	**Shared**	JV-greenfield (1)	Partial acquisition (JV-acquisition) (2)
	Full	WOS-greenfield (3)	Full Acquisition (WOS-acquisition) (4)

Source: Brouthers and Hennart 2007.

A few studies have combined ownership and establishment modes into the same empirical model. In these studies, the comparison of the shared ownership mode of a JV with the two establishment modes, greenfield investment and M&A, is the most commonly chosen research design (Li and Guisinger 1991, Woodcock et al. 1994, Li 1995, Nitsch et al. 1996, Siripaisalpipat and Hoshino 2000, Chang and Rosenzweig 2001).

The review of the applied definition of entry mode in the relevant literature reveals that only Dikova et al.'s study looked at the four possible combinations of ownership and establishment mode, however without testing for the interrelationship between these possibly endogenous two mode types (Dikova and van Witteloostuijn 2007). For example it is found that greater institutional advancement of the host country prompts firms to choose a JV ownership mode on the one hand and an acquisition on the other. Moreover, the transaction cost argument would predict FDI firms that have an interest to protect a specific asset (a technology, a patent, etc.) to cluster in the WOS-greenfield quadrant. The WOS ownership mode gives the parent maximum control over such an asset. The selection of a greenfield entry mode then becomes implicit: If the specific asset has been created by the investing foreign firm and is tested to sufficiently offset the liability of the foreignness of the MNE, there is little rationale for diluting this specific asset by acquiring yet another external asset and incurring risks of subsequent high integration costs. Unsurprisingly, some studies

89 A similar taxonomy on the basis of the UNIDO 2010/11 Investor Survey dataset has already been presented in Table 3.4.

found a superior performance in combined WOS-greenfield entry modes (Woodcock et al. 1994, Li 1995, Nitsch et al. 1996). In this context, Chapter 3.4 also found a high concentration of FDI subsidiaries in SSA in the WOS-greenfield quadrant. Following the above reasoning, such concentration effects might be the outcome of a deliberate strategic choice of the foreign investor. Neither can it however be ruled out that prevalent conditions in developing countries, in particular the lack of locally available assets for an M&A or absence of potential SSA joint venture partners, force the MNE to either enter through an WOS-greenfield mode or otherwise to dismiss the FDI project altogether.

The influence of knowledge-based theories and aspects of MNE learning have shed a fresh light on the FDI entry mode literature. The process of foreign market entry is no longer entirely considered as a static one-off decision to be taken at the beginning of the FDI project but is looked at as firm-level decision that can be subject to a dynamic performance review. The decision can be revisited and, if necessary, rectified or reversed depending on the outcome of such review. The previously experienced performance levels of the FDI project together with expectations of future growth prospects will determine whether the MNE, intentionally or unintentionally, changes its business strategy and opts for partial or full divestment, no further investment or sequential follow-up investment in the host country. The dynamic notion of FDI entry mode has been picked up by real option theory which emphasizes that firms keep a range of business options open in order to respond to uncertainties such as those related to policy reversals and changing host country conditions compared to originally prevalent conditions at the moment of FDI entry (Chung and Beamish 2005b, Brouthers et al. 2008a). A common strategy of FDI in host economies of high uncertainty is to begin the investment with a moderate financial commitment and to monitor the performance development of this initial investment before augmenting the financial commitment through a follow-up investment when new and more accurate information becomes available (Buckley and Tse 1996, Chang and Rosenzweig 2001). Reinvested earnings are thus a common financial instrument for sequential investment (Lundan 2006).

Against this backdrop, the variable of ownership mode in particular becomes a continuous and longitudinal variable measuring the foreign parent's control over its foreign operations at any point in time during the FDI life cycle. In this sense, one would do a disservice to dynamic research on JV performance if ownership mode were to be narrowly considered as a choice to be solely taken at the moment of FDI *entry*. This describes the main difference to the establishment mode which is rather a static variable that always refers back to the original timing of FDI entry. A foreign investor that has established the FDI project as a greenfield project will remain classified as greenfield investor throughout the FDI lifecycle unless the project is sold to another investor, in which case the market entry of the purchasing investor is determined as M&A[90] until the further sale of the FDI company to another M&A investor and so on.

The choice of the entry mode choice is naturally examined from an *ex post* perspective referring to a decision that has been taken by the foreign parent a long time ago (Kim and Hwang 1992). This increases the risks associated with retrospective reporting which is prone to errors due to limited cognitive and recall abilities of the respondent. This may be coupled with a hindsight bias of describing a past decision making process to be more systematic than it actually was (Huber and Power 1985, Miller et al. 1997). Of both variations of entry mode, the static nature of the establishment mode makes the latter more prone to suffer from retrospective rationalization. A robust empirical model would have to elicit determinants, in particular those related to transaction cost economics that prevailed at the time of FDI entry which is difficult if not impossible to accomplish for foreign market entries having occurred a long time ago.[91] This caveat does not exist or exists in a much weaker form in the case of a determinants analysis of ownership mode selection which was found to also maintain its explanatory value during the post-entry period (Puck et al. 2009).

4.1.2 FDI entry mode and performance

A plethora of studies exist that have focused on the specific nexus of entry mode and subsequent FDI performance (Simmonds 1990, Kent 1991, Li and Guisinger 1991, Chowdhury 1992, Woodcock et al. 1994, Li 1995, Nitsch et al. 1996, Hennart et al. 1998, McCloughan and Stone 1998, Shaver 1998, Pan and Chi 1999, Pan et al. 1999, Siripaisalpipat and Hoshino 2000, Lu and Beamish 2001, Shrader 2001, Brouthers 2002,

---

90 In the case that the investor is a foreign direct investor and not a domestic investor.

91 This is the case for the UNIDO 2010/11 Investor Survey sample under observation, where 1,709 firms (64.4 per cent) established their operations more than 10 year ago.

Chen and Hu 2002, Brouthers et al. 2003, Delios and Beamish 2004, Chung and Beamish 2005a, Zhan 2006, Gaur and Lu 2007, Brouthers et al. 2008a, Kim and Gray 2008, Slangen and Hennart 2008, Dhanaraj and Beamish 2009, Tan 2009, Chang et al. 2013, Brouthers et al. 2015). Despite the wealth of available literature, there exists no study that analyses the combined effect of FDI entry mode on FDI performance from a meta-level although two independent meta-studies exist on the transaction cost determinants of FDI entry mode (Zhao et al. 2004) and the measurement of performance in the international business literature (Hult et al. 2008).

In the 1990s, there was still a lack of understanding of endogeneity effects and how such effects could be accounted for to enhance the accuracy of predictive models of FDI entry mode. The majority of studies treated the entry mode as a randomly chosen variable. The findings have not been consistent in that one entry mode would outperform the other and they were highly contextual depending on which performance variable and which combinations of entry mode variables as per Table 4.1 had been chosen.[92] Long before the endogeneity issue in the entry mode/performance literature had become widely acknowledged, Chowdury had already stated that "the literature predicts that a given entry mode is not better or worse than others in an absolute sense, but it is only relatively superior (or inferior) to others in specific circumstances" (Chowdhury 1992, p. 131). For instance, in Chowdury's study, WOSs perform better than JVs in terms of intra-company sales and export sales whereas they tend to have shorter longevity than JVs (Chowdhury 1992). The study of Pan et al. found that FDI subsidiaries in China are more profitable, in terms of return on assets (ROA) if they operate under a JV arrangement whereas they have to compromise on market shares that would be larger in the case of WOSs (Pan et al. 1999). In another study in China, JVs were again more profitable than WOSs in terms of return on sales (ROS) (Pan and Chi 1999). Further authors found an interaction effect with the establishment mode and were able to illustrate that WOSs in Western Europe and North America led to a better subjective performance assessment by Japanese subsidiary managers than JVs, yet only in the case that the WOS had been established as a new greenfield venture and not through an acquisition (Woodcock et al. 1994, Nitsch et al. 1996). Despite using exactly the same

92 This is the case for all combinations, but particularly the combinations of ownership mode (JVs vs. WOSs) i.e. combined cell 1 and 2 vs. combined cell 3 and 4.

subjective performance variable, the results could not be reproduced in a cross-country study in Asia and led to mixed performance outcomes depending on the Asian FDI host country (Makino and Beamish 1998). The more recent study of Gaur and Lu found that WOSs have better chances of surviving than JVs if the regulative distance between home and host country is relatively larger (Gaur and Lu 2007).

With the realization that endogeneity and self-selection effects play an important role in the entry mode-performance literature because "firms purposely choose their strategies based on their capabilities and industry conditions [...] and will choose acquisitions when the expected value of entering by acquisition exceeds the expected value of entering by new plant" (Shaver 1998, p. 572–573), the results of studies that do not account for such effects should be seen in a different and generally more critical light. The statistical effect of endogeneity results in a correlation of the entry mode construct with the error term of the regression equation (Heckman 1979, Hult et al. 2008). To eliminate this self-selection effect, Keith Brouthers in 2002 spearheaded a two-staged research approach: The first step draws from transaction-based, institutional or resource-based predictors of entry mode. The second step then tests whether firms that exhibit a strategic fit between the actually realized and the predicted entry mode exhibit higher levels of performance (Brouthers 2002).[93] Accordingly, ownership modes which are in alignment with transaction-based, institutional or resource-based determinants ultimately perform better than ownership modes that are chosen without achieving the predictive fit of these variables. Further studies employ a similar contingency-based approach yet focus only on transaction-based variables (Chen and Hu 2002, Brouthers and Nakos 2004), on resource-based variables (Tan 2009) and on institution-based variables (Slangen and Hennart 2008), by adding the moderating influence of a national institutional environment to a resource-based perspective (Brouthers et al. 2008b) or through an extended set of transaction-based variables including institution-based perspectives (Kim and Gray 2008). Endogeneity issues have also been addressed in research on the performance of INVs as opposed to sequential FDI (Mudambi and Zahra 2007) and in a dynamic framework of conversion of JVs to WOSs (Chang et al. 2013).

93 For a detailed commentary on Brouthers' 2002 study, see Martin 2013.

One caveat to the majority of studies exploring the link between entry mode and performance, even if accounting for the endogeneity effect, is that the foreign firm's entry mode has often been treated as a one-off event in the FDI project's life time in inducing foreign subsidiary performance. As has been mentioned in the previous Chapter 4.1.1, real option theory takes post-entry volatilities in the business environment of the host country into account and provides a good framework in describing rational and transaction cost-minimizing responses of international investors (Buckley and Tse 1996, McGrath and Nerkar 2004, Brouthers et al. 2008a). Strategic JV alliances are the principal instrument in real options theory because they can be regarded as an intermediate stage permitting the foreign investor to examine the foreign market potential without being exposed to the full risk of a high-commitment ownership mode of the WOS (Folta and Miller 2002). At a certain point in time during the tenure of the JV, the foreign investor may reach more clarity of perception with regards to the correct valuation of the JV as well as its future growth potential. If the assessment is positive, the foreign investor would no longer be willing to share the expected rents from a favourable growth opportunity with the equity partner (Kogut 1991, Chi 2000, Kumar 2005). In this case, the foreign investor would increase its equity share in the JV which could in the extreme case result in totally buying out the local partner (Kogut 1991, Chi 2000). In such a scenario, a sequential investment takes place with the intention of switching from a formerly shared foreign ownership mode to a wholly foreign ownership mode (Puck et al. 2009, Chang et al. 2013). Host country government restrictions may however act as limiting factor and effectively bar the foreign JV partner from increasing its equity share beyond a certain threshold (Buckley 2007, World Bank et al. 2010, De la Medina Soto and Ghossein 2013).

Real option theory sees JVs as temporary vehicles until either partner exercises the option of divestment or sequential re-investment (partner buy-out). The mere existence of this real option can be regarded as an important determinant of JV instability (Beamish and Inkpen 1995, Inkpen and Beamish 1997, Hennart et al. 1999, Steensma et al. 2008). JVs become unstable if the partners get the impression that the initial JV contract is no longer reflective of a change in the real bargaining position (Inkpen and Beamish 1997). Tensions and conflicts may be the result of a creeping perception that either partner gives too much and receives too little as reciprocation by the other partner. Knowledge-intensive JVs that have been set up with the aim of fulfilling mutual learning objectives are prone to instability because both partners may fall into the "race to learn" dilemma. Here, both partners attempt to opportunistically extract business knowledge from the other partner while returning as little as possible (Hamel 1991, Larsson et al. 1998). The JV loses its raison d'être when one of the partners comes to the conclusion that the initially steep learning curve is flattening and that it would be opportune to dissolve the JV.

It is not always the case that subsequent adaptations and governance changes in existing JVs involve a buy-out of the local partner in order to transform into a WOS. In the few longitudinal analyses undertaken on this issue, it was found that ownership changes within JVs are a very common phenomenon. Between 50 to 75 per cent of observed JVs experienced an equity ownership change at least once in their lifetimes (Hennart et al. 1999, Brouthers and Bamossy 2006, Iriyama et al. 2014). Chung et al. found that an initial change in the ownership structure of a JV does not have a remedial effect on JV performance but instead triggers further and increasingly disruptive ownership changes. The JV falls into "the trap of continual change" as an expression of a "dysfunctional repetition of rearranging the structural arrangement, which locks the organization into bad choices and sends it into a downward spiral" (Chung and Beamish 2010, p. 1011).

Conversely, some authors argue that ownership and governance adaptations *within* existing JV agreements can actually have a long-term stabilizing effect as they are the expression of an organic and dynamic cooperation process that can actually help improve overall JV performance (Reuer 2000). In this connection, managers perceive JVs to be more successful if, during the post-formation processes, emphasis is put on the gradual increase of JV control compounded with continuous efforts to overcome cultural barriers (Brouthers and Bamossy 2006). It is possible that the renegotiation of the terms of the JV, including a power shift in terms of equity distribution, can unleash a series of positive feedback loops amongst the partners and eventually lead to balance in the relationship that had not existed before (Arino and de la Torre 1998). The points discussed above, as derived from the existing literature, lead to the following hypothesis:

Hypothesis 1 (H1): Foreign investors that have altered a given JV relationship through a recent increase of their foreign equity share (including the real option of buying out the local partner and making the transition to a WOS) will perform better than foreign investors that consider the partners' equity distribution within JVs as a static variable in spite of internal and external change dynamics.

4.2 FDI Performance

There are multiple approaches to FDI performance measurement and the findings differ depending on what criterion is being selected. The most common measures of performance are those based on objective financial indicators such as sales, exports, employment or profit indicators (Geringer et al. 1989, Chowdhury 1992, Pan et al. 1999, Makino et al. 2004, Ogasavara and Hoshino 2009, Chang et al. 2013, He et al. 2015), the survival rate or longevity of the subsidiary (Geringer and Hébert 1991, Chowdhury 1992, Pennings et al. 1994, Li 1995, McCloughan and Stone 1998, Delios and Beamish 2004, Chung and Beamish 2005a, Gaur and Lu 2007, Mudambi and Zahra 2007, Xu and Lu 2007, Alfaro and Chen 2012) and measures of performance perception (Woodcock et al. 1994, Nitsch et al. 1996, Andersson et al. 2001, Brouthers 2002, Beamish and Lee 2003, Delios and Beamish 2004, Brouthers et al. 2008b, Brouthers et al. 2015). Less common measures of subsidiary performance involve growth variables (Mata and Portugal 2004, Tan 2009) and stock market reactions (López-Duarte and Vidal-Suárez 2008). Some studies have shown that subjective and objective performance indicators display relatively high levels of correlation (Geringer and Hébert 1991, Ogasavara and Hoshino 2009).

A specific FDI performance variable is the survival of the subsidiary; this has received considerable attention particularly in longitudinal research designs. Although widely applied in the extant literature, the measurement of subsidiary survival or subsidiary longevity has some methodological limitations e.g. related to substitutability and interaction between objective or subjective performance indicators with variables of subsidiary survival (Yan and Zeng 1999). A foreign subsidiary is assumed to have exited if it ceases to appear in the yearly business directory that often forms the basis for the respective analyses (Chowdhury 1992, Li 1995, Delios and Beamish 2004). There can be other reasons for subsidiary exit besides those of liquidation and bankruptcy. A subsidiary can be sold to a new foreign investor which is not tantamount to dissolution but rather entails its continuation under a different parent firm. Hennart et al. argue that JV exit should not be misconstrued as failure and find that JV exit is explained by a higher probability of subsidiary selloff rather than its definite liquidation (Hennart et al. 1998). A further scenario is that both partners might have from the outset agreed to a limited life span of the JV as a vehicle for the attainment of mutual learning objectives (Hamel 1991, Lyles 1994). Subsidiary termination is therefore not always a result of unforeseen and insurmountable inter-partner conflicts but can also be foreseen and planned (Gomes-Casseres 1987, Inkpen and Beamish 1997).

In 2008, a meta-study on performance measurement in international business was undertaken (Hult et al. 2008). On the basis of a review of almost 100 articles in international business literature, Hult et al. arrive at a classification of the most frequently applied performance measures into three broad main categories, namely financial performance measures (ROS, ROA, return on investments (ROI), profitability, etc.), operational performance (market share, productivity, etc.) and overall effectiveness performance (perceived overall performance, perceived performance relative to competitors, perceived MNE reputation, etc.). The study cautions that measures of performance differences based on established financial indicators are sensitive to divergent management accounting practices across countries and firms.

The meta-analysis reveals that only one of the three performance metrics is used by about two thirds of empirical studies in the performance related literature. This is compounded by a strong tendency towards financial performance measures which are often extracted from secondary firm accounting data. The fewer studies that combine two performance metrics have most frequently chosen the combination of a financial or operational performance measure (21 studies). Hult et al's study further finds that there are only seven studies that have combined all three performance measures.

A comparison of different performance outcomes according to the same set of explanatory variables can sometimes lead to opposing results especially if the performance variables are not drawn from the same conceptual performance domain (Gomes and Ramaswamy 1999, Brouthers 2002). Hult et al. appeal for the broadened use of multi-dimensional performance measures: "different types of performance measure should become a natural ingredient in IB [international business] research to advance knowledge. At the same time, it is appropriate to suggest that researchers should consider using measures of multiple types of performance to comprehend more fully the relationships studied" (Hult et al. 2008, p. 1072).

4.3 Transaction cost determinants of FDI performance

The multinational firm incurs transaction costs when its products or services are transferred across a "technologically separable interface" (Teece 1984, p. 99), which is the case when the firm decides to invest outside its home country. A foreign investor is frequently exposed to different layers of market imperfections that vary in degree and impede the seamless transfer of goods and services between different economic players within and across borders (Buckley and Casson 1976). Buyers and sellers have opposing perspectives on the price and quality of a traded good or service and attempt to find a common ground by entering into a formal contractual relation (Williamson 1979). The efforts of a firm to identify suitable buyers or sellers, to monitor price developments, to negotiate an acceptable price for a product or service, to dissolve contracts through arbitration mechanisms, etc., entail costs that are commonly referred to as transaction costs (Williamson 1975, Buckley and Casson 1985). Market failures as well as the characteristic of the transaction according to the three dimensions of asset specificity, uncertainty and frequency determine the ultimate amount of these transaction costs (Williamson 1985). The transaction costs differ according to the institutional framework and governance system within which the transaction is concluded and monitored. These governance systems can vary between markets and hierarchies or hybrid forms of the two, such as licensing or franchising (Williamson 1975, Williamson 1991).

The different degrees of market failures and their associated transaction costs may prompt the MNE to reduce or supersede the role of markets as the interface for trading its intermediate goods or services, which is when partial or full market internalization occurs (Buckley and Casson 1976, Buckley and Casson 1985). A wealth of literature has thus studied the effect of transaction cost economics on the FDI ownership-based entry mode ranging from lower to higher levels of internalization and the corresponding forms of minority foreign-owned JVs, co-owned JVs, majority foreign-owned JVs and WOSs. The meta-analysis of Zhao et al. confirms that transaction costs economics are, with good cause, dominant determinants of the FDI entry mode although the results show sizable variations owing to moderating effects of location, industry and country of origin (Zhao et al. 2004). More recent reviews of the entry mode literature corroborate the influential role of transaction cost economics (Brouthers and Hennart 2007, Canabal and White III 2008). The transaction cost variable of asset specificity has been given considerably more attention than the other two variables of transaction uncertainty and transaction frequency. High degrees of asset specificity (e.g. a sophisticated and complex process or product technology) prompt MNEs to favour equity modes as an expression of a market internalization process (Maekelburger et al. 2012). Likewise, wholly-owned or greenfield entry modes are preferred against mixed equity modes because the FDI investor is anxious that its principal ownership advantage would be divulged to a JV partner without obtaining a fair and commensurate price in return (Erramilli and Rao 1993, Taylor et al. 1998, Brouthers and Brouthers 2003, Chiao et al. 2010). The risk of incomplete contracts for specific and complex assets is high which, in turn, heightens the risk that the foreign investor cannot adequately defend itself against a JV partner who starts shirking responsibility. Weak institutional contexts for contract enforcement can stoke fears in the foreign direct investor that opportunistic behaviour and free-riding of the JV partner would persist without any effective legal consequences (Williamson 1985, Gatignon and Anderson 1988).

Compared to the wealth of literature on the transaction cost determinants of FDI entry mode, there is relatively less literature that establishes a clear link between transaction costs and FDI performance. The majority of these studies were conducted by Brouthers et al. (Brouthers 2002, Brouthers et al. 2003, Brouthers and Nakos 2004, Brouthers et al. 2008a). The basic premise is that the multinational firm would be rational in choosing the least costly entry mode while being observant of the risks that arise by making difficult-to-reverse and often path-dependent resource commitments in the form of FDI. A foreign firm that has followed a strategy of transaction cost minimization at the time of foreign market entry, possibly combined with other determinants borrowed from Dunning's OLI approach, has probably gained a performance edge over other foreign firms that did not follow the entry mode as predicted by transaction cost economics (Brouthers 2002, Brouthers and Nakos 2004).

Extended transaction cost models with a focus on FDI performance have underpinned its proximity to institutional theory that posits a strong influence of host country conditions in either nurturing or impairing the value enhancement potential that should normally ensue soon after foreign market entry (Brouthers 2002, Maekelburger et al. 2012). "The logic of transaction cost economics suggest that difficulties encountered at any of the three stages of contracting for technology (specification of property rights, monitoring, or enforcement) will lead to an increase in appropriability hazards, and a move towards more hierarchical governance forms" (Oxley 1999, p. 287–288). In this connection, the efficiency of the host country's judicial system and whether it offers adequate enforcement of intellectual property rights in the case of disputes between two JV partners is of paramount importance. The JV partner's cognisance that the regulatory and legal system of contract enforcement of the host country is effective and intact may *a priori* deter opportunistic or obscure behaviour and increase JV stability (Beamish and Inkpen 1995). As a result, the performance of the JV will improve. An effective system of contract enforcement will not only enhance the performance in the case of JVs but also that of WOSs. In the day-to-day operations, JV firms as well as WOSs will engage in arms-length transactions with suppliers, distributors, import and export agents, etc., and adherence of these business entities to pre-established contracts will enhance the predictability of business operations and ultimately performance. The above leads to the following hypothesis:

Hypothesis 2 (H2): A high associated cost of contract enforcement will lead to lower levels of FDI performance.

Transaction costs considerations are also at play when the foreign subsidiary decides on the extent of local sourcing of raw materials and intermediary inputs supplied by local firms or agents. Supply chain localization constitutes a cost-efficient solution provided that two conditions are met: First, the internalization of upstream production steps, for example through vertical insourcing, is not cost-efficient because it would coerce the foreign firm to undertake unrelated diversification i.e. to establish production processes that are not part of the core activities and thus do not yield desirable levels of economies of scale (UNCTAD 2001). Second, the import of intermediary products might be expensive due to long transportation distances combined with a disadvantageous geographical location and topography of the FDI host country. These costs could be compounded with further costs related to import duties, tied up capital, lengthy customs procedures or a heightened risk of perishing or damaging goods during transport whose costs would be chargeable to the buyer.[94] Against this backdrop, an increase in local supply is not only desirable from the perspective of the host country that seeks to augment the local productivity spill-overs from FDI production but it may also coincidentally contribute in lowering input costs of the MNE subsidiary. Available literature on vertical supply chain spill-overs has placed relatively more emphasis on the local supplier as a unit of analysis rather than the performance-enhancing effect of input localization from the perspective of the multinational buyer. There is evidence of positive spill-over effects in terms of supplier productivity increase, learning effects or technology transfer (Moran 2001, Javorcik 2004, Jabbour and Mucchielli 2007, Blalock and Gertler 2008, Blalock and Simon 2009, Javorcik and Spatareanu 2009). In a recent study based on UNIDO's 2010/11 Investor Survey data in SSA, it was found that domestic suppliers of MNEs managed to improve their capacities for product innovation (Görg and Seric 2013). The extent of local procurement and ensuing channels for positive vertical spill-overs are stimulated through good infrastructure and the magnitude of the host country's components supply industry (Belderbos et al. 2001).

Relatively less empirical evidence exists with regard to the performance implications of an increase in local supply from the angle of the MNE buyer. UNCTAD argues that if "they [the MNEs] subcontract directly to local suppliers, they can increase their specialization and flexibility, and adapt technologies and products better and faster to local conditions. Technologically advanced suppliers can provide affiliates with access to a pool of external technological and skill resources, feeding into their own innovative efforts" (UNCTAD 2001, p. 129). It was found that transaction cost theory provides a suitable normative framework to explain a performance surplus whenever the buyer maintains relationship continuity with indigenous suppliers in the case that the asset of transaction is specific and its volume is difficult to predict (Heide and Stump 1995). In this connection, spatial proximity and availability of local supply clusters was found to contribute positively to the performance of the original equipment manufacturer (OEM) due to shorter delivery times and transportation costs in medium and high-tech sectors with a great degree of specialization such as in the automotive industry (Murray et al. 1995, Dyer 1996). Due to their

94 Such as in the case of free on board (FOB) agreements as opposed to cost, insurance and freight (CIF) agreements.

sector foci, these studies seem to have limited applicability in the specific context of SSA. The innovative and technological potential amongst local upstream suppliers, if they already exist, will in most cases not – yet – be on par to buyer requirements for high-value, innovative and strategic intermediary components. It is hence unsurprising that MNEs in high-tech sectors such as the machinery and equipment or the chemical sector have one of the lowest proportions of local inputs supply amongst all FDI firms in SSA compared to an average proportion of local content in material purchases of 38 per cent (UNIDO 2007).[95] Conversely, sourcing from local suppliers seems to be the dominant mode for low-technology foreign manufacturers or SSA's foreign construction sector. Here, local sourcing offers the greatest potential for transaction cost minimization compared to competing alternatives of vertical insourcing or importing (UNIDO 2007).[96]

Both the macro-economic review of Chapter 2 as well as the firm-level review of Chapter 3 revealed the prominent role of FDI in agriculture, agro-processing as well as the retail sector for agricultural products. Although foreign firms are occupying different stages in the agricultural value chain of SSA, there is an observable trend towards narrowing the scope of operations and thus avoiding unnecessary costs, administrative red tape and operational risks. FDI internalization of upstream value addition processes in terms of the foreign direct investor's direct involvement in land lease and farming loses importance and is increasingly replaced by vertically-organized arms-length market transactions (UNCTAD 2009f, Yumkella et al. 2011). The degree of MNE control on host country farmers varies and is particularly rigid in contract farming arrangements. Contract farming is rapidly gaining importance in SSA (Cotula et al. 2009, Oya 2012). In a contract farming arrangement, the MNE often dictates all aspects of local production covering the use of seeds or seedlings, the volume, quality, varieties, delivery times, etc., thereby giving it better control over product specifications and the local supply chain than through the procurement from agricultural spot markets (UNCTAD 2009f). As a con-

95 MNEs in machinery and equipment have a median local material share of 10 per cent and a mean of 27.4 per cent. MNEs in the chemical sector have a median local material share of 20 per cent and a mean of 28.6 per cent.

96 MNES in low-tech sectors such as food, beverage and tobacco have a median local material share of 40 per cent and a mean of 47.1 per cent, in the wood and furniture sector it is a median of 59 per cent and a mean of 52.4 per cent, in the construction sector it is a median of 60 per cent and a mean of 55.4 per cent.

sequence, the capacities and reliability of indigenous supply by farmers or agricultural cooperatives becomes a progressively more influential determinant in foreign agro-industrial production in SSA.

The above examples corroborate that the costs of foreign production in SSA are a great deal influenced by the ease of and options for accessing raw materials either directly within the boundaries of the MNE or via local suppliers. In this connection, it is not surprising that FDI investors in SSA have placed high importance on the local availability of production inputs (Kratzsch 2005, Bartels et al. 2008). Moreover, in its latest Africa Investor Survey Report, whose data will also underlie the empirical studies of the following Chapter 5, UNIDO found that foreign firms with many domestic suppliers are on average 1.7 per cent more productive than their peers without such linkages and that the productivity advantage is larger for foreign firms in the low-tech manufacturing sectors (UNIDO 2012a). The following hypothesis can therefore be developed:

Hypothesis 3 (H3): An overall improvement of the country's upstream vertical supply chain (raw materials and local suppliers) will lead to enhanced FDI performance.

4.4 Institutional and host country determinants of FDI performance

The performance of the FDI project is influenced by various factors, some of them are closely related to the specific FDI characteristics and some are determined by external host country factors which lie outside the control of the management of the subsidiary and which can preponderate resource-based performance determinants (Christmann et al. 1999). Host countries differ in terms of the development of their political, economic and social institutions. The host country's ability to address market failures will influence the level of transaction costs that the foreign subsidiary is exposed to. This may impact on the performance of the FDI project in a specific country context or explain different FDI performances in a cross-country context (Makino et al. 2004, Chan et al. 2008).

External firm factors have been subsumed under the theory of institutional environments which were to a large extent coined by the research of Douglass North who defines institutions as the "set of fundamental political, social and legal ground rules that establishes the basis for production, exchange, and distribution" (Davis and North 1971, p.6) and thereby "affect the performance of the economy by their effect on the costs of exchange and production" (North 1990, p.5). In this connection, external firm factors have been extensively examined from the perspective of host country determinants of FDI inflows and FDI entry modes, following the so-called "L" factors in John Dunning's OLI paradigm (Hymer 1976, Dunning 1993, Buckley and Casson 1998, UNCTAD 1998, Dunning 2000, UNCTAD 2005e). Pertaining to the array of literature on FDI determinants, institution-based variables such as the functioning of the host country's legal system, its regulatory environment, its political stability and others have been included in the models and were found to have a significant influence on the volumes of FDI inflows to a particular host country (Loree and Guisinger 1995, Gastanaga et al. 1998, Globerman and Shapiro 2003, Jensen 2003, Li and Resnick 2003, Bénassy-Quéré et al. 2007, UNCTAD 2009b). Macro-economic studies that have specifically focused on Africa conform to these former studies in that they found an equally positive relationship between the political business climate and the attraction of higher volumes of FDI inflows (Agodo 1978, Morisset 2000, Cotton and Ramachandran 2001, Pigato 2001, Bende-Nabende 2002, Asiedu 2004b, Mlambo 2005, Asiedu 2006, Naudé and Krugell 2007).

The literature on FDI inflow determinants underscores the role of institutional policy factors in predicting FDI flows from specific countries or by FDI groups of varying origins. The common limitation of these macroeconomic models is that the dependent variable of FDI inflows is the expression of *a realized decision* of foreign investors to invest in a certain host economy based on *expected* returns of investment. As a result, the volume of *unrealized* and *missed out* FDI and its associated opportunity costs for SSA are not part of the measurement because the latter would require complementary surveys at the level of the FDI parent in order to learn about the reasons for postponing or diverting FDI projects away from SSA. Furthermore, FDI inflows do not per se give any hints of subsequent subsidiary performance and whether it exceeded or fell below performance expectations that had been established at the time of FDI entry. Several scholars thus stated that macro-level FDI data is a spurious proxy for real value-added activities because the true extent of investment into human capacity development, fixed assets, brand development and others is not captured at the macro-economic level (Fujita 2008, Beugelsdijk et al. 2010, Kerner 2014). Chapter 2.3.6 has listed diverse factors that often lead to an erroneous recording of FDI flows or stocks due to over- or underestimation. Further variations stem from different reporting standards of IOs like the IMF, the World Bank or UNCTAD against the backdrop of overall rudimentary and sketchy FDI reporting in the majority of SSA countries (see Chapter 2.3.5).

Since institutional evolution is a "a process that is path-dependent, slow changing and uncertain" (Dunning and Lundan 2008a, p. 586), the same host country factors that had determined initial FDI entry are likely to further impact on the growth trajectory of the FDI subsidiary. Compared to the plethora of studies that explore the macro-level nexus between institutional environment and FDI inflows, there are relatively fewer studies that have gauged the effect of the institutional environment at FDI subsidiary-level and in a cross-country framework. One of them is that of Chan et al. that came to the unexpected conclusion of a negative relationship between the level of institutional development and foreign affiliate performance (Chan et al. 2008).[97] One explanation that was put forward is that new and profitable market opportunities may especially burgeon in a context of institutional voids and endow early FDI movers with a business advantage that outweighs higher transaction costs levels in countries with underdeveloped or ineffective institutions (Isobe et al. 2000). A recent institution-based study for SSA based on a sample of the 500 largest African companies refuted Chan et al's findings and found that country effects impact on sales profitability especially when the governance score increases from a low base (e.g. Nigeria, Cameroon) compared to a relatively higher governance score like in SA (Ngobo and Fouda 2012).

It seems undisputed that political and economic stability will overall lower business transaction costs for foreign investors. Improvements in the regulatory framework provide predictability to foreign investors in concluding and enforcing arms-length contracts with other business actors in the SSA host economy. Likewise, improvements in the rule-of-law curtail the discretion of individual government officials and may eventually reduce corruption, red tape, and the indirect costs of bribery (Khanna and Palepu 1997, Breslin and Samanta 2008). It is therefore hypothesized that:

97 Institutional development in Chan et al's study covered GDP per capita, economic conditions, distribution infrastructure, financial resources, intellectual property rights, political system, law and order, bureaucracy quality, justice, harassment and violence, corruption in government, and civil freedom.

Hypothesis 4 (H4): Improvements in economic and political stability as well as the host country's regulatory framework will lead to enhanced FDI performance.

Institutional determinants of FDI performance can be disaggregated into different underlying dimensions of country-level laws and regulations (Peng et al. 2008). A demarcation line is often drawn between formal vs. informal institutional infrastructure and enforcement mechanisms (Meyer and Nguyen 2005, Dunning and Lundan 2008a). The formal institutional infrastructure incorporates laws, regulations and conventions and their enforcement is assured through sanctions, penalties, taxes, incentives, etc. Conversely, the informal institutional context is shaped by norms, cultures, belief systems and definitions that can determine the extent of legitimacy that social actors in the host country bestow to the foreign enterprise (Kostova and Zaheer 1999, Chan and Makino 2007). Moral suasion and retaliation act as informal enforcement mechanisms which often result in a loss or gain of the MNE's reputation in the host country.

Formal institutional determinants of FDI are performance requirements that cover the extent to which host country governments impose rules and conditions for FDI firms to operate within. These comprise, for instance, a minimum proportion of the firm's output to be exported, import restrictions, local content requirements, labour regulations to employ a minimum proportion of indigenous staff, foreign equity restrictions in specific subsectors, etc. (UNCTAD 2003b, UNCTAD 2006a). From a neo-classical perspective, performance or entry requirements are considered a severe market distortion that create additional transaction costs for foreign investors and unduly limit their admissible activity space (Djankov et al. 2002, Moran 2002). Other economists consider performance requirements a necessary element of a new industrial policy (NIP) approach for SSA in order to spur and channel desirable investor behaviour and to attract FDI in strategic industrial sectors, of a certain size and in specific geographic spaces (UNCTAD and UNIDO 2011, Asche and Fritzen 2013). The NIP may usher in a comeback of a culture of bargaining between the FDI host country and the multinational investor especially in situations where the FDI framework cannot be easily standardized (Ramamurti 2001). Performance requirements can vary in restrictiveness and can be mandatory or voluntary depending on the perceived sensitivity of the FDI sector (UNCTAD 2003b). Priority sectors can be boosted through the granting of incentives to motivate FDI compliance. Performance requirements are established to prompt foreign investors to source a certain proportion of their inputs locally which the host country often reciprocates by granting tax discounts for a specified period. In this connection, the study of Loree and Guisinger is noteworthy because it underpins a negative relationship between FDI inflows and performance requirements and a positive relationship with incentives (Loree and Guisinger 1995). In the same vein, Woodward and Rolfe find a negative relationship of profit repatriation restrictions and a positive relationship of tax incentives on FDI location choice (Woodward and Rolfe 1993). In the light of the emerging paradigm of NIP which is suggesting a gradual reversal of across-the-board and unspecific incentives in SSA to be replaced by specific ones and linked to performance requirements, the outcome on FDI inflows would be less evident given the presence of two inter-connected but yet divergent effects: a deterring effect of performance requirements on FDI inflows linked to a positive effect of incentives on FDI attractiveness.

FDI equity ownership restrictions are prominent examples of performance requirements and they are implemented in a bid to generate direct transmission channels for technology and know-how transfer between a foreign investor and an indigenous JV partner. Sometimes they also aim at entirely locking out FDI in specific subsectors (UNCTAD 2003b). Given the allegedly limited success of such restrictions, SSA governments have over the last decades revisited a number of restrictions, including FDI ownership restrictions (Kobrin 2005, Djankov 2009, De la Medina Soto and Ghossein 2013). Exclusive domestic ownership requirements have become the exceptions and they reflect, where they still exist, the host country's attempt to let citizens partake in the associated rents of investment projects in "sensitive" and strategic sectors that impact large parts of the population such as in raw-materials exploitation or in service sectors e.g. in real estate, finance and insurance, the media and civil transport (UNCTAD 2003b). In 2005, OECD noted that "in terms of overall statutory FDI regulation African countries are on average not more restrictive than other developing nations" (OECD 2005b, p.3). UNCTAD also attested that the levels of African FDI restrictions are on a par with average global restrictions and significantly below FDI restrictions in Western or South East Asia (UNCTAD 2006a). This is re-confirmed by the 2010 World Bank Report "Investing Across Borders" and ensuing Reports which show that SSA countries are *de jure* less restrictive on foreign ownership in seven of the eleven subsectors examined by the Report (World Bank et al. 2010, De la Medina Soto and Ghossein 2013). The following

Box 2 will look into greater detail into the issue of FDI ownership restrictions and capital requirements in SSA.

Box 2: FDI ownership restrictions and minimum capital requirements of FDI entry in SSA

"Investing Across Borders 2010" data confirms that SSA has less ownership restrictions compared to the global average and is nearly as liberalized as high-income OECD countries (World Bank et al. 2010, De la Medina Soto and Ghossein 2013). Accordingly, foreign ownership restrictions are more relaxed than the global average in mining, oil and gas, agriculture, light manufacturing, electricity transportation, media, health care and waste management. The construction, tourism and retail sectors in SSA are also more liberalized than the global average in terms of FDI entry. Relatively more ownership restrictions exist for telecommunications, banking and the insurance sector (see Box Table 2 below).

Box Table 2: FDI ownership restrictions in different industry subsectors in SSA

Subsector	Country [maximum foreign ownership permitted in per cent]*
Mining, oil and gas	Angola [74.5], Burkina Faso [95], Cameroon [95], Ghana [90], Mali [95].
Agriculture and forestry	Sierra Leone [75], Sudan [75].
Light manufacturing	Angola [82.5], Sudan [87.5].
Telecommunications	Angola [75], Burkina Faso [87.5], Ethiopia [0], Kenya [70], Madagascar [74.5], Mozambique [75], SA [70], Sudan [50], Tanzania [65].
Electricity	Cameroon [71.4], Ethiopia [50], Kenya [92.9], Liberia [71.4], Madagascar [92.9], Sudan [50], Uganda [71.4].
Banking	Angola [10], Ethiopia [0], Nigeria [70], Sudan [50], Uganda [49].
Insurance	Angola [50], Ethiopia [0], Kenya [66.7], Sudan [50], Tanzania [66].
Transportation	Angola [80], Cameroon [49], Ethiopia [10], Kenya [70], Liberia [90], Madagascar [80], Sierra Leone [80], Sudan [60].
Media	Angola [30], Cameroon [49], Ethiopia [0], Kenya [75], Mali [49], Mauritius [60], Mozambique [20], SA [60], Sudan [0], Tanzania [24.5].
Sector group 1 (constr., tourism, retail)	Ethiopia [50]
Sector group 2 (healthcare, waste mgt.)	No restrictions

Source: World Bank et al. (2010).
*Countries not reported (from those covered by the Report) are allowing 100 per cent FDI ownership. Countries covered: Angola, Burkina Faso, Cameroon, Côte d'Ivoire, Ethiopia, Ghana, Kenya, Liberia, Madagascar, Mali, Mauritius, Mozambique, Nigeria, Rwanda, Senegal, Sierra Leone, South Africa, Sudan, Tanzania, Uganda and Zambia.

Of the 21 SSA countries under examination by the World Bank Report, Ethiopia came out to be the most restrictive in terms of foreign ownership. The Ethiopian telecommunications, banking, insurance and media sectors are not open to FDI. Sudan and Angola are likewise rather restrictive with regard to foreign ownership. In Sudan, no foreign ownership is allowed in the media sector and foreign investors cannot take the majority ownership in telecommunications, electricity, banking and insurance.

Countries with no ownership restrictions in any subsectors are Côte d'Ivoire, Rwanda, Senegal and Zambia. With minor exceptions, light manufacturing, agro-industries, forestry and healthcare are fully open to FDI entry all over SSA.

In the course of continuous efforts to liberalize FDI, African host countries have also removed or lowered the threshold for the minimum size of capital investment as a prerequisite for FDI approval by the national IPA or the registration agency. Information on minimal capital requirements need to be assessed with some caution due to constant changes and conflicting information depending on the source of information, differences according to the subsector in which the FDI is supposed to take place as well as variations from de jure regulations and their enforcement in actual practice (OECD 2005, UNCTAD 2008, World Bank et al. 2010). Relatively high minimum capital requirements continue to exist in Ethiopia (100,000 USD for a WOS and 50,000 USD for a JV), in Uganda (100,000 USD), in Nigeria (65,000 USD) and in Ghana (52,000 USD for a WOS and 10,000 USD for a JV). These requirements mirror the host countries' preferences towards attracting FDI by larger MNEs and/or FDI that comes in the form of a JV instead of a WOS. The minimum capital threshold should not constitute a severe barrier for large MNEs which would be investing more than the minimum capital requirement in most cases. The minimum capital requirement of 1,000,000 CFA Franc (approximately 2,000 USD) is applicable across all 17 member states of the Organization for the Harmonization of Business Law in Africa (OHADA). No minimum requirements exist in Kenya, Madagascar, Mauritius, Mozambique, Rwanda and Sudan.

The negative effect of FDI restrictions on FDI inflows or FDI stocks has been revealed by several studies however none of these studies have specifically covered SSA (Gomes-Casseres 1990, Nicoletti et al. 2003, UNCTAD 2006b, Busse and Groizard 2008). Concerning SSA, one could hypothesise that ownership restrictions should not play much of a role in deterring FDI. First, there are very few remnants of such restrictions (World Bank et al. 2010, De la Medina Soto and Ghossein 2013). Second, there exist palpable exceptions of relatively restricted countries with skyrocketing FDI inflows in the recent past. For instance, Ethiopia and Sudan remain to be two of the most restrictive countries in terms of ownership entry on the African continent. Notwithstanding, Ethiopia has increased its FDI inward stock between 2000 and 2010 by a factor of more than four (from 0.9 billion USD in 2000 to 4.2 billion USD in 2010) and Sudan by a factor of fifteen (from 1.4 billion USD in 2000 to 20.9 billion USD).[98]

98 Source: UNCTAD FDI Database.

In theory, firms that decide to enter the foreign market in spite of FDI restrictions may do so through a suboptimal entry mode which would have been different in a more liberalized scenario. On the one hand, an MNE that is forced by market restrictions to enter as JV and not as WOE could suffer from dampened FDI performance (Brouthers 2002, Chen and Hu 2002, Brouthers and Nakos 2004). On the other hand, countries that have liberalized their FDI entry regimes have soon after attracted investors with higher foreign equity shares (Contractor 1990, Padmanabhan and Cho 1996). Host country restriction on the share of foreign ownership might further limit the foreign investor's freedom in exercising the option of increasing its management control over the firm. This dilutes the real option of buying out the local partner for the purpose of maximizing the returns of the business venture. Quite unexpectedly, no clear relationship was found between ownership restrictions, entry mode choice and the financial performance of the subsidiary or the likelihood of FDI termination (Makino and Beamish 1998, Kim and Gray 2008). Makino and Beamish conclude that "local ownership restrictions *per se* are not necessarily an obstacle for the success of FDI. […] The likelihood of success for foreign subsidiaries in restrictive countries is equal to that of those in open countries. MNC managers should recognize that the key to FDI success is not the extent to which a foreign firm controls a subsidiary, but rather whether it can choose the right partner with which to form a cooperative relationship in a regulated local environment" (Makino and Beamish 1998, p. 133–134). Box 3 on the next page discusses the likelihood of detecting "forced JVs" in UNIDO's 2010/2011 Investor Survey database and concludes that their numbers would be insignificantly low.

A further institution-based variable that has received heightened attention in the FDI determinants and performance literature is related to BITs (UNCTAD 2009a). International Investment Agreements (IIAs) are concluded to signal the host country's commitment to respecting international investors' property rights. They are often implemented in an attempt to offset prevailing weaknesses in the general business climate.

Box 3: Assessing the likelihood of "forced JVs" in the UNIDO 2010/11 Investor Survey sample

In the UNIDO 2010/11 sample of foreign subsidiaries in SSA, it emerges that foreign ownership restrictions are not a major issue for the large majority of foreign firms. Some caveat to this finding may, however, still exist.* Of 2,708 foreign firms in the sample, less than 3 per cent or a total of 73 foreign firms operate in subsectors that might be subject to possible ownership restrictions. Here, foreign equity participation would be limited from 40 to 90 per cent. Most of these firms have established operations in Cameroon (18 firms), Ethiopia (16 firms), Kenya (10 firms) and Mali (10 firms) and operate in the postal and telecommunications sector (21 firms), transportation (11 firms) and the insurance sector (8 firms). Very surprisingly, only 44 per cent (30 firms) had actually formed a JV which might be due to either a misclassification or a lack of enforcement of de jure ownership restriction at the host country level. Either way, the occurrence of presumably "forced" JVs in the sample is very low. In terms of subjective performance self-evaluation (variable to be introduced in Chapter 5.2.1) there is no remarkable difference between the subsample and the results from the rest of the sample.

The performance regression model in Chapter 5 will be limited to manufacturing firms. There is no factual evidence that any of the 20 countries covered in the UNIDO 2010/11 Investor Survey sample have imposed FDI ownership restrictions on foreign firms in the manufacturing sector.** For this reason, a sample of manufacturing FDI is not suitable to test the hypothesis of a likely negative performance effect of forced local equity participation in a limited number of remaining subsectors in SSA. The only exceptions in this regard are Angola and Sudan where ownership restrictions also exist in the light manufacturing sectors. Such a test would require specific a priori sampling of potentially imposed JV FDI projects in specific sectors in order to compare the performance effect of the former group to a control group comprising freely chosen JV FDI projects in the same sectors of other SSA countries while controlling for other explanatory variables of performance in both groups.

*On a case-by-case basis, there are difficulties in converting the main sector classifications of World Bank et al.'s Report "Investing Across Borders 2010: Indicators of Foreign Direct Investment Regulation in 87 Economies." into the given sector categories of the UNIDO 2010/11 Investor Survey database without risking misclassifications especially in multi-product or multi-service firms. The latter would result in wrongly classifying a company in the UNIDO 2010/11 Investor Survey sample as being subject to ownership restrictions although there may not be such a restriction.

**According to World Bank et al. 2010, Burkina Faso, Cameroon, Côte d'Ivoire, Ethiopia, Ghana, Kenya, Madagascar, Mali, Mozambique, Nigeria, Rwanda, Senegal, Tanzania, Uganda and Zambia have fully liberalized FDI schemes. Burundi has fully liberalized its FDI entry regulations in all sectors, including manufacturing (De la Medina Soto and Ghossein 2013). UNCTAD also attests Cape Verde, Lesotho and Niger full openness to FDI, especially in the manufacturing sectors (UNCTAD 2008b). No FDI entry restrictions exist in Malawi (KPMG 2012).

Empirical studies on the impact of IIAs, or more specifically BITs on FDI inflows have led to mixed results.[99] Some studies have found a robust positive relationship with developing countries having signed BITs with developed countries aimed at attracting FDI inflows or stocks (Neumayer and Spess 2005, Busse et al. 2008, Büthe and Milner 2008).

The actual ratification of the BIT after its signing adds more credibility and is assumed to increase the attractiveness of the country for foreign investors (Egger and Pfaffermayr 2004). Other studies again argued that BITs are at best a complement to other institutional factors and would not succeed in attracting FDI in isolation unless they are accompanied by more wide-ranging political reforms (Hallward-Driemeyer 2003, Gallagher and Birch 2006, Yackee 2007).

Table 4.2: Top ten SSA signatories of BITs and other IIAs

Country	BITs		Other IIAs	
	Signed	In force	Signed	In force
Mauritius	42	25	10	8
South Africa	40	17	10	8
Zimbabwe	30	6	8	6
Ethiopia	29	21	6	5
Sudan	28	13	10	9
Senegal	27	12	10	8
Ghana	26	8	8	6
Mozambique	25	20	8	6
Nigeria	25	13	9	7
Guinea	20	6	8	6
Source: http://investmentpolicyhub.unctad.org (accessed on 6th September 2015).				

SSA countries have to date signed 653 BITs, of which 300 (46 per cent) are currently in force.[100] In terms of other IIAs, such as free trade agreements or other economic treaties with investment-related provisions[101], 375 have been signed of which 307 are in force (82 per cent). As illustrated in Table 4.2 above, Mauritius is the country that has signed and ratified the largest number of BITs (42 signed/25 ratified) and other IIAs (10

99 UNCTAD 2014a presents a comprehensive literature overview on the impact of IIAs on FDI.
100 See: http://investmentpolicyhub.unctad.org (accessed on 6 September 2015).
101 Excluding double taxation treaties (DTTs).

signed/8 ratified) which may have contributed to the country's attractiveness especially for SPEs (see Chapter 2.3.6). South Africa, Zimbabwe, Ethiopia, Sudan and Senegal have also signed several BITs although not all of them are yet enforced.

After almost twenty years of global proliferation of IIAs, from the 1990's until the beginning of the global financial crisis in 2009, IIAs have recently become subject to extensive reviews and reforms. One reason for this can be found in the rapid increase of investor–state dispute settlement (ISDS) cases that have been filed at the International Centre for Settlement of Investment Disputes (ICSID), the United Nations Commission on International Trade Law (UNCITRAL) and other international arbitration bodies. About 60 per cent of the decisions on the merits were made in favour of the foreign direct investor (UNCTAD 2015b). This fact has roused a more vigilant approach of FDI host countries that came to realize that IIAs or BITs are not only standard elements in the FDI promotion toolkit but can actually "bite" (Hallward-Driemeyer 2003) in the case of vague and unclear formulations that had been chosen without anticipating eventual interpretations through arbitral tribunals. UNCTAD thus calls to not only improve existing BITs or IIAs with regard to investor protection provisions but also to make more use of this instrument to prompt desirable and sustainable investor actions particularly with regard to environment, energy, health and labour conditions (UNCTAD 2015b). Similar to the argument made earlier on performance requirements in the framework of a New Industrial Policy (NIP), the trend thus goes towards tailored IIAs. The existence of an IIA would have per se little impact as an FDI determinant unless its provisions offer heightened investor protection for FDI in specific sectors, from specific countries of origin and with certain desirable characteristics.

In terms of statistical modelling, it is insufficient to treat BITs as simply a binary variable because its capacity to attract FDI depends on its content and not its mere existence (UNCTAD 2014a). Bilateral FDI flow data would be a prerequisite to model the real impact of bilateral BITs on bilateral FDI flows between two signatory countries. In SSA, FDI inflow data that is disaggregated by the country of origin of the foreign direct investor is scant und unreliable (see Chapter 2.4.2). Hence, there exists hitherto no study that has explored this relationship for SSA. A cursory look at the number of BITs concluded with specific OECD countries of investor origin and FDI outward stock data in SSA implies that the relationship would not be very strong and would probably be insignificant. Germany is the most frequent partner country with which SSA countries have signed BITs.[102] There is a total number of 41 BITs signed between SSA countries and Germany of which 38 are currently enforced.[103] This is followed by China which signed 30 BITs with SSA countries, of which only 13 are currently in force. Italy signed 23 BITs of which 19 are enforced, followed by Belgium (23 signed of which 11 are enforced) and the Netherlands (22 signed of which 21 are enforced). This ranking is blatantly incongruous with the volume of FDI outward stock of OECD countries in SSA, which is largest for the UK, the US and France. Germany, the most avid signatory of BITs with SSA, has an FDI outward stock of 7.5 billion USD and ranks only sixth in terms of volume (see Table 2.16 in Chapter 2.4.2). The pattern is not much different in the case of bilateral FDI inflow data (see Table 2.15 in Chapter 2.4.2) despite being patchy and fairly outdated.

Returning to the subject of FDI performance, no study has sought to establish a relationship between BITs and FDI subsidiary performance, not at the global-level and not at the SSA level. Foreign investors with operations in SSA might find comfort in the knowledge that the existence of a ratified BIT would in theory guarantee them additional legal protection against expropriation risks in the host country. Unless the foreign investor embarks on concrete recourse action for investor–state arbitration and wins the case in its favour, there is little reason to assume that the existence of a BIT would continuously and directly affect FDI performance in a positive direction. Until then, the existence of a BIT remains a rather abstract facet of the business climate with marginal value for the day-to-day business activities of the foreign investor. The effect of a BIT might at best be indirectly positive because the host government and other institutional actors might adopt a more cautious approach to dealing with an MNE from a BIT partner country. The above reasoning leads to the following hypothesis:

Hypothesis 5 (H5): The existence of or change of an SSA country's exposure to BITs will have no impact on FDI performance.

102 See: http://investmentpolicyhub.unctad.org (accessed on 6 September 2015)

103 Noteworthy is that the BIT between Germany and South Africa has been unilaterally denounced in 2014.

4.5 Industry and corporate determinants of FDI performance

Several scholars have focused on market concentration and structural characteristics of industries of the host country as determinants of the FDI entry mode and subsequent FDI performance (Porter 1980, Porter 1985, Schmalensee 1985, Wernerfelt and Montgomery 1988, Montgomery and Porter 1991, Rumelt 1991, Baum and Korn 1996, Powell 1996, Roquebert et al. 1996, McGahan and Porter 1997, UNCTAD 1997, Elango and Sambharya 2004, Miller and Eden 2006). Several studies estimate that industry effects explain between 17 to 20 per cent of a firm's financial performance (Schmalensee 1985, Wernerfelt and Montgomery 1988, Powell 1996, McGahan and Porter 1997).

In the 1950's, the economist Joe Bain developed the structure–conduct–performance (SCP) paradigm which postulates a causality between market structure, the reaction of the enterprise to a given market structure and the final performance outcome of the combination of the two (Bain 1956). The most important defining factors of the market structure are the levels of market concentration and competition among firms. A high market concentration finds its expression in oligopolistic or, in the extreme case, monopolistic seller structures and is usually characterized by a few large firms that have sufficient market power to influence the price level in a given industry. Classical theory suggests that highly concentrated markets have a positive performance and productivity effect on the few incumbent firms that participate in it especially when the institutional structures of host countries to counter firm collusion and anti-competitive behaviour are absent or ineffective (Caves 1974, Weiss 1974).

A further defining factor of market structure is the extent of entry barriers. Entry barriers in concentrated markets are usually high because significant levels of upfront investments, with a potentially large proportion of sunk costs, are required to exploit the same economies of scale and offer products at an equally competitive price as the firms of the oligopoly (Caves 1971, Elango and Sambharya 2004). That is the reason why foreign firms prefer to enter highly concentrated markets through an acquisition, thus leaving the total number of firms in the target industry unchanged and avoiding a sudden increase in supply and retaliation by the older members of oligopoly (Yip 1982, Caves and Mehra 1986, Baldwin and Caves 1991). High market concentration can for instance be observed in service industries such as telecommunications, power generation and financial services. M&As are more frequent than greenfield FDI entries in such industries (UNCTAD 2000). The costs of an acquisition can be prohibitive for FEs or INVs. Highly-internationalized MNEs command a large capital stock that permits them to not only carry the cost of the M&A purchase but also to cover subsequent costs associated with the seamless integration of the new organizational unit into the MNE's governance framework. The combination of the assets of the acquired company with the assets of the new market entrant can lead to superior performance over incumbent companies, for example when the well-established distribution networks of one firm are vertically combined with the technologically superior product of the other. The results in the literature show that foreign acquisitions exhibit excess performance levels compared to greenfield entry when the industry shows high levels of concentration (Georgopoulos and Preusse 2009).

The extent of entry barriers is also determined by the structure of the industry. Entry barriers are relatively higher in innovative industries with technology-intensive and patented production systems that invest significant portions of R&D into anticipating or responding to changing consumptions trends in the host market. Moreover, the ownership structure of the incumbent firms, i.e. whether large market shares are owned by foreign or local firms, plays a role in the survival rate of new foreign entrants. Accordingly, new FDI entries in sectors with an already high concentration of entrenched foreign competitors are expected to survive for a shorter period (Mitchell et al. 1994).

In line with previous findings, it can be hypothesized that a sizable portion of FDI performance variance can be explained by industry effects and that this effect would be moderated by the chosen FDI entry mode into that industry. As Elango and Sambharya put it: "Even though firms in an industry will vary in terms of resources, capabilities, size, etc., all firms in an industry face the dynamics of a particular market (e.g., competition, product differentiation costs, market demand). This industry-specific confluence of dynamics, to a large extent, influences the response of all companies within an industry. Therefore, the structure of an industry and its underlying economics influence [...] the profitability of all firms in that industry (Elango and Sambharya 2004, p. 111). Unfortunately, the FDI performance effect that might be attributable to prevalent dynamics within an industry e.g. in relation to entry barriers, market concentration and competition is not authoritatively measurable within the context of SSA due to vast gaps of year-by-year industrial output data (see Box 4 on the next page).

Box 4: The scenario of industrial statistics in SSA

The United Nations Industrial Development Organization (UNIDO) has the global mandate to report industrial output and growth statistics broken down by ISIC Revision 3 at 2-digit level and, in some instances, the updated ISIC Revision 4. The data is reported in UNIDO's yearly publication, the International Yearbook of Industrial Statistics (UNIDO 2015b) and can also be accessed on its website http://stat.unido.org (accessed on 06 March 2016).

Industrial output statistics are unknown for the majority of SSA countries. Only 18 SSA countries reported industrial output statistics between 2000 and 2012 (see Annex Table 8). In 2012, industrial output statistics were collected for only six SSA countries, namely Botswana, Eritrea, Kenya, Mauritius, Namibia and South Africa. Total manufacturing output is often not calculated from all ISIC, Rev. 3, 2-digit subsectors (ISIC 15 to 37) but only from those for which data exist particularly in low-technology sectors ranging from ISIC 15 to 22 (food, beverages, tobacco, textiles, wearing apparel, leather, wood, paper and printing) and for selected medium to high-tech sectors. The industrial output data is reported at the producer's price and in local currency which renders cross-country comparisons on a USD basis difficult and prone to errors. Industrial output growth can be calculated for Botswana, Burundi, Congo, Eritrea, Ethiopia, Kenya, Malawi, Mauritius, Namibia, Senegal, South Africa and Tanzania. However, the reference years differ from country to country. Inflation-unadjusted industrial output growth between 2005 and the latest reporting year has at least doubled in Botswana (+200.4 per cent), Ethiopia (+134.1 per cent), Malawi (+127.3 per cent), Tanzania (+119.7 per cent) and Kenya (+108.3 per cent). Conversely, industrial output growth was relatively moderate in Burundi (+11.8 per cent) and Eritrea (+22.3 per cent).

Besides industrial output, UNIDO also reports on the number of establishments (or identifiable units) for industrial production (see Annex Table 9). Data is available for 14 SSA countries. Comparability among countries should be better than in the case of industrial output because there are no inflation and exchange rate effects, although it remains unclear whether all countries adhere to the same definition when identifying and accounting the number of establishments. For example, Senegal had only half the number of establishments compared to its smaller neighbour Gambia and Cameroon had more than the quadruple of industrial establishments compared to the much larger economy Ethiopia. The largest number of industrial establishments exist in South Africa (72,316 establishments in 2011), followed by Sudan (24,098 establishments in 2001) and Cameroon (10,922 establishments in 2008). A sizable increase in the number of establishments occurred in Ethiopia (+83 per cent between 2005 and 2009), Senegal (+32.9 per cent between 2005 and 2012) and Kenya (plus 29.4 per cent between 2005 and 2012). The number of establishments shrank in Eritrea, Malawi and Mauritius.

This fact obstructs the development of a differentiated performance model based on industry structure such as has for instance been developed in a study in China undertaken by Yadong Luo. The study gauges the causality between international strategic alliance performance and industry-related variables like industry profitability, industry sales growth, industry asset intensity, growth in the number of firms and industry structure uncertainty (Luo 1999).

By definition, an MNE seeks to maximize its profits and tries to reduce unforeseen revenue variations that might scramble its future business plans. A commonly applied practice is therefore for the MNE to diversify its products and services to exploit new market niches within a given industry or by entering into new industries. In this connection, diversification into related sectors which leverages the MNE's central skills and expands upon its core product and process knowledge is more likely to generate performance advantages through economies of scope than diversification into unrelated industries (Rumelt 1974, Bettis 1981, Geringer et al. 1989). Foreign subsidiaries are exposed to a higher exit hazard if they are extensively engaged in unrelated diversification which comes on top of the general risk of foreign market entry (Li 1995).

Transaction cost economics asserts that the governance and coordination of different unrelated product categories in a simultaneously dynamic cross-border setting can at some point overstretch the capacities of a firm and produce suboptimal business performance outcomes (Markides 1992). In the same vein, a study of foreign subsidiaries in the computer and pharmaceutical industry found that diversification leads to higher firm exit rates (Li 1995). Consequently, it is argued that the diversification-performance relationship is that of an 'inverted-U' with a threshold up to which internal firm resources can be effectively channelled towards increased diversification and performance levels but beyond which performance levels start slackening due to ungovernable transaction costs in spheres of excessive diversification (Markides 1992, Palich et al. 2000, Chakrabarti et al. 2007). In summary, the maximum effects of diversification are achieved when a firm diversifies in such a manner that "all of its eggs are in similar baskets – not in the same baskets or in different baskets" (Lubatkin and Chatterjee 1994, p. 130).

As has been shown by Asche et al., one fundamental barrier to industrialization in SSA is caused by a lack of diversification in the manufacturing sector which leads to highly skewed export structures due to the dependency on one or only a few commodities (Asche et al. 2012). In such a general business climate, where domestic firms concentrate on the production of only a few and undiversified products, diversification is likely to yield a performance premium for FDI firms especially for those FDI firms that are equipped with commensurate know-how and resources from within the foreign entrepreneurial network or the foreign parent. Existing FDI firms will have an advantage over new FDI entrants because they are already able to rely on existing production systems and can leverage established marketing channels to influence African consumers' appetite for more diversified foreign products. By doing so, foreign firms create new internal markets (Chakrabarti et al. 2007). The earnings of the subsidiary made from the current product portfolio can be instantaneously ploughed back for the creation of the production infrastructure that is necessary for diversification. Reinvested earnings will be an easier financial channel for financing FDI expansion/diversification projects than mobilizing the entire capital through other internal corporate channels or the local or international banking system. However, the first mover may only enjoy the performance-enhancing effect of diversification for a certain period until the expectation of high profit margins attracts competitors or so-called "follow-the-leader" investors in the same industrial sector (Knickerbocker 1973, Head et al. 1995, Pan et al. 1999). General opacity and lack of information about actual FDI performance in SSA may however make this time span longer compared to other international FDI locations. The foreign firm can enjoy the diversification premium as long as this situation lasts. Consequently, it was found that the benefits from diversification are larger in emerging countries compared to developed countries with efficient markets and more advanced institutional structures (Khanna and Palepu 1997, Chakrabarti et al. 2007). Generally, the longer the firm can exploit the advantages of selling in a low density-low competition market, the greater its performance will be (Miller and Eden 2006) although performance increases will level off in scenarios of uninhibited and unrelated diversification (Tallman and Li 1996, Hitt et al. 1997). The hypothesis on diversification is therefore as follows:

Hypothesis 6 (H6): A foreign investor with a diversified product range in SSA (related and unrelated) will reap a performance premium compared to mono-product foreign investors.

4.6 Cultural and institutional distance determinants of FDI performance

The notion of measuring the cultural distance between the home and the host country of the foreign investor derives from the research of Geert Hofstede in the 1980s (Hofstede 1980). Most studies have combined Hofstede's four dimensions of cultural distance, namely *"power distance"*, *"uncertainty avoidance"*, *"individualism"* and *"masculinity"* into a composite index, as coined by the study of Kogut and Singh and applied in many subsequent studies (Kogut and Singh 1988, Barkema et al. 1996, Barkema and Vermeulen 1997, Hennart and Reddy 1997, Hennart and Larimo 1998, Chang and Rosenzweig 2001, Cho and Padmanabhan 2005, Wang and Schaan 2008). Hofstede has recently added two more dimensions of cultural distance, namely *"long term orientation"* and *"indulgence"* (Hofstede et al. 2010).

The results of the impact of cultural distance on the preferred FDI entry mode are mixed. Some authors found evidence that higher levels of cultural distance prompt multinational firms to lower their foreign equity contribution and to opt for JVs instead of hierarchical entry modes of WOSs (Kogut and Singh 1988, Hennart and Larimo 1998, Zhao et al. 2004). The argument is that elevated levels of cultural distance change the perception of country risk in the sense that JVs are regarded as the more conservative ownership modes in comparison to WOSs. Another group of scholars find an opposing effect whereby foreign investors avoid lower equity entry modes in culturally distant countries (Barkema et al. 1996, Pan 1996, Cho and Padmanabhan 2005).The main argument borrows from transaction cost economics and postulates that equity partnerships in culturally distant countries can give rise to costly conflicts and opportunistic behaviour amongst the business partners. Barkema et al. coined the term "double layered acculturation" that, on the one hand, expects the foreign firm to prevail within an unfamiliar economic context and, on the other hand, expects the foreign firm to cope with the unfamiliar corporate culture of the indigenous JV partner. A strategy to overcome corporate alienation would be to choose hierarchical entry modes instead (Barkema et al. 1996).

A specification of the concept of cultural distance is the notion that home and host country institutions can produce different regulatory, cognitive and normative environments and hence influence the extent of *institutional* distance. A large institutional distance creates an additional challenge to the foreign investor. The foreign firm may have to take steps to re-arrange established organizational practices and processes in order for its subsidiary to obtain legitimacy from the government and other institutional agents of the host country (Kostova and Zaheer 1999). Such adaptation processes might be costly and risky, prompting foreign firms to opt for low equity entry modes in institutionally distant environments (Xu and Shenkar 2002). In response to isomorphic pressures, external legitimacy can be (re)- gained through the formation of an alliance with an indigenous equity partner. A desirable outcome would be that outside social and institutional actors would begin to view the foreign-domestic JV as naturally integrated into the local business tissue and would change their perceptions in a positive direction (Davis et al. 2000, Xu et al. 2004). In this connection, Gaur and Lu find that the relationship between subsidiary survival and institutional distance follows an inverted "U-shaped" function which implies that not only very large institutional distance diminishes the positive returns of the foreign investment but also too much institutional proximity between the FDI home and the host country. Although institutional proximity reduces the liability of foreignness it also prevents the full exploitation of locational advantages and performance-enhancing learning opportunities (Gaur and Lu 2007). Gaur and Lu also found that a shift of the foreign investor towards full equity entry modes in institutionally distant host countries increases the chances of subsidiary survival. This contradicts the findings of Xu et al. who detected a trend towards low equity modes in a situation of high institutional distance, however without becoming specific on the performance outcome of such a choice (Xu and Shenkar 2002, Xu et al. 2004).

Similar to the inconclusive effects of cultural and institutional distance on entry mode choice, its effect on firm performance has been the subject of several studies and has led to equally differentiated results (Tihanyi et al. 2005). The effect of high cultural distance on firm performance has been positive in situations where the foreign firm places its emphasis on the knowledge-augmenting and innovative stimulus of a local JV partnership or the acquisition of an indigenous firm (Shane et al. 1995, Makino and Delios 1996, Gomez-Mejia and Palich 1997, Morosini et al. 1998). In SSA, the motive of FDI is seldom one of strategic asset-seeking which would place emphasis on harnessing the partners' capabilities for R&D and learning (UNIDO 2007, UNIDO 2012a). There is plausibility in the assumption that indigenous firm capabilities are fairly underdeveloped in the more technologically advanced industrial sectors in SSA. A foreign subsidiary might suffer from suboptimal performance levels if it decides to enter into a strategic alliance with such a low technology partner. Several studies found that firm performance decreases as cultural distance increases because the MNE may incur unforeseen transaction costs due to conflicts with the local partner or the management of the acquired firm, an incongruent perception of the appropriate business practices and a differing approach to marketing strategies and incompatible technologies (Li and Guisinger 1992, Kostova and Zaheer 1999, Luo and Peng 1999,

Palich and Gomez-Mejia 1999, Luo et al. 2001, Wang and Schaan 2008). Cultural distance can become particularly disruptive if it entails diverging assessments of business opportunities and risks by the different business partners (Barkema and Vermeulen 1997). Product and service adaptation to match the preferences of local consumers can pose unexpected challenges in culturally distant countries and can lead to unforeseen expenditures by the subsidiary, thereby curbing its financial profitability especially during the initially critical period after market entry. The above leads to the following hypothesis:

Hypothesis 7 (H7): Foreign investors exhibiting higher cultural proximity to the host country will experience higher performance levels compared to foreign investors from culturally more distant countries.

Closely related to the issue of cultural distance is the question of whether the home country and nationality of the investor have an effect on the entry mode choice (Makino and Neupert 2000, Mayrhofer 2004). For example, it was found that investors from home countries that are characterized by a higher degree of Hofstede's category of power distance (autocratic vs. democratic style of management) as well as uncertainty avoidance (tolerance for uncertainty) would, ceteris paribus, choose greater ownership levels for their foreign subsidiaries (Erramilli 1996, Pan 2002).

4.7 Firm resource and internationalization determinants of FDI performance

From a resource-based perspective, a given foreign firm derives its competitive advantage through the effective exploitation of its own resources which include "all assets, capabilities, organizational processes, firm attributes, information, knowledge, etc., controlled by a firm that enable the firm to conceive of and implement strategies that improve its efficiency and effectiveness" (Barney 1991, p. 101). Edith Penrose was the first scholar to describe the firm as "a collection of productive resources" (Penrose 1959, p. 24), which grows proportionally to its size and past experience. In this line of thinking, larger firms have a competitive edge vis-à-vis smaller and newer firms above and beyond the monopolistic advantages that may exist in a particular industry (Penrose 1956, Penrose 1959).

Sustained superior performance of a firm is influenced by the type of resources that the firm is able to control and harness (Wernerfelt 1984).

Mobile and homogenous resources that are acquired and traded in factor markets are insufficient to sustain superior performance unless they are combined with unique resources developed inside the firm, such as patents or brands that are difficult to replicate by its competitors (Dierickx and Cool 1989, Barney 1991). In an international context of FDI research, resource-based considerations connect to the notion of the MNE that requires specific ownership advantages stemming from privileged access to patented or otherwise private and unavailable technology, financial channels, management skills or economies of scale as a precondition for cross-border internationalization (Kindleberger 1969, Hymer 1976, Kogut and Zander 1993). The multinational firm that penetrates a foreign market will have to ensure that it possesses a reservoir of knowledge-based advantages over indigenous firms. These advantages will help to offset the costs of foreignness in operating in a political, legal and cultural environment that does not conform to previous business experiences of the multinational firm. The ability of the MNE to harness its resource-based advantages (e.g. technology intensity, patents, trademarks and brands) in a given institutional environment will determine its competitiveness in relation to indigenous firms. Brouthers et al. posit a moderating effect of the institutional environment on resource-based advantages in the sense that the "liabilities of foreignness" resulting from institutional context differences may lead to resource-based value erosion through increased costs, loss of time, or misunderstandings in terms of resources exploitation (Brouthers et al. 2008b).

The hypotheses H4 and H5 developed in Chapter 4.4 are expected to account for the most important external institutional effects impacting on MNE performance. From a resource-based perspective, the meta-analysis by Scott Newbert covered a sample of 55 studies and corroborates the positive effect of "valuable, rare, inimitable capabilities (dynamic and otherwise) and core competencies" (Newbert 2007, p. 142) on the firm's competitive position. As a consequence, a firm drawing from difficult-to-imitate patents, trademarks and brand names will enjoy superior performance compared to its competitors in the same sector and while controlling for institutional context variables. Newbert's meta-analysis reflects the research focus of previous studies on inimitability (Dierickx and Cool 1989, Barney 1991, De Carolis 2003) and confirms a consistent and strong effect of MNEs' inimitable resources on firm performance. Firms with a well-established brand name as an expression of a bundle of specific firm-specific resources also exhibit higher performance levels (Combs and

Ketchen 1999). The above leads to the development of the following hypothesis:

Hypothesis 8 (H8): Foreign investors that can draw on specific resources which are valuable, rare and difficult-to-imitate (patents, trademarks and brand names) will perform better than foreign investors with fewer such resources.

When the ownership advantage is primarily based on idiosyncratic, tacit and difficult-to-codify firm knowledge, the foreign market entry is likely to shift towards full equity modes to sustain the multinational firm's competitive advantage over indigenous firms (Kogut and Zander 1993). This resonates with the transaction cost reasoning which predicts a preference of WOSs over JV entry modes if the MNE is characterized by high asset specificity (Erramilli and Rao 1993, Taylor et al. 1998, Brouthers and Brouthers 2003, Chiao et al. 2010). Similar occurs when the firm exhibits larger levels of R&D intensity (Gatignon and Anderson 1988, Padmanabhan and Cho 1996, Delios and Henisz 2000).

More generally, R&D intensity has been a frequently employed variable in the FDI performance literature. Sometimes it has been labelled a transaction cost variable that proxies the multinational firm's asset specificity (Gatignon and Anderson 1988, Delios and Beamish 1999b, Brouthers 2002, Zhao et al. 2004) and sometimes it has been considered a resource-based variable as one of the conduits for expanded innovation and diversification in a multinational context (Hitt et al. 1997, Kotabe et al. 2002, UNCTAD 2005e). The extant literature finds robust evidence of a positive relationship between an MNE's R&D intensity and its FDI performance measured at the corporate MNE-level (Siripaisalpipat and Hoshino 2000, Lu and Beamish 2001, Shrader 2001, Andras and Srinivasan 2003, Mudambi and Zahra 2007). More specifically, there exists a positive moderating role of R&D intensity and the level of geographical expansion and diversification through FDI. This indicates that MNEs will perform better if they confront the inherent complexities of geographically dispersed business operations through skills development and innovation which, in turn, is a corollary of increased R&D intensity (Hitt et al. 1997, Lu and Beamish 2004).

The degree of decentralization of R&D activities across different multinational subsidiaries has also received heightened attention in the FDI literature. The general observation is that MNEs tend to protect their most vital technological ownership advantages by keeping them close to their headquarters. R&D activities geared towards the creation of new technologies and other frontier innovations will only in very exceptional cases be carried out away from the headquarters' sphere of action. However, recent trends in R&D internationalization also point towards the increased outsourcing of specific R&D activities to the subsidiary-level, including subsidiaries located in developing countries (UNCTAD 2005e, Dunning and Lundan 2009). The emergence of INVs has further boosted this trend. Flatter and less hierarchical organizational structures of INVs provide a fertile ground in teasing out the creative and innovative potential of subsidiary managers. Innovations that are originally developed at the periphery of the INV can subsequently be made available through feedback loops across the entire INV (Oviatt and McDougall 1994, Foss and Pedersen 2002, Williams and Lee 2011).

Following the taxonomy of international R&D activities of TNCs presented by UNCTAD (UNCTAD 2005e), it is plausible that the main motive for conducting R&D in SSA is for local adaptation. In this case, market-seeking MNEs run R&D units, either autonomously or with an indigenous JV partner, for "absorbing and adapting technologies, essentially to support product and process engineering departments in making existing technologies work more efficiently in new environments" (UNCTAD 2005e, p. 138). In such a scenario, the frontier innovations for new products and services remain centred at the MNE parent whereas subsidiaries are tasked with adapting the embodied innovative content of existing products or services to prevalent demand patterns in the SSA host economy. Such low-level transfer-related R&D can also include the experimentation with an optimal configuration of process and product parameters in a bid to enhance the operational efficiency of foreign plants. Such a process can be further spurred through the establishment of national innovation systems (NIS) in the host economy (UNIDO 2002b, Davis and Meyer 2004, Oyelaran-Oyeyinka 2006).

Previous results from the related literature and the above considerations lead to the following hypothesis:

Hypothesis 9 (H9): Foreign investors that carry out R&D will perform better than foreign investors that do not carry out R&D.

One fundamental thesis of Dunning's OLI paradigm is that MNEs seek to effectively combine the firm's ownership advantages with available production factors in a given FDI host country (Dunning 1993). The costs of the locally available labour force can be an important FDI determinant although different types of investors react differently to labour cost decreases or increases. Efficiency-seeking and export-oriented foreign investors in low-skill manufacturing or service sectors are usually attracted by low labour costs (Kumar 1994) whereas other types of foreign investors in more sophisticated service industries or medium- to high-tech manufacturing sectors might be deterred by low labour costs as they require a skilled but not necessarily a cheap labour force (UNCTAD 1998, Dunning 2006). Different sample compositions have led to mixed results due to the inverse relationship of labour costs and associated skill levels. Some studies find that FDI flows are negatively associated with rising labour costs (Schneider and Frey 1985, Bevan and Estrin 2000, Urata and Kawai 2000). Other studies, again, highlight that a higher skills level of a host country's human capital would attract higher levels of FDI (Wheeler and Mody 1992, Hanson II 1996, Borensztein et al. 1998, Noorbakhsh et al. 2001, Miyamoto 2003, Naudé and Krugell 2003). In SSA, a positive and significant relationship was found between the literacy rate as proxy for human capital with FDI inflows (Asiedu 2006, Naudé and Krugell 2007, Suliman and Mollick 2009) and between the literacy rate and the employment effects emanating from FDI (Asiedu 2004a). In combination with other FDI determinants, firm-level studies did not confirm a sizable effect of labour costs nor of the availability of skilled labour. Other factors such as political and economic stability or local market demand play a relatively more prominent role (Kratzsch 2005, Bartels et al. 2008).

Chapter 3.9 has illustrated that three quarters of foreign investors follow a local market-seeking motive. The proportion of firms with operations in low-technology manufacturing sectors is approximately the same as in the combined medium and high-tech manufacturing sectors (see Chapter 3.2). FDI firms in the latter two sectors are more technology-intensive which should trigger a demand for employees with higher skills levels. In the three FDI investor surveys that UNIDO undertook in 2003, 2005 and 2010/11, the availability of skilled labour was indeed ranked as relatively more important than labour costs, although the difference was not very large (UNIDO 2003, UNIDO 2007, UNIDO 2012a). The orientation of the large majority of MNEs towards SSA's local markets requires these firms to refine their skill sets in obtaining customer information and in developing strategic plans to develop swift and nimble responses to changing local consumer needs. To respond to the challenge of increased market orientation, foreign firms react by honing their human resource management practices (Wei and Lau 2008). In this light, foreign investors in SSA have in Chapter 3.5 adamantly stressed the critical capability of the indigenous JV partner in relation to the "Upgrading quality of staff". The JV becomes a device for the foreign direct investor to short-circuit a cumbersome recruitment process by tapping directly into the existing human resource pool of the indigenous partner.

Generally, MNEs make an increased effort to outcompete domestic firms in identifying and recruiting the highly skilled within the often scarce local labour force. Luring the local work force by paying better wages than indigenous firms falls in line with this strategy (Javorcik 2014). It guarantees that the foreign firm stays abreast of changes in local market structure and demand. UNIDO found that the output-to-labour ratios are proportional to the percentage of university graduates in the foreign subsidiary's workforce (UNIDO 2007). Given the specific composition of FDI motives in the sample i.e. high proportion of local market-seeking firms with presumably greater demand for skilled work force than efficiency-seeking firms (whose share in the sample is moderate), combined with the positive relation found in macro-level studies between human capital and FDI flows (Naudé and Krugell 2003, Asiedu 2004a, Asiedu 2006, Naudé and Krugell 2007, Suliman and Mollick 2009), it is hypothesized that:

Hypothesis 10 (H10): A high proportion of skilled workers in the foreign investor's work force will lead to enhanced FDI performance.

Previous internationalization experience on the part of the MNE is considered an important enabling factor for the augmentation of intangible assets through R&D (Lu and Beamish 2004). In the same vein, multinational expansion and diversification unfold their full potential when effectively coupled with increased research and marketing intensity, thus giving both a moderating effect on enhanced MNE performance (Kotabe et al. 2002). While industry effects are undoubtedly at play in a firm's decision to diversify, the endogenous firm's resources are another critical determinant for diversification (Wernerfelt 1984, Hoskisson and Hitt 1990, Chatterjee and Wernerfelt 1991). A firm with the intention to diversify must possess the requisite financial, tangible and intangible resources whose composition and availability will dictate the extent to which related or unrelated diversification becomes economically feasible. Apart from liquid financial assets which offer high flexibility regarding the type of diversification, the individual combination of tangible assets such as plants and equipment constitute a firm's manufacturing technology and make it suitable for related diversification (Hoskisson and Hitt 1990, Chatterjee and Wernerfelt 1991). Successful diversification on the basis of intangible resources requires know-how transfer at the level of different management units which is easier to achieve for less idiosyncratic and more cross-cutting skills (e.g. in marketing) and also if the communication culture and openness to innovation of the acquired and the acquiring firm are not too dissimilar (Capon et al. 1988).

Firm internationalization reflects the extent to which the operations of the multinational firm are being dispersed across different international markets. This exposes the firms to more potential market opportunities than less internationalized firms which, when successfully exploited, can translate into increased firm growth and performance. The internalization of cross-border market transactions facilitates learning due to interaction with actors in different markets and gives the MNE enhanced exposure to different innovation and technology systems (Zahra et al. 2000). Learning-by-doing is assumed to fine-tune the foreign firm's ability to more adequately predict the success factors of an anticipated new FDI engagement. This specifically includes the MNE's predictive capacity about superior combinations of collaborative vs. non-collaborative market entry modes in the light of the technological content of anticipated foreign operations and the diversity of products and services the foreign firm intends to sell in the targeted foreign market. In this context, foreign firms are likely to draw on their experience of successfully realized foreign market entries and tend to choose similar entry modes in new host countries with presumably similar institutional environments (Chang 1995, Padmanabhan and Cho 1999). Even experienced foreign firms may, however, encounter unexpected adaptation costs of foreign market entry. A foreign investor could make fallacious inferences about presumably similar market conditions. Based on this wrong judgment, MNEs might act less prudently than if they had invested in a foreign market that would have been a priori classified as unknown and culturally distant (Petersen et al. 2008).

The majority of studies found the link between international FDI experience and corporate FDI performance to be positive. For example, Delios and Beamish found that geographically dispersed FDI activities have a positive effect on the financial productivity of MNEs because the MNE has greater "ability to gain higher returns from exploiting proprietary assets, such as brand equity, patents, or unique processes, across a greater number of markets" (Delios and Beamish 1999a, p. 715). The results are reconfirmed in a later study and in relation to host country experience and the prospect of subsidiary survival (Delios and Beamish 2001). In this context, a stream of literature analysed the nexus between international market diversification and firm performance and posits the relationship to be non-linear across time (Hitt et al. 1997, Luo and Peng 1999, Lu and Beamish 2001, Lu and Beamish 2004). An argument that has often been put forward is that the liability of foreignness brings a range of business uncertainties and renders new FDI entrants easier victims of opportunistic behavior by business partners (Hymer 1976, Johanson and Vahlne 1977, Johanson and Vahlne 1990, Henisz and Delios 2001, Zhao et al. 2004). The costs associated with the liability of foreignness can considerably curb FDI performance during the first years of operation. Performance levels often improve soon after because the MNE has augmented its intangible assets through learning and innovation. The foreign direct investor is now fit to adapt to prevailing market conditions and may be ready to rectify any costly mistakes it had committed during the initial stage of the investment. A case in point is the real option of buying out the former joint venture partner (see Chapter 4.2.1).

The positive effect of increased internationalization is however time-bound and limited. Similar to the notion of the negative effect of excessive and unrelated product diversification, excessive internationalization can also entail heightened transaction costs. An MNE might have crossed a critical threshold in simultaneously managing too many foreign subsidiaries in geographically different markets up to a point where the potential benefits of internationalization are outweighed by disproportionately high costs (Geringer et al. 1989, Tallman and Li 1996, Hitt et al. 1997). Lu and Beamish came to the plausible conclusion that the relationship follows that of a horizontal S-curve with an initial performance decline at the beginning of the internationalization process, an increase in performance by tapping into the advantages of geographic diversification and an eventual performance decline due to large coordination and management costs in highly internationalized firms (Lu and Beamish 2001, Lu and Beamish 2004).

The overall positive effect of MNE experience and performance, albeit not necessarily a linear-one, was found not only at corporate-level but was also confirmed in studies that focus on the foreign subsidiary as the unit of analysis (Luo and Peng 1999, Siripaisalpipat and Hoshino 2000, Delios and Beamish 2001, Ogasavara and Hoshino 2009). International experiential knowledge measured as the parent firm's network of subsidiaries abroad had a significantly positive effect on the managerial assessment of subsidiary profitability on a scale of three performance levels (i.e. loss, break-even and gain) (Ogasavara and Hoshino 2009). This finding, combined with the finding that unbalanced geographical internationalization eventually leads to diminishing levels of FDI performance (Hitt et al. 1997, Lu and Beamish 2004), suggests that the experience of simultaneously operating a conservative number of other FDI subsidiaries in geographically related areas may offer a conducive mix for the maximization of FDI subsidiary performance. Transferring this reasoning to the sample of FDI firms in SSA, prior or current experience gained from operating subsidiaries in other SSA countries should lead to ownership advantages and hence to a performance premium. Although there are undoubtedly differences between different SSA countries, a regionally (i.e. SSA) diversified FDI investor would be exposed to common patterns of cultural behaviour and preferences of its different business partners and clients. This specific business knowledge of SSA gives "Africa experienced" foreign investors a competitive edge over newly internationalizing investors or investors that have gained their previous internationalization experience in other world regions but not in SSA. The hypothesis is thus as follows:

Hypothesis 11 (H11): Foreign investors that are operating other FDI subsidiaries in SSA will exhibit superior subsidiary performance.

4.8 Governance and subsidiary integration determinants of FDI performance

A relatively new branch of literature on FDI and international entrepreneurship has started to analyse the performance effects of the varying internal governance systems of MNEs. One fundamental aspect of internal governance is the extent to which the MNE parent tightens or loosens its control mechanisms for its network of foreign subsidiaries thereby allowing the subsidiary to seek and exploit market opportunities with a greater degree of autonomy (Dunning and Lundan 2009). The advent of INVs that derive their competitive advantage by organizing themselves in an entrepreneurial and flexible manner (Oviatt and McDougall 1994, Knight and Cavusgil 2004, Brouthers et al. 2015), prompted a debate amongst FDI scholars on whether "traditionally" and hierarchically structured multinational enterprises should reorganize themselves in order to establish a more conducive organizational framework for in-house entrepreneurial initiatives (Birkinshaw 1998, Birkinshaw 2000). The crucial role of the individual entrepreneur in driving the internationalization process through the exploitation of formal and informal networks of cooperative alliances, markets, financing channels, etc., impacts on the manner in which geographically dispersed MNE operations are organized, including organizational forms that imply a shift "away from the dyadic headquarters-subsidiary relationship in MNCs" (Ghoshal and Bartlett 1990, p. 603). Higher levels of risk tolerance within the multinational enterprise not only influence the speed of internationalization but also create a culture in which dispersed entrepreneurial tendencies within the multinational enterprise's network are spawned and reinforced within the context of an overall loosened headquarters-subsidiaries relationship (Birkinshaw and Morrison 1995, Birkinshaw 2000). A "heterarchical" instead of a hierarchical organization of subsidiaries is believed to unlock the innovative potential of subsidiary managers and provides them with the autonomy to act as entrepreneurs in their own right aimed at exploiting opportunities for localized innovation, learning or market growth (Hedlund 1986, Marschan et al. 1996, Lee and Williams 2007, Williams and Lee 2009). Suitable organizational mechanisms can facilitate a knowledge transfer loop from the subsidiary back to the MNE parent. Experiences are collected at the periphery of the MNE and may later be more widely diffused at the broader corporate level for upscaling and replication (Foss and Pedersen 2002, Williams and Lee 2011).

Studies that measure the direct effect of the extent of subsidiary autonomy on FDI performance are rather rare and are susceptible to changes of research design related to the measurement of subsidiary-headquarters interaction and ensuing autonomy. Birkinshaw et al. find that subsidiaries that are endowed with a "world mandate", coupled with higher levels of autonomy, generate the highest levels of ROI, productivity and profit compared to subsidiaries with a mandate of "local implementers" (i.e. subsidiaries with high product dependence on the parent and low autonomy), and compared to "specialized contributors" (i.e. subsidiaries with considerable expertise but with activities tightly coordinated with the activities of other subsidiaries) (Birkinshaw and Morrison 1995, Birkinshaw et al. 2005). Further evidence was found that operational decision-making autonomy in matters of local production and distribution improves the labour productivity and sales turnover of the MNE subsidiary whereas local embeddedness in the host location, in terms of locally-based networks and supply chains, shows only a weak effect on subsidiary performance (Mc-

Donald et al. 2008). The study of Gammelgard et al. confirms the positive effect of subsidiary autonomy and stressed that subsidiary autonomy and local partnership networks amplify each other and lead to superior performance (Gammelgaard et al. 2012).

The degree of subsidiary autonomy is moderated by the chosen establishment mode. It is more effective for the MNE to opt for the greenfield establishment mode if the parent firm is planning for lower subsidiary autonomy and tightened subsidiary integration. In the case of M&A subsidiaries, it is vice-versa more beneficial to allow for greater autonomy. Subsidiaries that evolved from an M&A continue to be influenced by previous management styles and the organizational culture of the acquired firm. As a consequence, a higher degree of subsidiary autonomy could mitigate resistance and detrimental conflicts during the post-acquisition phase and thus contribute positively to subsidiary performance (Slangen and Hennart 2008).

In the light of the aforementioned literature, the expectation would be to find a positive effect of subsidiary autonomy on FDI performance in SSA. Unfortunately, there is no enterprise-level variable in the UNIDO 2010/11 Investor Survey questionnaire that could lend itself to a reliable test of such a hypothesis.

5. Empirical analysis of FDI performance in SSA

A general conclusion of the extant literature review of the Chapter 4 was that transaction cost, resource-based, institutional, and cultural context considerations should play a crucial role in explaining firm-level FDI performance in SSA. A set of 11 hypotheses have been developed. The purpose of this chapter is to test these hypotheses and to analyse whether, and to what extent, different dependent variables influence FDI subsidiary performance in SSA.

First, the underlying sample for analysis will be described. The sample will be trimmed to facilitate and improve the accuracy of the subsequent empirical analysis. Second, the model will be developed together with a description of dependent, independent and control variables. A Principal Components Analysis (PCA) will be conducted to produce an additional subset of independent variables to be added to the regression model. The statistical model comprises different linear OLS regressions with changing combinations of dependent, independent and control variables. This statistical technique is hoped to achieve acceptable levels of explanatory power with which the hypotheses can be tested. The last sub-Chapter 5.4 will collate and discuss the findings.

5.1 Data and sample

Consistent with the descriptive analyses of Chapter 3, the sample will be based on the raw data from the UNIDO Investor Survey that was carried out in 2010/11 and which covered 2,692 foreign subsidiaries in 20 SSA countries (UNIDO 2012a). The modalities of data collection, sampling and stratification techniques have been described in greater detail in Chapter 3.1.

The subsequent analysis is based on a reduced sample which covers *industrial* FDI subsidiaries. In total, there are 1,499 foreign enterprises of which 1,340 are manufacturing enterprises and 159 are non-manufacturing industrial enterprises (see Chapter 3.2). In the following, the sample will be reduced further because missing observations for a single dependent, independent or control variable will lead to a list-wise exclusion of cases.

As a result, the number of observations in each particular model specification will be similar across the three different FDI performance variables to be introduced in the following sub-chapter.

The largest group of foreign investors in the sub-sample are based in Kenya (383 firms, 25.6 per cent), Uganda (177 firms, 11.8 per cent), Nigeria (119 firms, 7.9 per cent), Ghana (108 firms, 7.2 per cent), Tanzania (97 firms, 6.5 per cent), Ethiopia (94 firms, 6.4 per cent) and Mozambique (83 firms, 5.5 per cent). At the other end of the scale are countries that represent around 1 per cent or even less of the total sample, namely Burkina Faso, Burundi, Côte d'Ivoire and Niger. In terms of investor origin, the overall pattern of sample distribution has remained quite stable compared to the results of Chapter 3.3. Indian investors remain the largest group in industrial FDI with 16.8 per cent vs. 13.4 per cent in the whole sample. They are followed by investors from the UK (10.7 per cent), China (7.8 per cent), France (7.1 per cent), South Africa (6.3 per cent) and Kenya (4.8 per cent). The overall share of South-South investment is 57.2 per cent in industry-related FDI compared to a share of 53.6 per cent in the whole sample. This observation confirms the earlier finding that developing country foreign investors display a larger propensity to invest in the manufacturing, utilities or construction sector compared to their peers from developed countries. The share of FEs is also considerably larger in industry-related FDI than FDI covering all economic sectors. In the reduced sample, 71.9 per cent are FEs as compared to 65.2 per cent of FEs in the total sample (see Chapter 3.7).

5.2 Methodology

The methodology rests on the assumption that a set of explanatory or independent variables exists that influences the performance of FDI subsidiaries in SSA in a linear fashion. A linear regression model is formulated aimed at minimizing the sum of the squared differences between the observed values and the expected values as determined by the regression line. The applied method is therefore that of multiple OLS comprising more than one independent variable.

The model can be mathematically formulated as follows:

(1) $Y_i = \alpha + \beta_1 x_{1,i} + \beta_2 x_{2,i} + \ldots + \beta_p x_{p,i} + \varepsilon_i$

Where Y_i denotes the performance of FDI subsidiary i; α is the constant or intercept; $\beta_1, \ldots \beta_p$ are the set of parameters to be estimated; ε_i is the error term; and $x_{1,i}$, ...$x_{p,i}$ is the set of observations of FDI subsidiary i = 1, 2, ...n.

5.2.1 Dependent variables

One distinctive feature of the chosen research design is the inclusion of different performance measures and an analysis of how different domains of the complex construct of FDI performance change when measured against a constant set of independent variables. This research design responds to the critique by Hult et al. regarding the generally narrow scope of international business performance measurement which mostly focuses on only one performance variable at a time (Hult et al. 2008). One variable from each of Hult et al.'s proposed three main categorizations of international business performance will be selected i.e. one variable of financial performance, one variable of operational performance and one perception-based variable reflecting overall effectiveness performance.

The financial performance variable measures firm profitability by means of the profit margin (equal to ROS) before taxes (*PROFIT*). The measurement gives the mean annual profit margin i.e. the accrued earnings before tax from the sales of the company's product or service over the last three financial years. The coverage of three financial years makes the measurement more robust compared to a single-year measurement. The latter is more sensitive to extraordinary business related variations in the costs or turnover of foreign operations. The profit margin is a frequently chosen financial performance variable of MNEs (Geringer et al. 1989, Tallman and Li 1996, Andras and Srinivasan 2003, Makino et al. 2004, Chan et al. 2008, Ogasavara and Hoshino 2009, Shaner and Maznevski 2011, Mohamad and Hoshino 2012, Haar and Marinescu 2014) although it is not as frequently applied as sales growth or ROA (Hult et al. 2008). Some authors have argued that profit margin is a better financial measurement than ROA because its denominator term, sales, can be considered less sensitive to cross-country variability than assets whose valuation tends to fluctuate more widely in different host countries (Geringer et al. 1989, Makino et al. 2004, Chan et al. 2008).

There exists however a noisy element in profit-based performance measures (both profit margin/ROS or ROA) compared to, for example, sales or revenue growth indicators. The profit margin is quite susceptible to manipulation because TNCs might artificially raise the internal price that a foreign subsidiary is to pay for licenses or royalties in return of services offered by a holding company or the multinational parent. This effect lowers the taxable profit of the firm and is commonly referred to as transfer pricing (Christmann et al. 1999, OECD 2010). For example, in a survey approach for Viet Nam that largely resembles that of the survey underlying UNIDO's "Africa Investor Report 2011", UNIDO found hints of transfer pricing of MNEs at a considerable scale (UNIDO 2012c).[104] It is imaginable that similar effects are at play in the sample for analysis but it would be beyond the scope of this Book to make an attempt to determine the extent of transfer pricing activities of MNEs in SSA. By way of precaution, further performance variables will therefore be included in the statistical model.

The numerical value of *PROFIT* will be transformed to represent the decile rank of each case, resulting in the assignment of a score of 1 to 10 to each case. Each group will contain approximately the same number of cases representing about 10 per cent of the total sample. The transformation implies that *PROFIT* does not measure the foreign subsidiary's profit margin in absolute terms but relative to the profit margins of other firms in the sample. An advantage of decile rank transformation is that statistical outliers in terms of loss-making firms or firms with very high profit margins do not have to be excluded from the analysis but can be accorded a score of 1 or respectively 10. The transformation results in a nearly uniform distribution.[105]

The second performance variable relates to the capacity utilization of the international subsidiary (*CAPUTIL*) as a non-financial measure. Surprisingly, in their 2008 meta-study, Hult et al. did not make specific reference to capacity utilization but to closely related operational performance indicators such as market share, productive efficiency, productivity and production cycle times (Hult et al. 2008). Although not as common as other firm performance measures, capacity utilization has been used in a limited number of studies (Arnold and Javorcik 2005, Yasar et al. 2011). Ca-

---

104 In the sample of FDI subsidiaries in Viet Nam, there were numerous TNC subsidiaries that announced expansionary future sequential investments in Viet Nam despite reported profits being negative, zero or close to zero.

105 In strict statistical terms, each dependent variable in the OLS regression model should be normally distributed. Since this is not the case, extra caution will be on testing the variation of the residual term for normal distribution (i.e. test on heteroscedasticity).

pacity utilization is usually defined "as the ratio of actual output (Q) to some measure of potential output" (Nelson 1989, p. 273). There are two main interpretations of the concept of potential output. On the one hand, it could refer to the maximum output that is technically feasible from a firm's short-run availability of machinery and equipment. On the other hand, potential output could refer to an economically effective and steady mix of input vs. output factors in the sense that deviations from this potential output (underutilization or overutilization) would entail higher unit costs of production than necessary (Morrison 1993).[106] Given the methodological difficulties in obtaining an unambiguous measure of potential output or maximum capacity, capacity utilization is not normally measured for companies in the service sector. For example, the US Federal Reserve Bank reports regularly on industrial production and capacity utilization but it limits this indicator to industrial firms i.e. manufacturing firms as well as firms in mining and utilities.[107] Following this logic, the statistical model in this Book will also be limited to industrial firms.

The third dependent variable is a subjective performance variable (*SELFEVAL*) based on the respondent's perception on a 5-point Likert scale indicating whether the investment was *well below* (1), *below* (2), *in line with* (3), *above* (4), or *well above* (5) the foreign investor's initial expectation (UNIDO 2012a).[108] This measurement fulfils the definition of Hult et al's third performance category of overall effectiveness as being "a wider conceptualization of performance, and includes reputation, survival, perceived overall performance, achievement of goals, and perceived overall performance relative to competitors" (Hult et al. 2008, p. 1066). As

106 The difference in interpretation of "potential output" represents a methodological weakness because the UNIDO 2010/11 Investor Survey questionnaire simply asked respondents to "indicate the average level of capacity utilization in the company: Over the last three years before the global financial crisis/during global financial crisis" (UNIDO 2012a). *CAPUTIL* represents the mean of both values and ranges between 0 to 100 per cent.

107 See: http://www.federalreserve.gov/releases/g17/Current/table7.htm (accessed on 19 September 2015).

108 The UNIDO 2010/11 Investor Survey questionnaire made a distinction as to whether the subjective current FDI performance is referred to expectations that had been made before the outbreak of the global financial crisis in 2008/2009 or whether it is referred to readjusted expectations after the global financial crisis. Similar to the construction of variable *CAPUTIL*, the variable *SELFEVAL* represents the mean of both values.

shown in Chapter 4.2, measures of performance perception are common and have been widely applied by different FDI researchers (Woodcock et al. 1994, Nitsch et al. 1996, Andersson et al. 2001, Brouthers 2002, Beamish and Lee 2003, Delios and Beamish 2004, Brouthers et al. 2008b, Brouthers et al. 2015). In cross-country analytical frameworks such as in this Book, subjective performance measures are considered to have an advantage over financial performance indicators in that they remain impervious to divergent financial accounting standards and exchange rate fluctuations in the respective FDI host countries. Furthermore, the response rates tend to be higher in surveys that ask for information about subjective performance compared to objective performance indicators (Brouthers et al. 1999). In the subsequent analysis, numerical values from 1 to 5 will be assigned to the 5-point Likert scale which follows the methodology proposed by Labovitz (Labovitz 1970).

The sample consists of operational subsidiaries of foreign firms. As a result, other common measures such as the subsidiary survival rate or subsidiary longevity cannot be used as a criterion of FDI performance as in other mostly headquarters-based panel studies.

In the following section, the three dependent variables will be tested for correlation. As expected from previous studies (Geringer and Hébert 1991, Ogasavara and Hoshino 2009), all variables show a significantly positive correlation (see Table 5.1 below).

Table 5.1: Correlations of performance variables PROFIT, CAPUTIL and SELFEVAL

	PROFIT	*CAPUTIL*	*SELFEVAL*
PROFIT	1 (n=1,336)	0.074* (n=1,173)	0.192** (n=1,327)
CAPUTIL		1 (n=1,294)	0.305** (n=1,291)
SELFEVAL			1 (n=1,471)

**. Correlation is significant at the 0.01 level (2-tailed).
*. Correlation is significant at the 0.05 level (2-tailed).
Based on industrial firms (manufacturing; electricity, gas and water supply and construction).

The strongest positive correlation exists between *SELFEVAL* and *CAPUTIL* (+0.305**) and *SELFEVAL* and *PROFIT* (+0.192**). *PROFIT* and *CAPUTIL* show a weakly positive correlation of +0.074* with significance at the 0.05-level. The presence of positive and significant correlations gives a first indication that the three variables *PROFIT*, *CAPUTIL* and *SELFEVAL* pertain to the same empirical construct of FDI performance.

The multiple regression models can be further specified as follows:

(2) $PROFIT_i = \alpha_1 + \beta_{1,1}x_{1,i} + \beta_{1,2}x_{2,i} + \ldots + \beta_{1,p}x_{p,i} + \varepsilon_{1,i}$

(3) $CAPUTIL_i = \alpha_2 + \beta_{2,1}x_{1,i} + \beta_{2,2}x_{2,i} + \ldots + \beta_{2,p}x_{p,i} + \varepsilon_{2,i}$

(4) $SELFEVAL_i = \alpha_3 + \beta_{3,1}x_{1,i} + \beta_{3,2}x_{2,i} + \ldots + \beta_{3,p}x_{p,i} + \varepsilon_{3,i}$

α_1, α_2 and α_3 are the constants or intercepts pertaining to each of the three regression equations; $\beta_{1,1}, \ldots \beta_{1,p}$ and $\beta_{2,1}, \ldots \beta_{2,p}$ and $\beta_{3,1}, \ldots \beta_{3,p}$ are the set of parameters to be estimated in each of the three regression equations; $\varepsilon_{1,i}, \ldots \varepsilon_{3,i}$ are the three error terms; The index i = 1, 2, …n describing FDI subsidiary i is constant in each of the three regression models (list-wise case exclusion) to ensure maximum comparability.

5.2.2 Independent variables

The variables of MNE characteristics that will be employed as independent variables are mostly derived from the UNIDO 2010/11 Investor Survey dataset. This puts natural limitations on the inclusion of a wider set of independent variables as presented in other pertinent studies on FDI performance. Notwithstanding, the risk of a common method bias should be minor because the pertinent FDI performance determinants in the questionnaire are separated and not presented in a consecutive fashion. Such a questionnaire design reduces the likelihood that respondents grasp the theoretical concept behind the questions and attempt to "tune" answers in order to appear consistent and rational (Podsakoff et al. 2003). The independent variables will be selected based on their expected efficacy in testing the eleven hypotheses H1 to H11. Each hypothesis as well as its broader theoretical class is presented in the following Table 5.2 before the source and statistical treatment of each independent variable is presented in greater detail.

Due to the underlying effects of endogeneity, the first variable *OWNCHANGE* cannot be assigned to any specific theoretical domain (see Chapter 4.2.1). *OWNCHANGE* is constructed from two variables of the UNIDO 2010/11 Investor Survey questionnaire. The first variable denotes the current foreign equity share in the business venture and the second variable represents the foreign equity share of five years ago (UNIDO 2012a). Since the UNIDO Survey was conducted from 2010 to 2011, the second variable represents the foreign equity share from 2005 to 2006, with a few exceptions.[109]

OWNCHANGE takes a value of zero in the case that the foreign company experienced a decrease in foreign ownership or if foreign ownership remained the same. *OWNCHANGE* also takes a value of zero in the case that the ownership increase occurred within the context of an already existing WOS, namely a change from between 90 per cent of foreign equity up to 100 per cent, because H1 is to test for the performance outcome of a foreign ownership increase within the context of a JV partnership and not a WOS. Consequently, *OWNCHANGE* becomes 1 in the case that the foreign investor had been engaged in a JV five years ago and has since then increased its foreign equity.

The variable *CONTRACT* is one of three variables[110] in the regression model that does not specifically pertain to the UNIDO 2010/11 Investor Survey. *CONTRACT* represents a variable at host country-level and not at the firm-level. *CONTRACT* is developed from the World Bank's Doing Business 2009 Report which covered all 20 SSA host countries in the sample (World Bank 2009). It measures a percentage value based on the value of the claim, assumed to be 200 per cent of income per capita and related to a lawful transaction between two businesses, namely a buyer and a seller. The total costs include court costs, enforcement costs and average attorney fees (World Bank 2009). The reason for selecting the Doing Business data from 2009 is to ensure a one to two year time lag between the observed costs of contract enforcement and the year of data collection of the UNIDO 2010/11 Investor Survey sample which forms the basis for the three dependent variables *PROFIT*, *CAPUTIL* and *SELFEVAL*. Gener-

109 For firms younger than 2006 but older than 2009 i.e. for firms with a tenure of less than five years, the questionnaire variable "foreign ownership share at the time of the *initial* foreign investment" was used. For cases with missing value for the variable "foreign ownership five years ago" but values for "foreign ownership share at the time of the *initial* foreign investment" in firms established before 2006 and no change between that value and the *current* foreign ownership share observed, it was inferred that there was also no change compared to reference year 2005/2006. In such instance, the case would receive a value of zero for foreign equity change over the past five years.

110 The other two variables are *BIT_DUMMY* and *CULT_PROX*.

ally, the year-by-year costs of contract enforcements have seen almost no variation for the most relevant time frame of 2007 to 2010.[111]

Table 5.2: Summary of hypotheses and associated variables

	Hypothesis	Category	Expected sign with performance	Variable name
H1	Foreign investors that have altered a given JV relationship through a recent increase of their foreign equity share (including the real option of buying out the local partner and making the transition to a WOS) will perform better than foreign investors that consider the partners' equity distribution within JVs as a static variable in spite of internal and external change dynamics.	Not assignable (unspecific)	+	*OWNCHANGE*
H2	A high associated cost of contract enforcement will lead to lower levels of FDI performance.	Transaction costs	-	*CONTRACT*
H3	An overall improvement of the country's upstream vertical supply chain (raw materials and local suppliers) will lead to enhanced FDI performance.	Transaction costs	+	*RAW_SUPP*
H4	Improvements in economic and political stability as well as the host country's regulatory framework will lead to enhanced FDI performance.	Institution-based variable	+	*STABILITY*
H5	The existence of or change of an SSA country's exposure to BITs will have no impact on FDI performance.	Institution-based variable	0	*BIT_DUMMY*
H6	A foreign investor with a diversified product range in SSA (related and unrelated) will reap a performance premium compared to mono-product foreign investors.	Industry-effects	+	*PROD_DIV*
H7	Foreign investors exhibiting higher cultural proximity to the host country will experience higher performance levels compared to foreign investors from culturally more distant countries.	Cultural distance effects	+	*CULT_PROX*
H8	Foreign investors that can draw on specific resources which are valuable, rare and difficult-to-imitate (patents, trademarks and brand names) will perform better than foreign investors with fewer such resources.	Resource-based variable	+	*RESOURCES*

111 See: http://www.doingbusiness.org/data/exploretopics/enforcing-contracts (accessed on 20 May 2016).

H9	Foreign investors that carry out R&D will perform better than foreign investors that do not carry out R&D.	Resource-based variable	+	*R_AND_D*
H10	A high proportion of skilled workers in the foreign investor's work force will lead to enhanced FDI performance.	Resource-based variable	+	*SKILL_WF*
H11	Foreign investors that are operating other FDI subsidiaries in SSA will exhibit superior subsidiary performance.	Resource-based variable	+	*SSA_EXP*

Concerning the variables *RAW_SUPP* and *STABILITY,* it is expected that an exploratory principal components analysis (PCA) for a set of twelve location factors of the SSA host country will lead to a substantial data reduction. The twelve locational variables comprise political stability, economic stability, legal framework, quality of life, bilateral and double taxation agreements, local markets, export markets, labour costs, availability of skilled labour, costs of raw materials, availability of local suppliers and incentive packages (UNIDO 2012a). They are assessed on a 5-point Likert scale of perceived change over the past 3 years, covering the range of *much worse* (1), *worse* (2), *same* (3), *better* (4) and *much better* (5). The assignment of numerical to ordinal variables is a standard statistical procedure (Labovitz 1970). Previous factor analyses carried out on a location factor matrix with an analogue structure[112] generated factors for "Availability of Production Inputs" (Kratzsch 2005, Bartels et al. 2008) and "Vertical Integration Transaction Costs" (Bartels et al. 2009). The factors generated in these previous studies show great proximity to the variable *RAW_SUPP.* By the same token, *STABILITY* resembles the factor of "Political Economy of Investment Climate" (Kratzsch 2005, Bartels et al. 2008) and "Political Economy Infrastructure for Investment" (Bartels et al. 2009) of past studies. This bodes well for *RAW_SUPP* and *STABILITY* to emerge as separate components in the PCA of Chapter 5.3.2. The PCA will lead to the assignment of a score for each respondent foreign subsidiary. Factor scores are "composite variables which provide information

112 The data collected for UNIDO's Africa Foreign Investor Survey 2003 contained a list of 22 location factors each of which was evaluated on a Likert scale of 3 categories of ascending importance – *not important* (1), *important* (2) and *crucial* (3). The factor analysis was carried out on the basis of 718 valid responses from FDI subsidiaries in 11 SSA countries, namely Burkina Faso, Cameroon, Ethiopia, Kenya, Madagascar, Malawi, Mozambique, Nigeria, Senegal, Tanzania and Uganda.

about an individual's placement on the factor(s)" (DiStefano et al. 2009, p. 1). These standardized factor scores with a mean of zero and a standard deviation of one can subsequently be used as latent explanatory variables in a multiple regression model (Skrondal and Laake 2001, Wall and Li 2003, DiStefano et al. 2009). In the particular model at hand and subject to the emergence of the two factors *RAW_SUPP* and *STABILITY,* the standardized component scores of *RAW_SUPP* and *STABILITY* are expected to join with the other independent variables in explaining FDI performance.

The variable *BIT_DUMMY* is derived from UNCTAD's online database on BITs and IIAs.[113] It is a dummy variable that takes the value of 1 if the FDI host country has signed *and* enforced a BIT with the country of origin of the foreign investor. Otherwise, BIT takes the value of zero. A plausible cut-off date for the latest date of enforcement of the BIT is at the end of the year 2009 in order to have an effect on FDI performance in the year 2010/2011 when the UNIDO Investor Survey was conducted. BITs signed and enforced later than 2009 will lead to a coding of zero of the dummy variable *BIT_DUMMY.*

PROD_DIV will be derived from the Herfindahl index of product concentration based on the three main products of the foreign subsidiary and their current share in the annual turnover of the company (Herfindahl 1950, Hirschman 1964). The variable has its origin in the UNIDO 2010/11 Investor Survey questionnaire (UNIDO 2012a). The Herfindahl index represents the sum of the squared product shares of the firm in annual turnover and ranges from 0.33 for the most diversified to 1 for the most concentrated i.e. a mono-product firm.[114] To swap the sign from negative to positive in the sense of Hypothesis H6, namely that the diversified foreign firm achieves higher performance, *PROD_DIV* is transformed as 1 minus the firm's individual Herfindahl index. The Herfindahl index has previously been applied in the FDI performance literature (Lu and Beamish 2001).

113 Available under: http://investmentpolicyhub.unctad.org (accessed on 6 September 2015).

114 The Herfindahl index is calculated as $\sum_{j=1}^{3} S_j^2$, where S_j represents the product's share in the firm's total annual turnover. In cases where the respective shares of the three products did not add up to 100 per cent of total turnover, the shares have been normalized and were put in relation to the cumulative turnover generated only from these three products.

The construction of the variable *CULT_PROX* is complicated by the fact that Hofstede's six dimensions of national culture are only available for eleven of the 20 survey countries (Burkina Faso, Cape Verde, Ethiopia, Ghana, Kenya, Malawi, Mozambique, Nigeria, Senegal, Tanzania and Zambia).[115] Moreover, the cultural distance measure requires a pairing of data on national culture by both the SSA host country and the respective country of FDI origin. Data gaps at the level of the FDI host countries are aggravated by data gaps at the FDI country of origin. This applies especially for intra-SSA FDI causing omissions of observations from FDI investors from Mauritius, Sudan, Uganda and others for which Hofstede's national culture variables do not exist. It is hence impractical to apply Hofstede's measure of cultural distance because it would severely curtail the sample size of the analysis and consequently reduce the overall explanatory power of the FDI performance model.

A fitting alternative to cultural distance could be the linguistic diversity between the home and host country of FDI. Linguistic diversity goes beyond the concept of differences in business cultures and alludes to the meta-concept of *psychic* distance. Numerous scholars found that language differences can add to the liability of foreignness which, in turn, acts as an elevator of transaction costs (Johanson and Wiedersheim-Paul 1975, Stöttinger and Schlegelmilch 1998, Demirbag et al. 2007, López-Duarte and Vidal-Suárez 2010). The study of Dow and Karunaratra is persuasive in showing that Hofstede's composite measure of cultural distance represents a poor surrogate for psychic distance compared to language differences which have a significantly better predictive effect on international trade flows (Dow and Karunaratna 2006). In this context, West and Graham found that linguistic distance is linked to Hofstede's cultural value dimensions and they demonstrated that the "key predictor of employees' or managers' values and behaviours is the language they speak" (West and Graham 2004, p. 257). As a result, the construction of a language difference variable can be considered a good and perhaps even better substitute to Hofstede's measure of cultural distance. A further advantage of a language difference variable is that it enshrines antecedent colonial ties between the FDI country of origin and the FDI host country (Dow and Karunaratna 2006). This aspect is of particular relevance in the context of this Book. With the exception of Ethiopia, all other 19 SSA countries have

115 See http://geert-hofstede.com/countries.html (accessed on 28 November 2015).

a historical relationship with their last colonizer Belgium, France, the UK or Portugal. This colonial legacy has an effect to the present day because the languages commonly spoken in these SSA countries are indeed French, English or Portuguese. The construction of the variable *CULT_PROX* follows that of earlier studies that included language differences (Srivastava and Green 1986, Arora and Fosfuri 2000). *CULT_PROX* is a dummy variable that takes the value of 1 if the home and the host country have at least one of their official languages in common and 0 otherwise.

The first of the four resource-based variables in the analysis is *RESOURCES* which is a Likert scale variable that combines three different questions from the UNIDO 2010/11 Investor Survey questionnaire. The respondent makes a subjective assessment of how important the foreign parent company, the foreign JV partner or the owner of the business group is for assisting in the effective use of patents, trademarks or brand names (UNIDO 2012a). The Likert scale has five points ranging from *not important* (1), *slightly important* (2), *important* (3), *very important* (4), to *crucial* (5). Numerical values of 1 to 5 will be assigned to represent the corresponding rank (Labovitz 1970).

The second resource-based variable is *R_AND_D* which takes the value of 1 if the foreign investor has spent a positive amount on R&D for technological upgrading over the last three years. Otherwise the dummy variable takes a value of 0. The data source is the UNIDO 2010/11 Investor Survey (UNIDO 2012a).

The third resource-based variable *SKILL_WF* takes a value between 0 to 100 per cent and describes the aggregated share of the foreign investor's technical, supervisory or managerial staff in the full-time employees of the preceding financial year. The assumption is that employees in these categories should normally have higher skills levels compared to production workers and clerical or administrative staff.[116] The data source is the UNIDO 2010/11 Investor Survey (UNIDO 2012a). Moreover,

116 An important caveat is that the existence of supposedly highly-skilled job positions in the technical, supervisory or managerial domains does per se not give an indication of the *actual* skills level of the holder of the position. It might happen that the actual skills level of the incumbent is inadequate or insufficient for the job. To quantify this effect, additional data would have to be collected on the academic background, references, etc., of employees.

SKILL_WF mimics the skills variable that UNIDO had employed to predict labour productivity of FDI in Viet Nam (UNIDO 2012c).

The fourth resource-based variable *SSA_EXP* addresses the extent of SSA experience that a particular foreign investor has accumulated in parallel to business activities in the particular SSA host country under observation. To this end, UNIDO has collected data on the additional number of foreign establishments of the TNC or the FE in other SSA countries (UNIDO 2012a). A logarithmic transformation is employed to mitigate the right skew of the distribution[117] of the total number of subsidiaries in SSA and to draw in large values to converge the normal distribution. The subsidiary of the respective respondent is added to the other subsidiaries in SSA. The total number of subsidiaries is thus always an integer equal to or greater than 1 prior to logarithmic transformation. This avoids producing a log (0) which is not defined.

5.2.3 Control variables

The model will employ a number of control variables that are likely to influence FDI performance and which will help to reveal the explanatory power of the independent variables.

5.2.3.1 Subsidiary age

The model controls for the age of the subsidiary, which conforms to previous studies (Li 1995, Park and Russo 1996, Zhan 2006, Dhanaraj and Beamish 2009). Some found a non-monotonic relationship between subsidiary age and its performance levels (Park and Russo 1996, Dhanaraj and Beamish 2009). As an exception, the study of Chowdury constructs the age of the subsidiary as a dependent variable of entry mode performance which infers that older subsidiaries are an expression of longevity and high stability (Chowdhury 1992).

It is reasonable to assume that subsidiaries undergo a vulnerable phase during the first years of their existence during which they incur heightened transaction costs not only for setting up the actual operations but also due

117 The distribution is right skewed due to a large number of single-subsidiary observations in SSA.

to the required adaptation to the local environment and the costs of foreignness that are associated with such an adaptation process. Financial and subjective performance indicators are therefore likely to be below their optimum levels.

On the one hand, the initial infusion of resources and high levels of commitment by the parent firm may cushion performance discounts during the initial years and keep the risk of early termination relatively low regardless of the mode of initial entry (Kogut 1989, Hennart et al. 1998). This period is followed by a peak of higher risk of termination in the middle-age of the subsidiary when the parent firms start to critically scrutinize the ratio of resource commitment and the ensuing rates of financial return. Finally, performance levels often stabilize and the risk of termination declines again in older subsidiaries (Woodcock et al. 1994, Li 1995, McCloughan and Stone 1998).

On the other hand, overall resource constrains can make the parent firm reluctant to commit to a series of sequential capital boosts for a young and ailing subsidiary. There is no riskier phase for subsidiary failure than during the first couple of years of its operational existence. Li and Guisinger found that 70 per cent of foreign-controlled business failures occurred within the first five years of investments (Li and Guisinger 1991).

Age will be measured as the difference between the year of observation (2010) and the year when the subsidiary originally started regular operations (UNIDO 2012a). The distribution is skewed to the right with a mean value that is larger than the median. A logarithmic transformation is performed in order to normalize the distribution and pull closer larger age values pertaining to very old subsidiaries from colonial times. The control variable is named *CONTROL_AGE*.

5.2.3.2 Subsidiary size

The model also controls for the size of the subsidiary. Such an approach is in line with other studies, especially those with a focus on determinants of subsidiary survival and longevity (Li and Guisinger 1991, Li 1995, McCloughan and Stone 1998, Lu and Beamish 2001, Konopaske et al. 2002, Hewett et al. 2003, Gaur et al. 2007, Gaur and Lu 2007, Mudambi and Zahra 2007, McDonald et al. 2008, Slangen and Hennart 2008, Dhanaraj and Beamish 2009, Ogasavara and Hoshino 2009, Gammelgaard et al. 2012, Chang et al. 2013, He et al. 2015). Smaller firms are assumed to have a larger failure rate than large firms although their lower survival probability is often offset by higher profitability levels (Li and Guisinger 1991, Dhawan 2001).

The majority of studies have used the total number of employees or its logarithm to control for firm size (McCloughan and Stone 1998, Luo and Peng 1999, Lu and Beamish 2001, Gaur et al. 2007, Gaur and Lu 2007, McDonald et al. 2008, Dhanaraj and Beamish 2009, Ogasavara and Hoshino 2009, Gammelgaard et al. 2012). Luo and Peng, who also used the number of employees as proxy of subsidiary size, argued that "a large size may present a more diverse range of experience, thus giving the MNE more options for exploration and exploitation of opportunities" (Luo and Peng 1999, p. 280). Contrary to expectations, the results for a sample of foreign subsidiaries in China indicate that large subsidiaries underperform in terms of ROS or return on equity (ROE) compared to smaller subsidiaries (Luo and Peng 1999). Similar results have been found related to labour productivity performance (Gaur et al. 2007) and ROA (Lu and Beamish 2001). Concerning subsidiary survival or longevity, it is argued that large subsidiaries are the expression of a greater resource commitment by the MNE and that large subsidiaries can therefore expect greater financial support from the MNE parent which mitigates the risk of their mortality (Slangen and Hennart 2008). In some instances, larger subsidiaries (measured by the number of employees) do indeed stand a better chance of survival than their smaller counterparts (McCloughan and Stone 1998, Dhanaraj and Beamish 2009). Other studies, however, could not find a significant relationship (Slangen and Hennart 2008, Ogasavara and Hoshino 2009).

Alternative measures of subsidiary size can be the total sales of the subsidiary (Li 1995, Konopaske et al. 2002, Hewett et al. 2003) or the subsidiary's assets (Chang et al. 2013, He et al. 2015). Chang et al. observed that JVs that govern a larger volume of assets are less likely to be dissolved for conversion to a WOS because the foreign partner would have to mobilize more capital to buy out the local JV partner (Chang et al. 2013).

The variable *CONTROL_SIZE* will be based on the logarithmically normalized values of the subsidiary's total fixed assets[118] at the beginning of the last financial year (UNIDO 2012a). A small number of foreign firms whose fixed assets have been valuated at zero USD were converted to one USD so as to permit logarithmical transformation.

5.2.3.3 Entry mode

As discussed in Chapter 4.1, it is reasonable to address the choices of FDI entry mode as a two-dimensional construct that is influenced by industry, institutional and host country factors (Brouthers and Hennart 2007, Dikova and van Witteloostuijn 2007). On the one hand, a foreign firm will select the appropriate establishment mode which describes the firm's choice of entering the SSA host economy as a greenfield investment or through an M&A (Slangen and Hennart 2007). On the other hand, the foreign investor has the choice between sharing the investment costs with a JV partner or to fully bearing these costs from its own equity as WOS.

As discussed previously, firms will be rational in choosing the entry mode that is believed to propel future performance. The choice occurs against the background of the MNE's individual exposure to transaction costs due to the specificity of assets owned by it, its internal resources and the riskiness of location factors in the FDI host country. In the absence of a rigid experimental setting where entry mode strategies are randomly assigned to groups of firms to measure whether one strategy is unconditionally more successful than the other, the effect of entry mode on FDI performance might be endogenous (Shaver 1998, Brouthers 2002). Against such a scenario, the independent variables presented in the previous Chapter 5.2.2 might not only explain a significant degree of variation of the FDI performance outcome variable but might also have a causal effect on the entry mode choice. That would cause the entry mode to become an endogenous variable that correlates with the error term of the OLS regression model.

118 Fixed assets in the UNIDO 2010/11 Investor Survey questionnaire comprise a.) land improvements, buildings and other construction; b.) machinery and other equipment (except transport and ICT equipment); c.) ICT equipment; d.) Transport equipment; and e.) Intellectual property (including patents, software, copyrights).

The decision to classify entry mode variables as control variables instead as predictor variables is due to the fact that the results in the literature have been very mixed (see Chapter 4.2.1) and that no reasonable hypothesis on the direction of the relationship of entry mode on FDI performance could be developed under *ceteris paribus* conditions. The classification of a possibly endogenous variable as a control variable does not, however, fully rule out a contamination effect on the other remaining explanatory variables. A set of complex statistical techniques would be necessary to alleviate this effect. These entail the inclusion of additional instrumental variables or non-parametric estimation methods (Frölich 2008). Instrumental variables have either taken the form of an entry mode "fit" variable (Brouthers 2002, Brouthers and Nakos 2004) or a self-selection parameter (Heckman 1979, Shaver 1998, Mudambi and Zahra 2007, Brouthers et al. 2008a) for subsequent incorporation as a predictor variable into the second-stage OLS regression model.

Some caution is thus in order when interpreting the influence of the entry mode control variable on FDI performance. The risk of erroneous results will be somewhat mitigated by including model specifications that will present the results both with and without the entry mode control variable.[119] The two entry mode control variables will be named *ESTABLISH* and *OWNERSHIP.* Both are dummy variables and are generated from UNIDO's 2010/11 Investor Survey dataset (UNIDO 2012a). *ESTABLISH* takes a value of 1 if the foreign investor entered the SSA country as greenfield investor and it takes the value of 0 in the case of an M&A. *OWNERSHIP* takes a value of 1 if the foreign investor runs a WOS and it takes the value of 0 if the equity is shared with a local JV partner. A foreign subsidiary with a foreign equity share of equal or more than 10 per cent and lower than 90 per cent is classified as a JV. A WOS entails a foreign equity share of 90 per cent or more. No statistical distinction is made between whether the foreign company has engaged one or more local JV partners.

119 As recommended under http://marcfbellemare.com/wordpress/11057 (accessed on 13 December 2015) bearing in mind that the omission of the entry mode control variable reduces possible endogeneity effects but might, however, in turn induce an omitted-variable bias.

5.2.3.4 Export orientation

In the overall firm-level literature, the variable of export intensity is usually regarded as a non-random variable because the foreign firm can deliberately decide to increase or decrease its export share. More productive firms would self-select to become exporters and would be in a better position to cope with the costs of international market entry than less productive firms. The overview provided by Girma et al. illustrates that numerous previous studies have indeed found evidence for a self-selection effect of exporting firms in that these firms are more productive than domestic firms before starting to export (Girma et al. 2004). The majority of studies did not observe productivity gains after the firm had obtained the status of an exporter (Clerides et al. 1998, Bernard and Bradford Jensen 1999). Two studies with a focus on manufacturing exporters in SSA contradict this in that they both find a learning-by-exporting effect which translates into productivity gains after the company has become an exporter (Bigsten et al. 2004, Van Biesebroeck 2005). Bigsten et al. find no direct self-selection effect whereas Van Biesebroeck finds a self-selection effect compounded with a learning-by-exporting effect.

The application of the same research question away from an unspecific firm-level concept towards the foreign subsidiary as the unit of analysis has been quite rare in the international business literature. Notwithstanding, there is recognition that the export orientation of the foreign subsidiary would expose it, as much as any other firm, to fluctuations of international market demand combined with competitive pressures that may impact on the pricing policies of exported products, exchange rate fluctuations and distance to markets (Ellis 2007). FDI-related literature has focused on the link between export orientation and FDI subsidiary performance (Pan and Chi 1999, He et al. 2015), the role of export orientation as determinant of the chosen entry mode (Estrin et al. 2009) and the effect of export orientation on other MNE actions such as technological upgrading through sequential investments (Song 2002).

FDI subsidiaries with high export intensity are often the outcome of vertical or efficiency-seeking FDI which involves the shifting of labour-intensive production steps to locations with low factor and particularly low labour costs (Kumar 1994, UNCTAD 1998, Shatz and Venables 2000). The main motive of the original investment thus acts as a critical determinant of the subsidiary's export propensity (Dunning 1993). Unlike the results from domestic firm-level data which point towards a self-selection effect of competitive firms to become international exporters, a clear relationship is not observable in the case of foreign subsidiaries (Pan and Chi 1999). A ROA analysis amongst foreign subsidiaries in China has shown that lower levels of export propensity (higher levels of market orientation) translate into greater levels of profitability in the presence of other variables such as subsidiary age, subsidiary experience, host country institutional factors and other factors (He et al. 2015).

These somewhat controversial results between general firm-level vs. foreign subsidiary data make it difficult to establish a hypothesis on the direction of the relationship between FDI export orientation and performance. Export intensity is nevertheless likely to influence FDI performance through the mere fact that exporters face different market dynamics and a different mix of transaction costs compared to purely local market-seeking FDI subsidiaries. The variable *EXP_INTENSE* is thus added as a control variable. It is created from UNIDO's 2010/11 Investor Survey questionnaire and describes the percentage of exports in the sales of the foreign company during the last financial year (UNIDO 2012a).

5.2.3.5 Industry sector

Amongst the set of independent variables listed in the previous chapter, *PROD_DIV* has been classified as an industry-related variable that describes the degree of product diversification of the foreign subsidiary in SSA. Notwithstanding the relevance of product diversification to MNE performance (Geringer et al. 1989, Tallman and Li 1996), the variable of *PROD_DIV* appears to be blatantly insufficient in enveloping all other underlying and unobserved industry effects. As highlighted in Box 4 before, serious data paucity and obsolescence of industry-level data in SSA inhibit the development of a more sophisticated model that would incorporate important dimensions such as market concentration, intra-industry competition and industry-specific entry barriers on FDI performance. In recognition of the wealth of literature on industry-level effects on firm behaviour and performance (Porter 1980, Schmalensee 1985, Rumelt 1991, Powell 1996, Luo 1999, Elango and Sambharya 2004), it is indispensable to add at least one control variable that describes the main industrial sector of the foreign investor. The inclusion of industry-specific control variables is very common in the extant FDI performance literature (Brouthers 2002,

Brouthers et al. 2003, Gaur and Lu 2007, Dhanaraj and Beamish 2009, Ogasavara and Hoshino 2009, He et al. 2015).

Three different industry-specific control variables are created and they will be successively applied in the different model specifications. Since the sample consists of only firms in the secondary sector, a manufacturing dummy, *MF_DUMMY* is created which is 1 for FDI in the manufacturing sector and zero for FDI in non-manufacturing industries i.e. electricity, gas and water supply as well as the construction sector. A further control variable is *TECH_INT* which describes the technology intensity of a given manufacturing subsector. The sample will shrink to manufacturing foreign firms whenever *TECH_INT* is picked as control variable. Technology intensity is not defined for non-manufacturing industries. *TECH_INT* is an ordinal variable and follows the classification of the manufacturing sector into low-tech manufacturing (1), medium-tech manufacturing (2) and high-tech manufacturing (3). This classification was first presented in Chapter 3.2 and is consistent with classification schemes introduced by OECD and applied by UNIDO (OECD 2005a, UNIDO 2015a). The most granular disaggregation of the industrial sector of the foreign investor is provided in control variable *IND_SUBSEC* which covers 16 categories of industrial subsectors, of which eight subsectors fall under the category of low-tech manufacturing, four under medium-tech manufacturing, three under high-tech manufacturing and one representing non-manufacturing industry.[120] Taking into consideration that the degrees of freedom in the OLS regression residuals should be n-1, the *IND_SUBSEC* variable is

120 Some further aggregations had been necessary compared to the subsector categories presented in Chapter 3.2. This was the case for the dummy "Food, beverages and tobacco" which merges food and beverages (ISIC category 15) and tobacco (ISIC category 16); "Wood products and furniture" combines wood products except furniture (ISIC category 20) and furniture and n.e.c. (ISIC category 36); "Other low-tech manufacturing" combines leather and related products (ISIC category 19) and recycling (ISIC category 37); "Non-metallic minerals, coke and petroleum products" aggregate coke and refined petroleum products (ISIC category 23) and other non-metallic mineral products (26); "Machinery and equipment" combines machinery and equipment n.e.c. (ISIC category 29), office, accounting and computing machinery (ISIC category 30), electrical machinery and apparatus (ISIC category 31), radio, TV and communications equipment (ISIC category 32) and medical, precision and optical instruments (ISIC category 33); "Vehicles and transport equipment" merges motor vehicles, trailers and semi-trailers (ISIC category 34) with other transport equipment (ISIC Category 35).

transformed into 15 sectoral dummy variables which take the value of 1 if the foreign firm operates in the respective sector or zero otherwise.[121]

5.2.3.6 Host country

The literature review of Chapter 4.4 revealed that prevalent institutional factors and host country conditions are important determinants of FDI subsidiary performance (Christmann et al. 1999, Makino et al. 2004, Chan et al. 2008). This reasoning led to the creation of the two independent variables *STABILITY* (economic and political stability) and *BIT_DUMMY* (existence of a BIT between the FDI investor home country and the SSA host country). Although both variables are expected to explain a respectable portion of FDI performance variance, they still constitute an insufficient proxy of each host country's idiosyncratic mix of location factors such as capital, labour force availability, land availability, natural resources, geographical remoteness (e.g. landlocked vs. not landlocked) and other factors as delineated in the location-based (L) advantages of Dunning's eclectic OLI paradigm (Dunning 1993).

Two control variables are created to reflect the wider SSA region and the individual SSA host country in which the foreign investor has established FDI operations. The first control variable divides the set of 20 SSA countries that participated in UNIDO's 2010/11 Investor Survey into two broad subregions, namely Western/Middle Africa as opposed to Eastern/ Southern Africa.[122] The resulting dummy variable is named *SSAWEST-MID* and takes the value of 1 if the foreign investor has its operations in Burkina Faso, Cameroon, Cape Verde, Côte D'Ivoire, Ghana, Mali, Nigeria or Senegal and zero otherwise. As a more precise alternative, host country dummies, deducted from the variable *HOST_COUNTRY*, will be included in some model specifications.

121 The dummy variable to be dropped is "non-manufacturing industry".

122 The separation into these two groups follows UNCTAD's classification of SSA into Eastern Africa, Middle Africa, Southern Africa, Western Africa and Northern Africa (only Sudan), see UNCTAD FDI database http://www.unctad.org/fdistatistics (accessed on 11 February 2015).

5.3 Analysis and results

The following sub-chapter will start by providing descriptive results of the employed set of variables. It continues to present an exploratory PCA which is aimed at producing a set of principal components whose scores would complete the predefined set of independent variables. Ideally, the PCA will produce at least two components which match with the hypothesized variables *RAW_SUPP* and *STABILITY* for testing hypotheses H3 and H4. Finally, several OLS regression model specifications will be presented to measure the FDI performance outcomes against the set of independent variables and against varying combinations of control variables.

5.3.1 Descriptive results

The descriptive statistics, presented in the following Table 5.3, will cover the number of observations, the mean, the median, the minimum and maximum and the standard deviation of employed variables. In the case of ordinal or discrete variables, additional statistical results for skewness and kurtosis will help gauge the proximity of observed distributions to the normal distribution. The descriptive results need to be interpreted with caution especially where the variable has been subjected to a rank or logarithmic transformation, as is the case for *PROFIT*, *SSA_EXP*, *CONTROL_AGE* and *CONTROL_SIZE*.

Furthermore, the model contains several dummy variables whose minimum and maximum is naturally defined as zero and 1. In such cases, the most meaningful descriptive measure is the mean which provides the percentage of observations that have been coded as 1. In the case of *OWNCHANGE*, it means that 7.6 per cent of foreign firms in the sample activated higher levels of foreign equity and increased their control in the JV. Related to *BIT_DUMMY*, 30.7 per cent of foreign investors have their origin in a country that has concluded a BIT with the SSA host country. More than 55 per cent of foreign investors experience communality in terms of official language between their home and the SSA host country (*CULT_PROX*). Some form of R&D is conducted by 34.3 per cent of foreign investors. The greenfield establishment mode is clearly preferred by foreign investors, which explains the mean of 88 per cent for the variable *ESTABLISH*. Nearly 70 per cent of foreign firms prefer WOSs, as indicated by the descriptive results of the *OWNERSHIP* control variable. A total of 1,340 firms of 1,499 firms in the sample are manufacturing firms which explains the mean value of 89.4 per cent of variable *MF_DUMMY. SSAWESTMID* takes a value of 1 if the foreign subsidiary is based in Western or Middle Africa. This applies for 430 foreign subsidiaries (28.7 per cent). The standard deviations for dummy variables are reported for reasons of completeness although the respective means offer sufficient information on the dispersion of data values.

The skewness and kurtosis tests indicate that not all of the variables follow the normality assumption.[123] However, more important for the reliability of the OLS regression model is the absence of heteroscedasticity (to be tested later) which would cause the error term to deviate from a normal distribution (Ramanathan 1995). The sign of the skewness indicator designates the direction of the skew. For example, the mean capacity utilization of foreign firms in the sample is 65.5 per cent and hence less than the median of 70 per cent. *CAPUTIL* is thus skewed to the left. The mean of the dependent variable *SELFEVAL* is very close to "3" whereas the median is exactly "3". This indicates that the perceived performance is in line with prior expectations. The transformed Herfindahl index of product diversification has a mean value of 0.309 which is only slightly lower than its median of 0.368. This results in a close fit to the normality assumption. On average, 16.3 per cent of the full-time work force belongs to the company's technical, supervisory or managerial staff and can thus be classified as skilled (see *SKILL_WF*).

A further result is that the mean export intensity, *EXP_INTENSE,* accounted for 21.4 per cent of annual sales of the previous fiscal year. The median of *EXP_INTENSE* is zero. The ensuing high standard deviation confirms that the group is split into a very large group of local market-oriented foreign firms with no exports in contrast to global market-seeking firms that generate almost the totality of their sales abroad.

The descriptive results are followed by an analysis of variance (ANOVA) to test for significant differences between the means of the three performance variables *PROFIT, CAPUTIL* and *SELFEVAL* for different combinations of categorical variables. The following Table 5.4 displays the results.

123 Shapiro-Wilk and Kolmogorov-Smirnov tests were significant, which means that the null hypothesis of normality in distribution was in some instances rejected.

Table 5.3: Descriptive statistics of variables employed in the regression model

Variable Name	Type	N	Mean	Median	Min	Max	Standard deviation	Skewness		Kurtosis	
								Statistic	Std. Error	Statistic	Std. Error
PROFIT	Dependent	1,336	5.525	5.5	1	10	2.852	-0.007	0.0669	-1.208	0.134
CAPUTIL	Dependent	1,294	0.655	0.7	0.01	1	0.218	-0.798	0.068	0.533	0.136
SELFEVAL	Dependent	1,471	3.126	3	1	5	0.721	-0.166	0.0638	0.318	0.128
OWNCHANGE	Independent	1,415	0.0763	0	0	1	0.266				
CONTRACT	Independent	1,499	39.983	26.7	14.3	142.5	31.842	2.397	0.0632	4.966	0.126
BIT_DUMMY	Independent	1,389	0.307	0	0	1	0.461				
PROD_DIV	Independent	1,471	0.309	0.358	0	0.666	0.260	-0.091	0.064	-1.662	0.128
CULT_PROX	Independent	1,405	0.557	1	0	1	0.470				
RESOURCES	Independent	1,271	3.544	4	1	5	1.143	-0.683	0.0686	-0.103	0.137
R_AND_D	Independent	1,388	0.343	0	0	1	0.475				
SKILL_WF	Independent	1,430	0.163	0.121	0	1	0.153	2.326	0.065	7.119	0.129
SSA_EXP	Independent	1,324	0.315	0	0	4.615	0.654	2.248	0.0672	5.153	0.134
CONTROL_AGE	Control	1,474	2.663	2.708	0	4.727	0.866	-0.293	0.0637	-0.187	0.127
CONTROL_SIZE	Control	1,222	13.786	14.018	0	25.248	2.768	-1.702	0.067	8.339	0.14
ESTABLISH	Control	1,459	0.88	1	0	1	0.325				
OWNERSHIP	Control	1,439	0.697	1	0	1	0.46				
EXP_INTENSE	Control	1,399	21.381	0	0	100	33.322	1.453	0.0654	0.677	0.131
MF_DUMMY	Control	1,499	0.894	1	0	1	0.308				
TECH_INT	Control	1,340	1.742	2	1	3	0.79	0.492	0.0668	-1.234	0.134
SSAWESTMID	Control	1,499	0.287	0	0	1	0.452				

Note: The list does not include *RAW_SUPP* and *STABILITY* since the exploratory PCA is still to be carried out in the following sub-chapter.

With the exception of the variables *BIT_DUMMY* and *MF_DUMMY*, the null hypothesis of ANOVA that there are no mean differences between groups in the population can be rejected for at least one of the three performance variables at a significance level of $p<0.1$. Starting with the variable *OWNCHANGE,* a first surprising result is that, contrary to the hypothesized positive direction of Hypothesis H1, an increase of foreign equity in a JV does not translate into a performance surplus.

Table 5.4: Analysis of variance (ANOVA) of mean performance outcomes of categorical variables

Variable	Type	Mean		
		PROFIT	*CAPUTIL*	*SELFEVAL*
OWNCHANGE	No increase (0)	5.63**	66.5***	3.15***
	Increase (1)	4.95**	59.4***	2.95***
BIT_DUMMY	No BIT (0)	5.60	65.6	3.13
	BIT (1)	5.56	67.1	3.17
CULT_PROX	No common language (0)	5.25***	66.0	3.07***
	Common language (1)	5.83***	66.2	3.18***
R_AND_D	No R&D (0)	5.02***	62.9***	3.02***
	R&D (1)	6.40***	70.8***	3.36***
ESTABLISH	M&A (0)	5.29	62.3**	2.98***
	Greenfield (1)	5.57	66.0**	3.14***
OWNERSHIP	JV (0)	5.86**	65.5	3.18*
	WOS (1)	5.44**	65.9	3.11*
MF_DUMMY	Non MF Industry (0)	5.29	68.4	3.16
	Manufacturing (1)	5.56	65.4	3.12
TECH_INT	Low-tech (1)	5.49	66.6*	3.08*
	Medium-tech (2)	5.74	65.3*	3.14*
	High-tech (3)	5.44	62.9*	3.19*
SSAWESTMID	Eastern & Southern Africa (0)	5.87***	67.6***	3.22***
	Western & Middle Africa (1)	4.58***	59.9***	2.90***
*. Significant at $p < 0.1$ level; **. Significant at $p < 0.05$ level; ***. Significant at $p < 0.01$ level				

The opposite effect is indeed observable. The mean differences are highly significant at $p<0.05$ level for the variable *PROFIT* and at $p<0.01$ level for the variables *CAPUTIL* and *SELFEVAL.* As for *CULT_PROX,* language concomitance between the FDI host and home country has a positive and highly significant effect ($p<0.01$ level) on profit margin and the subjective performance perception but no effect on capacity utilization. R&D activities result into a distinct positive performance gap between MNE subsidiaries that conduct R&D versus those that do not. The ANOVA yields highly significant results at $p<0.01$ level for *PROFIT*, *CAPUTIL* and *SELFEVAL*. MNEs that have entered the SSA host country through a greenfield investment show a significantly positive mean difference in *CAPUTIL* and *SELFEVAL* compared to their M&A counterparts. Concerning the *OWNERSHIP* variable, the mean percentile ranking of *PROFIT* reaches 5.86 for JV investors compared to 5.44 of WOSs ($p<0.05$ level). The mean difference of *SELFEVAL* points in the same direction in favour of JVs and is significant at $p<0.1$. *TECH_INT* produces significance values at $p<0.1$ level for *CAPUTIL* and *SELFEVAL* but there is no clear pattern in that any category of technology intensity would consistently outperform the other two categories. Foreign investors with operations in the high-tech sector have the most positive outcome as compared to their initial performance expectation, as indicated by the mean of 3.19 of *SELFEVAL*. In contrast, the mean capacity utilization is highest in low-tech manufacturing FDI (66.6 per cent) whereas medium-tech manufacturing performs best in terms of profit margin, although the latter is statistically insignificant. Finally, all foreign investors perform considerably better in Eastern and Southern Africa compared to Western and Middle Africa. The results are statistically highly significant at $p<0.01$.

Annex Table 10 reports the performance effects that result from FDI affiliation to a specific industrial subsector. The largest subsector in terms of frequency of foreign firms is the food, beverages and tobacco sector.[124] No significant mean difference in performance exists between the food, beverages and tobacco sector and the rest of the sample. In the same vein, the second largest sector in terms of number of firms (161 firms in *PROFIT*, 178 firms in *CAPUTIL* and 179 firms in *SELFEVAL*), the rubber and plastics sector, is not performing significantly better or worse than the rest of the sample. With regards to statistically significant differences, there is a strikingly lower performance perception by foreign investors in the global market-seeking textiles and garment sector. A similar phenomenon was observed earlier in UNIDO's "Africa Foreign Investor Survey 2005" Report (UNIDO 2007). Foreign firms affiliated to the group of "other low-tech manufacturing" (mostly FDI in the leather sector as well as the recy-

124 The number of foreign subsidiaries in this sector ranges from 240 to 260, depending on the number of observations of the performance variable *PROFIT*, *CAPUTIL* and *SELFEVAL*.

cling sector), also expressed a significantly lower subjective performance perception compared to the rest of the sample (mean of 2.75 vs. remaining sample mean of 3.13). In contrast, the technology-intensive machinery and equipment sector excels in terms of performance self-evaluation (3.27 vs. remaining sample mean of 3.12). The combined group of non-metallic mineral products and refined petroleum products displays higher profit margins compared to the rest of the sample (6.12 vs. 5.53 in the total sample, significant at $p<0.05$ level). The only significant mean difference of *CAPUTIL* ($p<0.05$ level) is observed in the chemical sector which has a capacity utilization about 4 per cent above the mean of the rest of the sample.

The large observed FDI performance differences of foreign firms in Eastern and Southern Africa versus Western and Middle Africa had adumbrated that considerable host country effects might be at play in determining the extent of FDI firm-level performance. This is validated in Annex Table 11 which provides the ANOVA results of the three performance variables for individual SSA host country dummy variables. The largest number of foreign firms in the sample is located in Kenya, namely 378 firms in the case of *PROFIT*, 367 firms in the case of *CAPUTIL* and 383 firms in the case of *SELFEVAL*. Foreign firms in Kenya yield significantly ($p<0.01$ level) higher scores in profit margins (6.43 vs. 5.17 in rest of the sample), higher rates of capacity utilization (73.2 per cent vs. 62.4 per cent in the rest of the sample) and better subjective performance scores (3.41 vs. 3.03 in the rest of the sample). This is surpassed only by FDI in Mozambique which peak on *PROFIT*, *CAPUTIL* and *SELFEVAL* ($p<0.01$ level). Both countries fall under the Eastern and Southern Africa category and thus strongly determine the observed performance gap in comparison to Western and Middle Africa. More than half of foreign investor firms in the Western and Middle Africa grouping are located in Ghana and Nigeria. The fact that FDI in both countries is far off performance levels in the majority of Eastern and Southern African countries considerably pulls down the mean performance of the Western and Middle Africa group. In addition, foreign investors in Cameroon and Senegal achieve low results for all three performance variables, especially for *PROFIT* ($p<0.01$ level) and *CAPUTIL* ($p<0.05$ level). For example, the gap between the lowest performer Senegal and the highest performer Mozambique reaches almost three percentile ranks for *PROFIT* (3.94 vs. 6.85), more than 22 per cent for *CAPUTIL* (57.5 per cent vs. 79.9 per cent) and almost a full step in the ordinal variable *SELFEVAL* (2.66 vs. 3.61). The dichotomy in performance outcomes as cautioned by Hult et al. is palpable for foreign investors in Uganda and Lesotho (Hult et al. 2008). FDI in Uganda yields high on *PROFIT* ($p<0.05$ level) but low on *CAPUTIL* ($p<0.01$ level). Foreign investors in Lesotho are overly critical in terms of performance self-evaluation ($p<0.1$ level) despite a positive 10 percentage point gap in capacity utilization (75.5 per cent vs. 65.3 per cent for the rest of the sample, $p<0.01$ level).

5.3.2 Principal component analysis of the location factor change matrix

As intimated in chapter 5.2.2, a PCA will be performed to complete the current set of independent variables by at least two more variables pertaining to the transaction cost-based Hypothesis H3 and the institution-based Hypothesis H4.

A PCA or factor analysis is "a procedure that postulates that the correlations or covariance between a set of observed variables, $x' = [x_1, x_2, \ldots x_q]$ arise from the relationship of these variables to a small number of underlying, unobservable, *latent variables,* usually known as the *common factors*" (Everitt 2002, p. 140). There are less principle components or factors $f' = [f_1, f_2, \ldots f_k]$ than variables ($k<q$). The PCA analysis differs from linear regression in the sense that it analyses mutual interdependences in which all variables are simultaneously considered whereas the regression analysis explores or predicts a dependent variable.

The analysis is based on $q=12$ locational variables comprising "political stability" (*POL_STAB*), "economic stability" (*ECON_STAB*), "transparency of business regulations and legal framework" (*LEG_FRAME*), "quality of life" (*QUAL_LIFE*), "bilateral investment treaties and double taxation agreements" (*BIT_DTT*), "local market" (*LOC_MARK*), "export market" (*EXP_MARK*), "labour costs" (*LAB_COST*), "availability of skilled labour" (*SKILL_LAB*), "costs of raw materials" (*RAW_COST*), "availability of local suppliers" (*LOC_SUPP*) and "incentive package" (*INC_PACK*) (UNIDO 2012a). Each foreign investor was asked to indicate the perceived change of each location factor over the last three years on a 5-point Likert scale ranging from *much worse* (1), *worse* (2), *same* (3), *better* (4) to *much better* (5).

Figure 5.1 displays the mean change score in descending order. The means are clustered around the middle point i.e. the score of 3 of the Likert scale which indicates that there has been no perceived change in the location factor. The median for all 12 location factors is also the score of 3. The number of responses range between 1,365 firms (*EXP_MARK*) and 1,408 firms (*ECON_STAB*). Results for skewness and kurtosis suggest an acceptable goodness-of-fit to the normal distribution.[125]

Figure 5.1: Perceived change of 12 location factor variables in SSA

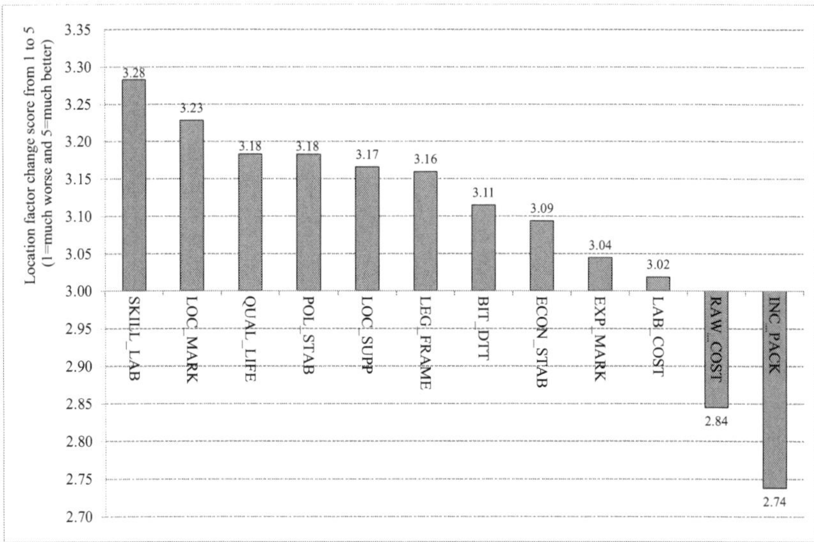

The availability of skilled labour (*SKILL_LAB*) has improved the most in the subjective assessment of foreign investors. This location factor has already been highly ranked in UNIDO's "Africa Foreign Investor Survey 2005" Report, which indicates that the perceived improvement has been consistent over a longer period of time and for different FDI sample structures in SSA (UNIDO 2007). The good score in terms of *SKILL_LAB* is corroborated by a review undertaken by the World Economic Forum (WEF) for the period of 2005 to 2012. It attributed competitive gains of SSA concerning "improvements in institutional quality, most noticeably in health and primary education, reflecting improved health conditions and gradually higher primary enrolment rates" (World Economic Forum 2012, p. 38). Location factors related to the local market, quality of life and po-

125 Shapiro-Wilk and Kolmogorov-Smirnov tests nevertheless indicate that the distribution is significantly different from a normal distribution.

litical stability have also improved as reflected in the respective scores of 3.18 and 3.23. Particularly noteworthy is the leap that the factor *QUAL_LIFE* has made compared to UNIDO's "Africa Foreign Investor Survey 2005" Report when this factor was most negatively ranked relative to other location factors (UNIDO 2007). At the more negative end of the spectrum, the two transaction cost factors of incentive package and raw materials have noticeably deteriorated in foreign investors' perceptions being quite consistent with previous results reported by UNIDO (UNIDO 2007). In particular, the low score of 2.74 of the incentive package might be explained by an emerging trend of SSA governments to gradually replace the paradigm of an across-the-board incentive policy through a more extensive application of tailored or smart incentives with the intention to foster the development of strategic industrial sectors (Asche and Fritzen 2013).

After analysing the means of the twelve locational variables, the next step consists in an analysis of their inter-correlations. The application of a list-wise exclusion of cases leads to a reduction to 1,335 cases. It is desirable that the variables share common variation as this will help in the extraction of distinctively different factors or components at a statistically larger explanatory power. Annex Table 12 confirms that all correlations are positive and highly significant at $p<0.01$ level (2-tailed). Of the 66 combinations of bivariate correlations, 47 are greater than 0.30 which, according to Tabachnik and Fidell, augurs well for a successful principal components analysis (Tabachnick and Fidell 2006). Large bivariate correlations of above +0.5 appear twice in the case of *ECON_STAB* and *POL_STAB* (+0.694; $p<0.01$) and between *ECON_STAB* and *LEG_FRAME* (+0.515; $p<0.01$). The level of correlation is still far from 1, hence there should be no problem of multicollinearity.[126] The variable *RAW_COST* also correlates significantly with *LAB_COST* (+0.493; $p<0.01$) and *INC_PACK* (+0.457; $p<0.01$). Relatively lower correlations are observable for the variable *EXP_MARK* with bivariate correlations to other variables below +0.3 except for variable *BIT_DTT* (+0.372; $p<0.01$) and *INC_PACK* (+0.327; $p<0.01$). *EXP_MARK* is also associated with the lowest bivariate correlations in the correlation matrix, namely with *POL_STAB* (+0.186; $p<0.01$) and *SKILL_LAB* (+0.213; $p<0.01$).

---

126 This is also confirmed by the Bartlett's test of sphericity whose null hypothesis is that the observed correlation matrix is equal to the identity matrix. The hypothesis can be rejected at a significance level of $p<0.001$.

An important statistical test is the Kaiser–Meyer–Olkin (KMO) measure of sampling adequacy which compares the magnitudes of the observed correlation coefficients with partial correlation coefficients. The KMO of the 12*12 correlation matrix achieves a KMO of 0.893 which is in the category of "meritorious" (KMO $\geq$ 0.8 and <0.9) and is actually close to the category of "marvellous" of greater than 0.9 and less or equal to 1 (Kaiser and Rice 1974).

Table 5.5: Explained total variance after component extraction

	Initial eigenvalues			Extraction sums of squared loadings		
Component	Total	Per cent of variance	Cumulative per cent	Total	Per cent of variance	Cumulative per cent
1	4.777	39.805	39.805	4.777	39.805	39.805
2	1.122	9.352	49.157	1.122	9.352	49.157
3	0.950	7.916	57.072	0.950	7.916	57.072
4	0.813	6.777	63.849			
5	0.713	5.945	69.794			
6	0.639	5.326	75.120			
7	0.625	5.205	80.325			
8	0.586	4.882	85.207			
9	0.542	4.513	89.720			
10	0.524	4.370	94.090			
11	0.424	3.537	97.628			
12	0.285	2.372	100.000			
Extraction Method: PCA; N=1,335.						

The objective of the analysis lies clearly in data reduction through a PCA instead of the detection of a structural relationship between variables which is the purpose of a Factor Analysis (Tabachnick and Fidell 2006). In the statistical practice, both approaches of PCA vs. Factor Analysis yield, however, nearly similar results (Velicer and Jackson 1990). The PCA is to identify components[127] that account for the maximum portion of variance i.e. common, specific and error variance innate to the set of twelve location factor change variables (Beavers et al. 2013). The sum of all squared component loadings, or the component communality, is highest for the

127 In the context of the analysis, the term "factor" or "component" might sometimes be used interchangeably, however bearing in mind that the extraction method was PCA and not Factor Analysis.

variables *ECON_STAB* (0.765), *POL_STAB* (0.713) and *BIT_DTT* (0.524) which indicates that these three variables might be instrumental in forming a component though not necessarily the same component.[128] The communality value for *SKILL_LAB* is the lowest of all twelve variables. Table 5.5 on the previous page shows the outcome of component extraction.

The extraction of the number of factors often follows the Kaiser-criterion. It stipulates that a factor should only be retained if it has an eigenvalue of greater than 1 and thus explains the variance of at least one single variable in the analysis (Kaiser 1960). This method has not been free of criticism and has prompted several researchers to stress that other aspects such as the form of the scree plot (Cattell 1966) and the total variance to be explained by all factors of the model deserve heightened attention (Fabrigar et al. 1999, Henson and Roberts 2006, Beavers et al. 2013). In this light, it is decided to override an overly strict application of the Kaiser-criterion and to retain three instead of two components for component rotation. The eigenvalue of 0.950 of the third component is considered to have enough numeric closeness to an eigenvalue of 1. The conservation of three components ensures that the total variance explained by the model exceeds the 50 per cent threshold and now explains 57 per cent of variation. No more than these three components will be extracted to avoid noisy results stemming from component over-extraction (Fava and Velicer 1992, Henson and Roberts 2006).

The un-rotated solution, not reported here, renders blurry results and fails to clearly delineate which variable items load more on one component as opposed to another. For this reason component rotation will be necessary. To enhance the interpretability of the final solution, the oblique rotation method of "Direct Oblimin" will be applied instead of an orthogonal rotation method. Allowing components to be correlated may lead to less clinical but usually more realistic empirical constructs in social science research (Fabrigar et al. 1999). To recapitulate, the objective of this PCA is to generate components that may eventually be inserted as explanatory variables in the regression model of FDI performance. Since some degree of inter-correlation amongst these explanatory variables is likely to occur, the insertion of component scores pertaining to forced and artificially uncorrelated and orthogonal components would introduce an unnecessary distortion into the regression model. Correlated component

128 The table of communalities is not reported.

scores are hence to be preferred. After 20 iterations, the oblique rotation produces two component matrices, the structure matrix and the pattern matrix, of which the pattern matrix better accentuates structural differences in variable item loadings on the different components. Component loadings that correspond to less than 20 per cent of explained variance ($\sqrt{0.2} = 0.447$) are blanked out and variables are sorted by descending size of their component loadings. The pattern matrix is reported as Table 5.6 below. The final step consists of a reasonable and meaningful labelling of the three principal components.

Table 5.6: Pattern matrix, oblique rotation, Direct Oblimin Method

Variable	Component		
	1	2	3
RAW_COST	0.820		
LAB_COST	0.780		
INC_PACK	0.524		
LOC_SUPP	0.477		
LOC_MARK	0.456		
SKILL_LAB			
BIT_DTT		0.748	
EXP_MARK		0.669	
ECON_STAB			0.842
POL_STAB			0.815
LEG_FRAME			0.646
QUAL_LIFE			0.499
Extraction Method: PCA. Rotation Method: Direct Oblimin with Kaiser Normalization (oblique rotation), 20 iterations; N=1,335.			

Generally, variables with higher loadings are considered more important in influencing the name of the component. All twelve variables, except the variable *SKILL_LAB*,[129] are assigned to one of the three components with at least 20 per cent of explained variance.

129 The highest loading of *SKILL_LAB* is +0.42 on "Component 1".

"Component 1", which explains 39.8 per cent of the overall variance, is largely impacted by the variable *RAW_COST*. This variable loads with a value of +0.820 on "Component 1" which means that it explains 67 per cent of the variance of *RAW_COST*. The second most important variable under "Component 1" is *LAB_COST* with a loading of +0.78, followed by *INC_PACK* which has a loading of +0.524. The emphasis on the transaction cost dimension in foreign production emerges quite blatantly from these first three variables. The PCA confirms that foreign investors perceive the changes in the mix of transaction costs in the host country as a common construct which can be subsumed under "Component 1". The fact that local suppliers and local markets are also associated with this component, albeit with lower respective loadings of +0.477 and +0.456, must not be in contradiction to this hypothesis. Both might entail transaction cost savings for the MNE stemming from lower dependence of potentially costly and unreliable import channels in the case of *LOC_SUPP* as well as economies of scale through increased volumes in market demand adherent to the variable *LOC_MARK*. *RAW_COST, LAB_COST* and *LOC_SUPP* also allude directly to *inputs* to foreign production. An accurate label of "Component 1" is therefore *"Costs in supply of input factors of production"*. This does justice to *RAW_COST* as the weightiest variable of "Component 1" and also to *LOC_SUPP*. Both are upstream production inputs that need to be organized, monitored and remunerated within the context of a vertically structured local supply chain. It is also in keeping with the results of previous factor analyses that were carried out on a related scale-based location factor matrix and that subsumed variables under a factor labelled "Availability of Production Inputs" (Kratzsch 2005, Bartels et al. 2008) and "Vertical Integration Transaction Costs" (Bartels et al. 2009). Recalling the literature review of Chapter 4.3 and the reasoning that led to the development of Hypothesis H3 "*An overall improvement of the country's upstream vertical supply chain (raw materials and local suppliers) will lead to enhanced FDI performance*", it is sound to allow component scores of "*Costs in supply of input factors of production*" to complement the regression model as independent variables. From now on, the component scores will be represented by the independent variable *RAW_SUPP*, as introduced before in Chapter 5.2.2.

"Component 2" had an eigenvalue of greater than 1 and explained somewhat more than 9 per cent of the overall variance. It consists of the two variables *BIT_DTT* and *EXP_MARK* each of which display a loading of +0.748 and +0.669. Both variables are perhaps the most unaffiliated location factors in that they point towards the extent of the international interrelatedness of the SSA host country into a globally dispersed production network governed and controlled by large multinationals in the form of a "global factory" (Buckley 2014). In the case of *BIT_DTT,* this specific form of connectedness between the SSA country and the outside world is established at government-level through one or more binding IIAs aimed at providing a sense of greater legal security to international investors. In the case of *EXP_MARK*, the element of connectedness between the SSA host country and the outside world is defined by the degree of global value chain integration in terms of trade intensity, embodied technology content in traded products as well as the available infrastructure for import and export logistics. Both variables can be tied together because bilateral or double taxation treaties can either be concluded to be a reaction to already existing commercial relations or to be the expression of a political desire to expand such relations in the future through increased market integration and liberalization (UNCTAD 2012b, UNCTAD 2015b). A general improvement of "Component 2" is likely to impact most on efficiency-seeking and export-oriented FDI (Kumar 1994, UNCTAD 1998). To sum up, "Component 2" is best described as "*International investment policy and trade connectedness*", or in short *INT_CONNECT*. It is also possible that the variable veils a latent variable related to the physical export infrastructure of the host country. Somewhat surprisingly, the location factor of infrastructure was not amongst the list of 12 location factors although its relevance as an FDI determinant has been corroborated by several studies (Agodo 1978, Wheeler and Mody 1992, Loree and Guisinger 1995, Urata and Kawai 2000, Akinkugbe 2005, Mlambo 2005, Asiedu 2006). In the next step, the component scores of *INT_CONNECT* will be added to the set of independent variables of the regression model, while bearing in mind a potential communality with the predictor variable *BIT_DUMMY* created for testing Hypothesis H5. This can easily be validated on the basis of pairwise inter-correlations of *INT_CONNECT* with other explanatory variables and especially *BIT_DUMMY.*

"Component 3" accounts for a variance of 7.9 per cent and comprises four location factors. *POL_STAB* and *ECON_STAB* have respectively high loadings of +0.842 and +0.815 on this component. It is also logical that *LEG_FRAME* and *QUAL_LIFE* have joined "Component 3", although their loadings are considerably lower. Transparency in business regulations and legal framework (*LEG_FRAME*) can be understood as crucial ingredient for political and economic stability whereas quality of life is the corollary of the presence or absence of such stability. The structure of "Component 3" does not come as a surprise and ascertains the earlier presumption that the principal PCA would contribute *STABILITY* as the final independent variable in the regression model for testing Hypothesis H4. "Component 3" is accordingly labelled as "*Investment climate stability and transparency*". It corresponds well to factors of a similar structure namely "Political Economy of Investment Climate" (Kratzsch 2005, Bartels et al. 2008) or "Political Economy Infrastructure for Investment" (Bartels et al. 2009) and strikes a balance to the macro-economic literature highlighting macro-economic and political stability as important determinant of FDI flows and stocks in SSA (Agodo 1978, Morisset 2000, Cotton and Ramachandran 2001, Bende-Nabende 2002, Asiedu 2004a, Mlambo 2005, Asiedu 2006, Naudé and Krugell 2007).

As a final step, a reliability test will be performed to ensure that the latent construct of changes in the host country's location factors made up by the 12 location factor variables is robust and reproducible. The reliability coefficient, known as Cronbach's α (Nunnally 1978, Peterson 1994), reaches a value of α=0.861 and attests to very high levels of reliability of the list of location factors. Further reliability tests performed only on the list of five variables pertaining to former "Component 1" (now variable *RAW SUPP*) achieve a very acceptable Cronbach's α of 0.756. Former "Component 2" (now *INT_CONNECT*) has a Cronbach's α=0.538 owed to the fact that it only contains two variables.[130] Former "Component 3" (now *STABILITY*) is reliable at α=0.781.

As a result of the PCA, each foreign firm will be assigned a component score based on the regression method (Skrondal and Laake 2001). It normalizes the mean as zero and the standard deviation as one (DiStefano et al. 2009). This applies to each of the 1,335 foreign subsidiaries that were subjected to the PCA under the list-wise exclusion condition. The component score is a numerical value that indicates the relative positioning of the foreign firm on the respective component. If the component score is positive, the firm has a position above the component mean and vice versa. The skewness and kurtosis values of the component score distribution are within reasonable ranges. The component scores can hence be employed in different multivariate analyses. Although the main purpose is the cre-

130 The reliability test can be considered acceptable as long as Cronbach's α is above 0.5.

ation of missing explanatory variables for the FDI performance regression model, interesting conclusions can also be drawn from an ANOVA analysis of the component scores for the twenty SSA host countries. Box 5 and Annex Table 13 present and discuss the results.

Box 5: ANOVA results of principal components' scores

The purpose of the analysis of variance (ANOVA) is to unearth host country differences along the three main dimensions of "*Costs in supply of input factors of production*" (*RAW_SUPP*), "*International investment policy and trade connectedness*" (*INT_CONNECT*) and "*Investment climate stability and transparency*" (*STABILITY*). Since the component scores are standardized to have a mean of zero, the results of the respective country dummy and the rest of the sample are naturally oriented towards the zero-point. Annex Table 13 provides the results. Many statistically significant differences were detected. In the perception of foreign investors, the conditions in supply of input factors of production have developed over-proportionally favourably in Malawi ($p<0.05$), Mozambique ($p<0.01$), Mali and Côte d'Ivoire. In contrast to that, the perception of foreign investors in Madagascar ($p<0.01$) and Niger is considerably below the mean of the *RAW_SUPP* component. In terms of international connectedness, it is noteworthy that the positive perception of foreign investors operating in member countries of the East African Community (EAC), with the exception of Burundi, outstrips all other SSA countries. Especially foreign investors in Kenya are pleased to see the country become increasingly connected in terms of investment policies and trade ($p<0.01$). Although many land-locked countries, especially Burkina Faso ($p<0.01$), Niger ($p<0.01$) and Mali, were judged to have deteriorated on the international connectedness dimension relative to other countries, also larger coastal economies like Cameroon ($p<0.01$), Ghana ($p<0.01$) or Madagascar ($p<0.01$) are not doing too well in the perception of foreign investors.

The component scores for "*Investment climate stability and transparency*" are a reflection of SSA's political and economic situation in 2010/2011 when the UNIDO Investor Survey had been carried out. The 2010/2011 crisis in Côte d'Ivoire and the coup d'états in 2009 in Madagascar and 2010 in Niger have left heavy marks on foreign investors' perceptions. Consequently, the three countries are the farthest away from the zero-point mean of *STABILITY*. On the other hand, foreign investors have particularly honoured strides towards improved stability in Malawi ($p<0.01$), Mozambique ($p<0.01$), Rwanda ($p<0.1$), and Ethiopia ($p<0.01$).

Interesting insights are also offered when comparing inter-factor score variations for a specific country. For instance, Ethiopia has outperformed most other countries in terms of relative perception of *STABILITY* but falls behind on *INT_CONNECT*. The same perception, albeit to a lesser extent, is shared by foreign investors in Malawi and Mozambique. Box Figure 1 plots the two dimensions of *STABILITY* and *INT_CONNECT*.

Box Figure 1: Scatter plot of host country factor scores of STABILITY and INT_CONNECT

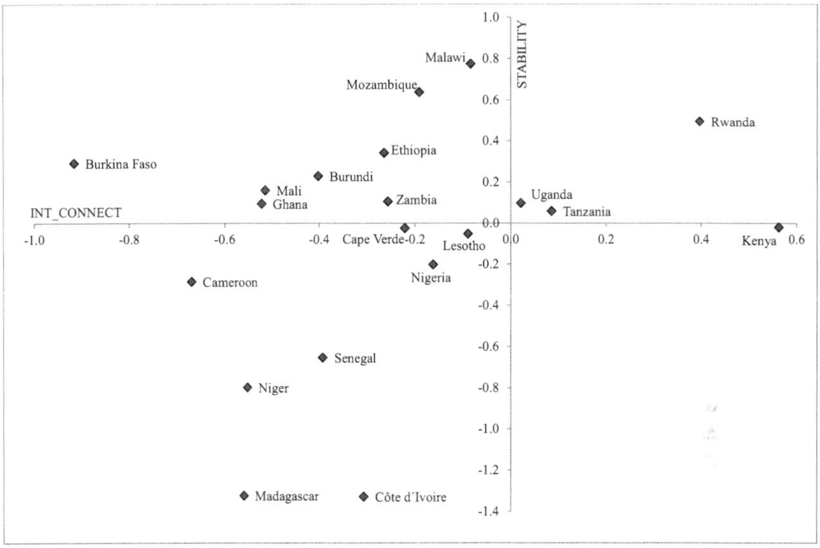

5.3.3 Regression results

The PCA of the previous chapter has provided the missing independent variables for the regression model. The models pertaining to each of the dependent variables *PROFIT*, *CAPUTIL* and *SELFEVAL* can now be written as follows:

(5)

$$\begin{aligned}
\mathrm{PROFIT_i} = {} & \alpha_1 + \beta_{1,1}OWNCHANGE_i + \beta_{1,2}CONTRACT_i \\
& + \beta_{1,3}RAW_SUPP_i + \beta_{1,4}INT_CONNECT_i + \beta_{1,5}STABILITY_i \\
& + \beta_{1,6}BIT_DUMMY_i + \beta_{1,7}PROD_DIV_i + \beta_{1,8}CULT_PROX_i \\
& + \beta_{1,9}RESOURCES_i + \beta_{1,10}R_AND_D_i + \beta_{1,11}SKILL_WF_i \\
& + \beta_{1,12}SSA_EXP_i + \beta_{1,13}CONTROL_AGE_i^* + \beta_{1,14}CONTROL_SIZE_i^* \\
& + \beta_{1,15}ESTABLISH_i^* + \beta_{1,16}OWNERSHIP_i^* + \beta_{1,17}EXP_INTENSE_i^* \\
& + \beta_{1,18}MF_DUMMY_i^* + \beta_{1,19}SSAWESTMID_i^* + \varepsilon_{1,i}
\end{aligned}$$

(6)

$$\text{CAPUTIL}_i = \alpha_2 + \beta_{2,1}OWNCHANGE_i + \beta_{2,2}CONTRACT_i + \beta_{2,3}RAW\_SUPP_i + \beta_{2,4}INT\_CONNECT_i + \beta_{2,5}STABILITY_i + \beta_{2,6}BIT\_DUMMY_i + \beta_{2,7}PROD\_DIV_i + \beta_{2,8}CULT\_PROX_i + \beta_{2,9}RESOURCES_i + \beta_{2,10}R\_AND\_D_i + \beta_{2,11}SKILL\_WF_i + \beta_{2,12}SSA\_EXP_i + \beta_{2,13}CONTROL\_AGE_i^* + \beta_{2,14}CONTROL\_SIZE_i^* + \beta_{2,15}ESTABLISH_i^* + \beta_{2,16}OWNERSHIP_i^* + \beta_{2,17}EXP\_INTENSE_i^* + \beta_{2,18}MF\_DUMMY_i^* + \beta_{2,19}SSAWESTMID_i^* + \varepsilon_{2,i}$$

(7)

$$\text{SELFEVAL}_i = \alpha_3 + \beta_{3,1}OWNCHANGE_i + \beta_{3,2}CONTRACT_i + \beta_{3,3}RAW\_SUPP_i + \beta_{3,4}INT\_CONNECT_i + \beta_{3,5}STABILITY_i + \beta_{3,6}BIT\_DUMMY_i + \beta_{3,7}PROD\_DIV_i + \beta_{3,8}CULT\_PROX_i + \beta_{3,9}RESOURCES_i + \beta_{3,10}R\_AND\_D_i + \beta_{3,11}SKILL\_WF_i + \beta_{3,12}SSA\_EXP_i + \beta_{3,13}CONTROL\_AGE_i^* + \beta_{3,14}CONTROL\_SIZE_i^* + \beta_{3,15}ESTABLISH_i^* + \beta_{3,16}OWNERSHIP_i^* + \beta_{3,17}EXP\_INTENSE_i^* + \beta_{3,18}MF\_DUMMY_i^* + \beta_{3,19}SSAWESTMID_i^* + \varepsilon_{3,i}$$

Control variables are indicated with an asterisk (*). List-wise exclusion of cases results in i = 1, 2, …n which oscillates between 757 cases in model specification 1 and 686 cases in model specification 3. In some specifications of the model, the variable *MF_DUMMY* will be substituted by *TECH_INT* or by the 15 sector dummy variables of *IND_SUBSEC*. Other model specifications will substitute *SSAWESTMID* by a maximum of 19 host country dummies *HOST_COUNTRY.* The component score variable *INT_CONNECT* will also be added to the regression models. Figure 5.2 portrays the variables of the regression model in visual form.

Figure 5.2: The complete regression model of FDI performance

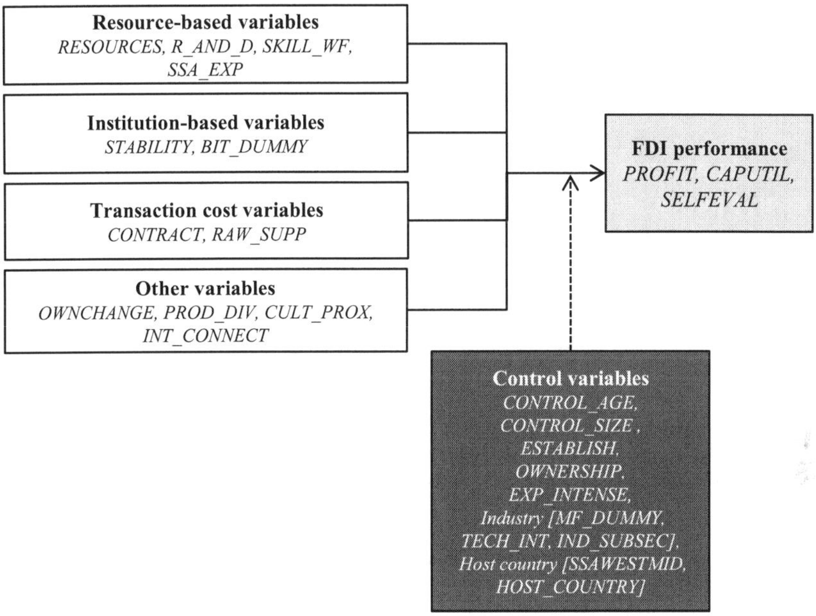

The following section checks for correlations between the three performance variables with the control and independent variables (see Table 5.7 on the following page). Amongst the control variables, *CONTROL_SIZE* exhibits positive and highly significant correlations with all three performance variables, especially *CAPUTIL* where the correlation coefficient is +0.204. A consistent inverse correlation exists between the Western and Middle Africa dummy variable and the three performance measures. *OWNERSHIP*, *EXP_INTENSE* and *MF_DUMMMY* have either no or only a weak correlation with *PROFIT*, *CAPUTIL* or *SELFEVAL*. In the case of individual host country variables, negative correlations with the three FDI performance variables are observable for Ethiopia, Ghana, Madagascar, Nigeria and Senegal (all $p<0.05$). These correlations are however quite weak and do not fall below a coefficient of minus 0.1. Kenya and Mozambique produce positive and significant correlation coefficients with *PROFIT*, *CAPUTIL* or *SELFEVAL* in the range of +0.198 and +0.232 (all $p<0.01$). Compared to country dummies, the subsector industry dummies produce only a few significant and moderate correlations with FDI performance. There is only one weakly positive correlation of +0.057 and with a significance level of $p<0.05$ between the "non-metallic minerals, coke and refined petroleum products" dummy and *PROFIT*.

Table 5.7: Pairwise correlation coefficients between PROFIT, CAPUTIL, SELFEVAL and control and independent variables

Variable	*PROFIT*	*CAPUTIL*	*SELFEVAL*
CONTROL_AGE	$+0.125^{***}$	$+0.038$	$+0.058^{**}$
CONTROL_SIZE	$+0.094^{***}$	$+0.204^{***}$	$+0.110^{***}$
ESTABLISH	$+0.031$	$+0.056^{**}$	$+0.074^{***}$
OWNERSHIP	-0.068^{**}	$+0.010$	-0.048^{*}
EXP_INTENSE	-0.015	$+0.035$	-0.065^{**}
MF_DUMMY	-0.029	-0.019	-0.015
TECH_INT	$+0.002$	$+0.075^{**}$	$+0.195^{***}$
SSAWESTMID	-0.201^{***}	-0.159^{***}	-0.198^{***}
OWNCHANGE	-0.063^{**}	-0.085^{***}	-0.073^{***}
CONTRACT	$+0.085^{***}$	$+0.094^{***}$	$+0.137^{***}$
RAW_SUPP	$+0.157^{***}$	-0.106^{***}	$+0.109^{***}$
INT_CONNECT	$+0.197^{***}$	-0.066^{**}	$+0.065^{**}$
STABILITY	$+0.144^{***}$	-0.051^{*}	$+0.102^{***}$
BIT_DUMMY	-0.007	$+0.033$	$+0.025$
PROD_DIV	-0.021	-0.137^{***}	-0.064^{**}
CULT_PROX	$+0.100^{***}$	$+0.005$	$+0.077^{***}$
RESOURCES	$+0.081^{***}$	$+0.086^{***}$	$+0.117^{***}$
R_AND_D	$+0.234^{***}$	$+0.174^{***}$	$+0.225^{***}$
SKILL_WF	-0.072^{***}	-0.090^{***}	-0.039
SSA_EXP	-0.035	$+0.098^{***}$	$+0.104^{***}$

*. Correlation is significant at the 0.1 level;
**. Correlation is significant at the 0.05 level;
***. Correlation is significant at the 0.01 level;
Pairwise exclusion of cases; N between 1,072 and 1,471.

The two high-tech manufacturing sectors, chemicals as well as vehicles and transport equipment, correlate negatively with *CAPUTIL* (-0.064 and -0.070 respectively; $p<0.05$). Textiles, garments, leather and recycling correlate weakly negatively with *SELFEVAL* ($p<0.01$) whereas machinery and equipment correlate positively with *SELFEVAL* (+0.052, $p<0.05$). In terms of the independent variables, there are consistently positive and significant correlations in the case of *CONTRACT*, *RESOURCES* and *R_AND_D* with regard to all three performance variables. *RAW_SUPP*, *INT_CONNECT* and *STABILITY* give mixed results as they display significantly positive correlation coefficients with *PROFIT* and *SELFEVAL* but a significantly negative correlation coefficient with *CAPUTIL*. The only independent variable that shows negligible levels of correlation is *BIT_DUMMY*.

The correlation matrix of independent and control variables, presented in Annex Table 14, serves to test for the presence of multicollinearity. There is no single pairwise correlation coefficient that would exceed ± 0.5. Multicollinearity becomes a matter of concern only if pairwise correlation coefficients exceed ± 0.7 (Tabachnick and Fidell 2006). The fact that most independent and control variables are either weakly correlated or not correlated at all attests to their distinctiveness in terms of describing underlying theoretical constructs. The largest correlation exists between the component scores of *STABILITY* and *RAW_SUPP* (+0.471, $p<0.01$) which is certainly an effect of the oblique PCA rotation method of "Direct Oblimin".[131] The PCA's second component "*International investment policy and trade connectedness*" *(INT_CONNECT)* shows no correlation whatsoever with the variable *BIT_DUMMY*. This is unexpected because the "bilateral investment treaties and double taxation agreements" *(BIT_DTT)* variable loaded highly on the component *INT_CONNECT*. In the light of this surprising outcome and the fact that *INT_CONNECT* emerged as a distinctive host country location factor besides *RAW_SUPP* and *STABILITY*, it appears reasonable to allow its entry to the regression model and regard it as a supportive variable for testing Hypothesis H5.

The correlations between individual country dummy variables and other independent and control variables (not reported) reveal the specific characteristic of *CONTRACT* as the only country-level variable which remains constant for all foreign firms within a specific SSA host country. The Mozambique dummy variable correlates very highly with *CONTRACT* (+0.852, $p<0.01$), a fact that warrants paying specific attention to the behaviour of this variable in the forthcoming regression model. Also noteworthy are the positive levels of correlations between the country dummy for Kenya and *CONTROL_SIZE* (+0.355, $p<0.01$) and *R_AND_D* (0.451, $p<0.01$). The subsector dummies generally correlate very weakly with the other variables. An exception is the garments subsector, which displays, as expected, a robust correlation with *EXP_INTENSE* (0.425, $p<0.01$). The

131 The effect of oblique component rotation is also visible in the pairwise correlations between *INT_CONNECT* and *STABILITY* (+0.325, $p<0.01$) and *INT_CONNECT* and *RAW_SUPP* (+0.371, $p<0.01$).

Variance Inflation Factor (VIF) is another measure to detect the extent of multicollinearity in the data. The VIF for all independent variables is between 1 and 1.5. The critical threshold for multicollinearity was set at a VIF of greater than 10 or even above (O'Brien 2007). Multicollinearity can hence be ruled out for the dataset at hand.

A first reduction of the sample to 757 FDI firms is caused by cases that have one or more missing values for *PROFIT*, *CAPUTIL* or *SELFEVAL* and that must consequently be dropped from the analysis. In this reduced sample, the variable *MF_DUMMY* has become meaningless for all subsequent model specifications because there are no more observations left that would represent non-manufacturing industries.

An iterative check on individual outliers in the data has been performed on the basis of the Mahalanobis Distance which follows a chi-square distribution with d degrees of freedom and a level of significance of $p<0.001$. With d=19 degrees of freedom for model specification M1, the acceptable level of Mahalanobis Distance would normally be 43.821. Of N=757 foreign firms, another 28 cases are eliminated because they are outside the acceptable Mahalanobis Distance range. The final sample for M1 thus consists of N=729 firms.[132]

Model specification M2 applies industrial subsector dummies instead of the control variable *TECH_INT*. With d=31 degrees of freedom for model specification 2, the acceptable level of Mahalanobis Distance is 61.098 with $p<0.001$. From originally N=757 foreign firms, 32 cases are eliminated so that the final sample for M2 consists of N=725 firms.[133] No more foreign firms with operations in the vehicles and transport equipment sector are left in this reduced sample. To ensure d-1 degrees of freedom for the dummy variables pertaining to *IND_SUBSEC*, no dummy variable will be created for the food, beverages and tobacco sector. In total, there are 12 subsector dummies.

The third model specification M3 includes subsector dummies substituting for the control variable *TECH_INT* as well as host country dummies substituting for the control variable *SSAWESTMID*. The variable *CONTRACT* displays unacceptable levels of multicollinearity with either one or

132 Due to the iterative process of outlier reduction, the objective is to get as close as possible to the acceptable Mahalanobis Distance. For Model specification 1, the maximum acceptable case had a Mahalanobis Distance of 48.311.

133 For Model specification 2, the maximum acceptable case had a Mahalanobis Distance of 68.444.

more of the country dummy variables. This is not surprising because *CONTRACT* is the only variable with no firm-level variations within a specific SSA host country whereas all other variables have such firm-level variations. *CONTRACT* will consequently be dropped from the list of independent variables for M3. There are no more cases of foreign firms located in Burkina Faso, Burundi, Cape Verde, Côte d'Ivoire, Malawi, Mali, Niger, Rwanda and Senegal. With d-1 degrees of freedom, there are 10 host country variables left. No dummy variable is generated in the case of Ghana. With d=39 degrees of freedom for M3, the acceptable level of Mahalanobis Distance is 72.055.[134] As a result, a total of 71 cases had to be dropped, leaving 686 foreign firms for analysis.

The fourth model specification (M4) includes host country dummies and the sector-specific variable *TECH_INT*. The inclusion of country dummies has made the variable *SSAWESTMID* redundant. With d=29 degrees of freedom for M4, the acceptable level of Mahalanobis Distance is 58.301.[135] A total of 36 cases had to be dropped, leaving N=719 cases for analysis. There are no more cases left from Burkina Faso, Burundi, Côte d'Ivoire, Malawi, Niger, Rwanda and Senegal. Ghana is the omitted host country dummy variable. The independent variable *CONTRACT* is discarded for the same reasons of multicollinearity as in M3.

The elimination of outliers had a positive effect on the goodness-of-fit of residual values to the normal distribution. A visual inspection of the scatterplot of residual values as well as the probability–probability plot[136] (not reported) does not find any alarming hints of heteroscedasticity in any of the four model specifications.

The regression is organized hierarchically (Hair et al. 1998), whereby the first level reports the isolated effect of control variables on FDI performance and the second level reports the combined effect of control and independent variables. The ΔR^2 indicates the level of additional variation of the dependent variables explained solely by the set of independent variables. The validity of the eleven Hypotheses will be checked based on the combined results of all four model specifications M1 to M4 and for the

134 For Model specification 3, the maximum acceptable case had a Mahalanobis Distance of 96.828.

135 For Model specification 4, the maximum acceptable case had a Mahalanobis Distance of 97.570.

136 The P-P plot is plotting the empirical distribution function against the normal distribution function.

three FDI performance variables *PROFIT*, *CAPUTIL* and *SELFEVAL* i.e. for a total of twelve combinations. These are reported in Tables 5.8 to 5.10 on the following pages as well as Annex Table 15. The F-values are all statistically significant at $p<0.01$ which signifies that control and independent variables have solid predictive capacities. In the case of *PROFIT*, R^2 values at second-level range from 0.128 for M1 and 0.169 for M3. For dependent variable *CAPUTIL,* the second-level R^2 values vary between 0.167 for M1 and 0.312 for M3. In the case of *SELFEVAL*, the second-level R^2 values are between 0.186 for M1 and 0.258 for M3.

As concerns Hypothesis H1 linked to the variable *OWNCHANGE*, the results are mixed. The hypothesized positive performance effect of an increase of foreign ownership in a given JV was only found in specification M3 and for the performance variable *PROFIT*. With a standardized β of +0.072 and $p<0.1$, the positive relation was not particularly strong.

Conversely, a negative relationship was found between *OWNCHANGE* and *CAPUTIL* at $p<0.1$ level in the case of M2 and between *OWNCHANGE* and *SELFEVAL* in all four model specifications M1–M4. The strongest negative relation was discovered for M3 and *SELFEVAL* with a standardized β of -0.081 and $p<0.05$. It confirms that there is an overall moderate effect of a foreign ownership increase on the financial or operational FDI performance as measured by *PROFIT* and *CAPUTIL*. In the subjective assessment of the foreign JV partner, however, a foreign ownership increase has a negative connotation. The foreign investor may be convinced that such a change was necessary to correct a misalignment in the JV but perceives the process of recovery and structural adjustments in the years after the change nevertheless as disruptive and detrimental, although this is not directly corroborated by objective FDI performance variables. The negative perception of the foreign JV partner could trigger further sequential changes which might have a further destabilizing effect on the JV as a whole. The results of FDI performance variable *SELFEVAL* seem to confirm the body of literature that finds a negative relation between ownership change and JV longevity (Beamish and Inkpen 1995, Inkpen and Beamish 1997, Steensma et al. 2008, Chung and Beamish 2010).

Table 5.8: Regression results for dependent variable PROFIT, model specifications M1–M3

Variables		Dependent variable: *PROFIT*					
		Specification 1 (M1)		Specification 2 (M2)		Specification 3 (M3)	
		Level 1 (Controls)	Level 2	Level 1 (Controls)	Level 2	Level 1 (Controls)	Level 2
	Intercept	4.982***	4.722***	3.895***	3.620***	4.184***	4.292***
Control variables	*CONTROL_AGE*	0.077*	0.058	0.072*	0.051	0.038	0.043
	CONTROL_SIZE	0.042	0.021	0.095**	0.069	0.108**	0.076
	ESTABLISH	0.038	0.026	0.028	0.012	0.047	0.043
	OWNERSHIP	-0.118***	-0.070*	-0.093**	-0.048	-0.109***	-0.073*
	EXP_INTENSE	-0.028	-0.008	0.001	0.018	0.011	0.016
	SSAWESTMID	-0.176***	-0.107***	-0.194***	-0.128***		
	TECH_INT	-0.004	-0.011				
	IND_SUBSEC	**No**	**No**	**Yes**	**Yes**	**Yes**	**Yes** [a]
	HOST_COUNTRY	**No**	**No**	**No**	**No**	**Yes**	**Yes** [b]
Indep. variables	*OWNCHANGE*		0.033		0.035		0.072*
	CONTRACT		0.077**		0.074*		
	RAW_SUPP		0.103**		0.094**		0.120***
	INT_CONNECT		0.052		0.063		0.041
	STABILITY		0.046		0.038		0.032
	BIT_DUMMY		-0.054		-0.040		-0.050
	PROD_DIV		0.013		0.015		0.045
	CULT_PROX		0.069*		0.055		0.024
	RESOURCES		0.015		0.021		0.053
	R_AND_D		0.142***		0.134***		0.086*
	SKILL_WF		-0.038		-0.010		-0.044
	SSA_EXP		-0.055		-0.036		-0.061
Stats.	No. of observations	729	729	725	725	686	686
	F-Value	7.119***	5.468***	3.732***	3.700***	3.374***	3.380***
	R^2	0.065	0.128	0.087	0.140	0.126	0.169
	Adjusted R^2	0.056	0.104	0.064	0.103	0.088	0.119
	ΔR^2		0.063		0.059		0.043

*. β significant at the 0.1 level; **. β significant at the 0.05 level; ***. β significant at the 0.01 level; [a] reported separately in Table 5.12; [b] reported separately in Table 5.13.

Table 5.9: Regression results for dependent variable CAPUTIL, model specifications M1–M3

Variables		Dependent variable: *CAPUTIL*					
		Specification 1 (M1)		Specification 2 (M2)		Specification 3 (M3)	
		Level 1 (Controls)	Level 2	Level 1 (Controls)	Level 2	Level 1 (Controls)	Level 2
	Intercept	0.369***	0.331***	0.365***	0.292***	0.454***	0.350***
Control variables	*CONTROL_AGE*	-0.005	-0.023	-0.015	-0.031	-0.008	0.001
	CONTROL_SIZE	0.242***	0.187***	0.244***	0.197***	0.220***	0.198***
	ESTABLISH	0.060*	0.029	0.045	0.013	0.010	0.010
	OWNERSHIP	-0.013	-0.035	-0.016	-0.039	0.048	0.019
	EXP_INTENSE	-0.062*	-0.067*	-0.044	-0.049	-0.031	-0.032
	SSAWESTMID	-0.153***	-0.094**	-0.160***	-0.086**		
	TECH_INT	-0.082**	-0.093***				
	IND_SUBSEC	**No**	**No**	**Yes**	**Yes**	**Yes**	**Yes** [a]
	HOST_COUNTRY	**No**	**No**	**No**	**No**	**Yes**	**Yes** [b]
Indep. variables	*OWNCHANGE*		-0.014		-0.067*		-0.024
	CONTRACT		0.086**		0.081**		
	RAW_SUPP		-0.094**		-0.147***		-0.122***
	INT_CONNECT		0.025		0.045		0.039
	STABILITY		-0.059		-0.021		-0.031
	BIT_DUMMY		0.021		0.011		-0.055
	PROD_DIV		-0.081**		-0.091**		-0.047
	CULT_PROX		-0.045		-0.036		0.003
	RESOURCES		0.112***		0.112***		0.076**
	R_AND_D		0.142***		0.141***		0.107***
	SKILL_WF		-0.051		-0.020		0.041
	SSA_EXP		0.079**		0.067*		0.084**
Stats.	No. of observations	729	729	725	725	686	686
	F-Value	10.420***	7.462***	4.419***	4.941***	8.789***	7.511***
	R^2	0.092	0.167	0.101	0.176	0.272	0.312
	Adjusted R^2	0.083	0.144	0.078	0.140	0.241	0.270
	ΔR^2		0.075		0.075		0.040

*. β significant at the 0.1 level; **. β significant at the 0.05 level; ***. β significant at the 0.01 level; [a] reported separately in Table 5.12; [b] reported separately in Table 5.13.

Table 5.10: Regression results for dependent variable SELFEVAL, model specifications M1–M3

Variables		Dependent variable: *SELFEVAL*					
		Specification 1 (M1)		Specification 2 (M2)		Specification 3 (M3)	
		Level 1 (Controls)	Level 2	Level 1 (Controls)	Level 2	Level 1 (Controls)	Level 2
	Intercept	2.452***	2.095***	2.681***	2.344***	3.051***	2.817***
Control variables	*CONTROL_AGE*	0.080**	0.067*	0.071*	0.062	0.035	0.061
	CONTROL_SIZE	0.089**	0.058	0.064	0.024	0.012	-0.021
	ESTABLISH	0.129***	0.110***	0.124***	0.100***	0.124***	0.120***
	OWNERSHIP	-0.063*	-0.040	-0.053	-0.036	-0.011	-0.007
	EXP_INTENSE	-0.123***	-0.093**	-0.058	-0.032	-0.056	-0.040
	SSAWESTMID	-0.154***	-0.059	-0.159***	-0.058	0.035	0.061
	TECH_INT	0.079**	0.067*				
	IND_SUBSEC	**No**	**No**	**Yes**	**Yes**	**Yes**	**Yes** [a]
	HOST_COUNTRY	**No**	**No**	**No**	**No**	**Yes**	**Yes** [b]
Indep. variables	*OWNCHANGE*		-0.066*		-0.073**		-0.081**
	CONTRACT		0.112***		0.103***		
	RAW_SUPP		0.044		0.038		0.081*
	INT_CONNECT		0.132***		0.135***		0.067
	STABILITY		0.003		-0.002		0.046
	BIT_DUMMY		-0.024		-0.027		-0.044
	PROD_DIV		-0.084**		-0.101***		-0.088**
	CULT_PROX		-0.023		-0.036		-0.052
	RESOURCES		0.055		0.046		-0.003
	R_AND_D		0.128***		0.139***		0.119***
	SKILL_WF		0.069*		0.075**		0.069*
	SSA_EXP		0.105***		0.095***		0.105***
Stats.	No. of observations	729	729	725	725	686	686
	F-Value	10.728***	8.524***	4.475***	5.515***	5.745***	5.758***
	R^2	0.094	0.186	0.101	0.192	0.197	0.258
	Adjusted R^2	0.086	0.164	0.080	0.158	0.162	0.213
	ΔR^2		0.092		0.091		0.061

*. β significant at the 0.1 level; **. β significant at the 0.05 level; ***. β significant at the 0.01 level; [a] reported separately in Table 5.12; [b] reported separately in Table 5.13.

Concerning the second Hypothesis H2, the associated variable *CONTRACT* takes the wrong sign and is positive for model specifications M1 and M2 and for all three performance variables *PROFIT*, *CAPUTIL* and *SELFEVAL*. The positive relationship is strongest for *SELFEVAL* with a standardized β of +0.112 ($p<0.01$) in M1 and a standardized β of +0.103 ($p<0.01$) in M2. *CONTRACT* was not retained in model specification M3 and M4 because most of its variation was absorbed by the SSA host country dummy variables. The results contradict conventional transaction cost and institution-based reasoning because they imply that high costs of contract enforcement may entail improved FDI performance. This outcome comes closest to that of Chan et al.'s study that finds that institutional voids may not always and immediately translate into diminishing FDI performance levels compared to institutionally better developed countries (Chan et al. 2008). A macro-level study on the effects of institutional development on Chinese FDI inflows in Africa also found a negative relationship and somewhat harshly concluded that "exploiting resources and weak institutions appears to be the name of the investment game in Africa" (Kolstad and Wiig 2011, p. 46). In a similar vein, Egger and Winner found that corruption acts as a stimulus for FDI (Egger and Winner 2005). A possible explanation for the positive sign of *CONTRACT* with FDI performance could be that high costs of contract enforcement not only act as barrier for the foreign investor to take recourse action via the host country's judicial system but also prevent other market actors from prosecuting their own claims directed at the foreign investor. The costs for contract enforcement are likely to be more prohibitive for local market actors than for foreign subsidiaries that belong to an MNE and that can tap, if necessary, into internally available financial channels. In the case of a mixed foreign-local JV, the foreign partner could get away with opportunistic behaviour because the local partner may either suffer from limited financial means to take legal action or be discouraged by the anticipated high costs and uncertainty of the lawsuit. Other examples could be non-payment or late payment by the foreign subsidiary to its local suppliers, wage arrears in relation to workforce employed by the foreign investor, substandard quality of goods and services supplied by foreign investors to local distributors or under public procurement, etc. Following this logic, an environment with high costs of contract enforcement can de facto protect foreign investors from legal culpability. Heightened levels of FDI performance might ensue if the advantage from a situation of de facto impunity surpasses the disadvantage of a costly enforcement of own claims towards third parties.

The variable *RAW_SUPP*, generated from the PCA, shows a positive sign for the four model specifications M1 to M4 of dependent variable *PROFIT* and for M3 and M4 of *SELFEVAL*. The positive relationship is more pronounced between *RAW_SUPP* and *PROFIT* than between *RAW_SUPP* and *SELFEVAL*. The standardized β coefficient (+0.120, $p<0.01$) between *RAW_SUPP* and *PROFIT* is largest when subsector and host country control variables are included (M3). This attests to the robustness of the relationship. While Hypothesis H3 is supported for *PROFIT* and *SELFEVAL*, it is rejected in the case of *CAPUTIL*. *RAW_SUPP* takes a highly significant negative sign for all four model specifications of *CAPUTIL*. Its predictive influence on *CAPUTIL* is the largest in model specification M2 reaching a standardized β coefficient of -0.147 at $p<0.01$. A possible explanation for the negative sign could be that lowered input factor costs of production lead to new market entries and stiffened competition amongst a widened range of manufacturing firm for the same but limited input factors e.g. labour or raw materials. Unless the supply of input factors can be enlarged in the short-term, the immediate consequence for the foreign firm would be to lower its capacity utilization and continue production on the basis of available input factors.

No support can be found for Hypothesis H4. None of the four model specifications for the three dependent variables *PROFIT*, *CAPUTIL* or *SELFEVAL* produces significant β coefficients of the *STABILITY* variable. That is particularly noteworthy in the light of numerous macro-economic studies that found a strong effect of stable and predictable host country business climate on FDI inflows into SSA (Agodo 1978, Morisset 2000, Cotton and Ramachandran 2001, Bende-Nabende 2002, Asiedu 2004b, Mlambo 2005, Asiedu 2006, Naudé and Krugell 2007).

As hypothesized under H5, there is no significant relationship between the variable *BIT_DUMMY* and FDI performance. The standardized β coefficient is weakly negative in most model specifications but never attains a level of $p<0.1$. This firm-level result is in line with macro-level studies that find either no or only a very weak relationship between the existence of BITs and FDI inflows (Hallward-Driemeyer 2003, Gallagher and Birch 2006, Yackee 2007). The results imply that the argument can be extended to firm-level performance of foreign subsidiaries. The second variable with relevance for testing H5 should be *"International investment policy and trade connectedness"* (*INT_CONNECT*), which emerged from the

PCA and which explained about 56 per cent of the variance of the single location factor "bilateral investment treaties and double taxation agreements" (*BIT_DTT*). In this context, it is rather surprising that the two variables *BIT_DUMMY* and *INT_CONNECT* are uncorrelated.[137] This nurtures the assumption that *INT_CONNECT* might be a proxy for a different theoretical construct than bilateral or other international agreements and that more weighting is placed on the "trade connectedness" aspect than the "international investment policy" aspect. Such unobserved "trade connectedness" location factors could be the quality of physical export infrastructure or the availability of industrial zones (IZs) or export processing zones (EPZs). *INT_CONNECT* has a positive and highly significant standardized β coefficient ($p<0.01$) of +0.132 in model specification M1 and +0.135 in M2 of dependent variable *SELFEVAL*. The simultaneous inclusion of host county and subsector dummy variables renders the standardized β coefficient in model specification M3 insignificant, however. In M4, *INT_CONNECT* again has a positive and significant effect on *SELFEVAL* with a standardized β coefficient of +0.071 and $p<0.1$. Although the results do not seem to carry much relevance in testing the validity of Hypothesis H5, they might indirectly suggest a positive effect of export infrastructure development on the subjective performance evaluation of FDI subsidiaries in SSA. Such an outcome is plausible when compared to the macro-level FDI determinants literature that found a positive effect of infrastructural development on FDI inflows (Wheeler and Mody 1992, Loree and Guisinger 1995, Urata and Kawai 2000), including FDI inflows directed to Africa (Agodo 1978, Akinkugbe 2005, Mlambo 2005, Asiedu 2006).

Hypothesis H6 anticipated a positive relationship between the foreign firm's product diversification and its performance. H6 has to be rejected because the outcomes in six different regression models point towards a significant and negative relationship. *PROD_DIV* has a significant standardized β coefficient of -0.081 in M1 ($p<0.05$) and -0.091 in M2 ($p<0.05$) of performance variable *CAPUTIL*. *PROD_DIV* is also negative for all four model specifications of *SELFEVAL*, especially for M2 with a standardized β coefficient of -0.101 ($p<0.01$). The results suggest that increased coordination costs and complexities in product-diversified firms do not engender the desired levels of economies of scope and consequently attenuate foreign subsidiary performance (Markides 1992, Li 1995).

137 The correlation coefficient is -0.013; List-wise exclusion of cases; N=1,276.

The characteristic of the *PROD_DIV* variable does not provide further insights into the inter-relatedness of the different products whose contribution to the annual turnover is measured through the Herfindahl index. If the different products are unrelated, the foreign firm distances itself too much from its core businesses competencies and faces the adversities of unrelated diversification as hypothesized by the 'inverted-U' model in the international business performance literature (Hitt et al. 1997, Palich et al. 2000). Although no terminal judgement can be made on the degree of relatedness on the basis of variable *PROD_DIV* alone, there is at least some plausibility as to the negative effect of *PROD_DIV* on capacity utilization. Each time the firm kicks off a new production lot for one of its (unrelated) products, it requires personnel to set up the machinery and to prepare the assembly work shop which takes away time and resources compared to production systems for single or multiple but closely related products. Unrelated diversification seems very common in "parallel entrepreneurs" (The Economist 2012) who "instead of investing and expanding a single firm in a clearly defined line of business, [...] engages in several unrelated businesses all at once. The firm becomes a cluster of disparate enterprises linked only by the owner and family members" (Kiggundu 2002, p. 247). The negative relationship of *PROD_DIV* on *CAPUTIL* and *SELFEVAL* somewhat dampens the notion that the "octopus organization" (Kiggundu 2002) might be a competitive and sustainable form of doing and organizing businesses in SSA or that this form would give FEs a performance edge vis-à-vis traditionally organized TNCs (UNIDO 2007). Multinational corporations take an increasingly hesitant approach to broad-based market internalization of business domains that are regarded as unrelated to their core businesses. A good example is the trend towards contract farming arrangements in agricultural FDI in SSA (Cotula et al. 2009, UNCTAD 2009f, Oya 2012). In the light of the results obtained, such an FDI business strategy focusing on the foreign investor's core competencies seems to pay off in achieving higher performance levels.

Concerning Hypothesis H7 and its associated variable *CULT_PROX*, the outcomes for model specifications M1 and M4 of the dependent performance variable *PROFIT* are in the expected positive direction. With a standardized β coefficient of +0.069 ($p<0.1$) in M1 and +0.074 ($p<0.1$) in M4, the positive effect on the foreign firm's profit margin is significant but not the strongest amongst the set of independent variables. The result confirms the finding from the literature that a common language background facilitates the adaptation of the foreign investor to the host country and lowers its barriers and transaction costs of cultural and psychic distance (Johanson and Wiedersheim-Paul 1975, Li and Guisinger 1992, López-Duarte and Vidal-Suárez 2010). For example, the group of French investors in Francophone Western Africa or investors from the UK in Anglophone Eastern Africa might achieve a somewhat higher profit margin compared to their peer foreign investors with a different linguistic background. The other two dimensions of FDI performance, *CAPUTIL* and *SELFEVAL*, are however insensitive to language proximity.

Hypothesis H8 is confirmed. The variable *RESOURCES* is positive and significant in all four model specifications of the performance variable *CAPUTIL*. The largest standardized β coefficients appear in M1 and M2 (both +0.112 and $p<0.01$). A recognized brand name or trademark has a positive effect on product sales which translates into a continuous stack of orders for the production department with a resulting positive impact on productive capacity utilization. In the other model specifications of *PROFIT* and *SELFEVAL*, the variable *RESOURCES* is still positive but insignificant. The result is in keeping with that of similar studies stressing the positive effect of valuable and non-substitutable resources and capabilities for the development of a competitive ownership advantage (Barney 1991, Newbert 2007).

The *R_AND_D* dummy variable emerges as the most potent predictor variable in all four model specifications of *PROFIT*, *CAPUTIL* and *SELFEVAL*. Consequently, Hypothesis H9 finds full support. The strongest effect on *PROFIT* is observed in M1 and M2 with standardized β coefficients of +0.142 ($p<0.01$) and +0.134 ($p<0.01$). Equally strong is the effect of *R_AND_D* on *CAPUTIL* with standardized β coefficients of +0.141 ($p<0.01$) in M1 and +0.142 ($p<0.01$) in M2. In model specifications M3 and M4, *R_AND_D* has the highest positive impact on *SELFEVAL* followed by *CAPUTIL* and *PROFIT*. The positive effect of R&D on FDI performance was anticipated in the light of previous findings in the extant literature (Siripaisalpipat and Hoshino 2000, Lu and Beamish 2001, Shrader 2001, Andras and Srinivasan 2003) but the power and robustness of the relationship at FDI subsidiary-level is still surprising.

Hypothesis H10 is tested through the *SKILL_WF* variable in the regression model. The variable takes the expected positive sign in model specifications M1, M2 and M3 of the performance variable *SELFEVAL*. The significance levels are fairly moderate at $p<0.1$. The firm-level FDI performance outcome is consistent with the findings at the macroeconomic-level namely that the quality and availability of skilled human resources is an important determinant of FDI inflows into SSA (Naudé and Krugell 2003, Asiedu 2006, Suliman and Mollick 2009). Interestingly, the share of skilled work force amongst the total workforce is insensitive to the technology intensity of the manufacturing subsector. The pairwise correlation coefficient between *SKILL_WF* and *TECH_INT* is positive but close to zero. Besides, the standardized β coefficient is largest for model specification M2 of *SELFEVAL* which includes industrial subsector dummies (β of +0.075, $p<0.01$). The conclusion is that the performance-enhancing effect of a skilled work force is not only limited to the medium- or high-tech sectors but affects all FDI subsectors alike.

After finding support for resource-based Hypotheses H8, H9 and H10, support is equally found for the fourth resource-based Hypothesis H11 measured by the variable *SSA_EXP*. In all four model specifications M1 to M4, there is a positive relationship between *SSA_EXP* and *CAPUTIL* and between *SSA_EXP* and *SELFEVAL*. The strongest relationship was identified for M4 of *SELFEVAL* where the standardized β coefficient takes a value of +0.107 with $p<0.01$. This indicates that managers who are running foreign subsidiaries that are embedded in a network of regionally-operating fellow subsidiaries take a more positive stance regarding past FDI performance. The effect on *CAPUTIL* was also fairly robust, in particular for M3 with a β coefficient of +0.084 ($p<0.05$). A network of subsidiaries thus acts as conduit for augmenting and harnessing business experience from different SSA countries and impacts positively on FDI subsidiary performance. The study of Ogasavara and Hoshino produced similar results for Japanese FDI in Brazil (Ogasavara and Hoshino 2009).

With regards to control variables, Table 5.11 on the next page provides an overview of the direction of the relationship between the seven control variables and *PROFIT*, *CAPUTIL* and *SELFEVAL*. Larger and older FDI subsidiaries have an overall better performance than smaller or younger foreign subsidiaries. Particularly noteworthy is the strong relationship between *CONTROL_SIZE* and *CAPUTIL* in all four model specifications. The link between firm size and profit margin emerges most explicitly in first-level model specification M3 with a standardized β coefficient of +0.108 and $p<0.05$. The positive signs in the control variables *CONTROL_AGE* and *CONTROL_SIZE* are generally consistent with the argument that the level of experience matters for FDI performance (Luo and Peng 1999, Delios and Beamish 2001, Ogasavara and Hoshino 2009). Similarly, larger subsidiaries usually receive more attention and support from the foreign parent and are under tighter control so as to prevent failure or extended periods of low subsidiary performance (Slangen and Hennart 2008). Despite the plausibility of the results, a note of caution is justified with regard to a likely survivor bias in the data, which does not take into account unsuccessful foreign subsidiaries that had already disappeared at the time of the UNIDO 2010/11 Investor Survey.

Table 5.11: Influence of control variables on dependent variables PROFIT, SELFEVAL and CAPUTIL

Control variables	Results (reported only if significant at p<0.1)
CONTROL_AGE	Positive for *PROFIT* (M1, M2) Positive for *SELFEVAL* (M1, M2)
CONTROL_SIZE	Positive for *PROFIT* (M2–M4) Positive for *CAPUTIL* (M1–M4) Positive for *SELFEVAL* (M1)
ESTABLISH	Positive for *CAPUTIL* (M1) Positive for *SELFEVAL* (M1–M4)
OWNERSHIP	Negative for *PROFIT* (M1–M4) Negative for *SELFEVAL* (M1)
EXP_INTENSE	Negative for *CAPUTIL* (M1, M4) Negative for *SELFEVAL* (M1, M4)
SSAWESTMID	Negative for *PROFIT* (M1, M2) Negative for *CAPUTIL* (M1, M2) Negative for *SELFEVAL* (M1, M2)
TECH_INT	Negative for *CAPUTIL* (M1, M4) Positive for *SELFEVAL* (M1, M4)

The two control variables *ESTABLISH* (1=greenfield) and *OWNERSHIP* (1=WOS) describe the FDI entry mode. Foreign investors operating under the greenfield establishment mode perform better than foreign investors that have invested and built their operations from existing assets through an M&A. The greenfield establishment mode shows a particularly strong effect on the *SELFEVAL* variable. In the first level of the hierarchical regression, the standardized β coefficient of *ESTABLISH* is +0.129 in M1, +0.124 in M2, +0.124 in M3 and +0.119 in M4 with significance levels of $p<0.01$. A weakly positive and significant relationship is also observed between *ESTABLISH* and *CAPUTIL*. This observation lends support to the argument that it can be complex and very costly to integrate previously external assets into the organizational structure of the TNC. Although a greenfield investor is obliged to build new business relationships, to establish new channels for input supply, to recruit a new work force, etc., from scratch, the long-term performance effect might still outstrip the performance levels associated with a poorly integrated M&A subsidiary (Woodcock et al. 1994, Hennart et al. 1998, Shaver 1998, Slangen and Hennart 2008). Concerning the *OWNERSHIP* variable, the regression results indicate that JVs outperform WOSs in at least two of the three FDI performance dimensions i.e. *PROFIT* and *SELFEVAL*. Being a JV exerts a positive effect on the profit margin as demonstrated by standardized β coefficients of level-one model specification M1 (-0.118, $p<0.01$), M2 (-0.093, $p<0.05$), M3 (-0.109, $p<0.01$) and M4 (-0.107, $p<0.01$). The positive effect of the JV mode somewhat abates after the inclusion of the set of independent variables in the second-level regression model which warrants a test of endogeneity as proposed in the more recent FDI entry mode literature (Shaver 1998, Brouthers 2002, Kim and Gray 2008, Martin 2013).[138] The independent variables are not, however, influential enough to swap the sign of *OWNERSHIP* from negative to positive. The negative and significant ($p<0.1$) association persists between *OWNERSHIP* and *PROFIT* in the second-level model specification M1 and M3. A similarly positive relationship between the JV ownership mode and profitability was detected in foreign subsidiaries in China (Pan and Chi 1999, Pan et al. 1999).

The control variable *EXP_INTENSE* shows a significantly negative relationship in model specifications M1 and M4 of *CAPUTIL* and *SELFEVAL*. The standardized β coefficient is most negative in the first-level model specification M1 of *SELFEVAL* with a value of -0.123 ($p<0.01$). The outcome confirms previous UNIDO FDI Surveys in SSA which identified a negative bias of export-oriented foreign investors in terms of their

138 The research design has neither included an entry mode "fit" variable (Brouthers 2002, Brouthers and Nakos 2004) nor a self-selection parameter (Heckman 1979, Shaver 1998, Brouthers et al. 2008a). As a second best alternative and in line with suggestions made under http://marcfbellemare.com/wordpress/11057 (accessed on 13 December 2015), model specification M5 (not reported) omits the control variable *OWNERSHIP* but kept an otherwise similar structure to model specification M1. In the case of dependent performance variable *PROFIT*, a remarkable change is only observed in the case of *CONTROL_AGE* (std. β increased from +0.058 to +0.067, $p<0.1$) and *CULT_PROX* (std. β increased from +0.069 to +0.077, $p<0.05$). There is no significant change in the case of *CAPUTIL*. As for *SELFEVAL*, the omission of *OWNERSHIP* led to a remarkable increase of the std. β in *CONTROL_AGE* from +0.067 to +0.072 ($p<0.1$), *CONTROL_SIZE* from +0.058 to +0.067, $p<0.1$ and *OWNCHANGE* from -0.066 to -0.062 ($p<0.1$). Since *OWNERSHIP* has a generally moderate effect on FDI performance in comparison to other control and independent variables, the spurious effect of endogeneity in the model should also be very limited.

subjective self-evaluation of past investment performance (UNIDO 2003, UNIDO 2007). A similar result was found in relation to profitability performance of FDI subsidiaries in China (He et al. 2015). Similar to FDI entry mode choice, the choice of market orientation can lead to an endogeneity problem because it is non-random and self-selected and may indirectly reflect strategic or industrial attributes of the foreign direct investor (He et al. 2015).[139] The significant effect of *EXP_INTENSE* on FDI performance disappears in model specifications M2 and M3 which include manufacturing subsector dummies. This indicates that the foreign investor's propensity to export is largely determined by the industrial subsector as shown in the descriptive statistics of Chapter 3.9.

Table 5.12 on the next page provides the standardized β coefficients of manufacturing subsector dummies and their significance levels in the case of model specification M3.

139 The methodological most rigorous approach would be to include a market orientation "fit" variable or a self-selection parameter (Martin 2013, He et al. 2015). Alternatively, model specification M6 (not reported) excludes control variable *EXP_INTENSE* but keeps an otherwise similar structure to model specification M1. The comparison of the model with and without the assumed endogenous control variable facilitates a judgement on whether endogeneity is likely to have a distortive effect or whether its effect is minor and hence acceptable, see: http://marcfbellemare.com/wordpress/11057 (accessed on 13 December 2015). The influence of *EXP_INTENSE* on *PROFIT* is minimal and so is also the variation in the standardized β coefficients between M1 and M6. In the case of *CAPUTIL*, a remarkable change occurs only in the standardized β coefficient of *TECH_INT* from -0.093 ($p<0.01$) in M1 to -0.079 ($p<0.05$) in M6 and *CONTRACT* from 0.086 ($p<0.05$) in M1 to 0.094 ($p<0.05$) in M6. As regards *SELFEVAL*, the most noteworthy change appears again in *TECH_INT* whose standardized β coefficient increases from +0.063 ($p<0.1$) in M1 to +0.083 ($p<0.05$) in M6. In the same vein, the standardized β coefficient of *SKILL_WF* climbs from +0.069 ($p<0.1$) in M1 to +0.075 ($p<0.05$) in M6. *EXP_INTENSE* has an overall very limited influence in altering the regression outcomes. Endogeneity should thus not be a major concern.

Table 5.12: Influence of manufacturing subsector control variables on PROFIT, CAPUTIL and SELFEVAL in level-one model specification M3

TECH_INT	Manufacturing subsector	*PROFIT* stand. β	*CAPUTIL* stand. β	*SELFEVAL* stand. β
Low-tech	Textiles	0.031	-0.041	-0.071^{*}
	Wearing apparel	0.003	-0.075^{*}	-0.085^{**}
	Wood products and furniture	-0.020	0.033	0.051
	Paper and paper products	-0.012	0.016	0.034
	Publishing and printing	0.012	0.030	0.062
	Other low-tech manuf.	0.061	-0.067^{*}	-0.097^{**}
Medium-tech	Rubber and plastics	0.011	-0.003	0.023
	Non-metal. min., coke and petrol.	0.060	-0.025	0.069^{*}
	Basic metals	-0.029	-0.083^{**}	0.006
	Fabricated metal products	-0.028	-0.037	0.024
High-tech	Chemical and chemical products	0.012	-0.074^{*}	0.062
	Machinery and equipment	0.031	-0.012	0.058
	Vehicles and transport equipm.	0.003	-0.038	0.041

Subsector aggregation as described in Chapter 5.2.3.5;
"Food, beverages and tobacco" is the omitted dummy variable; N=686;
*. β significant at the 0.1 level; **.β significant at the 0.05 level;

As expected, the export-oriented subsectors of wearing apparel and other low-tech manufacturing, in particular leather and footwear, display significantly negative standardized β coefficients for performance variables *CAPUTIL* and *SELFEVAL*. The chemical sector and the basic metals sector, albeit mainly oriented towards SSA's local or regional markets, struggle in terms of capacity utilization as indicated by standardized β coefficients of -0.083 ($p<0.05$) and -0.074 ($p<0.1$). Variations in profit margins are barely affected by the manufacturing subsector. If subsectors are aggregated according to their technological intensity, the results of control variable *TECH_INT* suggest that foreign investors in medium to high-tech sectors grapple more often with issues of lower capacity utilization compared to foreign investors in the lower-tech sectors. Despite lower levels of capacity utilization, foreign investors in the medium or high-tech sectors are more content with their overall FDI effectiveness. This is reflected in the positive standardized β coefficients of the level-one model specifications M1 and M4 of dependent variable *SELFEVAL*.

The control variable for Western and Middle Africa, *SSAWESTMID*, exerts a highly negative and statistically significant effect ($p<0.01$) on all three categories of FDI performance. This applies to model specifications

M1 and M2 that do not include individual host country dummy variables. The prevalent business environment in Western and Middle Africa has a particularly detrimental effect on *PROFIT* as indicated by a level-one standardized β coefficient of -0.176 ($p<0.01$) in model specification M1 and -0.194 ($p<0.01$) in model specification M2. Also in terms of *CAPUTIL* and *SELFEVAL*, the level-one standardized β coefficients are highly negative with -0.160 ($p<0.01$) and -0.159 ($p<0.01$) in model specification M2. This firm-level finding differs from the macro-economic evolution of FDI inflow statistics for Western and Middle Africa (see Figure 2.4). For example, Western Africa has seen steadily rising levels of year-by-year FDI inflows from 2000 until 2011 and with only one notable exception in the year 2010. The share of FDI inward stocks as a percentage of SSA's total FDI inward stocks remained relatively constant for the period 2000 until 2013 (see Figure 2.5), accounting for an average of 27 per cent in the case of Western Africa and around 14 per cent in the case of Middle Africa. This blatant difference between modest FDI firm-level performance on the one hand and robust new FDI inflows into the Western and Middle African region on the other hand, lends support to the argument that firm-level performance inferences from macro-economic FDI trends can be risky and often misleading (Stephan and Pfaffmann 2001, Beugelsdijk et al. 2010, Kerner 2014).

In contrast to the negative effect of the variable *SSAWESTMID* on FDI performance, there are several Eastern African host countries in which foreign subsidiaries performed outstandingly. As shown in Table 5.13 below, the front-runner is Kenya with level-one standardized β coefficients in M3 of +0.277 ($p<0.01$) for *PROFIT*, of +0.407 ($p<0.01$) for *CAPUTIL* and +0.379 ($p<0.01$) for *SELFEVAL*. It is followed by Mozambique which also displays highly significant and positive β coefficients for all three performance indicators. The high scoring of both countries is plausible in the light of results reported beforehand in Box 5. Kenya scored very highly in the *"International investment policy and trade connectedness"* Component (*INT_CONNECT*) due to its favourable location as distribution hub for exports to other members of the EAC (UNIDO 2007, AFDB 2010). In the case of Kenya, the *INT_CONNECT* Component seems to outbalance its mediocre level of perceived *"Investment Climate Stability and Transparency"* (*STABILITY*), which was certainly affected by Kenya's 2007 post-election crisis.

Table 5.13: Influence of SSA host country control variables on PROFIT, CAPUTIL and SELFEVAL in level-one model specification M3

SSA host country	*PROFIT* stand. β	*CAPUTIL* stand. β	*SELFEVAL* stand. β
Cameroon	-0.036	0.023	0.058
Ethiopia	0.045	0.130***	0.028
Kenya	0.277***	0.407***	0.379***
Lesotho	0.027	0.255***	0.015
Madagascar	-0.026	0.062*	0.054
Mozambique	0.191***	0.317***	0.230***
Nigeria	0.024	0.003	0.041
Tanzania	0.112**	0.177***	0.048
Uganda	0.217***	-0.014	0.133**
Zambia	0.045	0.020	0.091**

No observation for Burundi, Burkina Faso, Cape Verde, Côte d'Ivoire, Malawi, Mali, Rwanda, Senegal and Niger; Ghana is the omitted dummy variable in M3; N=686;
*. β significant at the 0.10 level; **.β significant at the 0.05 level; ***. β significant at the 0.01 level.

Mozambique achieved the second-best component score in terms of *STABILITY* combined with a positive result of the *"Costs in supply of input factors of production"* Component (*RAW_SUPP*). The two EAC member countries Tanzania and Uganda have a positive and significant bearing on the FDI profit margin and on the subjective performance self-evaluation. Ethiopia and Lesotho are attractive locations for FDI if emphasis is put on maximizing capacity utilization. The first intuitive explanation might be that both countries host a sizable proportion of global market-seeking FDI enterprises (UNCTAD 2003c, Lall 2005, Malefane 2007, Staritz 2011, World Bank 2012).[140] These enterprises can "escape" limited domestic market demand and benefit from a wider network of global buyers of the foreign firm's main product or commodity with a resulting positive effect on capacity utilization or productivity gains through learning-by-exporting (Bigsten et al. 2004, Van Biesebroeck 2005). Although intuitive, the positive effect of being located in Lesotho and Ethiopia on *CAPUTIL* is not determined by MNEs' export intensities. This has been controlled for in

140 In Ethiopia, 18.8 per cent of foreign firms are global market-seekers (24 of 128 foreign firms). In Lesotho, 52.2 per cent of foreign firms are global market-seekers (35 of 67 foreign firms). Basis: Total UNIDO 2010/11 Investor Survey sample of 2,692 foreign subsidiaries.

model specification M3 and produced a negative but insignificant standardized β coefficient of -0.032 (see Table 5.9).

5.4 Summary of findings and Chapter 5 conclusions

The purpose of Chapter 5 was to develop an appropriate empirical model to test a total of eleven hypotheses H1 to H11, which had been developed from the literature review of the previous Chapter 4. The chosen model was that of a multiple OLS regression with three different dependent FDI performance variables in accordance with the proposed classification of Hult et al. (Hult et al. 2008). The three performance variables *PROFIT*, *CAPUTIL* and *SELFEVAL* correlated weakly with each other. Neither did the control or independent variables show alarming levels of multicollinearity. The descriptive results were followed by an ANOVA of the three FDI performance variables. The ANOVA gave an early indication of the impact of four categorical independent variables on FDI performance. For instance, the group of foreign investors that have a common language between their country of origin and the SSA host country produced a higher mean of FDI performance than investors without such language communality. In the same vein, FDI subsidiaries that indicated an active pursuance of R&D activities had significantly higher means of *PROFIT*, *CAPUTIL* and *SELFEVAL*.

To produce the missing set of institutional variables, a PCA has been performed on a list of 12 location factors. Each location factor has been assessed by foreign investors in terms of its change during the past three years prior to the UNIDO 2010/11 Investor Survey. Foreign investors perceived that the most visible leap was made in terms of the availability of skilled labour (*SKILL_LAB*) and the evolution of local market opportunities (*LOC_MARK*). The analysis demarcated three distinct components, namely *"Costs in supply of input factors of production"* (*RAW_SUPP*), *"International investment policy and trade connectedness"* (*INT_CONNECT*) and *"Investment Climate Stability and Transparency"* (*STABILITY*). The firm-level component score of *RAW_SUPP* proved useful in testing Hypothesis H3. The *STABILITY* variable did not react in the hypothesized positive direction of H4 but remained insignificant in all model specifications.

The relationships between independent and control variables and the three FDI performance variables were assessed for the four different regression model specifications M1–M4 and in a hierarchical fashion. The set of control variables was entered at the first-level and the set of independent variables was entered at the second-level. Table 5.14 below provides the results for all independent variables.

Table 5.14: Summary of results in relation to the set of hypotheses

Hypothesis [hypothesized sign]	Category	Result (only if sign. at p<0.1)	Aggregated result [*]
H1: *OWNCHANGE* [+]	Unspec.	+ for *PROFIT* (M3)	**Rejected [67%]; Confirmed [33%]**
		+ for *CAPUTIL* (M2)	
		- for *SELFEVAL* (M1–M4)	
H2: *CONTRACT* [-]	TC	+ for *PROFIT* (M1, M2)	**Rejected [100%]**
		+ for *CAPUTIL* (M1, M2)	
		+ for *SELFEVAL* (M1, M2)	
H3: *RAW_SUPP* [+]	TC	+ for *PROFIT* (M1–M4)	**Rejected [40%]; Confirmed [60%]**
		- for *CAPUTIL* (M1–M4)	
		+ for *SELFEVAL* (M3, M4)	
H4: *STABILITY* [+]	IB	Insignificant for all models	**Neither confirmed nor rejected**
H5: *BIT_DUMMY* [0]	IB	Insignificant for all models	**Confirmed [100%]**
H6: *PROD_DIV* [+]	Ind.	- for *CAPUTIL* (M1, M2)	**Rejected [100%]**
		- for *SELFEVAL* (M1–M4)	
H7: *CULT_PROX* [+]	CD	+ for *PROFIT* (M1, M4)	**Confirmed [100%]**
H8: *RESOURCES* [+]	RB	+ for *CAPUTIL* (M1–M4)	**Confirmed [100%]**
H9: *R_AND_D* [+]	RB	+ for *PROFIT* (M1–M4)	**Confirmed [100%]**
		+ for *CAPUTIL* (M1–M4)	
		+ for *SELFEVAL* (M1–M4)	
H10: *SKILL_WF* [+]	RB	+ for *SELFEVAL* (M1–M3)	**Confirmed [100%]**
H11: *SSA_EXP* [+]	RB	+ for *CAPUTIL* (M1–M4)	**Confirmed [100%]**
		+ for *SELFEVAL* (M1–M4)	

* indicates the number of model specification with significant results as a percentage of all 12 combinations of M1–M4 and *PROFIT*, *CAPUTIL* and *SELFEVAL*;
IB – institution-based variable; TC – transaction cost variable; Ind. – Industry-based variable; CD – cultural distance variable; RB – resource-based variable.

Hypotheses H5, H7, H8, H9, H10 and H11 received unambiguous support. H2 and H6 were rejected in all models where the associated predictor variables *CONTRACT* and *PROD_DIV* had shown significant standardized β coefficients. The meta-level results of the *OWNCHANGE* variable suggested that H1 should be rejected rather than confirmed. The dependent variables *PROFIT* and *CAPUTIL* react in the hypothesized positive direction whereas all four model specifications of the dependent variable *SELFEVAL* show the opposite sign. The positive relationship between *RAW_SUPP* and FDI performance, hypothesized under H3, was robust for *PROFIT* and *SELFEVAL* but not for *CAPUTIL*. The only independent variable that was not directly linked to a particular hypothesis, *INT_CONNECT*, was positive for M1, M2 and M3 of the dependent variable *SELFEVAL*.

The influence of control variables on FDI performance parameters was generally quite strong. Unobserved and location-bound performance determinants have been encompassed by host country dummies whose inclusion has considerably improved the explanatory power of model specifications M3 and M4 compared to M1 and M2. Being an older and larger foreign subsidiary had a positive impact on FDI performance. The same applied to greenfield and JV FDI entry modes. Local market-seeking investors had an edge over export-oriented investors. Foreign investors located in Eastern Africa, particularly those located in the three EAC founding members Kenya, Uganda, Tanzania as well as Mozambique performed significantly better than investors in other parts of SSA and specifically in comparison to investors located in Western and Middle Africa. The manufacturing subsector of the foreign investor did generally not matter much in terms of FDI performance except when the characteristics of the subsector entailed a high export-orientation.

6. Conclusions, limitations and outlook

6.1 Summary of findings and contributions

This Book attempted to draw a picture of different forms of FDI in SSA, using both macro-economic information from the BOP and firm-level data of foreign subsidiaries. It rests on the premise that FDI in SSA can take very heterogeneous forms and constitutes a moving target in the investment promotion practice. Its results recall that different types of FDI are complex and anything but homogenous. FDI follows the different investment motives of one or more of its multinational corporate owners, they flow into different economic sectors, they have their origin in different home countries, they can be small or large in volume, they can come in a one-off fashion or sequentially and they can take different entry modes. The classification of these different forms of FDI in SSA was considered a necessary first step for the analysis of firm-level performance determinants. The objective of the host country government in maximizing the economic spill-over effects from FDI need to be harmonized with the objective of financial performance maximization of the foreign direct investor. There are ample examples in SSA wherein this potential win-win arrangement between the host country and the foreign investor has failed and has led to the disappointment of either or even both parties i.e. either a foreign investor who feels that its operating space is too confined and/or the host country government which realizes that the economic impact of FDI has been much lower than previously anticipated. The heated debate about the contribution of Chinese FDI in SSA (Corkin 2007, Wang 2007, Foster et al. 2008, GTZ 2008, Kaplinsky and Morris 2008, Bräutigam 2009, Bräutigam 2010, Kolstad and Wiig 2011) or the "land grab" discussion of FDI in the agricultural sector (Woertz et al. 2008, Bräutigam and Xiaoyang 2009, Cotula and Vermeulen 2009, Cotula et al. 2009) are only two of many examples.

The Book revealed that the quality of such political debates is compromised by the fact that SSA's FDI flows and stock statistics are produced in an environment where national central banks, NSOs or IPAs suffer from serious resource and capacity constraints. From a methodological point-of-view, the two flagship manuals, the 6th version of the Balance of Payment

Manual (BPM-6) and the 4th Edition of the "OECD Benchmark Definition" of FDI provide detailed instructions on the accurate measurement of FDI. The collection and compilation of FDI data is, however, a highly complex undertaking and poses challenge to even the most advanced Central Banks and Statistical Offices of developed countries (IMF 2003, De Nederlandsche Bank 2004, Patterson et al. 2004, Wacker 2013). While benchmarks for adequate FDI data collection and compilation are discussed at OECD country-level, SSA's central banks are at the other extreme as they attempt to record at least the most basic components of FDI, namely FDI equity capital, reinvested earnings and other capital (intercompany transactions).

Chapter 2 of this Book took a closer look at the multiple and simultaneous factors that lead to an over- or underestimation of FDI flows and hinder its accurate measurement (Bellak 1998). For instance, there seems to be systematic over-reporting of FDI intentions as opposed to actual FDI implementation as well as a skewed reporting of FDI from OECD countries at the expense of South-South or intra-African FDI. A consequence of different and often conflicting FDI measurement approaches is that the results of the three main providers of FDI inward statistics, the IMF, the World Bank and UNCTAD are strikingly incongruent in the context of a year-by-year comparison, even when controlling for the effects of different country coverage in SSA (see Chapter 2.3.5). A very blatant example is the total amount of FDI stocks in SSA which the CDIS initiative of the IMF recorded at 562.3 billion USD in 2012/2013 for 19 SSA countries whereas UNCTAD reported lower FDI inward stocks of 474.3 billion USD for the same year but for *all* SSA countries with the exception of South Sudan. From an accounting perspective it is imperative that such discrepancies are overcome because SSA countries need to know whether net FDI stocks result in either an asset or a liability (or a change thereof in the case of net FDI flows) to the outside world.

Disaggregated inward FDI statistics on SSA by industrial subsector or country of origin are of such poor quality that the literature review of macro-economic FDI studies could not identify a single study that would have used such data as opposed to firm-level FDI data. Even if the magnitude of FDI flows and stocks had been accurately captured, which is not the case, FDI flows or stocks still remain a noisy and unreliable proxy for foreign affiliates' value-adding activities (Beugelsdijk et al. 2010). The mere foreign financing of an investment from an accounting perspective does not per se guarantee that the foreign affiliate undertakes a real investment by increasing its current or fixed assets and increasing its productivity (Stephan and Pfaffmann 2001, Lipsey 2007). Chapter 2 of this Book comes to the perturbing conclusion that the scant and unreliable macro-level FDI statistics, even in aggregated form, are inadequate to provide an answer to the central topic of this Book, namely what different forms of FDI can be found in SSA and what are its performance drivers.

This Book heeds the advice of researchers and IOs that enterprise-level FDI data is a prerequisite for the analysis of different forms and motives of FDI (UNCTAD 2005d, Zhan 2006, Fujita 2008, UNCTAD 2009b). Until very recently, this has technically been impossible because such firm-level data simply did not exist. The scenario has changed owing to the unprecedentedly large data sample of 2,692 foreign subsidiaries that UNIDO has collected during its 2010/11 Investor Survey in 20 SSA countries (UNIDO 2012a). This dataset forms the basis for the firm-level analyses in this Book from both a descriptive (Chapter 3) as well as an econometric angle (Chapter 5). Although comprising the richest sample available to date, it naturally also suffers from limitations that are inherent to almost any sample. These limitations will be discussed at the end of this chapter.

Chapter 3 undertook a classification of different types of FDI in SSA and revealed structural patterns. A certain number of FDI trends stemming from macro-economic FDI statistics are equally reflected in the subsidiary-level data set. Other trends again do not find confirmation from subsidiary-level FDI data. Consistency between the micro- and macro-level views of FDI exists with regard to the rapid emergence of South-South and also intra-African FDI (Page and te Velde 2004, UNCTAD 2010a, UNOSAA 2010, AFDB et al. 2014, UNCTAD 2014d). The sample shows that there is now a majority of FDI subsidiaries from developing countries (53.6 per cent) compared to developed countries which also marks an increase compared to earlier UNIDO FDI firm-level samples (UNIDO 2003, UNIDO 2007). The typical foreign subsidiary from a developing country in SSA is younger, smaller and more entrepreneurially-oriented than its counterpart from a developed country. By the same token, South investors seem to own sufficient levels of financial resources that enable them to immediately enter SSA markets through higher commitment entry modes (i.e. the greenfield-WOS combination) and even in manufacturing subsectors where initial capital investments are usually higher than in most service-related FDI sectors. The high prevalence of small developing country greenfield-WOS investors in the manufacturing sector is in contrast to the "Uppsala"-Model which considers FDI to be the outcome of a long-term incremental learning process (Johanson and Wiedersheim-Paul 1975, Johanson and Vahlne 1977, Johanson and Vahlne 1990). It may suggest that the notion of rapid internationalization in INV theories is better suited to grasp the dynamic nature of this FDI group that is increasingly penetrating into low-technology and traditional manufacturing sectors (Oviatt and McDougall 1994, Knight and Cavusgil 2004, Ibeh 2005, Evers 2011, Puig et al. 2014).

In terms of entry mode choice, the analysis of subsidiary-level FDI data proves more rewarding than macro-economic statistics. It was found that the large majority of foreign investors had established greenfield operations (85.2 per cent) and WOSs (71.8 per cent). An analysis of entry mode at the macro-level is obscured by the fact that FDI statistics rely on two disparate data sources, namely the "Thomson One database" for M&As and "fDi Markets" for greenfield FDI. Both databases are skewed towards the largest "mega" FDI investments and confirm that the largest FDI transactions, both in terms of greenfield and M&A FDI in SSA, have occurred in the mining, oil and gas and the telecommunications sector (UNCTAD 2011a). Against this backdrop, UNCTAD's estimation that approximately 50 to 80 per cent of Africa's FDI stocks are assignable to natural-resource-seeking FDI may not be far from the unknown truth (UNCTAD 2004b). This combines with diverse signs that the proportion of manufacturing FDI in SSA (in terms of total volume) has been shrinking (UNCTAD 2005c, Kaplinsky and Morris 2008, UNCTAD 2008b, Staritz 2011, UNCTAD 2014d). As a matter of fact, the firm-level analysis of Chapter 3.2 confirms that the group of recent FDI arrivals have a remarkably lower share of manufacturing firms than the group of older FDI subsidiaries, which is mainly due to the fact that young FDI from developed countries is strongly skewed towards the services sector.

In more general terms, nearly 50 per cent of all foreign firms in the sample operate in the manufacturing sector with a large number of cases in food and beverages, rubber and plastics, chemicals and metal fabrication. This supports the notion that manufacturing FDI with a focus on local or regional markets is not simply a mirage but rather has become part of reality especially for larger SSA economies that are part of RECs. Despite its cumulative importance, this group has hitherto been below the radar of investment policy making and unwarrantedly receives much less public fanfare and attention compared to the "mega deals" happening in other FDI subsectors and dominating the "Africa Rising" storyline (The Economist 2013a). By the same token, the relevance of local and regional market orientation among foreign manufacturing subsidiaries contradicts the view that the exclusive and uninhibited promotion of export-oriented FDI e.g. in the export-oriented agro-food business or AGOA-induced FDI in the garment sector, is the only road to salvation to resolve SSA's challenges of a sluggish structural transformation. The results back up authors who call for a mixed FDI promotion approach that avoids the sole reliance on one type of FDI particularly if that type is by nature footloose and known to create no or at best shallow backward linkages with domestic firms (UNCTAD 2005c, Asche et al. 2012, UNIDO 2012a).

Chapter 4 provided an account of the wealth of literature on the determinants of FDI performance. Despite its richness at the global-level, with dozens of studies about FDI subsidiary performance in China alone e.g. Luo 1997, Pan et al. 1999, Luo and Park 2001, Wei and Lau 2008 and He et al. 2015, there is no quotable piece of research that has addressed this issue in SSA. The review reveals that the FDI determinants literature in SSA has misleadingly treated FDI flows as a measure of firm-level FDI performance. The body of FDI determinants literature is nearest to the "L" determinant of Dunning's OLI paradigm (see Chapter 4.4) and advocates almost unambiguously that SSA countries need to increase their effectiveness in reducing market failures and the ensuing transaction costs, that they need to improve their institutional business climate, to cut back corruption and red tape, to develop skills, etc., in order to attract more *new* FDI. In this context, it is found that SSA has already undertaken several steps to further abolish equity restrictions in most FDI sectors and to lower minimum capital requirements while increasing legal investment security by signing and ratifying a large number of new BITs. The summation of these measures has catapulted SSA into offering one of the world's most generous and liberal FDI environments (OECD 2005b, UNCTAD 2006a, World Bank et al. 2010, De la Medina Soto and Ghossein 2013). Given the fact that the UNIDO 2010/11 Investor Survey sample consists of *operational* FDI subsidiaries, meaning of MNEs or FEs that had already invested despite (or because) SSA's prevailing business climate constraints, the set of hypotheses has been considerably expanded beyond institutional theories and is deduced from resource-based theories, transaction cost-based theories, industry-based theories and cultural distance theories.

Chapter 5 began by giving descriptive results of the employed set of variables in the regression model. It continued to present an exploratory PCA which succeeded in producing three principal components whose scores complemented the set of independent variables of the OLS regression model. Finally, several versions of OLS regression models have been presented to measure the FDI performance outcomes against the predefined set of independent variables and with varying combinations of control variables. The sample is reduced to cover manufacturing subsidiaries in order to maintain comparability of the performance variable of productive capacity utilization.

Resource-based variables prove their relevance in influencing subsidiary-level FDI performance and lend clear support to the ostensibly trivial assumption that foreign investors are active architects of their own business successes in SSA as in any other business location: Parent firms that explicitly allow their subsidiaries to carry out R&D in SSA will be recompensed with significantly larger profit margins, higher productive capacity utilization and higher satisfaction rates of subsidiary managers. Likewise, gaining and sharing experience amongst fellow subsidiaries in SSA enhances FDI performance. The subjective performance evaluation is positively influenced if the subsidiary manager and higher management are embedded in an organizational framework that facilitates the harnessing of the creative and innovative potential of the firm's own skilled work force. Recognized and unique brands and trademarks guarantee that productive capacity utilization remains high. These findings remain robust across different manufacturing subsectors. The important role of resource-based variables in explaining FDI performance entails an important policy recommendation with regard to human capital and skills development. This resonates with findings from the macro-economic FDI determinants literature in SSA (Naudé and Krugell 2003, Asiedu 2006, Naudé and Krugell 2007, Suliman and Mollick 2009). In SSA, skills gaps between industry requirements and supply by vocational training and tertiary education systems are considered to be large (Oyelaran-Oyeyinka and Barclay 2004, Oyelaran-Oyeyinka 2006, Page 2012). A sufficient supply of locally available work force with appropriate skills, particularly in the fields of science, technology, engineering or mathematics (STEM), is imperative for MNEs to address their day-to-day production challenges and to continuously improve their production processes and quality systems. Literacy skills will enable workers to read and understand written instructions or blueprints whereas numeracy and engineering skills are necessary to operate complex machines. New industrial policies have indeed placed a new focus on education and skill-formation as a previously underrated driver for the structural transformation of SSA's manufacturing sector (UNCTAD and UNIDO 2011).

In contrast to the strong and positive effect of resource-based drivers of FDI performance, no effect has been detected for the two institutional-based variables in the regression model. The insignificance of the "Investment Climate Stability and Transparency" (*STABILITY*) variable on FDI performance is in stark contrast to the majority of macro-economic FDI studies that have ascribed an overarching role to political FDI determinants in SSA (Agodo 1978, Morisset 2000, Cotton and Ramachandran 2001, Bende-Nabende 2002, Asiedu 2004b, Mlambo 2005, Asiedu 2006, Naudé and Krugell 2007). A plausible explanation is that the firm-level sample consists of existing foreign subsidiaries which, at the time of entry, must have judged SSA's political and economic investment climate to be sufficiently conducive in order to undertake an initial foreign direct investment. The foreign investor has "found its way around" and got used to the prevalent business climate as long as the SSA host country is not affected by a severe economic shock or major political unrest. In this connection, a common language background facilitates and expedites the process of adaptation to the local environment and prevents the foreign investor from making too many costly mistakes. Although political and economic stability factors remain implicitly important, their critical role in determining the FDI entry decision seem to give way to other and relatively more influential FDI performance determinants during later phases in the FDI cycle.

With regard to transaction cost and other variables, it can be concluded that the possibility of backward linkages for accessing raw material or mobilizing in-country supply chains translates into higher levels of FDI performance. A reliable physical infrastructure could facilitate the creation of more of such linkages. Growth corridors or regional economic zones reduce the real and perceived distance between different actors in SSA's local supply chain (UNIDO 2009, Page 2012). The current lack of spatial industrial development in SSA might also explain why MNEs with a less diversified product range perform better than diversified firms. Governing the supply chains in a multi-product firm is in itself a complex undertaking but in most countries in SSA it is compounded by fragmented local supply chains and relatively weak local infrastructures for road, railway or air transportation.

The Book further revealed that cooperative ownership modes have a positive influence on FDI performance. Scholars have highlighted the relevance of complementary experience, local market knowledge and absorptive capacity of the JV partner(s) to be key factors for the sustainability in mixed foreign-domestic JVs. It is worthwhile for MNEs to make extra efforts in screening potentially viable indigenous JV partners. SSA's IPAs should pro-actively support this process through all its stages, including the post-JV formation phases where instabilities and conflicts might arise and "after care" support might be required to mediate between the partners (UNCTAD 2007a, UNIDO 2007, UNIDO 2012a). The empirical results indicated that foreign investors in SSA are not averse to changes or "corrections" to the initially chosen ownership mode. Such post-entry equity variations are common and respond to changing external investment conditions, strategy adjustments or changing cooperation dynamics between two JV partners (Puck et al. 2009). The lowest share of joint ventures appeared in the youngest age group of foreign investors whereas the highest share of joint ventures (41 per cent) was in the oldest age group. It is possible that a successful FDI trajectory would be to initially enter SSA's market as a WOS, to learn about local market dynamics and to map local companies or entrepreneurs in related subsectors with whom a JV could be concluded at a later stage. Being an older and larger foreign subsidiary as well as operating within the JV ownership mode had a positive effect on the three FDI performance variables. At the same time, a switch in the other direction i.e. from a joint venture to a WOS has not translated into the expected performance gain but has instead curbed FDI performance. Interestingly, in its penultimate "Africa Foreign Investor Survey 2005" Report, UNIDO noted that larger TNCs "endeavour to maintain their existing (dominant) market position and retain managerial control over operations. However, where feasible, they seek to reduce or concentrate their capital commitments in a smaller number of locations" (UNIDO 2007, p. 126). Panel data of FDI subsidiaries would be required to test the above assumption.

To sum up, the understanding of the factors that influence FDI success or failure are intrinsic to the broader political debate about the role of FDI for the achievement of SSA's industrialization and technology upgrading objectives. The purported positive impact of FDI in terms of employment effects, its effect on skills development, technology and know-how spillovers, etc., that SSA countries seek to maximize through different policy measures, presupposes adequate levels of enterprise-level FDI performance. The Book has shed light on a holistic set of drivers of FDI performance. Its recommendations are hoped to be of value to both MNEs and SSA host countries. MNEs might take advantage of the results to better define performance-maximization strategies in the context of a current or foreseen FDI engagement in SSA. Policy-makers and institutional decision-makers may be prompted to rethink established strategies for investment promotion and investor targeting or to develop such strategies where they do not yet exist.

6.2 Limitations and outlook

The research in this Book is subject to important limitations that may at the same time point to some interesting avenues for future theoretical and empirical refinements.

The limitations of macro-economic FDI statistics in SSA have been discussed at length in Chapter 2 and it emerged that there are various factors at play that may entail an under- or overestimation of SSA's FDI flows and stocks. Generally speaking, there are several indications that the current levels of FDI flows and stocks are under- rather than overestimated at the continental SSA level, although single SSA countries (e.g. Mauritius Seychelles or Liberia) seem to have bloated FDI inflow and stock figures. In the case of SSA, the error-prone practice of cumulating year-by-year FDI inflows to compute FDI stocks is still the rule rather than the exception.

The problems associated with FDI statistics in SSA point to the need of extensive and continent-wide capacity building of SSA's central banks and NSOs to ensure that the FDI methodologies under the BPM-5 are consistently applied. Most SSA countries are members of IMF's GDDS but such membership does not in itself guarantee the upgrading of FDI data compilation and dissemination techniques. Membership in the SDDS appears to be a distant and long-term goal for most SSA countries because the SDDS presupposes that its members have the capacity to implement the complex BPM-6 which is currently only the case for South Africa and Mauritius. An innovative example of a capacity building project in this area is the recently concluded "Enhanced Data Dissemination Initiative (EDDI) Project", which has been implemented by the IMF and was funded by the UK Department for International Development (DFID) for the period of 2010 until 2015 and which aimed at improving macro-economic statistics in 25 SSA countries. The sub-module for BOP statistics covered Gambia, Ghana, Kenya, Mauritius, Mozambique and Nigeria and the results of the Programme had a positive impact on the quality of IIP statements either through the continued use of ITRSs or through the regular implementation of annual enterprise surveys as the direct source for the BOP financial account transactions of enterprises (Morrison 2013, Quin et al. 2013). In this connection, the CDIS initiative of the IMF which started in 2009 has the potential to bring an unprecedentedly new understanding on the structure of SSA's IIP because it allows the separation between net equity and debt positions and the reporting of FDI "mirror" data i.e. inward stock data from the reporting economy shown side-by-side with outward stock data from all counterpart economies. It is to be hoped that the CDIS would eventually cover all of SSA together with complementary capacity building that follows the logic of the EDDI Project. The core group of 19 SSA countries under the CDIS should continue with the collection of panel data.

Besides the IMF-CDIS, there are two more IOs, namely UNIDO and the World Bank[141] that have collected FDI firm-level data in a cross-SSA framework. Although all IOs subscribe to the idea that more FDI establishment or subsidiary surveys are needed to obtain a fuller picture of FDI dynamics at the macro-, meso- and micro-level, the three datasets of CDIS, UNIDO and World Bank are completely disconnected from one another. For instance, there would be a great potential for knowledge enhancement by linking World Bank's rich perception data on the host country's business climate with UNIDO's data on FDI performance and impact. It would hence be desirable that the main providers of FDI data and other IOs with a mandate to report FDI statistics form a permanent Consultative Committee with the aim of aligning their methodological approaches and of defining criteria that enable cross-connections and data triangulation. Such a Committee could possibly be attached to the newly established "Inter-agency and Expert Group on SDG Indicators (IAEG-SDGs)".

Concerning the UNIDO 2010/11 Investor Survey sample underlying the analyses in Chapters 3 and 5, the first limitation is related to the generalizability of findings at the wider SSA-level. The sample consists of foreign subsidiaries in 20 SSA countries and thus disregards a large number of SSA countries, in particular countries in Central Africa. The regression analysis of Chapter 5 is further limited to manufacturing although it is

141 Subsidiary-level FDI data is a by-product of the World Bank's global Enterprise Survey Programme. Although the number of responding foreign subsidiaries is quite large, its use is limited by the fact that the World Bank country samples are not stratified according to investor ownership.

likely that the predictive capacity of the chosen FDI performance determinants would differ across the three main sectors.

UNIDO's 2010/11 Investor Survey data is cross-section data. This fact inhibits the analysis of the dynamic evolution of the foreign subsidiary in SSA. The analysis is based on the underlying and potentially misleading assumption that model parameters are time invariant and stable across firms (Bowen and Wiersema 1999). The risks of biased inferences due to unobserved heterogeneity cannot be fully ruled out although no alarming signs of heteroscedasticity have been detected. Furthermore, cross-section data samples are usually vulnerable to a survivor bias. As a result, the model measures the determinants of increased business success whereas it misses out on the reasons for business failure in terms of subsidiary termination or a complete divestment.

One of the methodological strengths of the survey was to approach managers of foreign subsidiaries and invite them to share their perceptions of FDI performance and of a wide range of host country factors. One the one hand, it permitted the survey to obtain detailed structural information about the subsidiary and its financial accounting data. On the other hand, assessments on the overall governance structure of the MNE (global sales, global diversification strategies, division of labour, etc.) may not be of the same quality and accuracy as those obtained from studies that directly target the MNE parent. From the perspective of the subsidiary manager alone, it would be impossible to determine the role of SSA's subsidiary in the global internationalization process of MNEs, e.g. whether internationalization into SSA occurs earlier or later in the lifetime of an MNE, whether subsidiaries in SSA are endowed with a different mandate than subsidiaries in other parts of the world or whether the size of the subsidiary is large or small, measured as a proportion of the MNE's global sales or global employment figures. The subsidiary's strategic position within the overall MNE will certainly influence its autonomy and the quality of managerial, financial and technological support (including "bailout" support during times of poor performance) that it can expect from the parent. Future research could emulate the design approach of the study by Gomez-Mera et al. which gauged the characteristics and motivations of MNE parent companies from four emerging economies on the basis of a "Potential Investor Survey" with specific questions on SSA (Gómez-Mera et al. 2015).

The Book does not claim to have presented an exhaustive set of firm-level determinants of subsidiary performance. The explanatory power of the regression model was acceptable for cross-section survey data. The adjusted R^2 was around 0.2 in the majority of model specifications. Data limitations obstructed the inclusion of other obvious predictor variables of firm performance that would most likely had improved the explanatory power of the statistical model. This is most evident for variables pertaining to industry-based theories and describing the foreign subsidiary's market share and the degree of inter-firm competition in a given industrial segment. By the same token, the inclusion of host country dummies may not have fully captured the emergence of geographical concepts in international business theory as well as the performance effects that stem from spatial agglomeration of FDI firms (Buckley 2014, Farole and Winkler 2014, Zschoche 2015). On the one hand, the likely negative performance effect of an otherwise poor general investment climate could be offset by the existence of a micro investment climate of relative stability inside an EPZ or an IZ. On the other hand, an overall positive investment climate could be exacerbated by a geographically disadvantaged and remote FDI location, creating a challenging micro investment climate with poor infrastructure, low institutional coverage and support, lack of a skilled work force and others. Future FDI research for SSA should possibly delve deeper into providing a link between the qualitative analysis of the institutional landscape of specific FDI service provision in confined geographical areas or specific industry subsectors, including newly emerging subsectors (e.g. the oil and gas sector in Ghana, Mozambique or Tanzania) and the quantitative analysis of foreign firm-level (re-)actions of backward and forward linkage creation, JV creation, human capital development and others.

Endogeneity is considered a common problem in multivariate analysis and even more so in studies that examine a relationship between MNE strategy and its performance (Hult et al. 2008, Martin 2013). MNEs self-select strategies based on the expectation that they would lead to superior performance than alternative strategies. To mitigate the risk of biased parameter estimations as a result of endogeneity, the two control variables of entry mode and export intensity have been alternately included and omitted from the OLS regression model while keeping track of changes between the different model specifications. Nonetheless, a limitation of the research design is that it did not include an instrumental variable, often referred to as the "Heckit variable", correcting for such a self-selection effect (Heckman 1979, Shaver 1998). An alternative methodology could have been the design of a "strategy fit" variable as first introduced by Brouthers (Brouthers 2002).

Besides the gaps in the set of independent variables, there is also room for future improvements of the dependent variable of FDI performance following by and large the propositions of Hult et al. (Hult et al. 2008). FDI performance is a multi-dimensional construct which goes beyond the three chosen measures of profit margin, productive capacity utilization and performance self-evaluation. Sales-based performance measures can include sales volume, export share in total sales, sales growth or export growth. Productivity measures, for example labour productivity or total factor productivity, have also been deployed in the extant FDI performance literature. The foreign subsidiary's market share and its survival are also relevant indicators of performance. Future studies with focus on FDI performance in SSA should make an attempt to include these additional measures of business performance.

The classification of FDI investment types led to the identification of several subgroups that would deserve more attention in any future qualitative and quantitative research. For instance, the FDI category of foreign entrepreneurs (FEs) is a very prominent group in SSA whose governance structures do not seem to follow the classical headquarters–subsidiary relationship. In the case of FEs, the boundaries between FDI and domestic investments often become blurred. An FE may combine own equity or savings with local financing and start a new business venture in SSA outside any central bank's ITRS. The FE group displays features of both INVs, especially INVs in low-technology and traditional subsectors (Ibeh 2005, Evers 2011, Puig et al. 2014) and so-called "parallel entrepreneurs" (The Economist 2012). A specific subgroup amongst these FEs are diaspora investors who are returning to their original SSA home country following classical FDI determinants coupled with an emotional bias towards their own SSA home country (African Courir 2010, Chacko and Gebre 2013, Boly et al. 2014). A number of case studies on FEs and diaspora FDI would help gain a better understanding of their business motives, their competitive advantages as against MNEs or purely domestic investors, their coping strategies to overcome the liability of foreignness, their typical growth trajectory as well as other business characteristics.

Another interesting subgroup is that of regional market-seeking FDI in SSA. A pertinent research question would be to assess whether the host country's membership in a REC has the potential to boost the arrival of a sizable number of regional market-seeking investors and whether the effect differs amongst SSA's multiple and often overlapping RECs or for specific member countries within a given REC. The available data indicated that regionalization of FDI in SSA is not instantaneous in the sense that some FDI subsidiaries would be "born-regional". Instead, foreign subsidiaries seem to take their time to test the initial host country market before they venture into neighbouring markets through exports or the establishment of fellow subsidiaries. A dynamic analysis of the determinants and the chosen timing of the switch from local market orientation towards regional market orientation would be an important contribution to the formulation of regional FDI promotion strategies by SSA's RECs.

Annex
Tables and Figures

Annex Table 1: IMF–CDIS Survey coverage in SSA during different years

Country	Inward Direct Investment Positions	Inward Equity Positions (Net)	Inward Debt Instruments Positions (Net)	Outward Direct Investment Positions	Outward Equity Positions (Net)	Outward Debt Instruments Positions (Net)
Benin	2011, 2012	2011, 2012	2011, 2012	2011, 2012	2011, 2012	2011, 2012
Botswana	2009, 2010, 2011, 2012, 2013	2010, 2011, 2012, 2013	2010, 2011, 2012, 2013	2009, 2010, 2011, 2012, 2013	2010, 2011, 2012, 2013	2010, 2011, 2012, 2013
Burkina Faso	2012, 2013	2012, 2013	2012, 2013	2012, 2013	2013	2012, 2013
Cape Verde	2012, 2013	2012, 2013	2012, 2013			
Ghana	2009, 2010, 2011, 2012	2009, 2010, 2011, 2012	2009, 2010, 2011, 2012			
Guinea-Bissau	2011, 2012	2011, 2012	2011			
Mali	2011, 2012, 2013	2011, 2012, 2013	2011, 2012, 2013	2011, 2012, 2013	2011, 2012, 2013	2011, 2012, 2013
Mauritius	2009, 2010, 2011, 2012, 2013	2009, 2010, 2011, 2012, 2013	2009, 2010, 2011, 2012, 2013	2009, 2010, 2011, 2012, 2013	2009, 2010, 2011, 2012, 2013	2009, 2010, 2011, 2012, 2013
Mozambique	2009, 2010, 2011, 2012	2009, 2010, 2011, 2012	2009, 2010, 2011, 2012	2009, 2010, 2011, 2012	2009, 2010, 2011, 2012	2009, 2010, 2011, 2012
Niger	2012	2012	2012			
Nigeria	2009, 2010, 2011, 2012, 2013	2009, 2010, 2011, 2012, 2013	2009, 2010, 2011, 2012, 2013			
Rwanda	2011, 2012	2011, 2012	2011, 2012			
Senegal	2011, 2012	2011, 2012	2011, 2012	2011, 2012	2011, 2012	2011, 2012
Seychelles	2009, 2010, 2011, 2012, 2013	2009, 2010, 2011, 2012, 2013	2009, 2010, 2011, 2012, 2013			
South Africa	2009, 2010, 2011, 2012, 2013	2009, 2010, 2011, 2012, 2013	2009, 2010, 2011, 2012, 2013	2009, 2010, 2011, 2012, 2013	2009, 2010, 2011, 2012, 2013	2009, 2010, 2011, 2012, 2013
Tanzania	2010, 2011, 2012					
Togo	2011, 2013	2011, 2013	2011, 2013	2011, 2013	2011, 2013	2011, 2013
Uganda	2009, 2010, 2011, 2012, 2013	2009, 2010, 2011, 2012, 2013	2009, 2010, 2011, 2012, 2013			
Zambia	2009, 2010, 2011, 2012, 2013	2009, 2010, 2011, 2012, 2013	2009, 2010, 2011, 2012, 2013	2009, 2010, 2011, 2012, 2013		

Source: IMF Coordinated Direct Investment Survey (CDIS); http://cdis.imf.org (accessed on 29 March 2015).

Annex Table 2: Meta-analysis of the main data sources of FDI in SSA from 2006 to 2012

SSA Country	2006	2007	2008	2009	2010	2011	2012
Angola	All same	All same	All same	All same	All same	All same	All same
Benin	IMF=UNCTAD; WB different	IMF=UNCTAD; WB different	IMF=UNCTAD; WB different	IMF=WB; UNCTAD different	IMF=WB; UNCTAD different	All same	All same
Botswana	All different	All different	All different	All same	All same	All same	All same
Burkina Faso	All different*	All different*	All different*	All different*	All different*	All same*	All same*
Burundi	All same	All same	All same	All same	All same	All same	All same
Cape Verde	All different	IMF=WB; UNCTAD different	All different	IMF=WB; UNCTAD different	IMF=WB; UNCTAD different	IMF=WB; UNCTAD different	IMF=WB; UNCTAD different
Cameroon	WB=UNCTAD; IMF different	WB=UNCTAD; IMF different	WB=UNCTAD; IMF different	WB=UNCTAD; IMF different	WB=UNCTAD; IMF different	IMF=WB; UNCTAD different	IMF=WB; UNCTAD different
Central African Republic	All same*	All same*	All same*	All same*	All same*	All same*	All same*
Chad	All same*	All same*	All same*	All same*	All same*	All same*	All same*
Comoros	All same*	All same*	All same*	All same*	All same*	All same*	All same*
Congo, Rep.	IMF=WB; UNCTAD different	IMF=WB; UNCTAD different	All same*	All same*	All same*	All same*	All same*
Côte d'Ivoire	IMF=UNCTAD; WB different	IMF=UNCTAD; WB different	IMF=UNCTAD; WB different	IMF=WB; UNCTAD different	IMF=WB; UNCTAD different	All same*	All same*
Djibouti	All same	All same	IMF=WB; UNCTAD different	IMF=WB; UNCTAD different	IMF=WB; UNCTAD different	IMF=WB; UNCTAD different	IMF=WB; UNCTAD different
DRC	All different*	All different*	All different*	All different*	All different*	All different*	All different*
Equatorial Guinea	All same*	All same*	All same*	All same*	All same*	All same*	All same*
Eritrea	All same*	All same*	All same*	All same*	All same*	All same*	All same*
Ethiopia	All same	All same	All same	All same	All same	All same	IMF=WB; UNCTAD different
Gabon	All same*	All same*	All same*	All same*	All same*	All same*	All same*
Gambia, The	IMF=WB; UNCTAD different	All different	IMF=WB; UNCTAD different	IMF=WB; UNCTAD different	IMF=WB; UNCTAD different	IMF=WB; UNCTAD different	IMF=WB; UNCTAD different
Ghana	IMF=WB; UNCTAD different	IMF=WB; UNCTAD different	IMF=WB; UNCTAD different	IMF=WB; UNCTAD different	All same	IMF=WB; UNCTAD different	IMF=WB; UNCTAD different
Guinea	All same	All same	All same	All same	All same	IMF=WB; UNCTAD different	IMF=WB; UNCTAD different

SSA Country	2006	2007	2008	2009	2010	2011	2012
Guinea-Bissau	All different	IMF=WB; UNCTAD different	IMF=UNCTAD; WB different	All different	All different	WB=UNCTAD; IMF different	WB=UNCTAD; IMF different
Lesotho	WB=UNCTAD; IMF different	WB=UNCTAD; IMF different	WB=UNCTAD; IMF different	All same	IMF=WB; UNCTAD different	IMF=WB; UNCTAD different	All different
Kenya	All same	IMF=WB; UNCTAD different	IMF=WB; UNCTAD different	IMF=WB; UNCTAD different	All same	All same	All same
Lesotho	WB=UNCTAD; IMF different	WB=UNCTAD; IMF different	WB=UNCTAD; IMF different	All same	IMF=WB; UNCTAD different	IMF=WB; UNCTAD different	All different
Liberia	IMF=WB; UNCTAD different	IMF=WB; UNCTAD different	All different	IMF=WB; UNCTAD different	IMF=WB; UNCTAD different	IMF=WB; UNCTAD different	WB=UNCTAD; IMF different
Madagascar	All same*	All same*	All same*	All same*	All same*	All same*	All same*
Malawi	All same	All same	All same	All same	All same	All same	All same
Mali	All different	All different	All different	IMF=WB; UNCTAD different	IMF=WB; UNCTAD different	All same	All same*
Mauritania	All same*	All same*	All same*	All same*	All same*	All same*	All same*
Mauritius	IMF=WB; UNCTAD different	IMF=WB; UNCTAD different	IMF=WB; UNCTAD different	IMF=WB; UNCTAD different	WB=UNCTAD; IMF different	WB=UNCTAD; IMF different	WB=UNCTAD; IMF different
Mozambique	All different	All different	All different	IMF=WB; UNCTAD different	IMF=WB; UNCTAD different	IMF=WB; UNCTAD different	IMF=WB; UNCTAD different
Namibia	All different	All different	All different	All different	All different	All different	All different
Niger	IMF=UNCTAD; WB different	IMF=UNCTAD; WB different	IMF=UNCTAD; WB different	IMF=WB; UNCTAD different	IMF=WB; UNCTAD different	WB=UNCTAD; IMF different	WB=UNCTAD; IMF different
Nigeria	IMF=WB; UNCTAD different	IMF=WB; UNCTAD different	IMF=WB; UNCTAD different	IMF=WB; UNCTAD different	IMF=WB; UNCTAD different	IMF=WB; UNCTAD different	IMF=WB; UNCTAD different
Rwanda	WB=UNCTAD; IMF different	WB=UNCTAD; IMF different	All different	All same	All same	All same	All same
São Tomé and Príncipe	IMF=WB; UNCTAD different	IMF=WB; UNCTAD different	IMF=WB; UNCTAD different	All same	All same	IMF=WB; UNCTAD different	IMF=WB; UNCTAD different
Senegal	IMF=UNCTAD; WB different	IMF=UNCTAD; WB different	IMF=UNCTAD; WB different	IMF=WB; UNCTAD different	All same	All same	All same*
Seychelles	IMF=WB; UNCTAD different	All different	All different	IMF=WB; UNCTAD different	IMF=WB; UNCTAD different	All different	All different
Sierra Leone	IMF=UNCTAD; WB different	All different	All different	IMF=WB; UNCTAD different	IMF=WB; UNCTAD different	All same	All different

SSA Country	2006	2007	2008	2009	2010	2011	2012
Somalia	All same*	All same*	All same*	All same*	All same*	All same*	All same*
South Africa	All different	All different	All different	IMF=WB; UNCTAD different	IMF=WB; UNCTAD different	IMF=WB; UNCTAD different	IMF=WB; UNCTAD different
South Sudan	No data	No data	No data	No data	No data	No data	No data
Sudan	All different	All different	All different	IMF=WB; UNCTAD different	IMF=WB; UNCTAD different	IMF=WB; UNCTAD different	IMF=WB; UNCTAD different
Swaziland	IMF=WB; UNCTAD different	IMF=WB; UNCTAD different	IMF=WB; UNCTAD different	IMF=WB; UNCTAD different	IMF=WB; UNCTAD different	IMF=WB; UNCTAD different	All same
Tanzania	All same	All same	IMF=WB; UNCTAD different	IMF=WB; UNCTAD different	IMF=WB; UNCTAD different	IMF=WB; UNCTAD different	All different
Togo	IMF=UNCTAD; WB different	IMF=UNCTAD; WB different	IMF=UNCTAD; WB different	IMF=WB; UNCTAD different	IMF=WB; UNCTAD different	All different*	All same*
Uganda	All same	All same	All same	All same	All same	All same	All same
Zambia	IMF=WB; UNCTAD different	All same	All same	All same	All same	All different	IMF=UNCTAD; WB different
Zimbabwe	All same*	All same*	All same*	All same*	All same*	All same*	All same*

Sources: IMF, http://elibrary-data.imf.org (accessed on 9 January 2015); WDI database (World Bank) and UNCTAD FDI Database.
*IMF BOP data not available (analysis only refers to UNCTAD and World Bank data sources);
The data sources were statistically treated as "same" in case the discrepancy between data sources was between +/- 1000 USD;
WB=World Bank

Annex Table 3: BOP reporting of SSA countries on the direct investment components of FDI assets (FDI outflows)

Country	Equity and Investment Fund Shares				Debt instruments		
	Equity other than reinvestment earnings						
	DI in DIE	DIE in DI (reverse inv.)	Between fellow enterprises	Reinv. Earnings	DI in DIE	DIE in DI (reverse inv.)	Between fellow enterprises
Angola	X				X		
Benin	X	X	X	X	X	X	X
Botswana	X	X		X	X	X	
Burkina Faso							
Burundi	X						
Cameroon	X	X		X	X	X	
Cape Verde	X	X			X	X	
Central African Republic							
Chad							
Comoros							
Congo, Rep.							
Côte d'Ivoire	X			X	X	X	
Djibouti							
DRC							
Equatorial Guinea							
Eritrea							
Ethiopia							
Gabon							
Gambia, The							
Ghana					X		
Guinea	X			X		X	
Guinea-Bissau	X			X	X	X	
Kenya	X						
Lesotho	X				X		
Liberia						X	
Madagascar							
Malawi	X			X	X		
Mali	X	X		X	X	X	
Mauritania							
Mauritius	X				X		
Mozambique	X				X	X	
Namibia	X			X	X	X	
Niger	X	X		X	X	X	
Nigeria	X			X			
Rwanda							
São Tomé and Príncipe	X				X		
Senegal	X	X	X	X	X	X	X
Seychelles	X			X			
Sierra Leone						X	
Somalia							
South Africa	X				X		
South Sudan							
Sudan							
Swaziland	X			X	X		
Tanzania							
Togo	X	X		X	X	X	
Uganda	X			X			
Zambia					X		
Zimbabwe							

Source: Financial account breakdown for direct investment, presented on http://elibrary-data.imf.org (accessed on 9 January 2015); Reported if SSA country has collected the direct investment item at least once between 2009 and 2013
DI – Direct Investment; DIE – Direct Investment Enterprise.

Annex Table 4: The 10 largest greenfield projects in SSA LDCs, 2003–2010

Host country	Name of company	Home country	Sector	Estimated amount, in million USD	Estimated no. of jobs created	Year
Angola	Total	France	Coal, oil and natural gas	9,000	2,013	2009
Angola	Chevron Corporation	US	Coal, oil and natural gas	8,300	1,967	2004
Mozambique	Ayr Logistics	US	Coal, oil and natural gas	5,500	1,267	2008
Uganda	Tullow Oil	UK	Coal, oil and natural gas	5,000	1,119	2008
Angola	Chevron Corporation	US	Coal, oil and natural gas	3,800	-	2008
Angola	CITIC Group	China	Real estate	3,535	3,000	2008
Angola	Total	France	Oil & Natural Gas Corp	3,400	806	2003
Angola	ExxonMobil	US	Oil & Natural Gas Corp	3,400	806	2004
Madagascar	Sumitomo Group	Japan	Metals	3,300	3,000	2007
Angola	ExxonMobil	US	Oil & Natural Gas Corp	3,000	839	2003

Source: UNCTAD 2011a.

Annex Table 5: FDI inward stock breakdown according to countries of origin

		Total CDIS stock (in million USD)	Main investor		2nd		3rd		4th		5th		6th		7th		8th		Other and unsp.
Country	Year		Country	Per cent	Country	Per cent	Country	Per cent	Country	Per cent	Country	Per cent	Country	Per cent	Country	Per cent	Country	Per cent	Per cent
Benin	2012	977	France	**39.8%**	Côte d'Ivoire	**11.8%**	UK	**8.0%**	Nigeria	**7.9%**	Senegal	**7.8%**	Togo	**4.8%**	Luxemb.	**3.6%**	UAE	**2.1%**	**14.1%**
Botswana	2013	4,921	Luxemb.	**43.9%**	China	**14.7%**	SA	**12.4%**	Australia	**10.3%**	Mauritius	**5.0%**	UK	**4.9%**	US	**2.8%**	Zimbabwe	**1.9%**	**4.0%**
Burkina Faso	2013	1,328	Barbados	**21.8%**	Canada	**11.9%**	France	**4.9%**	Côte d'Ivoire	**4.7%**	Togo	**4.5%**	Australia	**4.2%**	Cayman Islands	**2.3%**	Mali	**2.1%**	**43.5%**
Cape Verde	2013	1,611	Portugal	**26.0%**	Spain	**23.8%**	Italy	**11.0%**	UK	**10.2%**	Ireland	**5.7%**	Netherl.	**0.1%**	n/a	**n/a**	n/a	**n/a**	**23.2%**
Ghana	2012	13,076	UK	**23.9%**	Ireland	**18.1%**	Cayman Islands	**11.3%**	Brit. Virgin Islands	**9.4%**	France	**9.3%**	Panama	**6.7%**	Brit. Indian Ocean Terr.	**4.2%**	Belize	**3.6%**	**13.6%**
Guinea-Bissau	2012	150	Luxemb.	**42.9%**	Senegal	**23.7%**	Portugal	**15.5%**	Togo	**8.3%**	Mali	**6.4%**	SA	**2.3%**	Côte d'Ivoire	**0.4%**	Lebanon	**0.4%**	**n/a**
Mali	2013	2,355	UK	**33.0%**	Australia	**26.2%**	Senegal	**7.3%**	Canada	**6.8%**	Libya	**6.1%**	SA	**5.4%**	France	**3.5%**	Morocco	**2.8%**	**8.9%**
Mauritius	2013	238,002	US	**22.7%**	India	**9.6%**	UK	**8.8%**	Cayman Islands	**8.6%**	China	**7.0%**	Singapore	**5.7%**	Netherl.	**5.7%**	SA	**4.5%**	**27.4%**
Mozambique	2012	13,793	SA	**18.0%**	UAE	**17.4%**	US	**11.4%**	Mauritius	**9.0%**	Australia	**8.9%**	Portugal	**8.6%**	Italy	**6.5%**	UK	**4.8%**	**15.3%**
Niger	2012	1,552	France	**46.0%**	China	**27.8%**	Côte d'Ivoire	**6.8%**	Libya	**4.1%**	SA	**3.7%**	Tunisia	**3.5%**	Saudi Arabia	**2.3%**	Mali	**2.1%**	**3.8%**
Nigeria	2013	94,961	Netherl.	**18.1%**	China	**14.3%**	Bermuda	**13.7%**	Brit. Virgin Islands	**11.3%**	UK	**10.6%**	France	**6.1%**	US	**4.5%**	Saudi Arabia	**3.7%**	**17.6%**
Rwanda	2012	716	Mauritius	**24.8%**	SA	**16.2%**	Luxemb.	**10.4%**	Libya	**8.2%**	Kenya	**7.8%**	Netherl.	**6.9%**	Nigeria	**3.2%**	Togo	**2.7%**	**19.6%**
Senegal	2012	1,158	France	**45.5%**	India	**6.1%**	Morocco	**5.7%**	US	**4.3%**	Togo	**3.2%**	Côte d'Ivoire	**3.1%**	Libya	**2.3%**	Lebanon	**1.8%**	**28.1%**
Seychelles	2013	1,080	Mauritius	**40.5%**	Cyprus	**21.1%**	Russia	**11.7%**	UK	**5.1%**	US	**4.0%**	Brit. Virgin Islands	**3.6%**	France	**2.4%**	China	**2.1%**	**9.5%**
South Africa	2013	152,124	UK	**48.3%**	Netherl.	**16.8%**	US	**6.1%**	Germany	**4.7%**	China	**3.9%**	Japan	**2.2%**	Luxemb.	**1.9%**	Australia	**1.1%**	**14.9%**
Tanzania	2012	12,741	SA	**25.3%**	UK	**18.3%**	Barbados	**14.7%**	Canada	**10.5%**	Kenya	**4.9%**	Mauritius	**4.8%**	Switzerl.	**4.4%**	Netherl.	**2.5%**	**14.7%**

Country	Year	Total CDIS stock (in million USD)	Main investor		2nd		3rd		4th		5th		6th		7th		8th		Other and unsp.
			Country	Per cent	Country	Per cent	Country	Per cent	Country	Per cent	Country	Per cent	Country	Per cent	Country	Per cent	Country	Per cent	Per cent
Togo	2013	458	Côte d'Ivoire	**16.4%**	Gibraltar	**13.9%**	Benin	**11.3%**	UK	**11.1%**	US	**7.2%**	India	**6.7%**	Ghana	**6.6%**	France	**5.7%**	**21.1%**
Uganda	2013	9,214	Netherl.	**50.6%**	UK	**9.6%**	Kenya	**4.2%**	Mauritius	**3.7%**	Belgium	**1.6%**	Switzerl.	**1.1%**	US	**1.1%**	India	**1.0%**	**28.1%**
Zambia	2013	12,114	Australia	**15.8%**	China	**10.8%**	SA	**8.5%**	Switzerl.	**8.3%**	Ireland	**4.4%**	UK	**4.0%**	Netherl.	**2.3%**	Bermuda	**2.2%**	**43.8%**

Source: http://cdis.imf.org (accessed on 29 March 2015).

Annex Figure 1: Comparing SSA's FDI inflows with FDI greenfield and M&A databases, 2006 to 2013

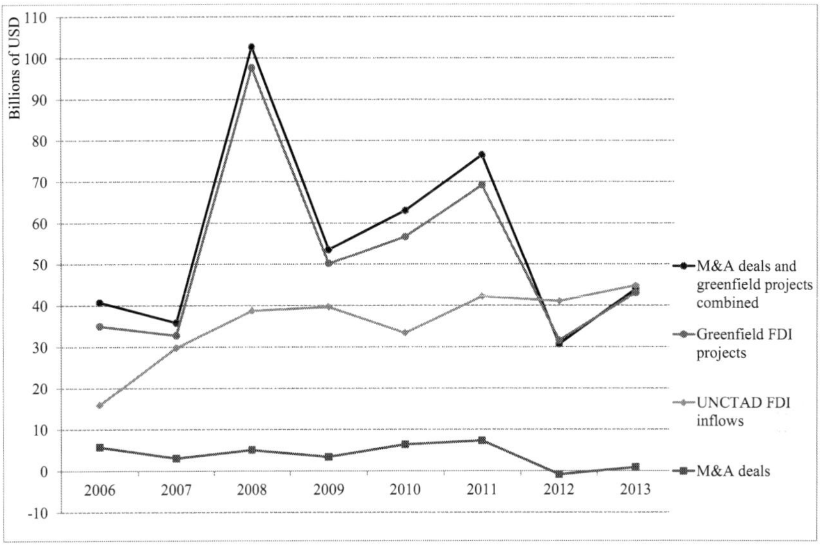

Source: Author's own calculation based on Thomson Reuters Financial (M&A) and "fDi Markets" data (greenfield) reported in UNCTAD 2011b, UNCTAD 2012b, 2013b and UNCTAD 2014d.

Annex Table 6: World Bank Enterprise Surveys in SSA and breakdown of domestic and foreign firms in the sample

Country	Year of most recent survey	Ownership status			Total	Per cent of Foreign in [Domestic + Foreign]	Year of previous survey(s)
		Domestic	Foreign	Unknown			
Angola	2010	246	104	10	360	29.7	2006
Benin	2009	127	22	1	150	14.8	n/a
Botswana	2010	137	129	2	268	48.5	2006
Burkina Faso	2009	336	54	4	394	13.8	n/a
Burundi	2014	127	30	0	157	19.1	2006
Cameroon	2009	297	66	0	363	18.2	n/a
Cape Verde	2009	131	24	1	156	15.5	n/a
Central African Rep.	2011	86	64	0	150	42.7	n/a
Chad	2009	103	47	0	150	31.3	n/a
Congo, Rep.	2009	111	33	7	151	22.9	n/a
Côte d'Ivoire	2009	433	92	1	526	17.5	n/a
Djibouti	2013	223	33	10	266	12.9	n/a
DRC	2013	437	90	2	529	17.1	2006, 2010
Eritrea	2009	170	6	3	179	3.4	n/a
Ethiopia	2011	515	42	87	644	7.5	n/a
Gabon	2009	69	110	0	179	61.5	n/a
Gambia	2006	122	52	0	174	29.9	n/a
Ghana	2013	604	115	1	720	16.0	2007
Guinea	2006	200	23	0	223	10.3	n/a
Guinea Bissau	2006	144	15	0	159	9.4	n/a
Kenya	2013	679	89	13	781	11.6	2007
Lesotho	2009	101	50	0	151	33.1	n/a
Liberia	2009	130	20	0	150	13.3	n/a
Madagascar	2013	372	146	14	532	28.2	2009

Country	Year of most recent survey	Ownership status			Total	Per cent of Foreign in [Domestic + Foreign]	Year of previous survey(s)
		Domestic	Foreign	Unknown			
Malawi	2014	355	101	67	523	22.1	2009
Mali	2010	304	40	16	360	11.6	2007
Mauritania	2014	125	23	2	150	15.5	2006
Mauritius	2009	346	42	10	398	10.8	n/a
Mozambique	2007	384	95	0	479	19.8	n/a
Namibia	2014	503	36	41	580	6.7	2006
Niger	2009	116	34	0	150	22.7	n/a
Nigeria	2014	2,162	320	194	2,676	12.9	2007
Rwanda	2011	190	50	1	241	20.8	2006
Senegal	2014	529	70	2	601	11.7	2007
Sierra Leone	2009	129	21	0	150	14.0	n/a
South Africa	2007	815	121	1	937	12.9	n/a
South Sudan	2014	438	292	8	738	40.0	n/a
Sudan	2014	647	9	6	662	1.4	n/a
Swaziland	2006	196	111	0	307	36.2	n/a
Tanzania	2013	721	44	48	813	5.8	2006
Togo	2009	108	47	0	155	30.3	n/a
Uganda	2013	648	108	6	762	14.3	2006
Zambia	2013	511	201	8	720	28.2	2007
Zimbabwe	2011	502	95	2	599	15.9	n/a
TOTAL		**15,629**	**3,316**	**568**	**19,513**	**17.5**	

Source: World Bank, http://www.enterprisesurveys.org (accessed and downloaded on 9 January 2016).

Annex Table 7: Top five investment subsectors in SSA by different countries of origin

Country	1. Rank	Per cent	2. Rank	Per cent	3. Rank	Per cent	4. Rank	Per cent	5. Rank	Per cent	Five top sectors
China	Rubber and plastics	**11.8%**	Wearing apparel	**8.5%**	Construction	**8.5%**	Wholesale trade and vehicle trade	**7.2%**	Fabricated metal products	**6.5%**	**42.5%**
France	Real estate, consulting, IT	**16.7%**	Wholesale trade and vehicle trade	**9.4%**	Construction	**8.1%**	Food and beverages	**8.1%**	Transport	**6.8%**	**49.1%**
Germany	Chemical and chemical products	**11.5%**	Other non-metallic mineral products	**9.6%**	Wholesale trade and vehicle trade	**9.6%**	Post and telecommunications	**7.7%**	Machinery and equipment n.e.c.	**5.8%**	**44.2%**
India	Food and beverages	**11.9%**	Wholesale trade and vehicle trade	**11.3%**	Rubber and plastics	**10.8%**	Chemical and chemical products	**9.3%**	Retail trade	**6.4%**	**49.7%**
Italy	Construction	**13.1%**	Hotels and restaurants	**11.9%**	Food and beverages	**10.7%**	Agriculture, forestry, fishing	**9.5%**	Real estate, consulting, IT	**8.3%**	**53.6%**
Kenya	Financial intermediation and insurance	**12.5%**	Rubber and plastics	**9.7%**	Food and beverages	**9.7%**	Real estate, consulting, IT	**8.3%**	Retail trade	**8.3%**	**48.6%**
Lebanon	Wholesale trade and vehicle trade	**17.6%**	Rubber and plastics	**14.1%**	Food and beverages	**9.4%**	Chemical and chemical products	**9.4%**	Retail trade	**9.4%**	**60.0%**
Netherlands	Agriculture, forestry, fishing	**30.8%**	Real estate, consulting, IT	**12.3%**	Wholesale trade and vehicle trade	**10.8%**	Food and beverages	**7.7%**	Transport	**6.2%**	**67.7%**
Portugal	Construction	**15.8%**	Wholesale trade and vehicle trade	**10.9%**	Hotels and restaurants	**7.9%**	Food and beverages	**7.9%**	Real estate, consulting, IT	**5.9%**	**48.5%**
South Africa	Wholesale trade and vehicle trade	**10.6%**	Fabricated metal products	**8.3%**	Food and beverages	**7.8%**	Financial intermediation and insurance	**7.8%**	Real estate, consulting, IT	**5.6%**	**40.0%**
UK	Food and beverages	**13.9%**	Chemical and chemical products	**10.2%**	Agriculture, forestry, fishing	**9.4%**	Wholesale trade and vehicle trade	**7.8%**	Rubber and plastics	**6.6%**	**48.0%**
US	Food and beverages	**14.4%**	Financial intermediation and insurance	**12.5%**	Real estate, consulting, IT	**11.5%**	Chemical and chemical products	**11.5%**	Transport	**5.8%**	**55.8%**
Others	Wholesale trade and vehicle trade	**10.0%**	Food and beverages	**9.2%**	Rubber and plastics	**6.9%**	Agriculture, forestry, fishing	**6.1%**	Financial intermediation and insurance	**6.0%**	**38.1%**

Source: UNIDO 2010/11 Investor Survey database.

Annex Table 8: Industrial output statistics in SSA

Country	Industrial Output	Currency	ISIC coverage	Last Reporting year	Industrial Output growth between last reporting year and 2005 (if available)
Botswana	23,713	Millions of Pula	15,17,19,35 (only 2002), 36	2012	200.4%
Burundi	2,276,998	Millions of Burundi-Francs	15, 17, 19, 20, 21, 22, 24, 26, 27	2010	11.8%[a]
Cameroon	2,565,190	Millions of CFA Francs	Most sectors covered, except ISIC 27, 29, 30	2008	n/a
Congo	439,297	Millions of CFA Francs	15, 16, 20, 21, 22, 23, 26, 27, 28, 36	2008	48.8%
Eritrea	3,350	Millions of Nakfa	All sectors	2012	22.3%
Ethiopia	28,829	Millions of Birr	All sectors	2009	134.1%
Gambia	66	Millions of Dalasis	15-22, 24, 26-28, 36	2004	n/a
Ghana	2,458	Millions of Cedis	All sectors, except 30 and 37	2003	n/a
Kenya	1,042,181	Millions of Shillings	All sectors, except 31 and 32 from 2007-2012 and 33, 37 (all years)	2012	108.3%
Madagascar	1,393,283	Millions of Ariary	Most sectors, except 21, 23, 30, 32-34, 37	2005	n/a
Malawi	244,270	Millions of Kwacha	All sectors, except 23, 27, 30, 32, 33, 35, 37	2010	127.3%
Mauritius	116,238	Millions of Rupees	All sectors, with few yearly omissions	2012	49.2%
Namibia	28,069	Millions of Namibia Dollars	15, 17-22, 24-29, 36	2012	50.0%[a]
Niger	13,347	Millions of CFA Francs	15, 22, 24, 26, 28, 36	2003	n/a
Senegal	2,076,272	Millions of CFA Francs	All sectors, except 37 from 2003-2012	2012	54.1%
South Africa	1,415,348	Millions of Rand	All sectors, except 30	2010	37.4%
Sudan[b]	7,642	Millions of Sudanese Pounds	All sectors, except 37	2001	n/a
Tanzania	5,198,431	Millions of Shillings	All sectors, except 23, 30, 32, 33, 37	2010	119.7%

Source: http://stat.unido.org (accessed on 06 March 2016).
[a] Referring to 2007 data as base year;
[b] includes South Sudan.

Annex Table 9: Industrial establishment statistics in SSA

Country	No of establishments	ISIC coverage	Last Reporting year	Establishment growth between last reporting year and 2005 (if available)
Botswana	1301	All except 16 and 23	2005	n/a
Cameroon	10,922	Most sectors covered, except ISIC 27, 29, 30	2008	n/a
Eritrea	248	All sectors	2012	-15.4%
Ethiopia	2,209	All sectors	2009	83.0%
Gambia	1,406	15-22, 24, 26-28, 36	2004	n/a
Ghana	3,796	All sectors, except 30 and 37	2003	n/a
Kenya	6,306	Data not available (only aggregated MF)	2012	29.4%
Malawi	101	All sectors, except 23, 27, 30, 32, 33, 35, 37	2010	-10.6%
Mauritius	634	All sectors, with few yearly omissions	2012	-28.2%
Niger	97	15, 18, 19, 22, 24, 25, 26, 28, 36	2003	n/a
Senegal	792	All sectors, except 37 from 2003-2012	2012	32.9%
South Africa	72,316	All sectors	2011	9.5% [a]
Sudan [b]	24,098	All sectors, except 37	2001	n/a
Tanzania	694	All sectors, except 23, 30, 32, 33, 37	2010	21.5%

Source: http://stat.unido.org (accessed on 06 March 2016).
[a] Referring to 2007 data as base year;
[b] includes South Sudan.

Annex Table 10: Analysis of variance (ANOVA) of manufacturing subsector performance

Subsector	Mean		
	PROFIT	*CAPUTIL*	*SELFEVAL*
Food, beverage and tobacco	5.60	66.0%	3.14
Other	5.51	65.3%	3.12
Textiles	5.16	64.8%	2.86***
Other	5.54	65.5%	3.14***
Wearing apparel	5.00	68.9%	2.89***
Other	5.55	65.2%	3.14***
Wood and furniture	5.43	67.1%	3.16
Other	5.53	65.3%	3.12
Paper and paper products	5.59	70.5%	3.27
Other	5.52	65.3%	3.12
Publishing and printing	6.12	65.9%	3.14
Other	5.53	65.4%	3.13
Other low-tech MF	5.25	63.1%	2.75***
Other	5.53	65.5%	3.13***
Rubber and plastics	5.65	67.0%	3.08
Other	5.51	65.2%	3.13
Non-metallic min., coke & petroleum prods.	6.25**	67.2%	3.22
Other	5.49**	65.4%	3.12
Basic metals	5.55	61.8%	3.26
Other	5.52	65.6%	3.12
Fabricated metals	5.64	62.9%	3.14
Other	5.52	65.7%	3.12
Chemicals	5.38	61.8%**	3.17
Other	5.54	66.0%**	3.12
Machinery and equipment	5.44	67.1%	3.27**
Other	5.53	65.3%	3.12**

*. Significant at $p < 0.1$ level;
**. Significant at $p < 0.05$ level;
***. Significant at $p < 0.01$ level.

Annex Table 11: Analysis of variance (ANOVA) of FDI performance in SSA host countries

Country	Mean		
	PROFIT	*CAPUTIL*	*SELFEVAL*
Burkina Faso	4.00*	72.6%	3.12
Other	5.54*	65.4%	3.13
Burundi	5.60	64.0%	2.97
Other	5.52	65.5%	3.13
Cameroon	4.07***	54.9%***	2.97
Other	5.57***	65.8%***	3.13
Cape Verde	4.32**	64.8%	3.15
Other	5.55**	65.5%	3.13
Côte d'Ivoire	4.50	58.9%	2.65**
Other	5.53	65.5%	3.13**
Ethiopia	4.76**	63.7%	2.90***
Other	5.58**	65.6%	3.14***
Ghana	4.79***	56.9%***	2.89***
Other	5.59***	66.1%***	3.14***
Kenya	6.43***	73.2%***	3.41***
Other	5.17***	62.4%***	3.03***
Lesotho.	4.97	75.5%***	2.95*
Other	5.54	65.3%***	3.13*
Madagascar	4.26***	70.1%	2.90**
Other	5.57***	65.6%	3.14**
Malawi	5.70	67.4%	3.41*
Other	5.52	65.4%	3.12*
Mali	5.29	72.3%*	2.94
Other	5.53	65.3%*	3.13
Mozambique	6.85***	79.9%***	3.61***
Other	5.44***	64.7%***	3.10***
Niger	4.83	65.8%	3.25
Other	5.53	65.5%	3.12
Nigeria	4.69***	58.0%***	2.85***
Other	5.59***	66.1%***	3.15***
Rwanda	5.13	61.4%	2.79**
Other	5.53	65.5%	3.13**
Senegal	3.94***	57.5%**	2.66***
Other	5.57***	65.7%**	3.14***
Tanzania	5.30	64.3%	3.04
Other	5.54	65.6%	3.13
Uganda	6.04**	53.6%***	3.17
Other	5.45**	66.9%***	3.12
Zambia	5.04	54.7%***	3.05
Other	5.54	65.9%***	3.13

*. Significant at $p < 0.1$ level; **. Significant at $p < 0.05$ level; ***. Significant at $p < 0.01$ level.

Annex Table 12: Correlation matrix of changes in12 locational factors in SSA

	POL_STAB	ECON_STAB	LEG_FRAME	QUAL_LIFE	BIT_DTT	LOC_MARK	EXP_MARK	LAB_COST	SKILL_LAB	RAW_COST	LOC_SUPP	INC_PACK
POL_STAB	1											
ECON_STAB	0.694**	1										
LEG_FRAME	0.410**	0.515**	1									
QUAL_LIFE	0.361**	0.430**	0.422**	1								
BIT_DTT	0.240**	0.268**	0.374**	0.374**	1							
LOC_MARK	0.402**	0.423**	0.308**	0.362**	0.298**	1						
EXP_MARK	0.186**	0.217**	0.281**	0.269**	0.372**	0.237**	1					
LAB_COST	0.372**	0.405**	0.271**	0.302**	0.241**	0.379**	0.294**	1				
SKILL_LAB	0.261**	0.266**	0.308**	0.339**	0.314**	0.325**	0.213**	0.321**	1			
RAW_COST	0.347**	0.400**	0.340**	0.287**	0.276**	0.393**	0.226**	0.493**	0.315**	1		
LOC_SUPP	0.305**	0.314**	0.311**	0.334**	0.327**	0.323**	0.295**	0.279**	0.380**	0.400**	1	
INC_PACK	0.349**	0.415**	0.363**	0.351**	0.348**	0.337**	0.327**	0.389**	0.310**	0.457**	0.414**	1

**Correlation is significant at the 0.01 level (2-tailed). List-wise exclusion of cases. N=1,335.

Annex Table 13: Analysis of variance (ANOVA) of component scores of RAW_SUPP, INT_CONNECT and STABILITY in SSA host countries

Country	Mean		
	RAW_SUPP	*INT_CONNECT*	*STABILITY*
Burkina Faso	-0.123240	-0.915094***	0.291743
Other	0.000743	0.005517***	-0.001759
Burundi	-0.086199	-0.401693	0.228658
Other	0.000585	0.002726	-0.001552
Cameroon	0.076413	-0.669040***	-0.285163
Other	-0.002666	0.023339***	0.009948
Cape Verde	-0.023923	-0.220999	-0.024566
Other	0.000550	0.005080	0.000565
Côte d'Ivoire	0.210640	-0.306581	-1.327760***
Other	-0.001590	0.002314	0.010021***
Ethiopia	-0.061451	-0.263875***	0.340680***
Other	0.004442	0.019075***	-0.024627***
Ghana	-0.107156	-0.520536***	0.094567
Other	0.008583	0.041693***	-0.007575
Kenya	-0.068372	0.561625***	-0.020585
Other	0.027306	-0.224297***	0.008221
Lesotho.	-0.199792	-0.088553	-0.051719
Other	0.007774	0.003446	0.002012
Madagascar	-0.448793***	-0.558793***	-1.323017***
Other	0.017826***	0.022195***	0.052550***
Malawi	0.497246**	-0.083029	0.774062***
Other	-0.006796**	0.001135	-0.010579***
Mali	0.232208	-0.513011***	0.159553
Other	-0.005520	0.012196***	-0.003793
Mozambique	0.311546***	-0.190546*	0.637419***
Other	-0.019859***	0.012146*	-0.040632***
Niger	-0.437391	-0.550955	-0.797346*
Other	0.001975	0.002487	0.003600*
Nigeria	-0.083890	-0.161786	-0.202304*
Other	0.005633	0.010863	0.013584*
Rwanda	0.135135	0.396539	0.494421*
Other	-0.001536	-0.004506	-0.005618*
Senegal	-0.070927	-0.392140**	-0.653511***
Other	0.001742	0.009630**	0.016049***
Tanzania	0.177239*	0.085849	0.058880
Other	-0.012965*	-0.006280	-0.004307
Uganda	0.148299**	0.021371	0.097938
Other	-0.020914**	-0.003014	-0.013812
Zambia	0.006112	-0.255841	0.105439
Other	-0.000189	0.007902	-0.003257

*. Significant at $p < 0.1$ level; **. Significant at $p < 0.05$ level; ***. Significant at $p < 0.01$ level.

Annex Table 14: Correlation matrix of control and independent variables

		1	2	3	4	5	6	7	8	9	10	11	12	13	14	15	16	17	18
1	*CONTROL_AGE*	1																	
2	*CONTROL_SIZE*	0.320***	1																
3	*ESTABLISH*	0.011	-0.036	1															
4	*OWNERSHIP*	-0.257***	-0.185***	0.008	1														
5	*EXP_INTENSE*	0.028	0.122***	-0.058*	0.027	1													
6	*MF_DUMMY*	0.006	-0.025	-0.037	0.033	0.158***	1												
7	*SSAWESTMID*	0.015	-0.093***	-0.050	-0.035	-0.060*	-0.064*	1											
8	*OWNCHANGE*	0.078**	0.012	-0.063*	-0.136***	-0.022	-0.041	0.110***	1										
9	*CONTRACT*	0.045	-0.133***	0.027	-0.020	-0.153***	-0.107***	-0.089***	-0.038	1									
10	*RAW_SUPP*	-0.010	-0.027	-0.008	-0.116***	-0.093***	0.029	0.026	-0.081**	0.068**	1								
11	*STABILITY*	-0.017	-0.042	0.015	-0.108***	-0.122***	-0.013	-0.042	-0.075**	0.154***	0.471***	1							
12	*BIT_DUMMY*	0.140***	0.041	-0.008	-0.066*	0.046	-0.039	0.012	0.018	0.196***	0.063*	0.057*	1						
13	*PROD_DIV*	0.094***	-0.053	-0.048	-0.074**	-0.019	0.029	0.102***	0.031	-0.044	-0.020	0.020	-0.017	1					
14	*CULT_PROX*	0.228***	0.002	-0.013	-0.114***	-0.009	0.022	-0.122***	-0.008	0.038	0.059*	0.041	-0.046	-0.030	1				
15	*RESOURCES*	0.007	0.062*	0.008	0.013	0.036	-0.008	-0.063*	-0.022	0.024	0.120***	0.128***	0.033	0.047	0.055	1			
16	*R_AND_D*	0.202***	0.252***	0.109***	-0.189***	0.002	-0.031	-0.244***	-0.022	0.154***	0.031	0.033	0.046	0.038	0.079**	0.025	1		
17	*SKILL_WF*	-0.053	-0.102***	-0.083**	-0.026	-0.088***	-0.085**	0.100***	-0.009	0.059*	0.102***	0.069**	0.067*	-0.062*	-0.013	0.048	-0.119***	1	
18	*SSA_EXP*	0.143***	0.133***	0.002	-0.022	-0.029	-0.006	-0.023	0.047	-0.035	-0.187***	-0.122***	-0.070**	0.040	0.036	-0.018	0.130***	-0.113***	1

*. Correlation is significant at the 0.1 level;
**. Correlation is significant at the 0.05 level;
***. Correlation is significant at the 0.01 level;
List-wise exclusion of cases; N=854.

Annex Table 15: Regression results for model specification M4 of dependent variables PROFIT, CAPUTIL, SELFEVAL

Variables		Model specification 4 (M4)					
		PROFIT		*CAPUTIL*		*SELFEVAL*	
		Level 1 (Controls)	Level 2	Level 1 (Controls)	Level 2	Level 1 (Controls)	Level 2
	Intercept	3.745***	4.008***	0.324***	0.275***	2.489***	2.481***
Control variables	*CONTROL_AGE*	0.051	0.050	0.009	0.021	0.047	0.068*
	CONTROL_SIZE	0.073*	0.050	0.197***	0.173***	0.010	-0.025
	ESTABLISH	0.005	-0.001	0.029	0.025	0.119***	0.113***
	OWNERSHIP	-0.107***	-0.063	0.020	-0.015	-0.033	-0.039
	EXP_INTENSE	-0.009	0.001	-0.066*	-0.067*	-0.083*	-0.070*
	SSAWESTMID						
	TECH_INT	-0.005	-0.006	-0.073**	-0.080**	0.090**	0.090**
	IND_SUBSEC	**No**	**No**	**No**	**No**	**No**	**No**
	HOST_COUNTRY	**Yes**	**Yes**	**Yes**	**Yes**	**Yes**	**Yes**
Indep. variables	*OWNCHANGE*		0.042		-0.038		-0.080**
	CONTRACT						
	RAW_SUPP		0.113***		-0.113***		0.088**
	INT_CONNECT		0.029		0.015		0.071*
	STABILITY		0.058		-0.043		0.026
	BIT_DUMMY		-0.050		-0.045		-0.032
	PROD_DIV		0.039		-0.044		-0.070**
	CULT_PROX		0.074*		-0.030		-0.061
	RESOURCES		0.020		0.096***		0.011
	R_AND_D		0.075*		0.103***		0.105**
	SKILL_WF		-0.030		0.030		0.029
	SSA_EXP		-0.042		0.072**		0.107***
Stats.	No. of observations	719	719	719	719	719	719
	F-Value	4.598***	4.061***	13.229***	9.891***	7.752***	6.696***
	R^2	0.106	0.146	0.254	0.294	0.166	0.220
	Adjusted R^2	0.083	0.110	0.235	0.264	0.145	0.187
	ΔR^2		0.04		0.04		0.054

*. β significant at the 0.1 level; **. β significant at the 0.05 level; ***. β significant at the 0.01 level; [a] reported separately in Table 5.12; [b] reported separately in Table 5.13.

Bibliography

Adams, S. (2009). 'Foreign Direct investment, domestic investment, and economic growth in Sub-Saharan Africa'. *Journal of Policy Modeling, 31*(6), 939–949.

African Courir (2010). *Back to Africa: Diaspora Returnees Making a Difference in Their Country of Origin*. August/September 2010 Issue, p. 26–31.

AFDB (2010). *Eastern Africa – Regional Integration Strategy Paper*. October 2010, Tunis: African Development Bank.

AFDB (2011a). *China and Africa: An emerging partnership for development?*. Edited by Schiere, S., Ndikumana, L. and Walkenhorst, P., Tunis: African Development Bank.

AFDB (2011b). *The Middle of the Pyramid: Dynamics of the Middle Class in Africa*. Market Brief, 20 April 2011, Tunis: African Development Bank.

AFDB (2014). *Tracking Africa's Progress in Figures*. Tunis: African Development Bank.

AFDB, OECD and UNDP (2014). *African Economic Outlook 2014*. Tunis, Paris and New York: African Development Bank, Organisation for Economic Co-operation and Development and United Nations Development Programme.

Agarwal, S. and Ramaswami, S. N. (1992). 'Choice of Foreign Market Entry Mode: Impact of Ownership, Location and Internalization Factors'. *Journal of International Business Studies, 23*(1), 1–27.

Agodo, O. (1978). 'The Determinants of U. S. Private Manufacturing Investments in Africa'. *Journal of International Business Studies, 9*(3), 95–107.

Ahmed, A. D. and Islam, S. M. N. (2010). *Financial Liberalization in Developing Countries: Issues, Time Series Analyses and Policy Implications*. Heidelberg: Physica-Verlag.

Ajakaiye, O. and Kaplinsky, R. (2009). 'China in Africa: A Relationship in Transition'. *European Journal of Development Research, 21*(4), 479–484.

Akinkugbe, O. (2005). 'A Two-part Econometric Analysis of Foreign Direct Investment Flows to Africa'. *Journal of World Trade, 39*(5), 907–923.

Akyut, D. and Ratha, D. (2003). 'South-South FDI flows: How big are they?'. *Transnational Corporations, 13*(1), 149–176.

Alfaro, L. and Chen, M. X. (2012). 'Surviving the Global Financial Crisis: Foreign Ownership and Establishment Performance'. *American Economic Journal: Economic Policy, 4*(3), 30–55.

Amendolagine, V., Boly, A., Coniglio, N. D., Prota, F. and Seric, A. (2013). 'FDI and Local Linkages in Developing Countries: Evidence from Sub-Saharan Africa'. *World Development, 50*, 41–56.

Ampiah, K. (1997). *The Dynamics of Japan's Relations with Africa – South Africa, Tanzania and Nigeria*. London and New York: Routledge.

Anand, J. and Delios, A. (1997). 'Location Specificity and the Transferability of Downstream Assets to Foreign Subsidiaries'. *Journal of International Business Studies*, *28*(3), 579–603.

Anderson, E. and Gatignon, H. (1986). 'Modes of Foreign Entry: A Transaction Cost Analysis and Propositions'. *Journal of International Business Studies*, *17*(3), 1–26.

Andersson, S., Evers, N. and Kuivalainen, O. (2014). 'International new ventures: Rapid internationalization across different industry contexts'. *European Business Review*, *26*(5), 390–405.

Andersson, U., Forsgren, M. and Pedersen, T. (2001). 'Subsidiary performance in multinational corporations: the importance of technology embeddedness'. *International Business Review*, *10*(1), 3–23.

Andras, T. L. and Srinivasan, S. S. (2003). 'Advertising Intensity and R&D Intensity: Differences across Industries and Their Impact on Firm's Performance'. *International Journal of Business and Economics*, *2*(2), 167–176.

Anyanwu, J. C. (2006). 'Promoting of Investment in Africa'. *African Development Review*, *18*(1), 42–71.

Arino, A. and de la Torre, J. (1998). 'Learning from Failure: Towards an Evolutionary Model of Collaborative Ventures'. *Organization Science*, *9*(3), 306–325.

Arnold, J. M. and Javorcik, B. S. (2005). *Gifted Kids or Pushy Parents? Foreign Acquisitions and Plant Performance in Indonesia.* Policy Research Working Paper No. 3597, Washington D.C.: World Bank Group.

Arora, A. and Fosfuri, A. (2000). 'Wholly Owned Subsidiary Versus Technology Licensing in the Worldwide Chemical Industry'. *Journal of International Business Studies*, *31*(4), 555–572.

Aryeetey, C., Barthel, F., Busse, M., Loehr, C. and Osei, R. (2008). *Empirical Study on the Determinants and Pro-Development Impacts of Foreign Direct Investment in Ghana*. Hamburgisches WeltWirtschaftsInstitut (HWWI) and Institute of Statistical, Social and Economic Research (ISSER) of the University of Ghana.

Asche, H. and Fritzen, A.-L. (2013). *Perspectives of Employment and Manufacturing Industry in resource-rich African Countries*. Eschborn: Gesellschaft für Internationale Zusammenarbeit (GIZ).

Asche, H., Neuerburg, P. and Menegatti, M. (2012). *Economic diversification strategies: A key driver in Africa's new industrial revolution*. Working Paper 2/2012, Vienna: United Nations Industrial Development Organization.

Asiedu, E. (2002). 'On the Determinants of Foreign Direct Investment to Developing Countries: Is Africa Different?'. *World Development*, *30*(1), 107–119.

Asiedu, E. (2004a). 'The Determinants of Employment of Affiliates of US Multinational Enterprises in Africa'. *Development Policy Review*, *22*(4), 371–379.

Asiedu, E. (2004b). 'Policy Reform and Foreign Direct Investment in Africa: Absolute Progress but Relative Decline'. *Development Policy Review*, *22*(1), 41–48.

Asiedu, E. (2006). 'Foreign Direct Investment in Africa: The Role of Natural Resources, Market Size, Government Policy, Institutions and Political Instability'. *World Economy*, *29*(1), 63–77.

Aulakh, P. S. and Kotabe, M. (1997). 'Antecedents and Performance Implications of Channel Integration in Foreign Markets'. *Journal of International Business Studies*, *28*(1), 145–175.

Autio, E., Sapienza, H. J. and Almeida, J. G. (2000). 'Effects of Age at Entry, Knowledge Intensity, and Imitability on International Growth'. *The Academy of Management Journal*, *43*(5), 909–924.

Aykut, D. and Goldstein, A. (2006). *Developing Country Multinationals: South-South Investment Comes of Age*. Working Paper No. 257, Paris: Organization for Economic Cooperation and Development.

Bain, J. (1956). *Barriers to New Competition*. Cambridge: Harvard University Press.

Baldwin, J. R. and Caves, R. E. (1991). 'Foreign multinational enterprises and merger activity in Canada'. In: Waverman, L. (Ed.), *Corporate Globalization through Mergers and Acquisitions*. Calgary: University of Calgary Press, 89–122.

Bame, J. (1995). *The Measurement of Reinvested Earnings in the Balance of Payments*. Washington D.C.: International Monetary Fund.

Barbosa, N. and Louri, H. (2002). 'On the determinants of multinationals' ownership preferences: evidence from Greece and Portugal'. *International Journal of Industrial Organization*, *20*(4), 493–515.

Barkema, H. G., Bell, J. H. J. and Pennings, J. M. (1996). 'Foreign Entry, Cultural Barriers, and Learning'. *Strategic Management Journal*, *17*(2), 151–166.

Barkema, H. G., Shenkar, O., Vermeulen, F. and Bell, J. H. J. (1997). 'Working Abroad, Working with Others: How Firms Learn to Operate International Joint Ventures'. *The Academy of Management Journal*, *40*(2), 426–442.

Barkema, H. G. and Vermeulen, F. (1997). 'What Differences in the Cultural Backgrounds of Partners are Detrimental fo International Joint Ventures?'. *Journal of International Business Studies*, *28*(4), 845–864.

Barkema, H. G. and Vermeulen, F. (1998). 'International Expansion through Start up or Acquisition: A Learning Perspective'. *The Academy of Management Journal*, *41*(1), 7–26.

Barney, J. (1991). 'Firm Resources and Sustained Competitive Advantage'. *Journal of Management*, *17*(1), 99–120.

Bartels, F. L., Alladina, S. N. and Lederer, S. (2009). 'Foreign Direct Investment in Sub-Saharan Africa: Motivating Factors and Policy Issues'. *Journal of African Business*, *10*(2), 141–162.

Bartels, F. L., Johnson, J. P. and Ahmed, Z. U. (2002). 'International Equity Joint Ventures in Ghana and Côte D'Ivoire: The Experience of British and French Firms'. *Journal of African Business*, *3*(3), 5–30.

Bartels, F. L., Kratzsch, S. and Eicher, M. (2008). *Foreign Direct Investment in Sub-Saharan Africa: Determinants and Location Decisions*. Working Paper 8/2008, Vienna: United Nations Industrial Development Organization.

Basdevant, O., Jonelis, A., Mircheva, B. and Slavov, S. (2014). *The Mystery of Missing Real Spillovers in Southern Africa – Some Facts and Possible Explanations*. Washington D.C.: International Monetary Fund.

Baum, J. A. C. and Korn, H. J. (1996). 'Competitive Dynamics of Interfirm Rivalry'. *The Academy of Management Journal*, *39*(2), 255–291.

Beamish, P. W. and Inkpen, A. C. (1995). 'Keeping international joint ventures stable and profitable'. *Long Range Planning*, *28*(3), 26–36.

Beamish, P. W. and Lee, C. (2003). 'The Characteristics and Performance of Affiliates of Small and Medium-Size Multinational Enterprises in an Emerging Market'. *Journal of International Entrepreneurship*, *1*(1), 121–134.

Beavers, A. S., Lounsbury, J. W., Richards, J. K., Huck, S. W., Skolits, G. J. and Esquivel, S. L. (2013). 'Practical Considerations for Using Exploratory Factor Analysis in Educational Research '. *Practical Assessment, Research & Evaluation*, *18*(6), 1–13.

Belderbos, R., Capannelli, G. and Fukao, K. (2001). 'Backward Vertical Linkages of Foreign Manufacturing Affiliates: Evidence from Japanese Multinationals'. *World Development*, *29*(1), 189–208.

Bellak, C. (1998). 'The measurement of foreign direct investment: A critical review'. *International Trade Journal*, *12*(2), 227–257.

Bellak, C. and Cantwell, J. (2004). 'Revaluing the capital stock of international production'. *International Business Review*, *13*(1), 1–18.

Bénassy-Quéré, A., Coupet, M. and Mayer, T. (2007). 'Institutional Determinants of Foreign Direct Investment'. *World Economy*, *30*(5), 764–782.

Bende-Nabende, A. (2002). 'Foreign direct investment determinants in sub-Sahara Africa: A co-integration analysis'. *Economics Bulletin*, *6*(4), 1−19.

Bernard, A. B. and Bradford Jensen, J. (1999). 'Exceptional exporter performance: cause, effect, or both?'. *Journal of International Economics*, *47*(1), 1–25.

Besada, H., Wang, Y. and Whalley, J. (2008). *China's Growing Economic Activity in Africa*. NBER Working Paper No. 14024, Cambridge: National Bureau of Economic Research.

Bettis, R. A. (1981). 'Performance Differences in Related and Unrelated Diversified Firms'. *Strategic Management Journal*, *2*(4), 379–393.

Beugelsdijk, S., Hennart, J.-F., Slangen, A. and Smeets, R. (2010). 'Why and how FDI stocks are a biased measure of MNE affiliate activity'. *Journal of International Business Studies*, *41*(9), 1444–1459.

Bevan, A. A. and Estrin, S. (2000). *The determinants of Foreign Direct Investment in Transition Economies*. Working Paper No. 342, William Davidson Institute.

Bewayo, E. (2009). 'Family Business In Africa: A Comparison with the U.S.-Western Model'. *Journal of Global Business Issues*, *3*(1), 171–181.

Bhaumik, S. K. and Gelb, S. (2005). 'Determinants of Entry Mode Choice of MNCs in Emerging Markets – Evidence from South Africa and Egypt'. *Emerging Markets Finance and Trade*, *41*(2), 5–24.

Biggs, T. and Shah, M. K. (2006). *African Small and Medium Enterprises, Networks, and Manufacturing Performance*. Policy Research Working Paper No. 3855, Washington D.C.: World Bank Group.

Bigsten, A., Collier, P., Dercon, S., Fafchamps, M., Gauthier, B., Gunning, J. W., Oduro, A., Oostendorp, R., Pattillo, C., Söderbom, M., Teal, F. and Zeufack, A. (2004). 'Do African Manufacturing Firms Learn from Exporting?'. *Journal of Development Studies*, *40*(3), 115–141.

Bigsten, A. and Söderbom, M. (2006). 'What Have We Learned from a Decade of Manufacturing Enterprise Surveys in Africa?'. *The World Bank Research Observer*, *21*(2), 241–265.

Birkinshaw, J. (1998). 'Corporate entrepreneurship in network organizations: How subsidiary initiative drives internal market efficiency'. *European Management Journal*, *16*(3), 355–364.

Birkinshaw, J. (2000). *Entrepreneurship in the global firm*. London: Sage Publications.

Birkinshaw, J., Hood, N. and Young, S. (2005). 'Subsidiary entrepreneurship, internal and external competitive forces, and subsidiary performance'. *International Business Review*, *14*(2), 227–248.

Birkinshaw, J. and Morrison, A. J. (1995). 'Configurations of Strategy and Structure in Subsidiaries of Multinational Corporations'. *Journal of International Business Studies*, *26*(4), 729–753.

Blalock, G. and Gertler, P. J. (2008). 'Welfare gains from Foreign Direct Investment through technology transfer to local suppliers'. *Journal of International Economics*, *74*(2), 402–421.

Blalock, G. and Simon, D. (2009). 'Do all firms benefit equally from downstream FDI? The moderating effect of local suppliers' capabilities on productivity gains'. *Journal of International Business Studies*, *40*(7), 1095–1112.

Boateng, A. and Glaister, K. (2002). 'Performance of international joint ventures: evidence for West Africa'. *International Business Review*, *11*, 523–541.

Boddewyn, J. J. (1983). 'Foreign Direct Divestment Theory: Is It the Reverse of FDI Theory?'. *Weltwirtschaftliches Archiv*, *119*(2), 345–355.

Boly, A., Coniglio, N. D., Prota, F. and Seric, A. (2014). 'Diaspora Investments and Firm Export Performance in Selected Sub-Saharan African Countries'. *World Development*, *59*, 422–433.

Borensztein, E., De Gregorio, J. and Lee, J. W. (1998). 'How does foreign direct investment affect economic growth?'. *Journal of International Economics*, *45*(1), 115–135.

Bowen, H. P. and Wiersema, M. F. (1999). 'Matching method to paradigm in strategy research: limitations of cross-sectional analysis and some methodological alternatives'. *Strategic Management Journal*, *20*(7), 625–636.

Bräutigam, D. (2009). *The Dragon's Gift: The Real Story of China in Africa*. New York and Oxford: Oxford University Press.

Bräutigam, D. (2010). *Africa's Eastern promise: What the West can learn from Chinese investment in Africa*. Foreign Affairs, Online at: http://www.foreignaffairs.com/articles/africa/2010-01-05/africa-s-eastern-promise (accessed on 6 July 2016).

Bräutigam, D. and Xiaoyang, T. (2009). 'China's Engagement in African Agriculture: "Down to the Countryside"'. *The China Quarterly*, *199*, 686–706.

Bräutigam, D. and Xiaoyang, T. (2011). 'African Shenzhen: China's special economic zones in Africa'. *The Journal of Modern African Studies*, *49*(1), 27–54.

Brenton, P. (2003). 'Integrating the Least Developed Countries into the World Trading System – The Current Impact of EU Preferences under "Everything but Arms"'. *Journal of World Trade*, *37*(3), 623–646.

Breslin, T. P. and Samanta, S. K. (2008). 'Investment Flows, Economic Growth, and Corruption in African Countries: An Analysis'. *Journal of African Business*, *9*(2), 287–307.

Broadman, H. G. (2007). *Africa's New Silk Road: China and India's New Economic Frontier*. Washington D.C.: World Bank Group.

Broadman, H. G. (2008). 'China and India go to Africa'. *Foreign Affairs*, *87*(2), 95–109.

Broadman, H. G. (2009). '"First Mover" Investment Advantages in Sub-Saharan Africa: Why Northern Multinationals Should React (Quickly) to Their Southern Counterparts'. *CESifo Forum*, *10*(4), 52–58.

Brouthers, K. D. (2002). 'Institutional, cultural and transaction cost influences on entry mode choice and performance'. *Journal of International Business Studies*, *33*(2), 203–221.

Brouthers, K. D. and Bamossy, G. J. (2006). 'Post-Formation Processes in Eastern and Western European Joint Ventures'. *Journal of Management Studies*, *43*(2), 203–229.

Brouthers, K. D. and Brouthers, L. E. (2000). 'Acquisition or Greenfield Start-up? Institutional, Cultural and Transaction Cost Influences'. *Strategic Management Journal*, *21*(1), 89–97.

Brouthers, K. D. and Brouthers, L. E. (2001). 'Explaining the National Cultural Distance Paradox'. *Journal of International Business Studies*, *32*(1), 177–189.

Brouthers, K. D. and Brouthers, L. E. (2003). 'Why Service and Manufacturing Entry Mode Choices Differ: The Influence of Transaction Cost Factors, Risk and Trust'. *Journal of Management Studies*, *40*(5), 1179–1204.

Brouthers, K. D., Brouthers, L. E. and Werner, S. (2003). 'Transaction Cost-Enhanced Entry Mode Choices and Firm Performance'. *Strategic Management Journal*, *24*(12), 1239–1248.

Brouthers, K. D., Brouthers, L. E. and Werner, S. (2008a). 'Real Options, International Entry Mode Choice and Performance'. *Journal of Management Studies*, *45*(5), 936–960.

Brouthers, K. D., Brouthers, L. E. and Werner, S. (2008b). 'Resource-Based Advantages in an International Context'. *Journal of Management*, *34*(2), 189–217.

Brouthers, K. D. and Hennart, J.-F. (2007). 'Boundaries of the Firm: Insights From International Entry Mode Research'. *Journal of Management*, *33*(3), 395–425.

Brouthers, K. D. and Nakos, G. (2004). 'SME Entry Mode Choice and Performance: A Transaction Cost Perspective'. *Entrepreneurship Theory and Practice*, *28*(3), 229–247.

Brouthers, K. D., Nakos, G. and Dimitratos, P. (2015). 'SME Entrepreneurial Orientation, International Performance, and the Moderating Role of Strategic Alliances'. *Entrepreneurship Theory and Practice*, *39*(5), 1161–1187.

Brouthers, L. E., Brouthers, K. D. and Werner, S. (1999). 'Is Dunning's Eclectic Framework Descriptive or Normative?'. *Journal of International Business Studies*, *30*(4), 831–844.

Brouthers, L. E., Brouthers, K. D. and Werner, S. (2000). 'Perceived Environmental Uncertainty, Entry Mode Choice and Satisfaction with EC-MNC Performance'. *British Journal of Management*, *11*(3), 183–195.

Buckley, A. and Tse, K. (1996). 'Real operating options and foreign direct investment: A synthetic approach'. *European Management Journal*, *14*(3), 304–314.

Buckley, P. J. (2007). 'The strategy of multinational enterprises in the light of the rise of China'. *Scandinavian Journal of Management*, *23*(2), 107–126.

Buckley, P. J. (2014). *The Multinational Enterprise and the Emergence of the Global Factory*. Basingstoke: Palgrave Macmillan.

Buckley, P. J. and Casson, M. (1976). *The Future of the Multinational Enterprise*. London: Macmillan Press.

Buckley, P. J. and Casson, M. (1985). *The Economic Theory of The Multinational Enterprise*. London: Macmillan Press.

Buckley, P. J. and Casson, M. (1998). 'Analyzing Foreign Market Entry Strategies: Extending the Internalization Approach'. *Journal of International Business Studies*, *29*(3), 539–561.

Buckley, P. J., Sutherland, D., Voss, H. and El-Gohari, A. (2015). 'The economic geography of offshore incorporation in tax havens and offshore financial centres: the case of Chinese MNEs'. *Journal of Economic Geography*, *15*(1), 103–128.

Buencamino, L. and Gorbunov, S. (2002). *Informal Money Transfer Systems – Opportunities and Challenges for Development Finance*. Discussion Paper No. 26, New York: United Nations Department of Economic and Social Affairs.

Burgel, O. and Murray, G. C. (2000). 'The International Market Entry Choices of Start-Up Companies in High-Technology Industries'. *Journal of International Marketing*, *8*(2), 33–62.

Busse, M. and Groizard, J. L. (2008). 'Foreign Direct Investment, Regulations and Growth'. *World Economy*, *31*(7), 861–886.

Busse, M., Königer, J. and Nunnenkamp, P. (2008). *FDI Promotion through Bilateral Investment Treaties: More Than a Bit?* Working Paper 1403, Kiel: Kiel Institute for the World Economy.

Büthe, T. and Milner, H. V. (2008). 'The Politics of Foreign Direct Investment into Developing Countries: Increasing FDI through International Trade Agreements?'. *American Journal of Political Science*, *52*(4), 741–762.

Canabal, A. and White III, G. O. (2008). 'Entry mode research: Past and future'. *International Business Review*, *17*(3), 267–284.

Cantwell, J. (1992). 'The methodological problems raised by the collection of foreign direct investment data'. *Scandinavian International Business Review*, *1*(1), 86–102.

Capon, N., Hulbert, J. M., Farley, J. U. and Martin, L. E. (1988). 'Corporate Diversity and Economic Performance: The Impact of Market Specialization'. *Strategic Management Journal*, *9*(1), 61–74.

Cattell, R. B. (1966). 'The Scree Test For The Number Of Factors'. *Multivariate Behavioral Research, 1*(2), 245–276.

Caves, R. E. (1971). 'International Corporations: The Industrial Economics of Foreign Investment'. *Economica, 38*(149), 1–27.

Caves, R. E. (1974). 'Industrial Organisation'. In: Dunning, J. (Ed.), *Economic Analysis and the Multinational Enterprise*, London: George Allen & Unwin, 115–146.

Caves, R. E. and Mehra, S. K. (1986). 'Entry of foreign multinational into U.S. manufacturing industries'. In: Porter, M. E. (Ed.), *Competition in Global Industries*, Boston: Harvard Business School Press. 449–481.

Chacko, E. and Gebre, P. H. (2013). 'Leveraging the diaspora for development: Lessons from Ethiopia'. *GeoJournal, 78*(3), 495–505.

Chakrabarti, A., Singh, K. and Mahmood, I. (2007). 'Diversification and performance: evidence from East Asian firms'. *Strategic Management Journal, 28*(2), 101–120.

Chan, C. M., Isobe, T. and Makino, S. (2008). 'Which country matters? Institutional development and foreign affiliate performance'. *Strategic Management Journal, 29*(11), 1179–1205.

Chan, C. M. and Makino, S. (2007). 'Legitimacy and Multi-Level Institutional Environments: Implications for Foreign Subsidiary Ownership Structure'. *Journal of International Business Studies, 38*(4), 621–638.

Chang, S.-J. (1995). 'International Expansion Strategy of Japanese Firms: Capability Building through Sequential Entry'. *The Academy of Management Journal, 38*(2), 383–407.

Chang, S.-J., Chung, J. and Moon, J. J. (2013). 'When do wholly owned subsidiaries perform better than joint ventures?'. *Strategic Management Journal, 34*(3), 317–337.

Chang, S.-J. and Rosenzweig, P. M. (2001). 'The Choice of Entry Mode in Sequential Foreign Direct Investment'. *Strategic Management Journal, 22*(8), 747–776.

Chatterjee, S. and Wernerfelt, B. (1991). 'The Link between Resources and Type of Diversification: Theory and Evidence'. *Strategic Management Journal, 12*(1), 33–48.

Chen, H. and Hu, M. Y. (2002). 'An analysis of determinants of entry mode and its impact on performance'. *International Business Review, 11*(2), 193–210.

Chi, T. (2000). 'Option to Acquire or Divest a Joint Venture'. *Strategic Management Journal, 21*(6), 665–687.

Chiao, Y. C., Lo, F. Y. and Yu, C. M. (2010). 'Choosing between wholly-owned subsidiaries and joint ventures of MNCs from an emerging market'. *International Marketing Review, 27*(3), 338–365.

Cho, K. R. and Padmanabhan, P. (2005). 'Revisiting the role of cultural distance in MNC's foreign ownership mode choice: the moderating effect of experience attributes'. *International Business Review, 14*(3), 307–324.

Chowdhury, J. (1992). 'Performance of international joint ventures and wholly owned foreign subsidiaries: A comparative perspective'. *Management International Review, 32*(2), 115–133.

Christmann, P., Day, D. and Yip, G. S. (1999). 'The relative influence of country conditions, industry structure, and business strategy on multinational corporation subsidiary performance'. *Journal of International Management*, *5*(4), 241–265.

Chung, C. C. and Beamish, P. W. (2005a). 'The Impact of Institutional Reforms on Characteristics and Survival of Foreign Subsidiaries in Emerging Economies'. *Journal of Management Studies*, *42*(1), 35–62.

Chung, C. C. and Beamish, P. W. (2005b). 'Investment mode strategy and expatriate strategy during times of economic crisis'. *Journal of International Management*, *11*(3), 331–355.

Chung, C. C. and Beamish, P. W. (2010). 'The Trap of Continual Ownership Change in International Equity Joint Ventures'. *Organization Science*, *21*(5), 995–1015.

Clarke, N. (2014). *Go out and manufacture: Policy support for Chinese FDI in Africa.* Columbia FDI Perspectives No. 107, New York: Vale Columbia Center on Sustainable International Investment.

Clerides, S. K., Lach, S. and Tybout, J. R. (1998). 'Is Learning by Exporting Important? Micro-Dynamic Evidence from Colombia, Mexico, and Morocco'. *The Quarterly Journal of Economics*, *113*(3), 903–947.

Combs, J. G. and Ketchen, D. J. (1999). 'Explaining interfirm cooperation and performance: toward a reconciliation of predictions from the resource-based view and organizational economics'. *Strategic Management Journal*, *20*(9), 867–888.

Contractor, F. J. (1990). 'Ownership Patterns of U.S. Joint Ventures Abroad and the Liberalization of Foreign Government Regulations in the 1980s: Evidence from the Benchmark Surveys'. *Journal of International Business Studies*, *21*(1), 55–73.

Contractor, F. J. and Lorange, P. (1988). 'Competition vs. Cooperation: A Benefit/Cost Framework for Choosing Between Fully-Owned Investments and Cooperative Relationships'. *Management International Review*, *28*(4), 5–18.

Corkin, L. (2007). 'The Strategic Entry of China's Emerging Multinationals into Africa'. *China Report*, *43*(3), 309–322.

Corkin, L. (2012). 'Chinese construction companies in Angola: A local linkages perspective'. *Resources Policy*, *37*(4), 475–483.

Cotton, L. and Ramachandran, V. (2001). *Foreign Direct Investment in Emerging Economies – Lessons from sub-Saharan Africa.* UNU-WIDER Discussion Paper No. 2001/82, Helsinki: United Nations University and World Institute for Development Economics Research.

Cotula, L. and Vermeulen, S. (2009). 'Deal or no deal: the outlook for agricultural land investment in Africa'. *International Affairs*, *85*(6), 1233–1247.

Cotula, L., Vermeulen, S., Leonard, R. and Keeley, J. (2009). *Land Grab or Development Opportunity? Agricultural Investment and International Land Deals in Africa.* London/Rome: International Institute for Environment and Development (IIED), Food and Agriculture Organization (FAO) and the International Fund for Agricultural Development (IFAD).

Coviello, N. E. and McAuley, A. (1999). 'Internationalisation and the smaller firm: A review of contemporary empirical research'. *Management International Review*, *39*(3), 223–256.

Coviello, N. E. and Munro, H. (1997). 'Network relationships and the internationalisation process of small software firms'. *International Business Review*, *6*(4), 361–386.

Coviello, N. E. (2006). 'The Network Dynamics of International New Ventures'. *Journal of International Business Studies*, *37*(5), 713–731.

Crick, D. and Jones, M. V. (2000). 'Small High-Technology Firms and International High-Technology Markets'. *Journal of International Marketing*, *8*(2), 63–85.

Cuervo-Cazurra, A. and Genc, M. (2008). 'Transforming Disadvantages into Advantages: Developing-Country MNEs in the Least Developed Countries'. *Journal of International Business Studies*, *39*(6), 957–979.

Cui, L. and Jiang, F. (2009). 'FDI entry mode choice of Chinese firms: A strategic behavior perspective'. *Journal of World Business*, *44*(4), 434–444.

Dabla-Norris, E., Honda, J., Lahreche, A. and Verdier, G. (2010). *FDI Flows to Low-Income Countries: Global Drivers and Growth Implications*. IMF Working Paper 10/132, Washington D.C.: International Monetary Fund.

Das, K. C. and Banik, N. (2015). 'What motivates Indian firms to invest abroad?'. *International Journal of Commerce and Management*, *25*(3), 330–355.

Davis, L. E. and North, D. C. (1971). *Institutional Change and American Economic Growth*. Cambridge: Cambridge University Press.

Davis, L. N. and Meyer, K. E. (2004). 'Subsidiary research and development, and the local environment'. *International Business Review*, *13*(3), 359–382.

Davis, P. S., Desai, A. B. and Francis, J. D. (2000). 'Mode of international entry: An isomorphism perspective'. *Journal of International Business Studies*, *31*(2), 239–258.

De Carolis, D. M. (2003). 'Competencies and Imitability in the Pharmaceutical Industry: An Analysis of Their Relationship with Firm Performance'. *Journal of Management*, *29*(1), 27–50.

De la Fontaine, D. and Seifert, J. (2009). *New Dynamics in the South-South Cooperation between Brazil and Africa*. Paper presented at the European Conference of African Studies (ECAS), Leipzig, 4–7 June 2009.

De la Medina Soto, C. and Ghossein, T. (2013). *Starting a Foreign Investment across Sectors*. Policy Research Working Paper No. 6707, Washington D.C.: World Bank Group.

De Nederlandsche Bank (2004). *FDI – Other Capital*. Issue Paper No. 22 prepared for the Direct Investment Technical Expert Group (DITEG), IMF Committee on Balance of Payments Statistics and OECD Workshop on International Investment Statistics.

Delios, A. and Beamish, P. W. (1999a). 'Geographic scope, product diversification, and the corporate performance of Japanese firms'. *Strategic Management Journal*, *20*(8), 711–727.

Delios, A. and Beamish, P. W. (1999b). 'Ownership Strategy of Japanese Firms: Transactional, Institutional, and Experience Influences'. *Strategic Management Journal*, *20*(10), 915–933.

Delios, A. and Beamish, P. W. (2001). 'Survival and Profitability: The Roles of Experience and Intangible Assets in Foreign Subsidiary Performance'. *The Academy of Management Journal*, *44*(5), 1028–1038.

Delios, A. and Beamish, P. W. (2004). 'Joint Venture Performance Revisited: Japanese Foreign Subsidiaries Worldwide'. *Management International Review*, *44*(1), 69–91.

Delios, A. and Henisz, W. J. (2000). 'Japanese Firms' Investment Strategies in Emerging Economies'. *The Academy of Management Journal*, *43*(3), 305–323.

Demirbag, M., Glaister, K. W. and Tatoglu, E. (2007). 'Institutional and transaction cost influences on MNEs' ownership strategies of their affiliates: Evidence from an emerging market'. *Journal of World Business*, *42*(4), 418–434.

Desbordes, R., Darby, J. and Wooton, I. (2011) *Institutional Quality and FDI to the South – An Analytical Approach*. Strathclyde Discussion Paper in Economics 11–31, Glasgow: University of Strathclyde.

Dhanaraj, C. and Beamish, P. W. (2009). 'Institutional Environment and Subsidiary Survival'. *Management International Review*, *49*(3), 291–312.

Dhawan, R. (2001). 'Firm size and productivity differential: theory and evidence from a panel of US firms'. *Journal of Economic Behavior & Organization*, *44*(3), 269–293.

Dierickx, I. and Cool, K. (1989). 'Asset Stock Accumulation and Sustainability of Competitive Advantage'. *Management Science*, *35*(12), 1504–1511.

Dikova, D. and van Witteloostuijn, A. (2007). 'Foreign direct investment mode choice: entry and establishment modes in transition economies'. *Journal of International Business Studies*, *38*(6), 1013–1033.

DiStefano, C., Zhu, M. and Mindrila, D. (2009). 'Understanding and Using Factor Scores: Considerations for the Applied Researcher'. *Practical Assessment, Research & Evaluation*, *14*(20), 1–11.

Djankov, S. (2009). 'The Regulation of Entry: A Survey'. *The World Bank Research Observer*, *24*(2), 183–203.

Djankov, S., La Porta, R., Lopez-de-Silanes, F. and Shleifer, A. (2002). 'The Regulation of Entry'. *The Quarterly Journal of Economics*, *117*(1), 1–37.

Djiofack-Zebaze, C. and Keck, A. (2009). 'Telecommunications Services in Africa: The Impact of WTO Commitments and Unilateral Reform on Sector Performance and Economic Growth'. *World Development*, *37*(5), 919–940.

Dobler, G. (2009). 'Chinese Shops and the Formation of a Chinese Expatriate Community in Namibia'. *The China Quarterly*, *199*, 707–727.

Dong, L. and Glaister, K. W. (2006). 'Motives and partner selection criteria in international strategic alliances: Perspectives of Chinese firms'. *International Business Review*, *15*(6), 577–600.

Dow, D. and Karunaratna, A. (2006). 'Developing a Multidimensional Instrument to Measure Psychic Distance Stimuli'. *Journal of International Business Studies*, *37*(5), 578–602.

Draper, P., Kiratu, S. and Samuel, C. (2010). *The Role of South African FDI in Southern Africa*. Discussion Paper 8/2010, Bonn: Deutsches Institut für Entwicklungspolitik.

Dunning, J. H. (1993). *Multinational Enterprises and the Global Economy*. Wokingham: Addison Wesley.

Dunning, J. H. (1998). 'Location and the Multinational Enterprise: A Neglected Factor?'. *Journal of International Business Studies*, *29*(1), 45–66.

Dunning, J. H. (2000). 'The eclectic paradigm as an envelope for economic and business theories of MNE activity'. *International Business Review*, *9*(2), 163–190.

Dunning, J. H. (2006). 'Towards a new paradigm of development: implications for the determinants of international business'. *Transnational Corporations*, *15*(1), 173–227.

Dunning, J. H. and Lundan, S. M. (2008a). 'Institutions and the OLI paradigm of the multinational enterprise'. *Asia Pacific Journal of Management*, *25*(4), 573–593.

Dunning, J. H. and Lundan, S. M. (2008b). *Multinational Enterprises and the Global Economy.* 2nd Edition. Cheltenham: Edward Elgar.

Dunning, J. H. and Lundan, S. M. (2009). 'The Internationalization of Corporate R&D: A Review of the Evidence and Some Policy Implications for Home Countries'. *Review of Policy Research*, *26*(1–2), 13–33.

Dupasquier, C. and Osakwe, P. N. (2006). 'Foreign direct investment in Africa: Performance, challenges, and responsibilities'. *Journal of Asian Economics*, *17*(2), 241–260.

Dyer, J. H. (1996). 'Specialized Supplier Networks as a Source of Competitive Advantage: Evidence from the Auto Industry'. *Strategic Management Journal*, *17*(4), 271–291.

EAC (2013). *EAC Investment Guidebook*. Arusha: East African Community Secretariat.

Egger, P. and Pfaffermayr, M. (2004). 'The impact of bilateral investment treaties on foreign direct investment'. *Journal of Comparative Economics*, *32*(4), 788–804.

Egger, P. and Winner, H. (2005). 'Evidence on corruption as an incentive for foreign direct investment'. *European Journal of Political Economy*, *21*(4), 932–952.

Elango, B. and Pattnaik, C. (2007). 'Building capabilities for international operations through networks: a study of Indian firms'. *Journal of International Business Studies*, *38*(4), 541–555.

Elango, B. and Sambharya, R. B. (2004). 'The influence of industry structure on the entry mode choice of overseas entrants in manufacturing industries'. *Journal of International Management*, *10*(1), 107–124.

Ellis, P. D. (2007). 'Distance, Dependence and Diversity of Markets: Effects on Market Orientation'. *Journal of International Business Studies*, *38*(3), 374–386.

Ernest and Young (2015). *EY's Attractiveness Survey Africa 2015 – Making Choices*.

Erramilli, M. K. (1996). 'Nationality and subsidiary ownership patterns in multinational corporations'. *Journal of International Business Studies*, *27*(2), 225–248.

Erramilli, M. K. and Rao, C. P. (1990). 'Choice of Foreign Market Entry Modes by Service Firms: Role of Market Knowledge'. *Management International Review*, *30*(2), 135–150.

Erramilli, M. K. and Rao, C. P. (1993). 'Service firms' international entry-mode choice: A modified transaction-cost analysis approach'. *Journal of Marketing*, *57*(3), 19–38.

Estrin, S., Baghdasaryan, D. and Meyer, K. E. (2009). 'The Impact of Institutional and Human Resource Distance on International Entry Strategies'. *Journal of Management Studies*, *46*(7), 1171–1196.

Everitt, B. S. (2002). *The Cambridge Dictionary of Statistics*. 2nd Edition. Cambridge: Cambridge University Press.

Evers, N. (2011). 'International new ventures in "low tech" sectors: a dynamic capabilities perspective'. *Journal of Small Business and Enterprise Development*, *18*(3), 502–528.

Fabrigar, L. R., Wegener, D. T., MacCallum, R. C. and Strahan, E. J. (1999). 'Evaluating the use of exploratory factor analysis in psychological research'. *Psychological Methods*, *4*(3), 272–299.

Farole, T. (2011). *Special Economic Zones in Africa – Comparing Performance and Learning from Global Experience*. Washington D.C.: World Bank Group.

Farole, T. and Winkler, D. (2014). *Making Foreign Direct Investment work for Sub-Saharan Africa: Local Spillovers and Competitiveness in Global Value Chains*. Directions in Development. Washington D.C.: World Bank Group.

Fava, J. L. and Velicer, W. F. (1992). 'The Effects of Overextraction on Factor and Component Analysis'. *Multivariate Behavioral Research*, *27*(3), 387–415.

Fernhaber, S. A., McDougall, P. P. and Oviatt, B. M. (2007). 'Exploring the Role of Industry Structure in New Venture Internationalization'. *Entrepreneurship Theory and Practice*, *31*(4), 517–542.

FIAS (2008). *Special Economic Zones – Performance, Lessons Learned, and Implications for Zone Development*. Washington D.C.: Foreign Investment Advisory Service (FIAS).

Financial Times (2011). *FDI Global Outlook Report – Manufacturing makes a comeback*. London: Financial Times Ltd.

Financial Times (2012). *The FDI Report 2012 – Global Greenfield Investment Trends*. London: Financial Times Ltd.

Folta, T. B. and Miller, K. D. (2002). 'Real options in equity partnerships'. *Strategic Management Journal*, *23*(1), 77–88.

Foss, N. J. and Pedersen, T. (2002). 'Transferring knowledge in MNCs: The role of sources of subsidiary knowledge and organizational context'. *Journal of International Management*, *8*(1), 49–67.

Foster, V., Butterfield, W., Chen, C. and Pushak, N. (2008). *Building Bridges: China's Growing Role as Infrastructure Financier for Sub-Saharan Africa*. Washington D.C.: World Bank Group.

Frölich, M. (2008). 'Parametric and Nonparametric Regression in the Presence of Endogenous Control Variables'. *International Statistical Review*, *76*(2), 214–227.

Fujita, M. (1995a). 'Small and medium-sized transnational corporations: Salient features'. *Small Business Economics*, *7*(4), 251–271.

Fujita, M. (1995b). 'Small and medium-sized transnational corporations: Trends and patterns of foreign direct investment'. *Small Business Economics*, *7*(3), 183–204.

Fujita, M. (2008). 'A critical assessment of FDI data and policy implications'. *Transnational Corporations*, *17*(2), 107–126.

Gallagher, K. B. and Birch, M. B. L. (2006). 'Do Investment Agreements Attract Investment?'. *The Journal of World Investment and Trade*, *7*(6), 961–974.

Games, D. (2004). *The experience of South African firms doing business in Africa – A preliminary survey and analysis*. Business in Africa Report No. 1, Johannesburg: South African Institute of International Affairs (SAIIA).

Gammelgaard, J., McDonald, F., Stephan, A., Tüselmann, H. and Dörrenbächer, C. (2012). 'The impact of increases in subsidiary autonomy and network relationships on performance'. *International Business Review*, *21*(6), 1158–1172.

Gastanaga, V. M., Nugent, J. B. and Pashamova, B. (1998). 'Host country reforms and FDI inflows: How much difference do they make?'. *World Development*, *26*(7), 1299–1314.

Gatignon, H. and Anderson, E. (1988). 'The Multinational Corporation's Degree of Control over Foreign Subsidiaries: An Empirical Test of a Transaction Cost Explanation'. *Journal of Law, Economics, & Organization*, *4*(2), 305–336.

Gaur, A. S., Delios, A. and Singh, K. (2007). 'Institutional Environments, Staffing Strategies, and Subsidiary Performance'. *Journal of Management*, *33*(4), 611–636.

Gaur, A. S. and Lu, J. W. (2007). 'Ownership Strategies and Survival of Foreign Subsidiaries: Impacts of Institutional Distance and Experience'. *Journal of Management*, *33*(1), 84–110.

Georgopoulos, A. and Preusse, H. G. (2009). 'Cross-border acquisitions vs. Greenfield investment: A comparative performance analysis in Greece'. *International Business Review*, *18*(6), 592–605.

Geringer, J. M., Beamish, P. W. and daCosta, R. C. (1989). 'Diversification Strategy and Internationalization: Implications for MNE Performance'. *Strategic Management Journal*, *10*(2), 109–119.

Geringer, J. M. and Hébert, L. (1991). 'Measuring Performance of International Joint Ventures'. *Journal of International Business Studies*, *22*(2), 249–263.

Ghoshal, S. and Bartlett, C. A. (1990). 'The Multinational Corporation as an Interorganizational Network'. *The Academy of Management Review*, *15*(4), 603–625.

Gil, A., Nakos, G., Brouthers, L. E. and Brouthers, K. D. (2006). 'Country-specific strategy and new venture formation in Central and East Europe'. *International Business Review*, *15*(1), 1–13.

Gilroy, B. M., Gries, T., Naudé, W., Schmidt, K.-H. and Bauer, N. (2001). *Multinational Enterprises in Africa – A Study of German Firms in South Africa*. Munich Personal RePEc Archive Paper No. 17868.

Girma, S., Greenaway, A. and Kneller, R. (2004). 'Does Exporting Increase Productivity? A Microeconometric Analysis of Matched Firms'. *Review of International Economics*, *12*(5), 855–866.

Glaister, K. W. and Buckley, P. J. (1996). 'Strategic Motives For International Alliance Formation'. *Journal of Management Studies*, *33*(3), 301–332.

Globerman, S. and Shapiro, D. (2003). 'Governance Infrastructure and US Foreign Direct Investment'. *Journal of International Business Studies, 34*(1), 19–39.

Gohou, G. and Soumaré, I. (2009). *Impact of FDI on Poverty Reduction in Africa: Are there Regional Differences?* Conference Paper presented at "African Economic Conference 2009 – Fostering Development in an Era of Financial and Economic Crises", 11–13 November 2009 in Addis Ababa, Ethiopia.

Gomes-Casseres, B. (1987). 'Joint Venture Instability: Is It A Problem?'. *Columbia Journal of World Business, 22*(2), 97–102.

Gomes-Casseres, B. (1989). 'Ownership structures of foreign subsidiaries: Theory and evidence'. *Journal of Economic Behavior & Organization, 11*(1), 1–25.

Gomes-Casseres, B. (1990). 'Firm Ownership Preferences and Host Government Restrictions: An Integrated Approach'. *Journal of International Business Studies, 21*(1), 1–22.

Gomes, L. and Ramaswamy, K. (1999). 'An Empirical Examination of the Form of the Relationship between Multinationality and Performance'. *Journal of International Business Studies, 30*(1), 173–187.

Gomez-Mejia, L. R. and Palich, L. E. (1997). 'Cultural Diversity and the Performance of Multinational Firms'. *Journal of International Business Studies, 28*(2), 309–335.

Gómez-Mera, L., Kenyon, T., Margalit, Y., Reis, J. G. and Varela, G. (2015). *New Voices in Investment: A Survey of Investors from Emerging Countries.* Washington D.C.: World Bank Group.

Görg, H. and Seric, A. (2013). *With a little help from my friends: Supplying to multinationals, buying from multinationals, and domestic firm performance.* Working Paper No. 1867. Kiel: Kiel Institute for the World Economy

Grobbelaar, N. (2004). *Every Continent Needs an America – The Experience of South African Firms Doing Business in Mozambique.* Business in Africa Report No. 2, Johannesburg: South African Institute of International Affairs (SAIIA).

GTZ (2008). *Chinas Engagement in Afrika – Chancen und Risiken für Entwicklung.* Eschborn: Deutsche Gesellschaft für Technische Zusammenarbeit.

Gu, J. (2009). 'China's Private Enterprises in Africa and the Implications for African Development'. *European Journal of Development Research, 21*(4), 570–587.

Haar, L. N. and Marinescu, N. (2014). 'Entry Modes and Firm Performance in a Transition Economy: Evidence from Inward FDI to Romania'. *Journal of East-West Business, 20*(1), 44–67.

Haberly, D. and Wójcik, D. (2015). 'Regional Blocks and Imperial Legacies: Mapping the Global Offshore FDI Network'. *Economic Geography, 91*(3), 251–280.

Hair, J. F., Tatham, R. M., Anderson, R. E. and Black, W. (1998). *Multivariate Data Analysis.* 5th Edition. New Jersey: Prentice Hall.

Hallward-Driemeyer, M. (2003). *Do bilateral investment treaties attract foreign direct investment? Only a bit…and they could bite.* Policy Research Working Paper No. 3121, Washington D.C.: World Bank Group.

Hamel, G. (1991). 'Competition for competence and inter-partner learning within international strategic alliances'. *Strategic Management Journal, 12*(S1), 83–103.

Hanson II, J. R. (1996). 'Human Capital and Direct Investment in Poor Countries'. *Explorations in Economic History*, *33*(1), 86–106.

Harding, T. and Javorcik, B. S. (2007). *Developing Economies and International Investors: Do Investment Promotion Agencies Bring Them Together?* Policy Research Working Paper No. 4339, Washington D.C.: World Bank Group.

Harding, T. and Javorcik, B. S. (2011). 'Roll Out the Red Carpet and They Will Come: Investment Promotion and FDI Inflows'. *The Economic Journal*, *121*(557), 1445–1476.

Harzing, A.-W. (2002). 'Acquisitions versus Greenfield Investments: International Strategy and Management of Entry Modes'. *Strategic Management Journal*, *23*(3), 211–227.

Hatch, N. W. and Dyer, J. H. (2004). 'Human capital and learning as a source of sustainable competitive advantage'. *Strategic Management Journal*, *25*(12), 1155–1178.

Hawawini, G., Subramanian, V. and Verdin, P. (2004). 'The home country in the age of globalization: how much does it matter for firm performance?'. *Journal of World Business*, *39*(2), 121–135.

He, X., Zhang, J. and Wang, J. (2015). 'Market Seeking Orientation and Performance in China: The Impact of Institutional Environment, Subsidiary Ownership Structure and Experience'. *Management International Review*, *55*(3), 389–419.

Head, K., Ries, J. and Swenson, D. (1995). 'Agglomeration benefits and location choice: Evidence from Japanese manufacturing investments in the United States'. *Journal of International Economics*, *38*(3–4), 223–247.

Heckman, J. J. (1979). 'Sample Selection Bias as a Specification Error'. *Econometrica*, *47*(1), 153–161.

Hedlund, G. (1986). 'The hypermodern MNC – A heterarchy?'. *Human Resource Management*, *25*(1), 9–35.

Heide, J. B. and Stump, R. L. (1995). 'Performance implications of buyer-supplier relationships in industrial markets: A transaction cost explanation'. *Journal of Business Research*, *32*(1), 57–66.

Henisz, W. J. and Delios, A. (2001). 'Uncertainty, Imitation, and Plant Location: Japanese Multinational Corporations, 1990–1996'. *Administrative Science Quarterly*, *46*(3), 443–475.

Henley, J., Kratzsch, S., Kulur, M. and Tandogan, T. (2008). *Foreign Direct Investment from China, India and South Africa in Sub-Saharan Africa: A New or Old Phenomenon?* UNU–WIDER Research Paper No. 2008/24, Helsinki: United Nations University and World Institute for Development Economics Research.

Hennart, J.-F. (1991). 'The Transaction Costs Theory of Joint Ventures: An Empirical Study of Japanese Subsidiaries in the United States'. *Management Science*, *37*(4), 483–497.

Hennart, J.-F., Kim, D.-J. and Zeng, M. (1998). 'The impact of joint venture status on the longevity of Japanese stakes in U.S. manufacturing affiliates'. *Organization Science*, *9*(3), 382–395.

Hennart, J.-F. and Larimo, J. (1998). 'The impact of culture on the strategy of multinational enterprises: Does national origin affect ownership decisions?'. *Journal of International Business Studies*, *29*(3), 515–538.

Hennart, J.-F. and Park, Y.-R. (1993). 'Greenfield vs. Acquisition: The Strategy of Japanese Investors in the United States'. *Management Science*, *39*(9), 1054–1070.

Hennart, J.-F. and Reddy, S. (1997). 'The Choice Between Mergers/Acquisitions and joint ventures: The case of Japanese Investors in the United States'. *Strategic Management Journal*, *18*(1), 1–12.

Hennart, J.-F., Roehl, T. and Zietlow, D. S. (1999). ''Trojan horse' or 'Workhorse'? The evolution of U.S.–Japanese joint ventures in the United States'. *Strategic Management Journal*, *20*(1), 15–29.

Henson, R. K. and Roberts, J. K. (2006). 'Use of Exploratory Factor Analysis in Published Research: Common Errors and Some Comment on Improved Practice'. *Educational and Psychological Measurement*, *66*(3), 393–416.

Herfindahl, O. (1950). *Concentration in the U.S. Steel Industry*. Unpublished doctoral dissertation. Columbia University.

Hewett, K., Roth, M. S. and Roth, K. (2003). 'Conditions Influencing Headquarters and Foreign Subsidiary Roles in Marketing Activities and Their Effects on Performance'. *Journal of International Business Studies*, *34*(6), 567–585.

Hirschman, A. O. (1964). 'The Paternity of an Index'. *The American Economic Review*, *54*(5), 761–762.

Hitt, M. A., Hoskisson, R. E. and Hicheon, K. (1997). 'International Diversification: Effects on Innovation and Firm Performance in Product-Diversified Firms'. *The Academy of Management Journal*, *40*(4), 767–798

Hofstede, G. (1980). *Culture's Consequences: International Differences in Work-Related Values*. Beverly Hills: Sage Publications.

Hofstede, G., Hofstede, G. J. and Minkov, M. (2010). *Cultures and Organizations: Software of the Mind.* 3rd Edition. New York: McGraw-Hill.

Hoskisson, R. E. and Hitt, M. A. (1990). 'Antecedents and Performance Outcomes of Diversification: A Review and Critique of Theoretical Perspectives'. *Journal of Management*, *16*(2), 461–509.

Huber, G. P. and Power, D. J. (1985). 'Retrospective reports of strategic-level managers: Guidelines for increasing their accuracy'. *Strategic Management Journal*, *6*(2), 171–180.

Hult, G. T. M., Ketchen, D. J., Griffith, D. A., Chabowski, B. R., Hamman, M. K., Dykes, B. J., Pollitte, W. A. and Cavusgil, S. T. (2008). 'An Assessment of the Measurement of Performance in International Business Research'. *Journal of International Business Studies*, *39*(6), 1064–1080.

Hymer, S. H. (1976). *The International Operations of National Firms: A Study of Direct Foreign Investment.* Cambridge: MIT Press.

Ibeh, K. I. N. (2005). 'Toward a Greater Level of International Entrepreneurship among Smaller Agribusiness Firms: Resource Levers and Strategic Options'. *Management International Review*, *45*(3), 59–81.

IMF (1993). *Balance of Payments Manual.* 5th Edition (BPM–5). Washington D.C.: International Monetary Fund.

IMF (2003). *Foreign Direct Investment Statistics: How Countries measure FDI.* Washington D.C.: International Monetary Fund.

IMF (2009). *Balance of Payments and International Investment Position Manual.* 6th Edition (BPM–6). Washington D.C.: International Monetary Fund.

IMF (2010). *Coordinated Direct Investment Survey Guide.* Washington D.C.: International Monetary Fund.

IMF (2011a). *Quarterly International Investment Position Statistics – Data Sources and Compilation Techniques.* Washington D.C.: International Monetary Fund.

IMF (2011b). *Regional Economic Outlook Sub-Saharan Africa – Sustaining the Expansion.* October 2011, Washington D.C.: International Monetary Fund.

IMF (2012). *Regional Economic Outlook Sub-Saharan Africa – Maintaining Growth in an Uncertain World.* October 2012, Washington D.C.: International Monetary Fund.

IMF (2013). *The General Data Dissemination System: Guide for Participants and Users.* Washington D.C.: International Monetary Fund.

IMF (2014a). *Balance of Payments and International Investment Position Compilation Guide.* Companion Document to the Sixth Edition of the Balance of Payments and International Investment Position Manual (BPM6). Washington D.C.: International Monetary Fund.

IMF (2014b). *Mozambique Rising: Building a New Tomorrow.* Washington D.C.: International Monetay Fund.

IMF (2014c). *Progress on BPM6 Implementation.* Paper prepared for the Twenty-Seventh Meeting of the IMF Committee on Balance of Payments Statistics, 27–29 October 2014 in Washington D.C., Washington D.C.: International Monetary Fund.

IMF (2014d). *World Economic Outlook – Legacies, Clouds, Uncertainties.* October 2014, Washington D.C.: International Monetary Fund.

Inkpen, A. C. and Beamish, P. W. (1997). 'Knowledge, bargaining power, and the instability of international joint ventures'. *The Academy of Management Review, 22*(1), 177–202.

Iriyama, A., Shi, W. and Prescott, J. (2014). 'Frequency and directional reversal of equity ownership change in international joint ventures'. *Asia Pacific Journal of Management, 31*(1), 215–243.

Isobe, T., Makino, S. and Montgomery, D. B. (2000). 'Resource Commitment, Entry Timing, and Market Performance of Foreign Direct Investments in Emerging Economies: The Case of Japanese International Joint Ventures in China'. *The Academy of Management Journal, 43*(3), 468–484.

Jabbour, L. and Mucchielli, J. L. (2007). 'Technology Transfer Through Vertical Linkages: The case of the Spanish Manufacturing Industry'. *Journal of Applied Economics, 10*(1), 115–136.

Javorcik, B. S. (2004). 'Does Foreign Direct Investment Increase the Productivity of Domestic Firms? In Search of Spillovers through Backward Linkages'. *The American Economic Review, 94*(3), 605–627.

Javorcik, B. S. (2014). *Does FDI Bring Good Jobs to Host Countries?* Policy Research Working Paper No. 6936. Washington D.C.: World Bank Group.

Javorcik, B. S. and Spatareanu, M. (2009). 'Tough Love: Do Czech Suppliers Learn from their Relationships with Multinationals?'. *Scandinavian Journal of Economics, 111*(4), 811–833.

Jensen, N. M. (2003). 'Democratic Governance and Multinational Corporations: Political Regimes and Inflows of Foreign Direct Investment'. *International Organization, 57*(3), 587–616.

Jerven, M. (2013). *Poor Numbers: How We Are Misled by African Development Statistics and What to Do about It.* Ithaca and London: Cornell University Press.

Johanson, J. and Vahlne, J.-E. (1977). 'The Internationalization Process of the Firm – A Model of Knowledge Development and Increasing Foreign Market Commitments'. *Journal of International Business Studies, 8*(1), 23–32.

Johanson, J. and Vahlne, J.-E. (1990). 'The Mechanism of Internationalisation'. *International Marketing Review, 7*(4), 11–24.

Johanson, J. and Wiedersheim-Paul, F. (1975). 'The Internationalization of the Firm – Four Swedish cases'. *Journal of Management Studies, 12*(3), 305–323.

Kabelwa, G. (2004). *Technology Transfer and South African Investment in Tanzania.* Globalisation and East Africa Working Paper 10, Dar es Salaam: Economic and Social Research Foundation.

Kaiser, H. F. (1960). 'The Application of Electronic Computers to Factor Analysis'. *Educational and Psychological Measurement, 20*(1), 141–151.

Kaiser, H. F. and Rice, J. (1974). 'Little Jiffy, Mark IV'. *Educational and Psychological Measurement, 34*(1), 111–117.

Kaplinsky, R. and Morris, M. (2008). 'Do the Asian Drivers Undermine Export-oriented Industrialization in SSA?'. *World Development, 36*(2), 254–273.

Kaplinsky, R. and Morris, M. (2009). 'Chinese FDI in Sub-Saharan Africa: Engaging with Large Dragons'. *European Journal of Development Research, 21*(4), 551–569.

Kaynak, E., Demirbag, M. and Tatoglu, E. (2007). 'Determinants of Ownership-based Entry Mode Choice of MNEs: Evidence from Mongolia'. *Management International Review, 47*(4), 505–530.

Kent, D. H. (1991). 'Joint Ventures vs. Non-Joint Ventures: An Empirical Investigation'. *Strategic Management Journal, 12*(5), 387–393.

Kerner, A. (2014). 'What We Talk About When We Talk About Foreign Direct Investment'. *International Studies Quarterly, 58*(4), 804–815.

Khanna, T. and Palepu, K. (1997). 'Why Focused Strategies May Be Wrong for Emerging Markets'. *Harvard Business Review, 75*(4), 41–51.

Kiggundu, M. N. (2002). 'Entrepreneurs and entrepreneurship in Africa: What is known and what needs to be done'. *Journal of Developmental Entrepreneurship, 7*(3), 239–258.

Kim, W. C. and Hwang, P. (1992). 'Global Strategy and Multinationals' Entry Mode Choice'. *Journal of International Business Studies, 23*(1), 29–53.

Kim, W. C., Hwang, P. and Burgers, W. P. (1993). 'Multinationals' Diversification and the Risk-Return Trade-Off'. *Strategic Management Journal*, *14*(4), 275–286.

Kim, Y. and Gray, S. (2008). 'The impact of entry mode choice on foreign affiliate performance: The case of foreign MNEs in South Korea'. *Management International Review*, *48*(2), 165–188.

Kindleberger, C. P. (1969). *Americal Business Abroad – Six Lectures on Direct Investment*. New Haven and London: Yale University Press.

Knickerbocker, F. T. (1973). *Oligopolistic Reaction and the Multinational Enterprise*. Cambridge: Harvard University Press.

Knight, G. A. and Cavusgil, S. T. (2004). 'Innovation, organizational capabilities, and the born-global firm'. *Journal of International Business Studies*, *35*(2), 124–141.

Knight, G. A. and Cavusgil, S. T. (2005). 'A Taxonomy of Born-global Firms'. *Management International Review*, *45*(3), 15–35.

Kobrin, S. (2005). 'The Determinants of Liberalization of FDI Policy in Developing Countries: A Cross-sectional Analysis, 1992–2001'. *Transnational Corporations*, *14*(1), 67–104.

Kogut, B. (1989). 'The Stability of Joint Ventures: Reciprocity and Competitive Rivalry'. *Journal of Industrial Economics*, *38*(2), 183–198.

Kogut, B. (1991). 'Joint Ventures and the Option to Expand and Acquire'. *Management Science*, *37*(1), 19–33.

Kogut, B. and Singh, H. (1988). 'The Effect of National Culture on the Choice of Entry Mode'. *Journal of International Business Studies*, *19*(3), 411–432.

Kogut, B. and Zander, U. (1992). 'Knowledge of the firm, combinative capabilities, and the replication of technology'. *Organization Science*, *3*(3), 383–397.

Kogut, B. and Zander, U. (1993). 'Knowledge of the Firm and the Evolutionary Theory of the Multinational Corporation'. *Journal of International Business Studies*, *24*(4), 625–645.

Kolstad, I. and Wiig, A. (2011). 'Better the Devil You Know? Chinese Foreign Direct Investment in Africa'. *Journal of African Business*, *12*(1), 31–50.

Konings, P. (2007). 'China and Africa: Building a Strategic Partnership'. *Journal of Developing Societies*, *23*(3), 341–367.

Konopaske, R., Werner, S. and Neupert, K. E. (2002). 'Entry mode strategy and performance: the role of FDI staffing'. *Journal of Business Research*, *55*(9), 759–770.

Kostova, T. (1999). 'Transnational Transfer of Strategic Organizational Practices: A Contextual Perspective'. *The Academy of Management Review*, *24*(2), 308–324.

Kostova, T. and Zaheer, S. (1999). 'Organizational Legitimacy under Conditions of Complexity: The Case of the Multinational Enterprise'. *The Academy of Management Review*, *24*(1), 64–81.

Kotabe, M., Srinivasan, S. S. and Aulakh, P. S. (2002). 'Multinationality and firm performance: The moderating role of R&D and marketing capabilities'. *Journal of International Business Studies*, *33*(1), 79–97.

KPMG (2012). Malawi – Country Profile. Online at: http://www.kpmg.com/Africa/en/KPMG-in-Africa/Documents/Malawi.pdf (accessed on 8 July 2016).

Kragelund, P. (2009). 'Part of the Disease or Part of the Cure? Chinese Investments in the Zambian Mining and Construction Sectors'. *European Journal of Development Research, 21*(4), 644–661.

Kratzsch, S. (2005). *The locational determinants of foreign direct investment activities: Implications for Sub-Saharan Africa.* Unpublished diploma thesis, Universität Karlsruhe (TH).

Kratzsch, S. (2010). *Migration and Remittances in Sub-Saharan Africa.* Unpublished Paper, Universität Leipzig.

Kumar, M. V. S. (2005). 'The value from acquiring and divesting a joint venture: a real options approach'. *Strategic Management Journal, 26*(4), 321–331.

Kumar, N. (1994). 'Determinants of Export Orientation of Foreign Production by U.S. Multinationals: An Inter-Country Analysis'. *Journal of International Business Studies, 25*(1), 141–156.

Labovitz, S. (1970). 'The Assignment of Numbers to Rank Order Categories'. *American Sociological Review, 35*(3), 515–524.

Lall, S. (2005). 'FDI, AGOA and Manufactured Exports by a Landlocked, Least Developed African Economy: Lesotho'. *Journal of Development Studies, 41*(6), 998–1022.

Lane, P., Salk, J. E. and Lyles, M. A. (2001). 'Absorptive capacity, learning, and performance in international joint ventures'. *Strategic Management Journal, 22*(12), 1139–1161.

Larsson, R., Bengtsson, L., Henriksson, K. and Sparks, J. (1998). 'The Interorganizational Learning Dilemma: Collective Knowledge Development in Strategic Alliances'. *Organization Science, 9*(3), 285–305.

Lee, S. H. and Williams, C. (2007). 'Dispersed entrepreneurship within multinational corporations: A community perspective'. *Journal of World Business, 42*(4), 505–519.

Li, J. (1995). 'Foreign entry and survival: Effects of strategic choices on performance in international markets'. *Strategic Management Journal, 16*(5), 333–351.

Li, J. and Guisinger, S. (1991). 'Comparative Business Failures of Foreign-Controlled Firms in the United States'. *Journal of International Business Studies, 22*(2), 209–224.

Li, J. and Guisinger, S. (1992). 'The Globalization of Service Multinationals in the "Triad" Regions: Japan, Western Europe and North America'. *Journal of International Business Studies, 23*(4), 675–696.

Li, Q. and Resnick, A. (2003). 'Reversal of Fortunes: Democratic Institutions and Foreign Direct Investment Inflows to Developing Countries'. *International Organization, 57*(1), 175–211.

Lipsey, R. E. (1999). *The role of foreign direct investment in international capital flows.* NBER Working Paper No. 7094, Cambridge: National Bureau of Economic Research.

Lipsey, R. E. (2007). *Defining and measuring the location of FDI output.* NBER Working Paper No. 12996, Cambridge: National Bureau of Economic Research.

Loane, S. and Bell, J. (2006). 'Rapid internationalisation among entrepreneurial firms in Australia, Canada, Ireland and New Zealand: An extension to the network approach'. *International Marketing Review*, *23*(5), 467–485.

López-Duarte, C. and Vidal-Suárez, M. M. (2008). 'Foreign Direct Investment through Partial Acquisitions: Hostage Effect or Conflicts Enhancement'. *Journal of Management and Governance*, *12*(3), 287–308.

López-Duarte, C. and Vidal-Suárez, M. M. (2010). 'External uncertainty and entry mode choice: Cultural distance, political risk and language diversity'. *International Business Review*, *19*(6), 575–588.

Loree, D. W. and Guisinger, S. (1995). 'Policy and Non-Policy Determinants of U.S. Equity Foreign Direct Investment'. *Journal of International Business Studies*, *26*(2), 281–299.

Lu, J. W. and Beamish, P. W. (2001). 'The Internationalization and Performance of SMEs'. *Strategic Management Journal*, *22*(6/7), 565–586.

Lu, J. W. and Beamish, P. W. (2004). 'International Diversification and Firm Performance: The S-Curve Hypothesis'. *The Academy of Management Journal*, *47*(4), 598–609.

Lu, J. W. and Beamish, P. W. (2006). 'Partnering strategies and performance of SMEs' international joint ventures'. *Journal of Business Venturing*, *21*(4), 461–486.

Lu, J. W. and Xu, D. (2006). 'Growth and Survival of International Joint Ventures: An External–Internal Legitimacy Perspective'. *Journal of Management*, *32*(3), 426–448.

Lubatkin, M. and Chatterjee, S. (1994). 'Extending Modern Portfolio Theory into the Domain of Corporate Diversification: Does It Apply?'. *The Academy of Management Journal*, *37*(1), 109–136.

Lumbila, K. N. (2005). *What Makes FDI Work? A Panel Analysis of the Growth Effect of FDI in Africa*. Africa Region Working Paper No. 80, Washington D.C.: World Bank Group.

Lundan, S. M. (2006). 'Reinvested earnings as a component of FDI: an analytical review of the determinants of reinvestment'. *Transnational Corporations*, *15*(3), 35–66.

Luo, Y. (1997). 'Partner Selection and Venturing Success: The Case of Joint Ventures with Firms in the People's Republic of China'. *Organization Science*, *8*(6), 648–662.

Luo, Y. (1999). 'The Structure-Performance Relationship in a Transitional Economy: An Empirical Study of Multinational Alliances in China'. *Journal of Business Research*, *46*(1), 15–30.

Luo, Y. (2001). 'Determinants of Entry in an Emerging Economy: A Multilevel Approach'. *Journal of Management Studies*, *38*(3), 443–472.

Luo, Y. and Park, S. H. (2001). 'Strategic Alignment and Performance of Market-Seeking MNCs in China'. *Strategic Management Journal*, *22*(2), 141–155.

Luo, Y. and Peng, M. W. (1999). 'Learning to Compete in a Transition Economy: Experience, Environment, and Performance'. *Journal of International Business Studies*, *30*(2), 269–295.

Luo, Y., Shenkar, O. and Nyaw, M.-K. (2001). 'A Dual Parent Perspective on Control and Performance in International Joint Ventures: Lessons from a Developing Economy'. *Journal of International Business Studies*, *32*(1), 41–58.

Lyles, M. A. (1994). 'The impact of organizational learning on joint venture formations'. *International Business Review*, *3*(4), 459–467.

Lyles, M. A. and Salk, J. E. (1996). 'Knowledge acquisition from foreign parents in international joint ventures: An empirical examination in the Hungarian context'. *Journal of International Business Studies*, *27*(5), 877–903.

Maekelburger, B., Schwens, C. and Kabst, R. (2012). 'Asset specificity and foreign market entry mode choice of small and medium-sized enterprises: The moderating influence of knowledge safeguards and institutional safeguards'. *Journal of International Business Studies*, *43*(5), 458–476.

Mahnke, V. and Venzin, M. (2003). 'The Internationalization Process of Digital Information Good Providers'. *Management International Review*, *43*(1), 115–143.

Makino, S. and Beamish, P. W. (1998). 'Local Ownership Restrictions, Entry Mode Choice, and FDI Performance: Japanese Overseas Subsidiaries in Asia'. *Asia Pacific Journal of Management*, *15*(2), 119–136.

Makino, S. and Delios, A. (1996). 'Local knowledge transfer and performance: Implications for alliance formation in Asia'. *Journal of International Business Studies*, *27*(5), 905–927.

Makino, S., Isobe, T. and Chan, C. M. (2004). 'Does country matter?'. *Strategic Management Journal*, *25*(10), 1027–1043.

Makino, S. and Neupert, K. E. (2000). 'National culture, transaction costs, and the choice between joint venture and wholly owned subsidiary'. *Journal of International Business Studies*, *31*(4), 705–713.

Malefane, M. R. (2007). 'Determinants of foreign direct investment in Lesotho: Evidence from cointegration and error correction modeling'. *South African Journal of Economic and Management Sciences*, *10*(1), 99–106.

Markides, C. C. (1992). 'Consequences of Corporate Refocusing: Ex Ante Evidence'. *The Academy of Management Journal*, 35(2), 398–412.

Marschan, R., Welch, D. and Welch, L. (1996). 'Control in less-hierarchical multinationals: The role of personal networks and informal communication'. *International Business Review*, *5*(2), 137–150.

Martin, X. (2013). 'Solving theoretical and empirical conundrums in international strategy research: Linking foreign entry mode choices and performance'. *Journal of International Business Studies*, *44*(1), 28–41.

Mata, J. and Portugal, P. (2004). 'Patterns of Entry, Post-Entry Growth and Survival: A Comparison Between Domestic and Foreign Owned Firms'. *Small Business Economics*, *22*(3), 283–298.

Mayrhofer, U. (2004). 'International Market Entry: Does the Home Country Affect Entry-Mode Decisions?'. *Journal of International Marketing*, *12*(4), 71–96.

McCloughan, P. and Stone, I. (1998). 'Life duration of foreign multinational subsidiaries: Evidence from UK northern manufacturing industry 1970–93'. *International Journal of Industrial Organization*, *16*(6), 719–747.

McDonald, F., Warhurst, S. and Allen, M. (2008). 'Autonomy, Embeddedness, and the Performance of Foreign Owned Subsidiaries'. *Multinational Business Review*, *16*(3), 73–92.

McGahan, A. M. and Porter, M. E. (1997). 'How Much Does Industry Matter, Really?'. *Strategic Management Journal*, *18*, 15–30.

McGrath, R. G. and Nerkar, A. (2004). 'Real options reasoning and a new look at the R&D investment strategies of pharmaceutical firms'. *Strategic Management Journal*, *25*(1), 1–21.

McKinsey Global Institute (2010). *Lions on the move: The progress and potential of African economies*. Online at: http://www.mckinsey.com/global-themes/middle-east-and-africa/lions-on-the-move (accessed on 7 July 2016).

McLure, J. (2008). 'Ethiopia's rosy harvest'. *The Africa Report*, No. 11 (June–July), 62–64.

McMillan, M. S. and Harttgen, K. (2014). *What is driving the 'African Growth Miracle'?* NBER Working Paper No. 20077, Cambridge: National Bureau of Economic Research.

Meyer, K. E. and Nguyen, H. V. (2005). 'Foreign Investment Strategies and Sub-national Institutions in Emerging Markets: Evidence from Vietnam'. *Journal of Management Studies*, *42*(1), 63–93.

Meyer, K. E. and Sinani, E. (2009). 'When and where does foreign direct investment generate positive spillovers? A meta-analysis'. *Journal of International Business Studies*, *40*(7), 1075–1094.

MIGA (2014). *World Investment and Political Risk 2013*. Washington D.C.: Multilateral Investment Guarantee Agency.

Miller, C. C., Cardinal, L. B. and Glick, W. H. (1997). 'Retrospective Reports in Organizational Research: A Reexamination of Recent Evidence'. *The Academy of Management Journal*, *40*(1), 189–204.

Miller, S. R. and Eden, L. (2006). 'Local Density and Foreign Subsidiary Performance'. *The Academy of Management Journal*, *49*(2), 341–355.

Mitchell, W., Shaver, J. M. and Yeung, B. (1994). 'Foreign entrant survival and foreign market share: Canadian companies' experience in United States medical sector markets'. *Strategic Management Journal*, *15*(7), 555–567.

Miyamoto, K. (2003). *Human Capital Formation and Foreign Direct Investment in Developing Countries*. OECD Development Centre Working Paper No. 211, Paris: Organisation for Economic Co-operation and Development.

Mlachila, M. and Takebe, M. (2011). *FDI from BRICs to LICs: Emerging Growth Driver?* Working Paper 11/178, Washington D.C.: International Monetary Fund.

Mlambo, K. (2005). 'Reviving Foreign Direct Investments in Southern Africa: Constraints and Policies'. *African Development Review*, *17*(3), 552–579.

Mohamad, N. and Hoshino, Y. (2012). 'Survival and Financial Performance of Japanese Subsidiaries in Malaysia and Thailand'. *Business and Management Review*, *2*(4), 21–41.

Mohan, G. and Lampert, B. (2013). 'Negotiating China: Reinserting African agency into China – Africa relations'. *African Affairs*, *112*(446), 92–110.

Montgomery, C. A. and Porter, M. E. (Eds.) (1991). *Strategy: Seeking and Securing Competitive Advantage*. Boston: Harvard Business School Press.

Moran, T. H. (2001). *Parental Supervision: The New Paradigm for Foreign Direct Investment and Development*. Washington D.C.: Peterson Institute for International Economics.

Moran, T. H. (2002). *Strategy and Tactics for the Doha Round: Capturing the Benefits of Foreign Direct Investment*. Manila: Asian Development Bank.

Morisset, J. (2000). 'Foreign Direct Investment in Africa: Policies also Matter'. *Transnational Corporations*, *9*(2), 107–125.

Morosini, P., Shane, S. and Singh, H. (1998). 'National Cultural Distance and Cross-Border Acquisition Performance'. *Journal of International Business Studies*, *29*(1), 137–158.

Morrison, C. J. (1993). *A Microeconomic Approach to the Measurement of Economic Performance*. New York: Springer-Verlag.

Morrison, T. (2013). *Mid-Term Evaluation Report on the Enhanced Data Dissemination Initiative Project*. Washington D.C.: Internatonal Monetary Fund.

Morrissey, O. and Osei, R. (2004). 'Capital Flows to Developing Countries: Trends, Volatility and Policy Implications'. *IDS Bulletin*, *35*(1), 40–49.

Mudambi, R. (1998). 'The Role of Duration in Multinational Investment Strategies'. *Journal of International Business Studies*, *29*(2), 239–261.

Mudambi, R. and Zahra, S. A. (2007). 'The survival of international new ventures'. *Journal of International Business Studies*, *38*(2), 333–352.

Murray, J. Y., Wildt, A. R. and Kotabe, M. (1995). 'Global Sourcing Strategies of U. S. Subsidiaries of Foreign Multinationals'. *Management International Review*, *35*(4), 307–324.

Mutinelli, M. and Piscitello, L. (1998a). 'The entry mode choice of MNEs: an evolutionary approach'. *Research Policy*, *27*(5), 491–506.

Mutinelli, M. and Piscitello, L. (1998b). 'The Influence of Firm's Size and International Experience on the Ownership Structure of Italian FDI in Manufacturing'. *Small Business Economics*, *11*(1), 43–56.

Naidu, S. and Lutchman, J. (2004). *Understanding South Africa's Engagement in the Region: Has the Leopard Changed its Spots?* Paper presented at Conference "Stability, Poverty Reduction, and South African Trade and Investment in Southern Africa", 29–30 March 2004 in Pretoria, South Africa.

Nanda, R. and Khanna, T. (2010). 'Diasporas and Domestic Entrepreneurs: Evidence from the Indian Software Industry'. *Journal of Economics & Management Strategy*, *19*(4), 991–1012.

Naudé, W. and Krugell, W. (2003). 'Developing human resources to attract foreign direct investment in Africa'. *Management Dynamics*, *12*(3), 2–12.

Naudé, W. and Krugell, W. (2007). 'Investigating geography and institutions as determinants of foreign direct investment in Africa using panel data'. *Applied Economics*, *39*(10), 1223–1233.

Nelson, R. A. (1989). 'On the Measurement of Capacity Utilization'. *Journal of Industrial Economics*, *37*(3), 273–286.

Neumayer, E. and Spess, L. (2005). 'Do bilateral investment treaties increase foreign direct investment to developing countries?'. *World Development*, *33*(10), 1567–1585.

Newbert, S. L. (2007). 'Empirical research on the resource-based view of the firm: an assessment and suggestions for future research'. *Strategic Management Journal*, *28*(2), 121–146.

Ngobo, P. V. and Fouda, M. (2012). 'Is 'Good' governance good for business? A cross-national analysis of firms in African countries'. *Journal of World Business*, *47*(3), 435–449.

Nicoletti, G., Golub, S., Hajkova, D., Mirza, D. and Yoo, K.-Y. (2003). *Policies and International Integration: Influences on Trade and Foreign Direct Investment.* OECD Economics Department Working Paper No. 359, Paris: Organization for Economic Cooperation and Development.

Nitsch, D., Beamish, P. and Makino, S. (1996). 'Entry mode and performance of Japanese FDI in Western Europe'. *Management International Review*, *36*(1), 27–43.

Noorbakhsh, F., Paloni, A. and Youssef, A. (2001). 'Human Capital and FDI Inflows to Developing Countries: New Empirical Evidence'. *World Development*, *29*(9), 1593–1610.

North, D. C. (1990). *Institutions, Institutional Change and Economic Performance.* Cambridge: Cambridge University Press.

Nunnally, J. C. (1978). *Psychometric Theory*. 2nd Edition. New York: McGraw-Hill.

O'Brien, R. M. (2007). 'A Caution Regarding Rules of Thumb for Variance Inflation Factors'. *Quality & Quantity*, *41*(5), 673–690.

Ocampo, J. A., Kregel, J. and Griffith-Jones, S. (2007). *International Finance and Development.* London: Zed Books.

OECD (2005a). *OECD Science, Technology and Industry Scoreboard 2005.* Paris: Organisation for Economic Cooperation and Development.

OECD (2005b). *Regulatory environment for foreign direct investment.* Draft overview study prepared by the Organisation for Economic Cooperation and Development Secretariat for "NEPAD/OECD Investment Initiative Roundtable – Investment for African Development: Making it Happen", 25–27 May 2005 in Entebbe, Uganda.

OECD (2008). *OECD Benchmark Definition of Foreign Direct Investment.* 4th Edition. Paris: Organisation for Economic Co-operation and Development.

OECD (2010). *OECD Transfer Pricing Guidelines for Multinational Enterprises and Tax Administrations 2010.* Paris: Organisation for Economic Co-operation and Development.

OECD (2014a). *Geographical Distribution of Financial Flows to Developing Countries: Disbursements, Commitments, Country Indicators.* Paris: Organisation for Economic Co-operation and Development.

OECD (2014b). *OECD International Direct Investment Statistics.* Paris: Organisation for Economic Co-operation and Development.

OECD (2014c). *Tax Transparency 2014: Report on Progress*. Global Forum on Transparency and Exchange of Information for Tax Purposes, Paris: Organisation for Economic Co-operation and Development.

OECD (2015). *Progress Report to the G20 Finance Ministers and Central Bank Governors: Update on Effectiveness and On-Going Monitoring*. Report prepared by the Secretary-General of the Organisation for Economic Co-operation and Development for the G20 Finance Ministers and Central Bank Governors Meeting. 9–10 February 2015 in Istanbul, Turkey.

Ogasavara, M. H. and Hoshino, Y. (2009). 'Implications of Firm Experiential Knowledge and Sequential FDI on Performance of Japanese Subsidiaries in Brazil'. *Review of Quantitative Finance and Accounting*, *33*(1), 37–58.

Okeahalam, C. C. and Wood, S. (2009). 'Financing internationalisation: a case study of an African retail transnational corporation'. *Journal of Economic Geography*, *9*(4), 511–537.

Onyeiwu, S. and Shrestha, H. (2004). 'Determinants of Foreign Direct Investment in Africa'. *Journal of Developing Societies*, *20*(1–2), 89–106.

Oviatt, B. M. and McDougall, P. P. (1994). 'Toward a Theory of International New Ventures'. *Journal of International Business Studies*, *25*(1), 45–64.

Oviatt, B. M. and McDougall, P. P. (2005). 'Defining International Entrepreneurship and Modeling the Speed of Internationalization'. *Entrepreneurship Theory and Practice*, *29*(5), 537–554.

Oxley, J. E. (1999). 'Institutional environment and the mechanisms of governance: the impact of intellectual property protection on the structure of inter-firm alliances'. *Journal of Economic Behavior & Organization*, *38*(3), 283–309.

Oya, C. (2012). 'Contract Farming in Sub-Saharan Africa: A Survey of Approaches, Debates and Issues'. *Journal of Agrarian Change*, *12*(1), 1–33.

Oyelaran-Oyeyinka, B. (2006). *Learning to Compete in African Industry: Institutions and Technology in Development*. Aldershot: Ashgate Publishing.

Oyelaran-Oyeyinka, B. and Barclay, L. A. (2004). 'Human Capital and Systems of Innovation in African Development'. *African Development Review*, *16*(1), 115–138.

Padmanabhan, P. and Cho, K. R. (1995). 'Methodological issues in International Business Studies: The case of foreign establishment mode decisions by multinational firms'. *International Business Review*, *4*(1), 55–73.

Padmanabhan, P. and Cho, K. R. (1996). 'Ownership strategy for a foreign affiliate: An empirical investigation of Japanese firms'. *Management International Review*, *36*(1), 45–65.

Padmanabhan, P. and Cho, K. R. (1999). 'Decision Specific Experience in Foreign Ownership and Establishment Strategies: Evidence from Japanese Firms'. *Journal of International Business Studies*, *30*(1), 25–43.

Page, J. (2012). 'Can Africa Industrialise?'. *Journal of African Economies*, *21* (AERC Supplement 2), ii86–ii124.

Page, S. and te Velde, D. W. (2004). *Foreign direct investment by African countries*. Paper prepared for "InWent/UNCTAD meeting on FDI in Africa", 22–24 November 2004 in Addis Ababa, Ethiopia.

Palich, L. E., Cardinal, L. B. and Miller, C. C. (2000). 'Curvilinearity in the Diversification-Performance Linkage: An Examination of over Three Decades of Research'. *Strategic Management Journal*, *21*(2), 155–174.

Palich, L. E. and Gomez-Mejia, L. R. (1999). 'A Theory of Global Strategy and Firm Efficiencies: Considering the Effects of Cultural Diversity'. *Journal of Management*, *25*(4), 587–606.

Pan, Y. (1996). 'Influences on Foreign Equity Ownership Level in Joint Ventures in China'. *Journal of International Business Studies*, *27*(1), 1–26.

Pan, Y. (2002). 'Equity ownership in international joint ventures: The impact of source country factors'. *Journal of International Business Studies*, *33*(2), 375–384.

Pan, Y. and Chi, P. S. K. (1999). 'Financial performance and survival of multinational corporations in China'. *Strategic Management Journal*, *20*(4), 359–374.

Pan, Y., Li, S. and Tse, D. K. (1999). 'The Impact of Order and Mode of Market Entry on Profitability and Market Share'. *Journal of International Business Studies*, *30*(1), 81–103.

Park, S. H. and Russo, M. V. (1996). 'When Competition Eclipses Cooperation: An Event History Analysis of Joint Venture Failure'. *Management Science*, *42*(6), 875–890.

Park, S. H. and Ungson, G. R. (1997). 'The Effect of National Culture, Organizational Complementarity, and Economic Motivation on Joint Venture Dissolution'. *The Academy of Management Journal*, *40*(2), 279–307.

Patterson, N., Montanjees, M., Motala, J. and Cardillo, C. (2004). *Foreign Direct Investment: Trends, Data Availability, Concepts, and Recording Practices*. Washington D.C.: International Monetary Fund.

Peng, M. W., Wang, D. Y. L. and Jiang, Y. (2008). 'An Institution-Based View of International Business Strategy: A Focus on Emerging Economies'. *Journal of International Business Studies*, *39*(5), 920–936.

Pennings, J. M., Barkema, H. and Douma, S. (1994). 'Organizational Learning and Diversification'. *The Academy of Management Journal*, *37*(3), 608–640.

Penrose, E. (1956). 'Foreign Investment and the Growth of the Firm'. *The Economic Journal*, *66*(262), 220–235.

Penrose, E. (1959). *The Theory of the Growth of the Firm*. Oxford: Blackwell.

Petersen, B., Pedersen, T. and Lyles, M. A. (2008). 'Closing Knowledge Gaps in Foreign Markets'. *Journal of International Business Studies*, *39*(7), 1097–1113.

Peterson, R. A. (1994). 'A Meta-Analysis of Cronbach's Coefficient Alpha'. *Journal of Consumer Research*, *21*(2), 381–391.

Phelps, N. A., Stillwell, J. C. H. and Wanjiru, R. (2008). 'Missing the GO in AGOA? Growth and constraints of foreign direct investment in the Kenyan clothing industry'. *Transnational Corporations*, *17*(2), 67–106.

Pigato, M. A. (2000). *Foreign Direct Investment in Africa: Old tales and new evidence*. Africa Region Working Paper No. 8, Washington D.C.: World Bank Group.

Pigato, M. A. (2001). *The Foreign Direct Investment Environment in Africa*. Africa Region Working Paper No. 15, Washington D.C.: World Bank Group.

Podsakoff, P. M., MacKenzie, S. B., Jeong-Yeon, L. and Podsakoff, N. P. (2003). 'Common Method Biases in Behavioral Research: A Critical Review of the Literature and Recommended Remedies'. *Journal of Applied Psychology*, *88*(5), 879–903.

Porter, M. E. (1980). *Competitive Strategy: Techniques for Analyzing Industries and Competitors*. New York: Free Press.

Porter, M. E. (1985). *Competitive Advantage: Creating and Sustaining Superior Performance*. New York: Free Press.

Powell, T. C. (1996). 'How Much Does Industry Matter? An Alternative Empirical Test'. *Strategic Management Journal*, *17*(4), 323–334.

Power, M. and Alves, A. C. (Eds.) (2012). *China and Angola: A Marriage of Convenience?* Cape Town: Pambazuka Press.

Prabhakar, A. C. (2008). *An Evaluation of Indian Joint-ventures in East Africa*. Geneva: South Centre.

Puck, J. F., Holtbrügge, D. and Mohr, A. T. (2009). 'Beyond Entry Mode Choice: Explaining the Conversion of Joint Ventures into Wholly Owned Subsidiaries in the People's Republic of China'. *Journal of International Business Studies*, *40*(3), 388–404.

Puig, F., González-Loureiro, M. and Ghauri, P. N. (2014). 'Internationalisation for Survival: The Case of New Ventures'. *Management International Review*, *54*(5), 653–673.

Quin, S., Egesa, K. and Murad, H. (2013). *Direct Reporting of Private Sector Cross-Border Financial Flows and Stocks in Selected African Countries*. Technical Notes and Manuals No. 13/02, Washington D.C.: International Monetary Fund.

Ramachandran, V. and Shah, M. K. (1999). 'Minority Entrepreneurs and Firm Performance in Sub-Saharan Africa'. *Journal of Development Studies*, *36*(2), 71–87.

Ramamurti, R. (2001). 'The Obsolescing 'Bargaining Model'? MNC-Host Developing Country Relations Revisited'. *Journal of International Business Studies*, *32*(1), 23–39.

Ramanathan, R. (1995). *Introductory Econometrics with Applications*. 3rd Edition. Fort Worth: Dryden Press.

Reuer, J. J. (2000). 'Parent firm performance across international joint venture life-cycle stages'. *Journal of International Business Studies*, *31*(1), 1–20.

Roquebert, J. A., Phillips, R. L. and Westfall, P. A. (1996). 'Markets vs. Management: What 'Drives' Profitability?'. *Strategic Management Journal*, *17*(8), 653–664.

Rumelt, R. P. (1974). *Strategy, Structure and Economic Performance*. Cambridge: Harvard University Press.

Rumelt, R. P. (1991). 'How Much Does Industry Matter?'. *Strategic Management Journal*, *12*(3), 167–185.

Rumney, R. and Pingo, M. (2004). *Mapping South Africa's Trade and Investment in the Region*. Paper presented at Conference "Stability, Poverty Reduction, and South African Trade and Investment in Southern Africa", 29–30 March 2004 in Pretoria, South Africa.

Rundell, S. (2010). Angola is latest investment magnet. *African Business*, June 2010, 24–26.

Saunders, R. (2008). *South African Investment in Africa: Restructuring and Resistance*. Online at: http://www.africafiles.org/atissueezine.asp?issue=issue8#art1 (accessed on 8 July 2016).

Schmalensee, R. (1985). 'Do Markets Differ Much?'. *The American Economic Review*, *75*(3), 341–351.

Schneider, F. and Frey, B. S. (1985). 'Economic and political determinants of foreign direct investment'. *World Development*, *13*(2), 161–175.

Schroath, F. W., Hu, M. Y. and Chen, H. (1993). 'Country-of-origin effects of foreign investments in the People's Republic of China'. *Journal of International Business Studies*, *24*(2), 277–290.

Schroeder, R. A. (2008). South African Capital in the Land of Ujamaa: Contested Terrain in Tanzania. Online at: http://www.africafiles.org/atissueezine.asp?issue=issue8#art5 (accessed on 8 July 2016).

Shan, W. (1991). 'Environmental Risks and Joint Venture Sharing Arrangements'. *Journal of International Business Studies*, *22*(4), 555–578.

Shane, S., Venkataraman, S. and MacMillan, I. (1995). 'Cultural differences in Innovation Championing Strategies'. *Journal of Management*, *21*(5), 931–952.

Shaner, J. and Maznevski, M. (2011). 'The relationship between networks, institutional development, and performance in foreign investments'. *Strategic Management Journal*, *32*(5), 556–568.

Sharife, K. (2010). 'Flying a Questionable Flag: Liberia's Lucrative Shipping Industry'. *World Policy Journal*, *27*(4), 111–118.

Shatz, H. J. and Venables, A. J. (2000). *The Geography of International Investment*. Policy Research Working Paper No. 2338, Washington D.C.: World Bank Group.

Shaver, J. M. (1998). 'Accounting for Endogeneity When Assessing Strategy Performance: Does Entry Mode Choice Affect FDI Survival?'. *Management Science*, *44*(4), 571–585.

Shen, X. (2013). *Private Chinese Investment in Africa: Myths and Realities*. Policy Research Working Paper No. 6311, Washington D.C.: World Bank Group.

Shenkar, O. (2001). 'Cultural Distance Revisited: Towards a More Rigorous Conceptualization and Measurement of Cultural Differences'. *Journal of International Business Studies*, *32*(3), 519–535.

Shrader, R. C. (2001). 'Collaboration and Performance in Foreign Markets: The Case of Young High-Technology Manufacturing Firms'. *The Academy of Management Journal*, *44*(1), 45–60.

Sichei, M. M. and Kinyondo, G. (2012). 'Determinants of Foreign Direct Investment in Africa: A Panel Data Analysis'. *Global Journal of Management and Business Research*, *12*(18), 84–97.

Simmonds, P. G. (1990). 'The Combined Diversification Breadth and Mode Dimensions and the Performance of Large Diversified Firms'. *Strategic Management Journal*, *11*(5), 399–410.

Siripaisalpipat, P. and Hoshino, Y. (2000). 'Firm-specific advantages, entry modes, and performance of Japanese FDI in Thailand'. *Japan and the World Economy*, *12*(1), 33–48.

Skrondal, A. and Laake, P. (2001). 'Regression among factor scores'. *Psychometrika*, *66*(4), 563–575.

Slangen, A. and Hennart, J.-F. (2007). 'Greenfield or acquisition entry: A review of the empirical foreign establishment mode literature'. *Journal of International Management*, *13*(4), 403–429.

Slangen, A. and Hennart, J.-F. (2008). 'Do Foreign Greenfields Outperform Foreign Acquisitions or Vice Versa? An Institutional Perspective'. *Journal of Management Studies*, *45*(7), 1301–1328.

Song, J. (2002). 'Firm capabilities and technology ladders: sequential foreign direct investments of Japanese electronics firms in East Asia'. *Strategic Management Journal*, *23*(3), 191–210.

Srivastava, R. K. and Green, R. T. (1986). 'Determinants of Bilateral Trade Flows'. *The Journal of Business*, *59*(4), 623–640.

Staritz, C. (2011). *Making the Cut? Low-Income Countries and the Global Clothing Value Chain in a Post-Quota and Post-Crisis World*. Washington D.C.: World Bank Group.

Steensma, H. K., Barden, J. Q., Dhanaraj, C., Lyles, M. and Tihanyi, L. (2008). 'The Evolution and Internalization of International Joint Ventures in a Transitioning Economy'. *Journal of International Business Studies*, *39*(3), 491–507.

Stephan, M. and Pfaffmann, E. (2001). 'Detecting the Pitfalls of Data on Foreign Direct Investment: Scope and Limits of FDI Data'. *Management International Review*, *41*(2), 189–218.

Stöttinger, B. and Schlegelmilch, B. B. (1998). 'Explaining export development through psychic distance: enlightening or elusive?'. *International Marketing Review*, *15*(5), 357–372.

Suliman, A. H. and Mollick, A. V. (2009). 'Human Capital Development, War and Foreign Direct Investment in Sub-Saharan Africa'. *Oxford Development Studies*, *37*(1), 47–61.

Tabachnick, B. G. and Fidell, L. S. (2006). *Using Multivariate Statistics*. 5th Edition. Boston: Pearson/Allyn & Bacon.

Tallman, S. and Li, J. (1996). 'Effects of International Diversity and Product Diversity on the Performance of Multinational Firms'. *The Academy of Management Journal*, *39*(1), 179–196.

Tan, D. (2009). 'Foreign Market Entry Strategies and Post-Entry Growth: Acquisitions vs Greenfield Investments'. *Journal of International Business Studies*, *40*(6), 1046–1063.

Tatoglu, E. and Glaister, K. W. (1998). 'Performance of international joint ventures in Turkey: perspectives of Western firms and Turkish firms'. *International Business Review*, *7*(6), 635–656.

Taylor, C. R., Zou, S. and Osland, G. E. (1998). 'A Transaction Cost Perspective on Foreign Market Entry Strategies of US and Japanese Firms'. *Thunderbird International Business Review*, *40*(4), 389–412.

Teece, D. J. (1984). 'Economic Analysis and Strategic Management'. *California Management Review*, *26*(3), 84–110.

The Economist (2000). *The hopeless continent.* 13–19 May 2000 edition.

The Economist (2012). *African entrepreneurs: Parallel players.* Article in 23–29 June 2012 edition, online at: http://www.economist.com/node/21557373 (accessed on 8 July 2016).

The Economist (2013a). *Africa rising: A hopeful continent.* Article in 2–8 March 2013 edition.

The Economist (2013b). *Supermarkets in Africa: The grocers' great trek.* Article in 21–27 September 2013 edition.

The Economist (2014). *Dangote Group: Building on concrete foundations.* Article in 12–18 April 2014 edition.

Tihanyi, L., Griffith, D. A. and Russell, C. J. (2005). 'The effect of cultural distance on entry mode choice, international diversification, and MNE performance: a meta-analysis'. *Journal of International Business Studies*, *36*(3), 270–283.

UNCTAD (1993). *World Investment Report 1993: Transnational Corporations and Integrated International Production.* New York: United Nations Conference on Trade and Development.

UNCTAD (1996). *World Investment Report 1996: Investment, Trade and International Policy Arrangements.* New York and Geneva: United Nations Conference on Trade and Development.

UNCTAD (1997). *World Investment Report 1997: Transnational Corporations, Market Structure and Competition Policy.* New York and Geneva: United Nations Conference on Trade and Development.

UNCTAD (1998). *World Investment Report 1998: Trends and Determinants.* New York and Geneva: United Nations Conference on Trade and Development.

UNCTAD (1999a). *Foreign Direct Investment in Africa: Performance and Potential.* New York and Geneva: United Nations Conference on Trade and Development.

UNCTAD (1999b). *World Investment Report 1999: Foreign Direct Investment and the Challenge of Development.* New York and Geneva: United Nations Conference on Trade and Development.

UNCTAD (2000). *World Investment Report 2000: Cross-border Mergers and Acquisitions and Development.* New York and Geneva: United Nations Conference on Trade and Development.

UNCTAD (2001). *World Investment Report 2001: Promoting Linkages.* New York and Geneva: United Nations Conference on Trade and Development.

UNCTAD (2002). *World Investment Report 2002: Transnational Corporations and Export Competitiveness.* New York and Geneva: United Nations Conference on Trade and Development.

UNCTAD (2003a). *The African Growth and Opportunity Act: A Preliminary Assessment*. New York and Geneva: United Nations Conference on Trade and Development.

UNCTAD (2003b). *Foreign Direct Investment and Performance Requirements: New Evidence from Selected Countries*. New York and Geneva: United Nations Conference on Trade and Development.

UNCTAD (2003c). *Investment Policy Review: Lesotho*. New York and Geneva: United Nations Conference on Trade and Development.

UNCTAD (2004a). *Prospects for Foreign Direct Investment and the Strategies of Transnational Corporations, 2004–2007*. New York and Geneva: United Nations Conference on Trade and Development.

UNCTAD (2004b). *World Investment Report 2004: The Shift Towards Services*. New York and Geneva: United Nations Conference on Trade and Development.

UNCTAD (2005a). *Case study on outward foreign direct investment by Indian small and medium-sized enterprises*. Document prepared by the United Nations Conference on Trade and Development Secretariat for the "Expert Meeting on Enhancing Productive Capacity of Developing Country Firms through Internationalization", 5–7 December 2015 in Geneva, Switzerland.

UNCTAD (2005b). *Case study on outward foreign direct investment by South African enterprises*. Document prepared by the United Nations Conference on Trade and Development Secretariat for the "Expert Meeting on Enhancing Productive Capacity of Developing Country Firms through Internationalization", 5–7 December 2015 in Geneva, Switzerland.

UNCTAD (2005c). *Economic Development in Africa: Rethinking the Role of Foreign Direct Investment*. New York and Geneva: United Nations Conference on Trade and Development.

UNCTAD (2005d). *FDI Statistics: Data compilation and policy issues*. Document prepared by the United Nations Conference on Trade and Development Secretariat for the "Expert Meeting on Capacity Building in the Area of FDI: Data Compilation and Policy Formulation in Developing Countries", 12–14 December 2015 in Geneva, Switzerland.

UNCTAD (2005e). *World Investment Report 2005: Transnational Corporations and the Internationalization of R&D*. New York and Geneva: United Nations Conference on Trade and Development.

UNCTAD (2006a). *Measuring Restrictions on FDI in Services in Developing Countries and Transition Economies*. New York and Geneva: United Nations Conference on Trade and Development.

UNCTAD (2006b). *World Investment Report 2006: FDI from Developing and Transition Economies: Implications for Development*. New York and Geneva: United Nations Conference on Trade and Development.

UNCTAD (2007a). *Aftercare: A Core Function in Investment Promotion*. Investment Advisory Series A, No. 1, New York and Geneva: United Nations Conference on Trade and Development.

UNCTAD (2007b). *World Investment Report 2007: Transnational Corporations, Extractive Industries and Development*. New York and Geneva: United Nations Conference on Trade and Development.

UNCTAD (2008a). *FDI and Tourism: The development dimension – East and Southern Africa*. New York and Geneva: United Nations Conference on Trade and Development.

UNCTAD (2008b). *World Investment Directory: Volume X – Africa*. New York and Geneva: United Nations Conference on Trade and Development.

UNCTAD (2009a). *The Role of International Investment Agreements in Attracting Foreign Direct Investment to Developing Countries*. Geneva and New York: United Nations Conference on Trade and Development.

UNCTAD (2009b). *UNCTAD Training Manual on Statistics for FDI and the Operations of TNCs – Volume I: FDI Flows and Stocks*. New York and Geneva: United Nations Conference on Trade and Development.

UNCTAD (2009c). *UNCTAD Training Manual on Statistics for FDI and the Operations of TNCs – Volume II: Statistics on the Operations of Transnational Corporations*. New York and Geneva: United Nations Conference on Trade and Development.

UNCTAD (2009d). *UNCTAD Training Manual on Statistics for FDI and the Operations of TNCs – Volume III: Collecting and Reporting FDI/TNC Statistics: Institutional Issues*. New York and Geneva: United Nations Conference on Trade and Development.

UNCTAD (2009e). *World Investment Prospect Survey 2009–2011*. New York and Geneva: United Nations Conference on Trade and Development.

UNCTAD (2009f). *World Investment Report 2009: Transnational Corporations, Agricultural Production and Development*. New York and Geneva: United Nations Conference on Trade and Development.

UNCTAD (2010a). *Economic Development in Africa Report 2010: South-South Cooperation: Africa and the New Forms of Development Partnership*. New York and Geneva: United Nations Conference on Trade and Development.

UNCTAD (2010b). *World Investment Report 2010: Investing in a Low-Carbon Economy*. New York and Geneva: United Nations Conference on Trade and Development.

UNCTAD (2011a). *Foreign Direct Investments in LDCs: Lessons Learned from the Decade 2001–2010 and the Way Forward*. New York and Geneva: United Nations Conference on Trade and Development.

UNCTAD (2011b). *World Investment Report 2011: Non-Equity Modes of International Production and Development*. New York and Geneva: United Nations Conference on Trade and Development.

UNCTAD (2012a). *World Investment Prospects Survey 2012–2014*. New York and Geneva: United Nations Conference on Trade and Development.

UNCTAD (2012b). *World Investment Report 2012: Towards a New Generation of Investment Policies*. New York and Geneva: United Nations Conference on Trade and Development.

UNCTAD (2013a). *Review of Maritime Transport 2013*. New York and Geneva: United Nations Conference on Trade and Development.

UNCTAD (2013b). *World Investment Report 2013: Global Value Chains: Investment and Trade for Development*. New York and Geneva: United Nations Conference on Trade and Development.

UNCTAD (2014a). *The Impact of International Investment Agreements on Foreign Direct Investment: An Overview of Empirical Studies 1998–2014*. IIA Issues Note September 2014, New York and Geneva: United Nations Conference on Trade and Development.

UNCTAD (2014b). *Review of Maritime Transport 2014*. New York and Geneva: United Nations Conference on Trade and Development.

UNCTAD (2014c). *World Investment Prospects Survey 2014–2016*. New York and Geneva: United Nations Conference on Trade and Development.

UNCTAD (2014d). *World Investment Report 2014: Investing in the SDGs: An Action Plan*. New York and Geneva: United Nations Conference on Trade and Development.

UNCTAD (2015a). *Generalized System of Preferences: List of Beneficiaries*. New York and Geneva: United Nations Conference on Trade and Development.

UNCTAD (2015b). *World Investment Report 2015: Reforming International Investment Governance*. New York and Geneva: United Nations Conference on Trade and Development.

UNCTAD (2016). World Investment Report 2016: *Investor Nationality – Policy Challenges*. New York and Geneva: United Nations Conference on Trade and Development.

UNCTAD and UNDP (2007). *Asian Foreign Direct Investment in Africa: Towards a New Era of Cooperation among Developing Countries*. New York and Geneva: United Nations Conference on Trade and Development and United Nations Development Programme.

UNCTAD and UNIDO (2011). *Economic Development in Africa Report 2011: Fostering Industrial Development in Africa in the New Global Environment*. New York, Geneva and Vienna: United Nations Conference on Trade and Development and United Nations Industrial Development Organization.

UNECA (2006). *Economic Report on Africa 2006: Capital Flows and Development Financing in Africa*. Addis Ababa: United Nations Economic Commission for Africa.

UNECA (2014). *Frontier Markets in Africa: Misperceptions in a Sea of Opportunities*. Note prepared by the United Nations Economic Commission for Africa for the "US-Africa Leaders Summit 2014", 4–6 August 2014 in Washington D.C., USA.

UNIDO (2002a). *Foreign Direct Investor Perceptions in Sub-Saharan Africa: UNIDO Pilot Survey in Ethiopia, Nigeria, Uganda, United Republic of Tanzania*. Vienna: United Nations Industrial Development Organization.

UNIDO (2002b). *Industrial Development Report 2002/2003: Competing through Innovation and Learning*. Vienna: United Nations Industrial Development Organization.

UNIDO (2003). *Africa Foreign Investor Survey 2003: Motivations, Operations, Perceptions and Future plans – Implications for Investment Promotion*. Vienna: United Nations Industrial Development Organization.

UNIDO (2005). *Industrial Development Report 2005: Capability building for catching-up*. Vienna: United Nations Industrial Development Organization.

UNIDO (2007). *Africa Foreign Investor Survey 2005: Understanding the contributions of different investor categories to development – Implications for targeting strategies*. 2nd Edition. Vienna: United Nations Industrial Development Organization.

UNIDO (2009). *Industrial Development Report 2009: Breaking In and Moving Up: New Industrial Challenges for the Bottom Billion and the Middle-Income Countries*. Vienna: United Nations Industrial Development Organization.

UNIDO (2010). *The International Yearbook of Industrial Statistics 2010*. Vienna: United Nations Industrial Development Organization

UNIDO (2012a). *Africa Investor Report 2011: Towards Evidence-Based Investment Promotion Strategies*. Vienna: United Nations Industrial Development Organization.

UNIDO (2012b). *Tanzania Industrial Competitiveness Report 2012*. Vienna: United Nations Industrial Development Organization.

UNIDO (2012c). *Viet Nam Industrial Investment Report 2011: Understanding the Impact of Foreign Direct Investment on Industrial Development*. Vienna: United Nations Industrial Development Organization.

UNIDO (2015a). *Industrial Development Report 2016: The Role of Technology and Innovation in Inclusive and Sustainable Industrial Development*. Vienna: United Nations Industrial Development Organization.

UNIDO (2015b). *The International Yearbook of Industrial Statistics 2015*. Vienna: United Nations Industrial Development Organization.

UNOSAA (2010). *Africa's Cooperation with New and Emerging Development Partners: Options for Africa's Development*. New York: United Nations Office of the Special Advisor on Africa.

Urata, S. and Kawai, H. (2000). 'The Determinants of the Location of Foreign Direct Investment by Japanese Small and Medium-sized Enterprises'. *Small Business Economics*, *15*(2), 79–103.

Van Biesebroeck, J. (2005). 'Exporting raises productivity in sub-Saharan African manufacturing firms'. *Journal of International Economics*, *67*(2), 373–391.

Velicer, W. F. and Jackson, D. N. (1990). 'Component Analysis versus Common Factor Analysis: Some issues in Selecting an Appropriate Procedure'. *Multivariate Behavioral Research*, *25*(1), 1–28.

Wacker, K. (2013). *On the measurement of Foreign Direct Investment and its relationship to activities of multinational corporations*. Working Paper No. 1614/November 2013, Frankfurt am Main: European Central Bank.

Wall, M. M. and Li, R. (2003). 'Comparison of multiple regression to two latent variable techniques for estimation and prediction'. *Statistics in Medicine*, *22*(23), 3671–3685.

Wang, H. and Schaan, J.-L. (2008). 'How much distance do we need? Revisiting the “National cultural distance paradox”'. *Management International Review*, *48*(3), 263–278.

Wang, J.-Y. (2007). *What Drives China's Growing Role in Africa?* Working Paper 07/211, Washington D.C.: International Monetary Fund.

Wang, J.-Y. and Bio-Tchané, A. (2008). 'Africa's Burgeoning Ties: Maximizing the benefits of China's increasing economic engagement with Africa'. *Finance & Development*, *45*(1), 44–47.

Wei, L.-Q. and Lau, C.-M. (2008). 'The Impact of Market Orientation and Strategic HRM on Firm Performance: The Case of Chinese Enterprises'. *Journal of International Business Studies*, *39*(6), 980–995.

Weiss, L. W. (1974). 'The concentration-profits relationship and antitrust'. In Goldschmid H. J., Mann, H. M. and Weston, J. F. (Eds.), *Industrial Concentration: The New Learning*. Boston: Little-Brown. 184–233.

Wells, L. T. and Wint, A. G. (2000). *Marketing a Country: Promotion as a Tool for Attracting Foreign Investment*. Washington D.C.: Foreign Investment Advisory Service.

Wernerfelt, B. (1984). 'A Resource-Based View of the Firm'. *Strategic Management Journal*, *5*(2), 171–180.

Wernerfelt, B. and Montgomery, C. A. (1988). 'Tobin's q and the Importance of Focus in Firm Performance'. *The American Economic Review*, *78*(1), 246–250.

West, J. and Graham, J. L. (2004). 'A Linguistic-based Measure of Cultural Distance and Its Relationship to Managerial Values'. *Management International Review*, *44*(3), 239 260.

Wheeler, D. and Mody, A. (1992). 'International investment location decisions: The case of U.S. firms'. *Journal of International Economics*, *33*(1–2), 57–76.

White, L. (2010). 'Understanding Brazil's new drive for Africa'. *South African Journal of International Affairs*, *17*(2), 221–242.

Wilkinson, T. J., Peng, G. Z., Brouthers, L. E. and Beamish, P. W. (2008). 'The diminishing effect of cultural distance on subsidiary control'. *Journal of International Management*, *14*(2), 93–107.

Williams, C. and Lee, S. H. (2009). 'International management, political arena and dispersed entrepreneurship in the MNC'. *Journal of World Business*, *44*(3), 287–299.

Williams, C. and Lee, S. H. (2011). 'Political Heterarchy and Dispersed Entrepreneurship in the MNC'. *Journal of Management Studies*, *48*(6), 1243–1268.

Williamson, O. E. (1975). *Markets and Hierarchies: Analysis and Antitrust implications*. New York: Free Press.

Williamson, O. E. (1979). 'Transaction-Cost Economics: The Governance of Contractual Relations'. *Journal of Law and Economics*, *22*(2), 233–261.

Williamson, O. E. (1985). *The Economic Institutions of Capitalism*. New York: The Free Press.

Williamson, O. E. (1991). 'Comparative Economic Organization: The Analysis of Discrete Structural Alternatives'. *Administrative Science Quarterly*, *36*(2), 269–296.

Woertz, E., Pradhan, S., Biberovic, N. and Jingzhong, C. (2008). *Potential for GCC Agro-investments in Africa and Central Asia*. Dubai: Gulf Research Center.

Woodcock, C. P., Beamish, P. W. and Makino, S. (1994). 'Ownership-Based Entry Mode Strategies and International Performance'. *Journal of International Business Studies*, *25*(2), 253–273.

Woodward, D. P. and Rolfe, R. J. (1993). 'The Location of Export-Oriented Foreign Direct Investment in the Caribbean Basin'. *Journal of International Business Studies*, *24*(1), 121–144.

World Bank (2009). *Doing Business 2009*. Washington D.C.: World Bank Group.

World Bank, IFC and MIGA (2010). *Investing Across Borders 2010: Indicators of Foreign Direct Investment Regulation in 87 Economies*. Washington, D.C.: World Bank, International Finance Corporation and Multilateral Investment Guarantee Agency.

World Bank (2012). *Chinese FDI in Ethiopia: A World Bank Survey*. Washington D.C.: World Bank Group.

World Bank (2013). *Doing Business 2014: Understanding Regulations for Small and Medium-Size Enterprises*. Washington D.C.: World Bank Group.

World Bank (2014). *Foreign Direct Investment Flows into Sub-Saharan Africa*. Washington D.C.: World Bank Group. Online at: http://documents.worldbank.org/curated/en/2014/03/19259750/foreign-direct-investment-flows-sub-saharan-africa (accessed on 8 July 2016).

World Bank (2016). Enterprise Survey Database. Washington D.C.: World Bank Group. Online at: http://www.enterprisesurveys.org (accessed on 8 July 2016).

World Economic Forum (2012). *The Global Competitiveness Report 2012–2013*. Geneva: World Economic Forum.

Xu, D. and Lu, J. W. (2007). 'Technological knowledge, product relatedness, and parent control: The effect on IJV survival'. *Journal of Business Research*, *60*(11), 1166–1176.

Xu, D., Pan, Y. and Beamish, P. W. (2004). 'The Effect of Regulative and Normative Distances on MNE Ownership and Expatriate Strategies'. *Management International Review*, *44*(3), 285–307.

Xu, D. and Shenkar, O. (2002). 'Institutional Distance and the Multinational Enterprise'. *The Academy of Management Review*, *27*(4), 608–618.

Yackee, J. W. (2007). 'Do BITs Really Work? Revisiting the Empirical Link between Investment Treaties and Foreign Direct Investment'. Legal Studies Research Paper No. 1054, University of Wisconsin Law School.

Yan, A. and Gray, B. (1994). 'Bargaining Power, Management Control, and Performance in United States-China Joint Ventures: A Comparative Case Study'. *The Academy of Management Journal*, *37*(6), 1478–1517.

Yan, A. and Zeng, M. (1999). 'International Joint Venture Instability: A Critique of Previous Research, a Reconceptualization, and Directions for Future Research'. *Journal of International Business Studies*, *30*(2), 397–414.

Yasar, M., Paul, C. J. M. and Ward, M. R. (2011). 'Property Rights Institutions and Firm Performance: A Cross-Country Analysis'. *World Development*, *39*(4), 648–661.

Yip, G. (1982). 'Diversification Entry: Internal Development versus Acquisition'. *Strategic Management Journal*, *3*(4), 331–345.

Yli-Renko, H., Autio, E. and Tontti, V. (2002). 'Social capital, knowledge, and the international growth of technology-based new firms'. *International Business Review*, *11*(3), 279–304.

Yumkella, K. K., Kormawa, P. M., Roepstorff, T. M. and Hawkins, A. M. (Eds.) (2011). *Agribusiness for Africa's prosperity*. Vienna: United Nations Industrial Development Organization.

Zacharakis, A. L. (1997). 'Entrepreneurial Entry Into Foreign Markets: A Transaction Cost Perspective'. *Entrepreneurship Theory and Practice*, *21*(3), 23–39.

Zafar, A. (2007). 'The Growing Relationship Between China and Sub-Saharan Africa: Macroeconomic, Trade, Investment, and Aid Links'. *The World Bank Research Observer*, *22*(1), 103–130.

Zahra, S. A. (2004). 'A theory of international new ventures: a decade of research'. *Journal of International Business Studies*, *36*(1), 20–28.

Zahra, S. A., Ireland, R. D. and Hitt, M. A. (2000). 'International Expansion by New Venture Firms: International Diversity, Mode of Market Entry, Technological Learning, and Performance'. *The Academy of Management Journal*, *43*(5), 925–950.

Zhan, J. J. (2006). *FDI Statistics: A Critical Review and Policy Implications*. Geneva: World Association of Investment Promotion Agencies (WAIPA).

Zhao, H., Luo, Y. and Suh, T. (2004). 'Transaction cost determinants and ownership-based entry mode choice: a meta-analytical review'. *Journal of International Business Studies*, *35*(6), 524–544.

Zhao, H. and Zhu, G. (1998). 'Determinants of ownership preference of international joint ventures: new evidence from Chinese manufacturing industries'. *International Business Review*, *7*(6), 569–589.

Zhao, X. and Decker, R. (2005). 'Modeling SMEs' Choice of Foreign Market Entry: Joint Venture vs. Wholly Owned Venture'. *Operations Research Proceedings 2004*, 221–229.

Zschoche, M. (2015). 'The Effects of Foreign Direct Investment Colocation: Differences Between Manufacturing and Service Firms'. *Managerial and Decision Economics*, Early online publication: http://onlinelibrary.wiley.com/doi/10.1002/mde.2730/abstract (accessed on 8 July 2016).